Religion & Politics
in East Africa

Eastern African Studies

*forthcoming

Religion & Politics in East Africa

The Period
Since Independence

Edited by

HOLGER BERNT HANSEN
& MICHAEL TWADDLE

James Currey
LONDON

E.A.E.P
NAIROBI

Fountain Publishers
KAMPALA

Ohio University Press
ATHENS

James Currey Ltd
54b Thornhill Square
Islington
*London N1 1BE, England

East African Educational Publishers
PO Box 45314
Nairobi, Kenya

Fountain Publishers
PO Box 488
Kampala, Uganda

Ohio University Press
Scott Quadrangle
Athens, Ohio 45701, USA

95 96 97 98 99 5 4 3 2 1

British Library Cataloguing in Publication Data

Religion and Politics in East Africa:
Period Since Independence. — (Eastern
African Studies)
I. Hansen, Holger Bernt II. Twaddle,
Michael III. Series
967.604

ISBN 0-85255-384-6 (Paper)
ISBN 0-85255-385-4 (Cloth)

Library of Congress Cataloging-in-Publication Data

Religion and politics in East Africa since independence / edited by Holger Bernt Hansen
& Michael Twaddle.
    p.   cm. — (Eastern African studies)
  Includes bibliographical references and index.
  ISBN 0-8214-1085-7 (hard). — ISBN 0-8214-1086-5 (pbk.)
    1. Religion and politics—Africa, Eastern. 2. Religion and state—Africa,
Eastern. 3. Africa, Eastern—Politics and government—1960-
4. Christianity—Africa, Eastern—20th century. 5. Islam—Africa,
Eastern—20th century. I. Hansen, Holger Bernt. II. Twaddle, Michael. III.
Series: Eastern African studies (London, England)
BL65.P7R43233 1995
322'.1'09676—dc20   94-3513
                                                                       CIP

Typeset in 10/11 pt Baskerville by Colset Pte Ltd, Singapore
Printed and Bound in Great Britain by Villiers Publications, London N3

Contents

Contents

Part Two

Christianity, Sectarianism & Politics in Uganda

Five

Six

Seven

Eight

Part Three

Christians & Muslims in Kenyan politics

Nine

Contents

Ten

Ideological Politics versus Biblical Hermeneutics
Kenya's Protestant Churches & the *Nyayo* State   177
G.P. BENSON

Eleven

Coping with the Christians
The Muslim Predicament in Kenya   200
DONAL B. CRUISE O'BRIEN

Part Four

Cross-Cultural Complications

Twelve

*Christian–Muslim Inputs into Public Policy Formation
in Kenya, Tanzania & Uganda*   223
A.B.K. KASOZI

Thirteen

*The Churches & Human Rights
in Kenya & Uganda since Independence*   247
M. LOUISE PIROUET

Fourteen

Church & State in Eastern Africa
Some Unresolved Questions   260
MARTIN DOORNBOS

Index   270

vii

Contributors

Heike Behrend is Professor of Anthropology at the University of Cologne and author of *Alice und die Geister: Krieg im norden Ugandas* (Munich: Trickster, 1993)

G. P. Benson was previously on the staff of Bishop David Gitari in Kenya

Holger Bernt Hansen is Professor of Third World Church History at Copenhagen University and Director of its Centre for African Studies

François Constantin is Professor of Public Law at the University of Pau and Director of its Centre of East African Studies

Donal Cruise O'Brien is Professor of Politics with special reference to Africa at SOAS, University of London

Martin Doornbos teaches African politics at the Institute of Social Studies at The Hague in the Netherlands, where he also edits the quarterly journal *Development and Change*

A. B. K. Kasozi is the author of *The Spread of Islam in Uganda* (Nairobi: Oxford University Press, 1986). Previously he taught history at Makerere

Ronald Kassimir recently completed field research in Uganda and now teaches African politics at Columbia University, New York

Omari Kokole is Professor of Political Science at the State University of New York at Binghamton

Rex O'Fahey specializes in African and Middle Eastern studies at the University of Bergen and is the author of many publications on Islam in the Sudan

Louise Pirouet wrote *Black Evangelists* (London: Rex Collings, 1978) and has taught at Makerere, Nairobi and Cambridge Universities

Michael Twaddle specializes in East African history and politics at the Institute of Commonwealth Studies at London University

John Mary Waliggo wrote *A History of African Priests* (Nairobi: Mariatum Press, 1988), after which he became Secretary to the Uganda Constitutional Commission

Kevin Ward taught church history for many years at Bishop Tucker Theological College in Uganda. Presently he is a vicar in the north of England and a lecturer at Leeds University

Thanks

Holger Bernt Hansen and Michael Twaddle wish to thank colleagues in the Universities of Copenhagen and London for logistical support for the third conference at Lyngby Landbrugsskole, at which most of the material in this book was first presented; the Kuliika Trust of London for enabling Godfrey Okoth and John Mary Waliggo to attend this conference; the Danish Research Council for the Humanities for meeting most of its other expenses through the Special Research Professorship held by Holger Bernt Hansen at the time; staff at Lyngby Landbrugsskole for taking care of material arrangements for the conference so efficiently; Copenhagen University's Faculty of Theology for a memorable dinner; and Hugh Dinwiddy, Carl Hallencreutz, Godfrey Okoth and Lillian and Neville Sanderson for making the conference memorable in other ways. We sadly give our condolences and thanks to the families of the late Anne Marie Bak Rasmussen and Per Frostin for their contributions. We also thank Professor G. N. Sanderson for commenting on parts of the final manuscript; and staff at James Currey Ltd, particularly Lynn Taylor, for their quiet but essential assistance in transforming this manuscript into a book. Thanks, also to Danchurchaid, Copenhagen, for their assistance in making copies available in East Africa.

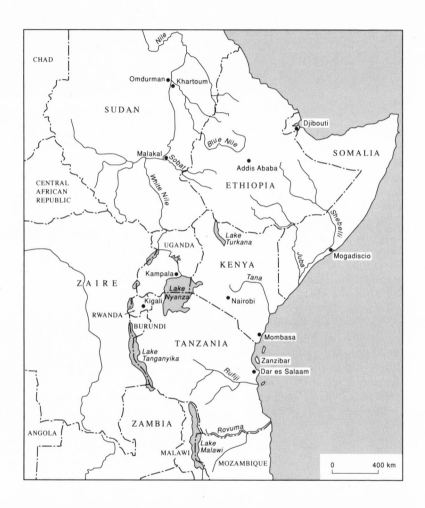

East Africa

One

The Character
of Politico-Religious Conflict
in Eastern Africa

MICHAEL TWADDLE

This collection of essays arose out of two earlier international workshops held at Lyngby Landbrugsskole in Denmark. Both gatherings were concerned with recent history, politics and development in one particular African country: Uganda. The first workshop's proceedings were published in 1988, under the title *Uganda Now: Between decay and development.*[1] These were concerned with issues and events between independence from Britain and the coming to power of Yoweri Museveni's National Resistance Movement in 1986. The second meeting's proceedings dealt with developments shaped by, and themselves shaping, the Museveni government's first five years in power. These were published in a volume entitled *Changing Uganda: The dilemmas of structural adjustment and political change* (1991).[2] Needless to say, the organizers and editors of these two workshops and publications were concerned to make them as comprehensive as possible. Currently, we are arranging to publish proceedings from further gatherings at Lyngby Landbrugsskole covering topics incompletely debated at the first two workshops as well as to bring discussion of the dilemmas of democratization and economic and political development in Uganda up to date. But one topic popped up repeatedly in our earlier workshops and yet appeared impossible to deal with satisfactorily solely within a further single-country workshop: politico-religious conflict and change. We therefore organized our third international gathering of scholars at Lyngby Landbrugsskole between 20 and 23 September 1990 on 'Religion and politics in East Africa since independence', in order to consider this subject within a wider regional setting. That, essentially, is why this volume contains studies of politico-religious groupings in Kenya and Sudan as well as in Uganda, and why there are references in it to religion and politics in Tanzania and Zaïre too.

Others would broaden the backcloth to politico-religious conflict still further. In a post-Cold War world still reeling from blows struck by resurgent politico-religious groupings in countries as wide apart as Christian Poland and Muslim Iran, or Christian–Muslim Nigeria and Muslim–Hindu India, only a global approach seems sufficient to cope with their complications. Yet the global approach, too, has drawbacks. Amongst the most serious are tendencies to hubris, superficiality and mere listing of surface characteristics. An adequate appreciation of politico-religious dynamics is more likely to be obtained within a regional setting, large enough in extent to provide politico-religious groupings in sufficient number for comparative study and yet small enough in area for them to be investigated in sufficiently contrasting and overlapping detail. That is another reason why this collection of studies is concerned with East (or, more precisely, Eastern) Africa rather than with just one of its constituent countries.

To be sure, some scholars might consider that even one African country forms too broad a remit, let alone a cluster of several countries. Only more detailed and locally focused studies bring true wisdom. This would appear to be the position Terence Ranger comes close to adopting in his review of 'Religious movements and politics in sub-Saharan Africa' in the *African Studies Review* for June 1986. An anthropologist obtains his encomium for warning that:

> Much of the [more recent] work on black religious movements in central and southern Africa has failed to match [Bishop] Sundkler's sensitivity [in his *Bantu Prophets in South Africa* (1948)] to their broad cultural significance, and to their character as complex symbolic systems. A host of more explicitly sociological studies have provided ample evidence of their mediating role under conditions of rapid and uneven transformation, often viewing them as buffers in the wake of social dislocation. In reaction to the limitations of such sociological analysis, there have been efforts to understand the religious movements in idealist terms. But like the sociological focus it ostensibly opposes, this idealist perspective fails to situate these movements within [the] more encompassing structural orders of colonial domination.[3]

On the other hand, Ranger points out that:

> In other parts of Africa, where the power of the colonial state was much less omnipresent, the task of integrating indigenous cultural structures and global determination is a rather different one. The vigor of indigenous cultural structures in many parts of West Africa, for example, is more readily apparent than the structures of national and international political economy.[4]

The Character of Politico-Religious Conflict in Eastern Africa

In Zambia, during its political incarnation as Northern Rhodesia, Ranger agrees with Karen Fields that British colonial rule 'depended on two irreconcilable religious ideologies – on progressive Christianity as taught by the missionaries and on the traditional [African] religious beliefs which gave authority to chiefs within systems of Indirect Rule'.[5] He quotes approvingly Fields's view that:

> How cultural patterns are articulated to systems of political domination is a question as important to pose as it is elusive to answer systematically. But we can say for certain that, in times of upheaval, those who move into action grasp its importance immediately, whatever side they are on. There is no genuine revolution which is not at the same time cultural revolution. And there is no serious political repression which does not invade the realm of culture.[6]

But there are problems with this formulation too. The distortions of idealism aside, the sheer variety of African religious movements is such that it is extremely difficult to build any broader interpretations upon the recent or more distant experiences of only one or two of them. There is also, almost by definition, their millenarian exceptionalism. This makes very shaky ground upon which to base any longer-term trajectory of change in religion and politics. However, Ranger is surely right to stress that African religious movements should be seen, at least to start with, in their own terms as systems of cultural signification. He is surely right, too, to stress that Western colonialism has been a crucial cluster of influences in their histories, but by no means the only factor shaping them. They had important histories before the era of Western colonialism in Africa.[7] They have, and doubtless will have, important histories after it. But, as so many African ethnographic zones are nowadays divided between one or more successor states as a direct consequence of Western colonial rule, sometimes it is necessary to study African religious movements and their backgrounds in more than one African country in order to understand them at all adequately. This is yet another reason for the regional approach adopted in this volume.

Omari Kokole's discussion of the Nubians in Ugandan politics (Chapter 4) and Heike Behrend's account of 'The Holy Spirit Movement and the forces of nature in the north of Uganda, 1985–1987' (Chapter 5) are two case studies illustrating this point.

The Nubians considered by Kokole ('Nubi' in his terminology) are not the peoples of the Nuba mountains in the heart of modern Sudan, studied by the German photographer Leni Riefenstahl, or more distant descendants from the kingdom of Nubia which flourished in Upper Egypt during late antiquity. They are the offspring of mercenaries recruited in the 1890s by the first British colonial administrators of what are today Uganda, Kenya and Tanzania, from the remnants of earlier Turco-Egyptian armies cut off in what is nowadays southern Sudan and northeastern Zaïre by the Mahdist revolt. During British colonial rule

3

they and their descendants petitioned for a more privileged legal status than ordinary Africans. But their petitions were unsuccessful. Following independence from Britain, they continued to work as soldiers or petty traders on the edges of towns and formed a secondary category of folk known primarily as members of other, better-known tribes, Bantu, Nilotic and Sudanic. When Idi Amin seized power in Uganda in 1971 and called them the most important tribe in East Africa, most scholars were astounded. The Nubi were so few in number, and seemingly so unimportant, that they had not even been mentioned in some censuses and sociological surveys. Amin's period of power in Uganda underlined their strategic significance as an Islamic minority on the margins of non-Muslim society. Omari Kokole suggests that when Amin seized power in January 1971 his Kakwa identity straddling the Sudan–Uganda border proved more important than his Nubian affiliation. Subsequently, it became steadily less important as Amin sought to broaden internal support for his regime and his policies in general became more favourable to Islam. Indeed, Kokole stresses that 'perhaps the most consistent aspect of his policies as President of Uganda [was his] anti-Israeli/anti-Zionist orientation and strong pro-Palestinian/ pro-Arab stand'.

Heike Behrend deals with another religious movement straddling the Sudan–Uganda border, this time a movement arising much more recently and within the more confined Nilotic ethnographic zone overlapping these two countries and edging into western Kenya. As Behrend relates, it arose initially in Acholiland in 1986 in response to the seizure of central power in Uganda by Yoweri Museveni's National Resistance Movement.

> [A] 'holy spirit', called the Lakwena, was sent to Uganda by the Christian God. Under the leadership of the spirit, his medium, Alice Auma, a young woman of Gulu, built up the Holy Spirit Mobile Forces (HSMF) to over-throw the government, to cleanse the world of evil and to build a new world in which man and nature were reconciled. [To this end] not only men and women fought as Holy Spirit soldiers, but also 140,000 spirits and parts of animate and inanimate nature, such as bees, snakes, rivers, rocks and moun-tains ... The war of the HSM [Holy Spirit Movement] was a cosmic uprising in which human forces, spiritual forces and the forces of nature actively took part together.

Behrend reports that: 'On the road to Kampala, Alice took the same route as the Lwoo-speaking people took when they migrated from Sudan into their present area of settlement a few centuries ago.' Behrend also stresses other aspects of Alice's cultural inventiveness:

> Alice had had recourse to the role of [chief or] *rwot* (pl. *rwodi*) in pre-colonial times and activated particularly those aspects that had retreated into the background since the colonial period, namely the ecological concerns. Like

a *rwot*, she ensured the rain and made sacrifices to reconcile injured and insulted nature. Like a *rwot*, she passed judgment and set up regulations (the twenty Holy Spirit safety precautions), so that the people once again had clean hearts and the moral community was reconstituted. And, like a *rwot*, she made war against her enemies.

Alice was defeated in war once her Holy Spirit Movement army moved out of its Nilotic ethnographic homeland in northern Uganda into the Bantu-speaking area of Busoga district and her troops were confronted with Museveni's soldiers equipped with precision firearms. But, before that happened, 'Alice and her followers [had] succeeded in reinforcing "the instant millennium" . . . which they inaugurated by cleansing [themselves and] their followers from witchcraft and sorcery, through Christian eschatological expectations'.

Islam is not mentioned by Heike Behrend in her account of Alice Lakwena's Holy Spirit Movement. But we know from other sources that Nubian Muslims introduced Islam into Acholiland and other areas of northern Uganda and southern Sudan during the preceding 100 years.[8] However, Islam appears to have been compromised by association with slave-raiding marauders from Khartoum, Cairo and elsewhere immediately before a British protectorate was declared over Uganda in the 1890s, and thereafter it never became more than a minority faith in Acholiland.[9] Instead, Christian missionaries made many more converts.

Essentially, it was Christians rather than Muslims who battled for independence from Britain in Tanganyika (1961), Uganda (1962) and Kenya (1963), though each colony or protectorate contained economically important Muslim minorities, South Asian as well as African in character, at the moment of independence.[10] Only in Sudan (1956) and Zanzibar (1963) was Islam predominant in the independence struggle. In Zanzibar this was basically because the great majority of its inhabitants were themselves Muslims.[11] In Sudan, it was basically because pressure for independence (from Egypt as well as Britain, as it was formally an Anglo-Egyptian condominium) came initially from its northern Arab and Muslim areas rather than from its southern non-Arab and more Christianized peoples.

However, in neither Sudan nor Zanzibar was Islam itself a major issue in the independence struggle. In Zanzibar conflict centred upon communal differences originating in the main island's nineteenth-century history as an Arab-administered slave state, and in its record in the twentieth century of 'local ethnic and class divisions, and . . . the very nature of British rule, which had for so long compartmentalised the communities' there.[12] In 1963 came 'independence for Arabs only' and 1964 brought an African seizure of power. It also brought a pogrom against Zanzibaris of Arab and South Asian descent, led by a Ugandan migrant worker and former house painter, John Okello, and the incorporation of the tiny mini-state alongside Tanganyika within a United Republic of Tanzania. This followed astute diplomacy by Julius Nyerere and considerable activity of other kinds by Britain and the USA designed to forestall a communist takeover masterminded by the Zanzibari revolutionary Abdulrahman Muhammad Babu. After all, for Babu, 'Marx was much more important than Islam' at this time,[13] and the Cold War was then at its height.

Rex O'Fahey (Chapter 3) points out that in Sudan the first nationalist parties emerging in the northern parts of the condominium during the 1930s and 1940s were both based on avowedly Islamic organizations. Their strengths might have derived from Islamic sentiments of solidarity, 'but these were used to articulate basically secular nationalist positions'. It was only as these politicians lost office or credibility over time that more consciously Islamist leaders increased in popularity. O'Fahey considers two alternative, or overlapping, explanations for this outcome: disenchantment with recently overthrown or newly empowered politicians because of their mistakes, and the growing influence of Muslim Brothers from Egypt.

> The preoccupation of this [Western-orientated] élite with a row of 'isms', pan-Arabism, communism, socialism, the one-party state (the Sudan Socialist Union under al-Numayri) concealed the truly Islamic nature of northern Sudanese society. Moreover, with increasing urbanization and education, more and more northern Sudanese were being exposed to an urban form of Islam that derived many of its patterns of behaviour from Egypt.

It was into this explosive setting that the charismatic Dr al-Turabi returned in 1962, with his demand that 'Islamic jurisprudence shall be the general source of law'.

O'Fahey points out that over the centuries Islamic law had prevailed in Sudan in matters of marriage and divorce, but regarding criminal and property law there had been local variations. During the condominium period, a number of laws were codified and compromises made with Western jurisprudence. 'It is this compromise,' O'Fahey notes, 'where the modern compromise over law is but one of a range of concessions in the face of the Western secular impact, that is unacceptable to all Islamist movements, from Morocco to Malaysia.' What makes demands for 'restoration of the Sharia' additionally contentious in Sudan is the civil war which has continued with interruptions between the northern and southern parts of the country since 1955.

In other areas of Eastern Africa, where non-Muslim and Muslim populations live in close proximity, demands for the imposition of Islamic law have also been made in recent years. The Coast Province of Kenya is one example. There, as in Sudan, a Muslim population has lived alongside non-Muslim peoples for a considerable period of time.

Profiting modestly from Indian Ocean trade, it was settled in a series of city states. Following the British colonial takeover at the close of the nineteenth century, cities like Lamu or Malindi came to serve as centres of tourism or, in the case of Mombasa, as a major international port too. In the process, as Donal Cruise O'Brien points out (Chapter 11), the morale of Kenyan Muslims slumped. They were marginalized economically by the development of commercial agriculture up-country. They were out numbered ten-to-one in Kenya as a whole by Christians as a result of Protestant and Roman Catholic missionary endeavour. Educationally, they were left behind as regards the English language. Reverse migration by labourers as well as literate clerks from up-country areas turned even Muslims living at Mombasa into a minority community. Morally, these Muslims were affronted by much tourist behaviour there and elsewhere along the Kenyan coast. In these circumstances, it is hardly surprising that demands arose amongst them for a revival of Islam.

Donal Cruise O'Brien is uncertain about the prospects for Islamic revival or reform in Kenya. However, since the OPEC-inspired oil-price rises of the 1970s, Kenyan Muslims have received considerable assistance from Middle Eastern and Gulf states in support of overseas study and, as A. B. K. Kasozi demonstrates (Chapter 12), Muslims have much to make up for educationally throughout East Africa. The Iranian revolution of the Ayatollah Khomeini has also been an inspiration to many. Precisely what impact returning Muslim teachers from Al-Azhar or Madina may have in future, it is impossible to predict. East African governments have attempted to control many Muslim activities through the establishment of national organizations, as François Constantin relates (Chapter 2). But the establishment of the Islamic Party of Kenya (IPK) shortly before the national elections in 1992 provides evidence of increased political activism by Muslims on the East African coast. As it happened, the IPK was banned by the Moi government. But Ali Mazrui's prediction of a future *intifada* against the Kenyan government by Swahili-speaking peoples in Kenya's Coast Province, should the IPK be prevented from participating in future general elections, is not to be dismissed out of hand. It is one form of possible politico-religious conflict in future. Nor should the position of Somali-speaking Muslims as soldiers and petty traders be ignored as another source of potential political strife in Kenya. After all, Nubians formed a comparable strategic constituency in Uganda immediately before the seizure of power by a Nubian head of the armed forces there in 1971, and the current head of the Kenyan armed forces is a Somali.

None the less, the principal forms of politico-religious conflict in Kenya since independence have concerned Christians rather than Muslims. It is with their conflicts that David Throup (Chapter 9) and G. P. Benson (Chapter 10) are concerned. Both quote the comment by John Lonsdale, Stanley Booth-Clibborn and Andrew Hake that: 'Apart from the Roman Catholic Church, the churches in Kenya – and there are many – have historically possessed a very limited theology of secular power.'[14] Both provide accounts of how this changed to a considerable extent after independence from Britain.

David Throup's account is a story familiar to analysts of military seizures of power in independent Africa, but as yet undocumented to any considerable extent by students of religion and politics – increased governmental interference in institutional life, and institutional reactions. In the first years of independence, the Christian churches in Kenya kept a low profile because of their earlier very close association with the European colonial power. But in 1969 a government minister was assassinated. In 1969, too, several church leaders expressed anxieties about oathing in Kikuyuland. Government ministers for their part by this time were anxious about pastors and priests making 'political' comments. However, while Jomo Kenyatta remained president of Kenya, government attacks upon individual churchmen did not get out of hand. After all, his wife's brother was Roman Catholic chaplain to the University of Nairobi, another relative was the first African Anglican bishop in Kenya and other Kikuyu were prominent as leaders in other Christian churches. But in 1978 Kenyatta died. Daniel arap Moi now became president of Kenya and embarked upon his own 'hegemonic project'.[15] This included advancing people from his own home area, to the west of Kikululand, into positions of influence and power in the country. In 1982–1983 the process was speeded up considerably, following an abortive *coup d'état* and the fall from power of a leading Kikuyu politician and Anglican layman: 'Njonjo's downfall coincided with the ascension of a new, populist generation of politicians in the ruling Kenya African National Union (KANU).' These new politicians sought to revivify KANU. They were not backward in attacking anybody who stood in their way. Partly because of their international connections, and partly because church services and sermons are extremely difficult to censor in advance, David Throup is probably correct to point out that:

> Only church leaders have the freedom to criticize the government without risking detention [in Kenya]. The CPK [Church of the Province of Kenya – the Anglican Church], Presbyterian and Roman Catholic Churches have occupied the ground emptied by the silencing of serious political opposition since the attempt coup and Njonjo's downfall.

In other words, they became a surrogate opposition to the government of Daniel arap Moi. Subsequently, with the collapse of one-party states in Eastern Europe, and pressure for multi-party democracy throughout Africa from Western European countries and the USA following this collapse, the churches' role as a surrogate opposition in Kenya has increased rather than diminished in salience.

G. P. Benson does not dispute the importance of the regional, international and personal factors in church–government relations in Kenya stressed by David Throup. But Benson is more interested in the cultural factors underlined earlier by Terence Ranger in his survey of African religious movements in Southern and Central Africa. Throup is disparaging of Moi's ideology, *Nyayo* ('footsteps'). Benson takes it more seriously as an amalgam of African cultural, Christian and politically pragmatic discourse. Essentially, Benson sees it as an ideology designed to encapsulate other forms of leadership in Kenya within a single, top-down structure. After 1982–1983, the new KANU politicians attempted to put the structure into operation with more vigour than honesty. A number of Kenyan church leaders protested. Like Throup, Benson has much to say about charismatic critics like the Anglican Henry Okullu and the Presbyterian Timothy Njoya.[16] But he devotes most space to the culturally sensitive and provocative David Gitari, Anglican bishop of Mount Kenya East:

> We have inherited from the Western Church a concept of evangelism as winning individuals to Jesus Christ . . . But an individual making a major decision in his life alone is alien to African culture . . . We are convinced that in our primary evangelism among nomadic peoples, our approach must not be that of rescuing individuals from a sinking boat but rather winning communities . . . The gospel can also be preached in the household of a nomadic people, respecting and preserving their traditional communitarian culture.

Regarding other Kenyan peoples, Gitari's sermons struck chords KANU politicians would have rather not heard. Some concerned a story of Daniel in the Old Testament:

> [King Darius] chose three ministers who were to receive reports from the 120 administrators. We might describe them as 'Ministers in the Office of the President, responsible for provincial administration'. . . .
>
> If Daniel was an administrator in Kenya today, he would sell KANU tickets to every citizen who qualifies and he would not register anybody as a voter who was not supposed to be registered . . .
>
> The conspirators having failed to find fault in Daniel's work, they had to look for faults elsewhere. After much consideration, they decided to remove Daniel by changing the constitution . . .
>
> King Darius made the mistake of allowing the constitution to be changed before this matter which affected fundamental human rights was thoroughly discussed by all concerned.

Benson sees the Kenyan churches' engagement with politics as 'the result of a sustained hermeneutical enterprise' with the Christian Bible as well as with African culture and Kenyan social life. Yet, like David

Michael Twaddle

Throup, he sees the Kenyan churches' contemporary involvement with politics as essentially reactive: 'the churches threw down a challenge just by existing as separate institutions, outside the framework of the *Nyayo* leadership corps'.

If the fragility of the Kenyan state was underlined by the abortive coup of 1 August 1982, the precariousness of its mainland Tanzanian counterpart had been brought home to Julius Nyerere by the army mutinies of 1964.[17] These mutinies led Nyerere to formulate his ideology of African socialism or 'brotherhood' (*Ujamaa*). As a Roman Catholic politician in an immediately adjacent country with a larger Muslim minority than Kenya, concentrated largely but not exclusively along the East African coast, Nyerere stressed that it was a political philosophy based upon man rather than God. References to religion within it were minimal, no attempt being made formally to incorporate insights from liberation theology elsewhere in Africa or the Third World. In an unpublished paper Per Frostin recognizes that its Africanist anthropology ('We are all Africans') is widely regarded nowadays by scholars as mythological, invented more to mask class divisions within the country than to describe or to deal with them directly. Economically, many of its prescriptions have proved disastrous. Internally, much of Nyerere's ideology is incoherent. None the less, Frostin praises his commitment to human liberation:

> The present condition of men [and women] must be unacceptable to all who think of an individual person as a unique creation of a living God. We say man was created in the image of God. I refuse to imagine a God who is poor, ignorant, superstitious, wretched - which is the lot of the majority of those He created in his own image.

Though refusing to situate this God specifically within Christianity, Frostin considers that Nyerere's thought here 'fits into the conceptual framework of liberation theology'. As such, it has 'important implications for the definition of the mission of the church'.

In Uganda, Milton Obote's 'Common Man's Charter' and 'Move to the Left' ideology (1969–1970) was a pale reflection of Nyerere's documentary socialism in Tanzania. These deceived nobody in Uganda, though possibly they assisted Idi Amin's seizure of power in 1971 by convincing local shareholders in the Lake Victoria Bottling Company and comparable enterprises that even these investments were now unsafe. Obote had come to power in 1962 as leader of the Uganda Peoples' Congress in alliance with the *Kabaka Yekka* ('the king alone') movement flourishing in the Buganda kingdom. After the constitutional crisis of 1966–1967, Obote ruled Uganda as executive president, without further election but with army support - until the army commander himself seized power. As Louise Pirouet (Chapter 14) makes clear, the Christian churches were largely silent about infringements of human rights during these early years of power of both Milton Obote and Idi Amin. Together with the Chief Kadhi, the Anglican and Roman Catholic archbishops of Uganda did protest directly to Amin about the mass expulsion of South Asian traders in 1972. But this protest was made privately rather than publicly. Only after the Anglican archbishop himself was murdered, in February 1977, did Christian leaders go public and a critical commentary by the Christian churches upon public affairs commence substantively in Uganda.

None the less, and paradoxically, both the Anglican and the Roman Catholic Churches have been hindered as much as helped in this endeavour by the size of their public support. As Kevin Ward points out in his account of 'The Church of Uganda amidst conflict' (Chapter 6), the Roman Catholic and the Anglican Churches in Uganda are both 'great "folk" churches; that is, they have become integrated at a very basic level into the social, cultural and political fabric' of the country, 'both at the local and the national level'. This is because both denominations came to Uganda nearly two decades before the imposition of the British protectorate, and built up church support and schooling massively in subsequent years. There were never as many competing Christian missionary societies at work in colonial Uganda as in colonial Kenya or Tanganyika, and no Islamic 'no-go' area limiting their room for manoeuvre as in colonial Sudan. As a result, Uganda has one of the highest percentages of professing Christians in Africa today, the great majority of them either Anglicans or Roman Catholics. Roman Catholics were not as successful as Anglicans politically during colonial days and instead concentrated upon building up their spiritual kingdom. Ward points out that since independence political power has also largely eluded Ugandan Roman Catholics. 'The sense that it has been denied its rightful position has helped to give the [Roman] Catholic Church a certain degree of internal unity and cohesion . . . a powerful critical voice *vis-à-vis* the state' and 'probably a majority of the Ugandan population as a whole' as its members.

These considerations inform both John Mary Waliggo's discussion of 'The Catholic Church and the root cause of political instability in Uganda' (Chapter 7) and Ronald Kassimir's case study of 'Catholics and political identity in Toro' (Chapter 8).

Noting Michael Mann's distinction between the 'extensive' and 'intensive' powers of social organizations, Kassimir presents the Roman Catholic Church as 'historically an institution of "extensive" power second to none' in his area of research. Regarding 'intensive' power, he sees the Roman Catholic Church as less successful because of its embeddedness in local social structures and divisions among local Catholics. Clergy and laity who are charismatics are divided from those who are not, paralleling the division between those who are and are not 'saved ones' (*balokole*) in Protestant churches in Eastern Africa. There are also divisions between Roman Catholic clergy and the laity belonging to the Toro Catholic Council on the question of pre-Christian culture. Kassimir quotes one warning by this body that clergy were becoming too remote and that, unless halted, this gap might lead to Catholicism losing its grasp on local Catholics. 'It took less than forty days for the Hebrews to adore the calf and for us paganism is still on the threshold and naturally we are inclined to it.'

Divisions of other kinds among Roman Catholic clergy throughout Eastern Africa are highlighted by Martin Doornbos (Chapter 14). Doornbos draws attention to the tensions created by Catholic missionaries and organizations acting as developmental agencies as well as evangelistic bodies in the post-colonial era. Some elderly missionaries still find it difficult to come to terms with these changes. Other younger ones have an entirely different difficulty. Noting that many African clergy were ordained at a time when clerical prestige was much higher than it is nowadays, Doornbos reports being told

> of African priests who sit reading in their porches, not to be disturbed by people who come to ask for help on rural development projects. They claim that some African clergy oppose reforms, particularly in the nature of the priesthood, because it would devalue the status positions they have reached after prolonged sacrifice.

Doornbos suggests that the basic choice confronting the Roman Catholic Church in Eastern Africa is

> between the continuation of a cautious status quo policy on the one hand . . . and the adoption of a more militant orientation and closer identification with the African world and its problematics, though in doing so risking a collision with the state, as well as friction with Rome as to what is still permissible in terms of universal norms.

John Mary Waliggo is probably an advocate of the latter approach. In his chapter, he draws attention to the views of the first Catholic African bishop (and subsequently archbishop) of Uganda, Joseph Kiwanuka, whose biography he is currently completing. In November 1961 Archbishop Kiwanuka issued an important pastoral letter attacking sectarian politics, 'whereby Protestants came first, Catholics second, Muslims third and traditionalists last'. Waliggo also suggests that:

> Several people have rather uncritically glorified the performance of the first Obote government in the first four years of the country's independence in order to emphasize the point that the root-cause of Uganda's subsequent instability should be sought, not in the past, but in the crisis of 1966. Archbishop Kiwanuka was of an entirely different view. He had strongly opposed the indirect election of Buganda's representatives to the National Assembly, the continued existence of KY [Kabaka Yekka] and its alliance with the Uganda People's Congress (UPC). He had warned that the issue of the 'Lost Counties' would cause trouble, especially as the campaign to

move Baganda into those areas was highly resented by the inhabitants of the counties. To him, Uganda had attained independence [from Britain] before eradicating completely the root-cause of sectarian politics.

Today Father Waliggo is Secretary to the Constitutional Commission, appointed to 'find lasting solutions' to Uganda's problems of 'divisive politics based on tribe, region, religion and political parties'. It is an onerous task, not made easier by the recent revival of kingdoms in southern and western Uganda or by continuing close ties between certain sections of the Anglican Church and the Uganda Peoples' Congress.

It is now possible to comment critically upon the suggestions in a recent number of the *Review of African Political Economy (ROAPE)* devoted to 'Fundamentalism in Africa: religion and politics': (i) that 'religious resurgence, conversion and *belief*, on a grand scale [have been] occurring in Africa and, we emphasize, throughout the world'; (ii) that therefore 'it does seem to matter what people believe in, for it can be argued that it is the *beliefs* themselves which provide the means whereby people negotiate the personal, social and political conditions they experience and through which they may even be empowered'; but (iii) that 'dispensationalist' acceptance by conservative evangelical Christians of contemporary disasters as evidence of the 'last days' immediately preceding the inauguration of a millennium, and their consequent opposition to current development project work, is to be deplored both because of its opposition to development and its evidence of a new variety of Western imperialism.[18] To be sure, the editors of this particular issue of *ROAPE* are uneasy with the view that only 'bad' or conservative evangelical Christians oppose development projects in Africa today. This is sensible scepticism. As Martin Doornbos (Chapter 14) suggests, opposition to development projects is shared nowadays also by some older Roman Catholic priests – and these have not previously been identified as supporters of Protestant dispensationalism. The leading Protestant and conservative evangelical churchmen in Kenya considered by David Throup (Chapter 9) moreover, are all enthusiastic supporters of development projects. Indeed, as Throup reveals, the tragic death of Bishop Muge was partly prompted by one government supporter's opposition to Muge's enthusiasm for development and famine relief work in western Kenya.

It is also too simplistic to say that resurgence in religious belief has itself caused political problems throughout Eastern Africa in recent years. Exponential growth in religious belief is impossible to verify in this part of Africa. Even if it were, political impact would not follow automatically. Louise Pirouet (Chapter 13) quotes a revealing comment in this regard by the conservative evangelical Anglican bishop, Festo Kivengere, during the early 1980s:

> We have a government in Uganda which is almost entirely made up of members of our church. That should make things very easy for us, you may think. But I am sure you know that that makes things very difficult for us. The government does not stand in our way at all . . . in fact we are constantly appealed to by members of the government to take the lead in 'spiritual rehabilitation' . . . this sounds tremendous but underneath it is very difficult because words do not mean actions . . . When the government is putting us in this position of favour, speaking the truth becomes doubly difficult.

Perhaps we should draw attention again to the distinction made by Michael Mann between the 'intensive' and 'extensive' characteristics of social organizations in shaping their political clout. Religious organizations may be penetrated deeply by other social forces and they themselves only influence those other forces in a politically superficial manner.

To be sure, I am using the adjective 'political' here in the sense of 'pertaining to the state', and in his earlier article Terence Ranger rightly remarked that religious organizations have their own imperatives to which the adjective 'political' may also be applied. Indeed, it is regarding millenarian movements in Southern and Central Africa in recent years that some of the most interesting scholarly work has been done regarding politico-religious conflict. Here, with due regard for social context as well as the particularities of belief, subaltern groups recruited into religious organizations may, in another scholar's words, legitimate 'new kinds of leaders while eliciting potential leadership cadres from hitherto passive or suppressed groups'.[19] While therefore agreeing with this writer in rejecting the hubris of 'much instant scholarship, which now attributes to religion all the decisive impact once reserved for Marxism or modernization', we note his endorsement of Max Weber's earlier point about 'the "elective affinities" between religious and political ideas, institutional forms, and practices' and fully support his acceptance of

> religion's tremendous *consolidating* power . . . the peculiar ability of religious metaphors, places and rituals to sum up and intensify experience . . . by joining everyday events to a sense of supernatural intervention and by reinforcing religious ideas with material resources and . . . repeated human interactions. This is what religious organizations and rituals *do*, and this is why they are so powerful in unifying behaviour across social levels . . . in different arenas and walks of life.[20]

This is what makes even a minuscule community of African Jews in eastern Uganda appear deeply subversive to Idi Amin,[21] and comparatively small Muslim populations in neighbouring countries sufficiently worrying for these countries' political leaders to attempt to encapsulate them within a succession of country-wide associations controlled by themselves.

The Character of Politico-Religious Conflict in Eastern Africa

Notes

1. Published by James Currey, London; Ohio University Press, Athens, Ohio, USA; and Uganda Bookshop, Kampala, Uganda.
2. Published by James Currey, London, in association with Ohio University Press, Athens, Ohio, and Fountain Publishers, Kampala.
3. *African Studies Review* (June 1986), p. 12.
4. Ibid.
5. Ibid., p. 19.
6. Ibid., p. 18.
7. T. O. Ranger and I. Kimambo, eds, *The historical study of African religion* (London, 1972) is the pioneering symposium.
8. See Holger Bernt Hansen, 'Pre-colonial immigrants and colonial servants: The Nubians in Uganda revisited', *African Affairs* 90 (1991), pp. 559–580; G. N. Sanderson, *England, Europe and the Upper Nile 1882–1889* (Edinburgh, 1965), pp. 6–9; R. Gray, *A history of the southern Sudan 1839–1889* (London, 1961) for the background.
9. N. King, A. Kasozi and A. Oded, *Islam and the confluence of religions in Uganda* (Tallahassee, 1973), p. 37; interview with Eria Olet, Lira, Uganda, November 1965.
10. See J. S. Mangat, ch. 12 in D. A. Low and Alison Smith, eds, *History of East Africa*, vol. III (Oxford, 1976); F. Constantin, ed., *Les Voies de l'Islam en Afrique orientale* (Paris, 1987).
11. See J. Middleton, ch. 13 in Low and Smith, *History of East Africa*, vol. III; M. Lofchie, *Zanzibar: Background to revolution* (Princeton, 1965).
12. A. Clayton, *The Zanzibar revolution and its aftermath* (London, 1981), pp. 48 ff.
13. Ibid., p. 45.
14. In their contribution to the important *Christianity in independent Africa*, edited by E. Fashole-Luke, R. Gray, A. Hastings and G. Tasie (London, 1978), p. 267.
15. This notion is developed systematically in Jean-François Bayart, *L'Etat en Afrique: La politique du ventre* (Paris, 1989); now available in an English translation as *The State in Africa: The politics of the belly* (London 1993).
16. See Timothy Njoya, *Human dignity and national identity* (Nairobi, 1987) and *Out of silence* (Nairobi, 1987); Henry Okullu, *Church and politics in East Africa* (Nairobi, 1979) and *Church and state in nation building and human development* (Nairobi, 1984).
17. See further H. Bienen, *Armies and parties in Africa* (New York, 1978).
18. *Review of African Political Economy* 52 (Nov. 1991), pp. 3, 7.
19. Daniel H. Levine, 'Religion and politics in comparative and historical perspective', *Comparative Politics* 19 (1986), p. 100.
20. Ibid., pp. 95, 97.
21. Michael Twaddle, *Kakungulu and the creation of Uganda* (London, 1993), p. 300.

Part One

The Challenge of Islam

Two

Muslims & Politics

The Attempts to Create
Muslim National Organizations
in Tanzania, Uganda & Kenya

FRANÇOIS CONSTANTIN

Very few scholars have interested themselves in research into the development of national Muslim organizations in post-colonial Africa.[1] One reason may be that these organizations are comparatively inefficient and not yet particularly important in either religious, social or political terms. Yet even this opinion needs to be substantiated through serious (and that means scientific) research. Such research is still at a comparatively early stage in Eastern Africa. This chapter is a preliminary attempt at suggesting some aspects requiring further reflection and study.

One question in particular requires further attention. This is the attempted bureaucratization of Muslim communities and its impact upon religions and political affairs in Eastern Africa. This involves complex issues associated with the articulation of what Gramsci called civil and political societies. This is a complex matter, firstly, because religions differ so much in character, from the heavily centralized Roman Catholic Church at one end of the spectrum to the more or less decentralized Muslim sects at the other extreme. Among Muslims, organizational principles can be both democratic (regarding management of mosque affairs) and autocratic (through the agency of spiritual charismatic leadership). Moreover, religious pluralism is not the same in Kenya, Uganda and Tanzania, and even in one of these countries policies towards religious affairs may vary considerably. It is highly speculative to suggest general propositions about the significance of organizational changes which are valid for all three countries, let alone further afield. Secondly, we should remember that political systems may vary widely also within single countries. It is not necessary to emphasize here the differences in the political development of Kenya, Tanzania and Uganda at state level. Last but not least, the articulation of religion and politics is an even more complex matter when we consider that, with few exceptions, the religious believer is a human being required to play a variety of interacting social roles that are not necessarily congruent with one another. The believer may be at the same time a peasant, an urban worker or an entrepreneur, living in town or countryside, young or old, male or female, of high or low education having to deal with his or her own material and affective affairs. Religion is just one of many daily troubles (and/or delights).

None the less, keeping in mind these basic considerations, some general factors transcend them. One is that, following Max Weber, we must consider bureaucratic organization to be a vital structure in modern societies reinforcing the legitimacy and effectiveness of a centralized power. Bureaucracy is a formidable 'multiplier of power'. That is one reason why Weber predicted its generalization in complex, modern societies. This hypothesis will be borne in mind throughout our case study.[2] We should also perhaps note here the general historical background to Islam in East Africa. Let us just remember that, before European colonialism, Islam was a core element of the Arab–Omani hegemony on the East African coast. It was the monopoly of a (politically and economically) ruling minority. None the less, the prestige of Muslimhood (which was in turn associated with the Swahilization process) was disturbed by the development of a popular Islam (through brotherhoods) and then by the domination of Christian European rulers. During the anti-colonial struggle, the status of Islam was still ambiguous because of the historical memory of Arab domination (actualized in the continuance of the Sultanate of Zanzibar), and because of the support accorded by some literate Muslims to British colonial rule itself.[3] Thus nowadays Muslims in ex-British East Africa are not only a minority at national level (even in Tanzania) but a minority divided along religious, social and political lines.

However, throughout Eastern Africa, from Kenya to Zimbabwe, politicians and Muslim leaders have attempted to unite Muslim communities into single national associations. These are supposed to co-ordinate, regulate and centralize the various activities more or less related to religious (meaning, in these contexts, Islamic) matters. Whatever conclusions may be drawn regarding the effectiveness or otherwise of these national associations, such a widespread process cannot be regarded as politically insignificant. These organizations are SUPKEM (Supreme Council of Kenya Muslims), BAKWATA (Baraza Kuu Waislamu wa Tanzania) and the Uganda Muslim Supreme Council (UMSC) or, for a time in Uganda, the National Association for the Advancement of Muslims (NAAM). Their 'supremacy' is rather dubious and, even when their legal positions and statuses are made public in printed regulations, their legitimacy and social impact remain ambiguous.

At first sight, it would seem that the statutory recognition of a national Muslim association is a signal success for a much divided minority group. It would seem to be a positive step for Muslims seeking to increase social influence and to secure their corporate identity more firmly at nation-state level. For these very reasons, Muslim leaders lobby, too, for the legalization of Islamic law, for the development of Muslim educational facilities and for greater access to state radio and TV. Compared with a situation in which numerous subordinate Muslim associations selfishly compete with one another for attention, one national Muslim association acting on behalf of all believers should enable it to overcome the problems of leadership in pluralist and complex groups and indeed to be more efficient in operating as an interest group in support of Muslim concerns.[4]

However, such success could be more apparent than real as institutionalization (bureaucratization) gives central government legal and political opportunities for closer control of the activities of Muslim communities, particularly those troubling the political system. Moreover, we should remember R. Michels' findings on the effects of the bureaucratization process on associative movements. Centralization often creates oligarchy even when leaders are elected, and new conflicts develop within communities whose leaders compete for access to new strategic cores of power or influence.[5] Centralization also creates a marginalized militant minority, or minorities, opposing the oligarchy and likely to initiate political troubles for central governments.

This pessimistic perspective draws sustenance not only from current events in Kenya and Tanzania, but also from historical investigations into the development of Muslim supreme councils in Eastern Africa in recent years. But, before reflecting upon the way in which national associations were created and their ensuing problems, we should first understand why the post-colonial African state requires closer control over Muslim communities.

Muslims and politics in Eastern African states

Most Eastern African post-colonial states' constitutions acknowledge freedom of worship, and most of their governments do not harass religious leaders openly. They prefer to get their support. Every day Eastern African rulers defer to religious piety in speeches, public attitudes and behaviour.[6] The only exception to this general rule is Mozambique during its Marxist-Leninist phase, when Muslims were criticized for alleged laziness and alliance with Portuguese colonial rule.[7] Elsewhere, individual restrictions have been imposed upon a cult or sect when suspected of creating disturbance or opposition to the ruling party. On unsafe Ugandan and Kenyan roads, it has also happened that some prominent priests and bishops have died in unexpected car crashes. Except for localized troubles and repressive actions, one can, however, say that there is no 'Muslim issue' as such in Eastern Africa. Even during Idi Amin Dada's dictatorship and the years immediately afterwards in Uganda, the problem was less one of religious repression than of widespread tyrannic power.[8] Yet Eastern African governments are still confronted with more specific thorny issues concerning Muslim peoples in the region.

Local and regional issues

Many Muslim people are concentrated in specific areas of big cities as well as on the coast. Historically, the question of the 'coastal strip' was an important issue during the independence negotiations in Kenya. Subsequently, the Kenyan government has had to deal with security problems in the North Eastern Province, inhabited by Muslim Somali-speaking inhabitants. Recent developments in the history of the union of Zanzibar and mainland Tanzania also demonstrate that the Islamic factor can be used by factions opposed to the union. More contentious debate, however, arises during general elections. Muslim issues are then debated hotly by competing candidates canvassing for votes in constituencies in which Muslim minorities both reside and are registered as electors. That happened, for instance, in Nairobi during the early 1980s.[9] In the same way, the intensification of multi-party democratic debates throughout Eastern Africa is nowadays contributing to the further activation of Islamic political militancy in the region.

Economic stakes

Sometimes specialized jobs may be the virtual monopoly of Muslim people (taxi-drivers or butchers in Uganda, boat-builders on the Swahili-speaking East African coast), who thereby increase in social influence as they work to satisfy the needs of the wider population, as too does the hard-working retail shopkeeper (*dukawallah*) of Arab or Asian origin who happens to be a Muslim. More important is the national or even international power of private dynastic corporations linking Eastern African economies with the wider world (Arabia, India and North America especially). The power of these networks is increasing with the intensification of economic crisis throughout Eastern Africa, basically because they are the only people able to supply essential goods, albeit at inflated prices. They tend at the same time to be loosely protected by the dominant African authorities (as shown, for example, by the official comeback of the Aga Khan in Tanzania at the time of the Economic Recovery Programme) and to be hated strongly by the urban poor (as shown by sporadic pogroms in Kenya or Uganda).[10]

Cultural concerns

Until the end of the nineteenth century, particularly on the East African coast, Islamic culture was regarded as superior, as indicated by the Kiswahili word *ustaarabu* for 'civilization', and Muslims (particularly Arab Muslims) were highly respected. But European colonialism introduced Christian denominations, which proved to be more efficient agents of social promotion, not only during the era of European domination but afterwards too. None the less, Islam is still highly regarded in Eastern Africa, and not only by conservative people. Modernist attitudes towards education and politics emerged in the 1930s among some members of the Muslim élite – particularly among Asians – who propagated the view that Muslim values were not outdated in the modern world. But, today, Islam is used as the ideology of protest against the current social and political order. Islamic dynamics are active among troubled, destabilized groups such as the young and disgruntled people who rioted in Mombasa in November 1987 or on Zanzibar during May 1989. Actually, this is not so much a cultural problem as a political and ideological one, closely related to the socio-economic issues noted in the previous section.

International considerations

Religion, among other things, implies transnationality, and most of the Islamic holy centres are not far from any part of Eastern Africa in strictly geographical terms. Pilgrims go constantly to Mecca and to other sacred cities in Arabia, and students go to study at Islamic universities in Egypt, Sudan and Arabia. At the same time, networks related to kinship and business and criss-crossing the western Indian Ocean are very active. Africans can find well-paid jobs in Arabia, in most of the emirates or in North Africa, and improve their social status at home through the prestige and relative wealth accumulated through their sojourns in Arab countries. African governments expect to obtain financial support from the richer Arab oil-producing countries. Black markets and official deals are more important here than diplomatic links (of course, sometimes they overlap), and uncontrolled private transactions constitute a problem for governments on both the oil-producing and non-oil-producing sides: both are losing money (through unpaid export or import duties and non-taxed profits), Arabs fear uncontrolled immigration and African governments are afraid of subversion by either radical Islamic propaganda from Libya or Iran or through capitalist domination by returning Omanis.[11]

The construction of national Muslim associations is also directly related to concerns by East African governments about each of these overlapping clusters of issues.

Creating supreme councils for Muslims

A government may increase control over or influence with Christian private networks by negotiating with local religious leaders (a cardinal or an Anglican archbishop) or with a central religious authority (the Pope). Such hierarchical power does not really exist within Islam, especially among the Sunni.[12] Thus, when confronted with what it considers to be subversive activities (in the political or economic sphere) closely related to identifiable groups, an Eastern African government looks for authoritative leaders. Creating a national Muslim association may therefore be seen as part of a general policy of social control initiated by post-colonial governments. But Muslims themselves are also directly involved in this bureaucratization process.

Three groups are mainly concerned – the national Muslims themselves, local politicians and foreign governments and organizations.

In Kenya, Tanzania and Uganda, certain Muslim associations existed for a long time without any intervention by state authorities in their affairs. But the first important territorial or regional religious associations were generally initiated by Asian Muslims in British East Africa. Arab (Omani) authority was based more traditionally upon clanship and upon *ulama*'s religious authority. Many Africans were relative newcomers to Islam, some initiated into it through brotherhoods.[13] Formal territorial and regional Muslim associations were first organized in the 1930s and 1940s in Uganda and on the Kenyan coast. Acting essentially as instrumental interest groups, they articulated demands of members, who were initially mostly Asians. Nevertheless, they were efficient negotiators. They were able to obtain a certain recognition for Muslim laws as well as government approval of Muslim schools and other activities, such as the development of welfare centres. The most important of these Asian-led associations was the East African Muslim Welfare Society (EAMWS), created by the

Aga Khan's Ismaili community in 1945. More specialized associations were created to deal with education or health upon a more restricted, communal basis. This pluralism fed further splits in Muslim leadership, adding to divisions over religious ceremonial and secular issues and differences between the various Muslim legal schools and brotherhoods, not to mention further strains induced by the segregationist policy of the British colonial government, which ranked Asians, Arabs and 'Natives' in separate educational hierarchies. Granted such divisions, ambitious Muslim politicians tended to use religious associations as aids to career development in a negative rather than a positive manner, accentuating divisions among Muslims instead of attempting to bridge them, especially in Uganda.[14]

With the creation of post-colonial states in Tanganyika (Tanzania in 1964), Uganda and Kenya, it quickly became evident that the strengthening of social control required Muslim minorities to be unified into bureaucratically centralized bodies. This became especially evident by the end of the 1960s. Top-level politicians were therefore directly involved in the conferences and negotiations which led to the creation of supreme councils for Muslims in Uganda (A. Nekyon and NAAM), Tanzania (A. Karume and R. Kawawa and BAKWATA) and Kenya (A. Abdullah and SUPKEM), though not all of them subsequently became formal members of the leading boards of these supreme councils.

Through the respective national councils, social attitudes of Muslim believers were to be regulated. Because of the top-down nature of their formation, council leaders were members of the appropriate national establishments. In the prevailing one-party states, this meant that they had to be in harmony with the political leadership or at least with some leading faction within it. Government expected the supreme council's staff to help control Muslim people. Conversely, Muslim believers accepted these leaders in so far as they promoted Islamic values and interests at the national level. Thus it was important for those leaders to have access to state-administered resources which they could share with their Muslim brethren. These resources might be symbolic (participation by Muslim religious leaders in state ceremonies), political (direct access to decision-makers) or economic (funding for Muslim buildings or activities). These were all classic clientelist strategies, requiring Muslim leaders to act as faithful clients of politicians (this was the price to pay for resources received) and leading grass-roots level believers to consider their superiors in the Muslim national association as respected authorities – as long as funds, jobs, air tickets and self-esteem continued to flow.[15]

At the various levels of any hierarchical clientelist structure, the price to be paid for access to resources is political conformism. This is the case whether the client is president of the supreme council, a multinational capitalist businessman, a hard-working *dukawallah* or a jobless believer. All are expected to accept the system and to behave as loyal citizens of a political order which is legitimate because it helps to perform Muslim religious tasks.

Such clientelist logic sometimes fails. This was shown in Tanzania in 1967, when the interests of some Muslim (economic) leaders differed too much from the ideology and related regulations of the new socialist-oriented *Ujamaa* policy. This contradiction developed into a conflict within the ruling élite of Tanzania, which ended in the banning of the EAMWS and the establishment of BAKWATA in 1968.[16]

The importance of the international dimension is indicated by the intervention of Arab organizations (such as the Islamic Call Organization) and some Arab governments (in southern Arabia and some emirates) in the establishment and running of Muslim supreme councils. Examples are SUPKEM in Kenya, which was subsidized by the Islamic Foundation, and later the creation of BAMITA (Association of Mosques of Tanzania) under the sponsorship of the Islamic World League in Tanzania. Such involvement may be explained in terms of religious piety, whereby wealthy rulers consider it their religious obligation to help poorer brethren and to contribute to the spread of Islam in Eastern Africa. More pragmatically, granted the prevailing political climate of conflict in the Middle East, and even between Arab states themselves, bureaucratic structures may have been considered helpful as channels for Arab financial aid to East Africa because of the possibilities of creating thereby new clientelist networks linking kings, emirs and colonels in the Arab world to a wide range of indebted African governments.

According to their legal instruments, the supreme councils are the only acknowledged Muslim associations at the national level in Kenya, Tanzania, Uganda, Mozambique and Malawi. As such, the supreme council is both an institutionalized interest group and an adviser to government on secular matters concerning Muslims. Official participation in the state system inevitably sometimes creates contradictions amongst Muslims, as shown in Kenya in the early 1980s in the cautious attitude of SUPKEM during the Succession (Inheritance) Law crisis, which was strongly criticized by radical Kenyan Muslims.[17]

The council is supposed to be in charge of the management of national religious activities, particularly organization of the pilgrimage to Mecca, collecting and allocating national and foreign funds for religious activities, maintenance of social services (education, health) and the organization of religious festivals, such as Idd or Maulidi. Councils may have a diplomatic role concerning accommodation for pilgrims in Mecca or managing international funds for Muslim schools or hospitals. But the domain of the supreme council is limited to secular matters as it has no authority in theological or intra-Islamic legal disputes. These fall within the competence of learned *ulama* or sheikhs and of kadhi courts nominated by government. None the less, such disputes can create troubles within the national organization, as was spectacularly the case in Uganda.

Some councils look like federations of pre-existing associations – they retain their identity but are required to participate in the supreme council. Such is the case of SUPKEM. However, in Kenya some Asian and more localized Muslim associations are not members of SUPKEM while remaining registered bodies. Other supreme councils are organized on the principle of bureaucratic centralism. BAKWATA's structure, for example, is more centralized and was supposed to parallel the structure of the government party (TANU/CCM), with about 55 local branches, district and regional offices covering mainland Tanzania and, at the top, a central board. BAKWATA, however, does not extend to Zanzibar. Even on the Tanzanian mainland, other Muslim associations emerge from time to time, more or less opposed to BAKWATA's domination. The Tanzanian government does not appear to ban these rivals systematically except when they are suspected of supporting subversive opposition.[18]

The leaders and directors of Muslim supreme councils in Eastern Africa are supposed to be elected. In fact, they tend to be re-elected, except at times of serious internal crisis or of conflict with public authorities. The oligarchical process is clearly at work here, to the extent that the legitimacy of the leadership in some supreme councils or even of the councils themselves is a permanent challenge to other Muslims. This is merely one of a number of current issues.

Current issues

As noted already, not all Muslim religious groups or secular associations are associated with supreme councils. Coastal Muslims in Kenya, Shi'a sects and fundamentalist groupings in general are reluctant to integrate with seemingly state-related and centralized councils. At the same time, brotherhoods seem sometimes to be active and their leaders to be at best formal members of the national council. Because of their international links and spiritual leadership, these unintegrated, or only partially integrated, groupings can be more powerful than the supreme council itself. The Ramiya family leading the Qadiriyya brotherhood and Sheikh Musa's Simbon Centre in Tanzania are further examples of Muslim organizations largely outside a supreme council's control. Were it to wish to take such action, the central government concerned probably would not feel strong enough to impose total integration upon these bodies or to ban them completely. The supreme council's supremacy is further weakened by its sharing of religious authority in even minor matters with sheikhs, imams and kadhis. Indeed, as in Islam there is no clear-cut distinction between religious and secular affairs, the leadership of a supreme council may eventually appear fictional. Certainly, none of them appears to have proved capable thus far of forming any really effective form of institutionalized authority or charismatic domination.

The basic issue confronting Muslims in Eastern Africa nowadays is perhaps who in Islam has the right to speak authoritatively throughout all Muslim communities. This issue is linked to a fundamental characteristic of Muslimhood. The existence of a world-wide shared feeling of the unity of the *Umma* has never meant acceptance of any one centralized power. This is possibly one explanation for continuing political instability among Muslim peoples. Some commentators even argue that modern bureaucratic organization, as a typical product of Western European ideology and culture, implies a strict distinction between religious and secular affairs, a distinction which does not exist in Islam.[19] The creation of a Muslim national organization is therefore considered by Muslims to create one more structure which might be used to extend social influence and economic and/or political power over them by ambitious 'big men'. These characteristically struggle for control of the Muslim national organization, either openly or covertly through intermediaries. Thereby the perverse logic of organizational development on the eve of the twentieth century described by R. Michels (1958) plays itself out within Muslim supreme councils in Eastern Africa. Democratic rules (elections, participation, discussion) are all marginalized with the concentration of power in the hands of a small oligarchy whose legitimacy arises from the political élite rather than the social base.[20]

In so far as the Muslim national association seems only to be an instrument for individual prestige, profit and power, it does not perform its statutory duties. For many ordinary Muslims, schools are not built on schedule, scholarly duties are not performed honestly, health centres are neglected: 'They mix religion and money, and that is wrong' is a common complaint, implying that business is considered by the leaders as more important than spiritual or welfare issue. The Muslim national organization therefore comes to be seen as just another extension of the corruption system. The believer as such no longer feels concerned and prefers to return to 'informal' or underground structures, to structures that are strongly independent of any direct governmental influence. The influence of charismatic leaders, such as the famous readers of the Koran or of learned sheikhs, and political mobilization through rival bodies (such as BALUKTA – the National Association of Koran Readers in Tanzania) or parties (such as the still unregistered Islamic Party of Kenya) are evidence of the crises of the supreme councils.[21]

Where legitimacy, too, is seriously declining, reactions come from central government, which considers it has to intervene through changing leaders (as has happened several times in Uganda) or through the creation of a new association, as did the Tanzanian government in the early 1980s, when the then Vice-President of the Republic and President of Zanzibar, A. Jumbe, toured the mainland in support of BAMITA to replace the run-down BAKWATA. But changing structures or men generally does not alter the roots of problems. It seems that, after Jumbe's resignation, BAMITA (which eventually did not work on the mainland) was no longer active even in Zanzibar. Now management of the religious activities of the Muslims there is the responsibility of the Waqf Commission. This is another institution created by the government of Zanzibar, with members appointed by the same government.[22] The only alternative is again the popular one, where Muslims create new local bodies to counter the inefficiency or corruption of the national supreme council.

But bureaucratic inefficiency and corruption are but one aspect of the dangers of increasing interventions in religious affairs by governments and political parties. The official recognition of Muslim law in the national legal system seems to be a triumph for Muslim minorities when legal unification drafts are first published. But the application of that law is in the hands of Muslim judges (kadhis), themselves generally appointed by government and therefore appearing as governmental civil servants. Under cover of the unification of law (and even of just Islamic law), the government even tries to 'adapt' the Muslim (Koranic) rules, for instance, on family or inheritance matters. But this creates conflicts, not only between Muslim and non-Muslims, but among Muslims themselves, as shown by the Succession Law dispute in Kenya in the early 1980s, to which reference has already been made.[23]

The teaching of Islam in public schools is, in the same way, controlled by governmental officers, who can decide on the appointment of the teachers and control the syllabus according to recommendations of experts only partly representative of the Muslim people. Access to national media, radio and TV, especially, also depends on a Ministry of Information which can choose Muslim speakers without considering their religious reputation. When bargaining with the central political system, a religious group has to be careful and to remember that a major consideration for the government is to increase its control over all social groups. But, when Muslim communities are rich enough to organize their own educational system and their own information structures, they impose upon the state authorities a more cautious attitude. The relations of East African governments with the Aga Khan's Ismailis or with the Islamic Foundation are contemporary examples of such cautiousness.

In short, for Muslims the advancement of religious interests requires both them and their governments to behave like interest groups. Very often there is a negotiated deal where the government agrees to take into account some religious demand. But, at the same time, the state is enabled thereby to penetrate religious affairs – by appointing teachers, speakers, judges or whatever. Even where Machiavellian intentions are absent, the government will organize such affairs according to national rules and what it considers to be the national interest. A first risk is then the 'nationalization' of Islam, much as Christianity was 'nationalized' nearly two millennia ago with the Emperor Constantine's intervention in God's affairs. But this development requires first an effectively strong Emperor of another sort to emerge, which is not yet the case in Eastern Africa. Another risk is an increasing mobilization of disgruntled Muslims opposing the state system as a whole and embarking upon political unrest before considering their actual powers to influence events in Eastern Africa.

Notes

1. The only noteworthy exception is Abdu K. Kasozi, 'The Uganda Muslim Supreme Council: an experiment in Muslim administrative centralization and institutionalization, 1972–1982', *Journal of the Institute of Muslim Minority Affairs* 6 (1) (1985). Some information can be found in K. Mayanja Kiwanuka, *The Politics of Islam in Bukoba district*, BA Dissertation, University of Dar es Salaam (1973); David Westerlund, *Ujamaa na dini* (Stockholm, Almquist & Wiksell, 1980).

2. For theoretical developments on modern bureaucracy: Bengt Abrahamsson, *Bureaucracy or participation: The logic of organization* (Beverly Hills/London, Sage Publications, 1977; Michel Crozier, *The Bureaucratic phenomenon* (London, Tavistock, 1964); H. H. Gerth and C. Wright Mills, eds, *From Max Weber: Essays in sociology* (London/Boston, Routledge & Kegan Paul, 1982).

3. The historical background is developed in the three volumes of *History of East Africa* published by Clarendon Press, Oxford. Political and social aspects are outlined particularly in Frederick Cooper, 'Islam and cultural hegemony: The ideology of slaveowners on the East African coast', in Paul Lovejoy, ed., *The ideology of slavery in Africa* (London, Sage Publications, 1981); François Constantin, *Les Communautés musulmanes d'Afrique orientale* (Pau, CREPAO, 1983); id., 'De l'Arabie du sud à l'Afrique orientale: Réflexions à propos d'une hégémonie imparfaite', *Canadian Journal of African Studies* 3 (1987) id., 'Social stratification on the Swahili coast: from race to class?', *Africa* 59 (2) (1989).

4. This was the first argument developed by the director of SUPKEM, interview, Nairobi, June 1985.

5. Robert Michels, *Political parties* (Glencoe, Free Press, 1958). On Ugandan conflicts, see François Constantin, 'Minorité religieuse et luttes politiques dans l'espace ougandais', *Politique Africaine* 4 (1981).

6. President Daniel arap Moi is one of the best example of such public piety. See Stephen M. Njiro, *Daniel arap Moi, man of peace, love and unity* (Nairobi, Transafrica, 1980).

7. *Tempo*, 30 August (1981); *Al Islam* (Dar es Salaam) 1 (2) (1980).

8. Remember Archbishop Luwum's (1977) and Bishop Muge's (1990) deaths and the banning of the *Watchtower* in Kenya and Malawi. On Idi Amin, see Constantin, *Politique Africaine* 4 (1981); John A. Rowe, 'Islam under Idi Amin: A case of *déjà vu?*', in Holger B. Hansen and Michael Twaddle, eds, *Uganda now, between decay and develop-*

ment (London, James Currey, 1988); and Kokole's contribution in this volume.

9. See Ahmed I. Salim, 'The Movement of "Mwambao" or coast autonomy in Kenya, 1956-1963', in Bethwell A. Ogot, ed, *Hadith 2* (Nairobi, East African Publishing House, 1975); *The Weekly Review* from February to September 1979 (elections in Nairobi); the 'Bismillah' opposition campaign in Zanzibar in 1989.

10. See Mougo Nyaggah, 'Asians in East Africa: The case of Kenya', *Journal of African Studies* 1 (2) (1974). The Madhvanis and Mehtas are just two examples of famous East African Asian transnational families whose expulsion from Uganda under Amin was not seriously criticized by African opinion. See Gérard Prunier, *L'Ouganda et la question indienne, 1896-1972* (Paris, ERC, 1990) and Michael Twaddle, ed., *Expulsion of a minority: Essays on Ugandan Asians* (London, The Athlone Press, 1975). Another study is John I. Zarwan, *Indian businessmen in Kenya during the twentieth century: A case study*, PhD, Yale University (1977). On those networks, see François Constantin 'Sur les modes populaires d'action diplomatiques: Affaires de famille et affaires d'état en Afrique orientale', *Revue Française de Science Politique* 36 (5) (1986).

11. François Constantin and Françoise Le Guennec Coppens, 'Dubaï Street, Zanzibar . . . ', *Politique Africaine*, 30 (1988). See also the informative page 12 chronicles in the fortnightly *Africa Analysis*.

12. Shi'a sects are more centralized, as shown by the Aga Khan's leadership of the Ismailis, or the Dai's leadership of the Dawoodi Bohras.

13. B. G. Martin, *Muslim brotherhoods in nineteenth-century Africa* (Cambridge, Cambridge University Press; 1976); August H. Nimtz, *Islam and politics in East Africa* (Minneapolis, University of Minnesota Press, 1980); A. H. M. El Zein, *The sacred meadows: A structural analysis of religious symbolism in an East African town (Lamu)* (Evanston, Northwestern University Press, 1974); François Constantin, ed., *Les Voies de l'islam en Afrique orientale* (Paris, Karthala, 1988); id., 'Charisma and the crisis of power in East Africa', in Donal Cruise O'Brien and Christian Coulon, eds, *Charisma and brotherhoods in African Islam* (Oxford, Clarendon Press, 1988).

14. On conflicts concerning rituals (Maulidi, drumming), see Alan W. Boyd, *To praise the Prophet: A processual symbolic analysis of 'Maulidi', a Muslim ritual in Lamu, Kenya*, PhD, Indiana University (1981). See also Abdu B. K. Kasozi, *The spread of Islam in Uganda* (Nairobi/Khartoum, Oxford University Press/Islamic African Centre, 1986).

15. On clientelism, see S. N. Eisenstadt and René Lemarchand, *Political clientelism, patronage and development* (Beverly Hills/London, Sage Publications, 1981). The problem of self-esteem is implicit in the militant paper of Mohammed Saïdi, *Islam and politics in Tanzania* (Nairobi, Conference on Daawa in East Africa, mimeo, 1989); for a field analysis, see Pamela W. Landberg, *Kinship and community in a Tanzania coastal village*, PhD, University of California (1977).

16. See Kiwanuka, *Politics of Islam*, or Westerlund, *Ujamaa na dini*.

17. See further François Constantin 'Loi de l'islam contre loi de l'état: petite chronique d'un été kenyan', *Islam et sociétés au Sud du Sahara*, 3 (1989).

18. See Kiwanuka, *Politics of Islam*; local information, Tanzania, May 1987, June 1989.

19. Bertrand Badie, *Les Deux états: Pouvoir et société en Occident et en terre d'Islam* (Paris, Fayard, 1986).

20. Michels, *Political parties*.

21. Local information, Bagamoyo (May 1987), Dar es Salaam, Zanzibar (May 1987, June 1989), Moshi (June 1989).

22. Interview, Zanzibar, June 1989.

23. Constantin, *Islam et Sociétés au Sud du Sahara* 3 (1989); Abdu B. K. Kasozi, *The Influence of Christian–Muslim relations on public policy formation and implementation in East Africa since 1900* (Roskilde, mimeo, 1990), a revised version of which appears in this volume.

Three

The Past
in the Present?

The Issue of the Sharia
in Sudan

R. S. O'FAHEY

The issue of the Sharia or Islamic law has become central to the political
and military conflicts of modern Sudan. At one end of the ideological
spectrum is the National Islamic Front (*al-jabhat al-Islamiyya al-qawmiyya*:
NIF) led by Dr Hasan al-Turabi, which is the dominant civilian force
behind the military regime of Umar al-Bashir which seized power in
July 1989; at the other end is the Sudan People's Liberation Army/
Sudan People's Liberation Movement (SPLA/SPLM), the creation of
Dr John Garang, now seemingly hopelessly factionalized. Between the
poles of the NIF and the SPLA sit uncomfortably the old, largely
northern, political parties, which cannot quite decide on which side of
the Sharia fence to be.

The Islamic resurgence and the Sharia issue

The 'restoration' of the Sharia as the law of the land has become the
touchstone of Islamist movements throughout the Muslim world.[1] The
Sharia is God's revealed law; it is therefore a collective duty of Muslims
to obey it, just as it is the duty of the jurisprudents to determine what
the Sharia is. Historically, the law that prevailed in any given Muslim

---

*A study of this issue risks being out of date before it is published. The present contribu-
tion is based on the sources cited and on conversations held by the author with northern
Sudanese intellectuals, including Dr al-Turabi, during a visit in December 1992/
January 1993.

country was in practice a compromise between divine law, local custom and the fiat of the rulers. Generally, the Sharia prevailed in matters of personal status (marriage, divorce and the like), while criminal and property law was subject to local variations. By the late nineteenth century, the Sharia's domain narrowed even more as secular codes were imported or imposed on more and more Muslim countries. It is this compromise, where the modern compromise over law is but one of a range of concessions in the face of the Western secular impact, that is unacceptable to all Islamist movements, from Morocco to Malaysia. At one level, the demand for the 'restoration') of the Sharia is an innovation since the Islamists, admit now of no possibility of compromise; in another sense, it is a traditional demand in that all revolutionary movements in the Islamic world have demanded a return to the precedents of *al-salaf al-salih*, 'the pious ancestors', that is to the pristine state of the Prophet and his Companions.

For the student of Sudan's recent past and present, a problem lies in where to pitch discussion of the debate. The actors on all sides of the Sudanese political divide are highly articulate men (little has been written by women); a stream of books, pamphlets and manifestos pours out, some highly abstract tomes, some very concrete ephemera. Their authors are usually fluent in both Arabic and English (at least) and tailor their writings to their desired readership.[2] It becomes hard to tie down the theoretical debate to the realities on the ground; the former conceals the latter.

On the ground now

What is the present (1993) situation in Sudan?[3] Frankly, it is horrendous. A civil war, which started in 1955 with a short intermission between 1972 and 1983, continues its inexorable devouring of people and resources with no one able or seemingly willing to bring it to an end. The present talks being held under the auspices of the Nigerian government at Abuja appear to offer very little hope of a genuine negotiated settlement. Moreover, the conflict is no longer an 'organized' war between a northern Sudanese army and a rebel southern movement (the SPLA has now split into at least three factions); rather, it has fragmented into dozens of local tribal conflicts, pitting Arab nomads against their southern neighbours, Dinka against Nuer. The old Sudanic African 'fracture belt' between Muslim and non-Muslim, an arena of slave- and cattle-raiding has returned. In desperation, the previous democratic regime of Sadiq al-Mahdi (1985–June 1989) and the present military regime of Umar al-Bashir have armed the Arab nomads of the west, leading to the resurgence of slave-raiding[4] and vicious intertribal warfare. Certain ethnic groups, particularly the Dinka, Fur and Nuba, seem to have been targeted by the government for 'ethnic cleansing'. Ecological degradation in the savannahs has brought a new dimension to the conflict as Arab nomads look for new land, often in alliance with traders from the capital interested in mechanized farming, at the expense of local communities.

Dissent among the intellectuals is silenced by torture, imprisonment, loss of jobs and exile. The country is bankrupt, while famine revisits the land and food, or rather its denial, is a recognized weapon of war. An estimated 3 million Sudanese live outside their country; by no means all are exiles, but many, especially the educated, are.

In the midst of all this tragedy, the NIF insists that Sudan must become a truly Muslim state, specifically that 'Islamic jurisprudence shall be the general source of law'.[5] Two attempts have so far been made to realize this, in 1983 by Ja'far al-Numayri with the so-called 'September Laws' and in January/February 1991 with the formal resuscitation of the *hadd* punishments of Islamic law by the present regime. Here I want to consider two questions. Has this call for the implementation of Islamic law or the Sharia as the law of the land roots in Sudan's past, or is it something new? And, further, what is the ideological significance of this demand within the present crisis in Sudan?

Islam in Sudan or Sudanese Islam?[6]

The coming of Islam to northern and western Sudan is associated with the immigration of Arab nomads in the Middle Ages. While the nomads brought with them Arabic, they are not seen as the primary agents of Islamization; the latter were above all the peripatetic holy men (*faqih*, 'jurisconsult', but in Sudan with the anomalous plural, *fuqara*, 'poor, medicant' - a term with Sufi overtones). These frontier missionaries were responsible for the primary Islamization of northern and western Sudan.[7] In the secondary literature these holy men are described as Sufis and the type of Islam they taught as 'popular'. This may to a degree be true, but it is as incorrect to equate Sufism with popular or folk Islam as it is to equate Sufism with antinomianism, that all Sufis were careless of or ignorant of the law. What is true is that, *pace* the cliché about the indivisibility of church and state in Islam (a cliché that despite its importance to modern Islamists flies in the face of the realities of the history of most Muslim countries), the Islamization of northern and western Sudan, whose dominant political structures were the Funj (*fl.* 1504–1820) and Darfur (*c.* 1650–1916) Sultanates, was accompanied by only a limited introduction of the Sharia. Briefly, the Sharia became the law in certain spheres, for example, commercial law, marriage and divorce and court procedure, but never replaced state or local law in its entirety. In certain major spheres, such as inheritance and control over natural resources like land and water, the Sharia was not applied.[8]

It is worth noting that this long period of Arabicization and Islamization (approximately 1400–1800) did not lead to the confrontation of a 'mixed' Muslim society by Muslim reformers comparable to the *jihad* or holy war led by the Fulani leader Usuman dan Fodio in West Africa. Occasionally, holy men would reprove local rulers or other holy men for alleged lapses from Islamic norms, but the displacement of local practices by Islamic norms was a slow and largely non-confrontational process.[9]

However, the Islamization of Sudan entered a new phase in the late eighteenth and early nineteenth centuries with the coming of new Sufi brotherhoods introduced by students of the Meccan Muhammad b. Abd al-Karim al-Samman (d. 1775) or the Moroccan Ahmad b. Idris (d. 1837).[10] Whether these brotherhoods were doctrinally different from the Sufi affiliations, mainly Qadiriyya and Shadhiliyya, present in Sudan from before is a disputed point, but what is undoubted is that they created the first supra-tribal and relatively centralized religious organizations in the region.[11] Their coming also coincided with the destruction of the old political order by the Egyptians, who conquered most of the region from 1820 onwards. In other words, the disappearance of indigenous political structures whose primary legitimization was not Islamic but 'African' took place at about the same time as the emergence of new mass organizations, the Khatmiyya, Sammaniyya, Isma'iliyya, Rashidiyya, Tijaniyya and others, whose legitimacy rested on mystical Islam.

The interaction between these new forms of mystical Islam and the social and economic burdens of an oppressive colonial regime has yet to be fully charted. The Egyptian rulers of Sudan between 1820 and 1882 did not have a coherent religious policy; they supported with money or tax exemptions some Sufi leaders, but viewed others with disfavour. They were seemingly indifferent to the attempts of the Catholic Church to establish a foothold in southern Sudan.[12] A small cadre of Sudanese were educated at the Azhar mosque/school in Cairo, but the nature of their activities and writings did not differ greatly from the products of the Sufi orders. For their part, some of the local religious leaders collaborated, some were critical, most simply ignored the government, which was after all at least in name Muslim.

In 1882, a sheikh belonging to the Sammaniyya brotherhood, Muhammad Ahmad b. Abd Allah, revealed that he was the expected Mahdi, the one sent at the end of time to establish righteousness upon the earth before the Last Day. The Mahdist revolution (1882–1885), one of the great cataclysms in modern Islamic history, swept the colonial regime of the Egyptians away and established what was the first ostensibly theocratic state in Sudan (1885–1890).[13] But again, to go back to our original question, it is a moot point as to how far the Mahdist state was in reality a theocracy based on the Sharia. This is in turn related to the, in practice, unanswerable question as to whether the Mahdist revolt was primarily nationalist, directed against the hated Turk (as the Egyptian regime was called) or primarily an expression of religious messianism. The very partial evidence we have suggests that while both the Mahdi and his successor, the Khalifa Abdallahi (1885–1898), attempted to enforce the Sharia as they understood it (a question complicated by the fact that theologically the Mahdi *qua* Mahdi had the right to abrogate the pre-existing schools of Islamic law), in reality matters continued very much as before, namely a combination of Sharia and 'customary' law.

In sum, the slow Islamization of Sudan was a Sufi phenomenon, as elsewhere in Muslim frontier lands.[14] In certain spheres of individual and social life, Islamic norms came to prevail, but, except perhaps for the Funj state at the very end of its existence, there was no institutional takeover. Darfur, for example, remained a Sudanic African kingdom until its final destruction in 1916. The first colonial period, that is, Egyptian rule (1820–1882), 'opened up' Sudan in a limited way to Western capitalist penetration and to new forces within the Muslim Arab heartlands, but there is no evidence, for example, that the Mahdi was influenced by Wahhabism.

The British interlude

A conscious Islamic policy in Sudan is a British invention. The British were obsessed by the fear of a rerun of Islamic messianism in a land whose conquest ('reconquest' on behalf of Egypt in official parlance, to legitimize their actions) had taken them three years (1896–1899), in contrast to the surgically swift annexation of Egypt in 1882 in the face of a largely secular nationalist movement. Consequently, they watched over Sudanese Muslim leaders like hawks. Politically, the history of the British in Sudan is a complex dance conducted by the colonial power, the revived Mahdist movement led by a son of the Mahdi, Sir Sayyid Abd al-Rahman al-Mahdi (d. 1959), the Khatmiyya brotherhood led by Sir Sayyid Ali al-Mirghani (d. 1968) and various lesser Sufi figures. In the early years of colonial rule, the Mahdists were suspect and the Khatmiyya favoured; in later years; as the Khatmiyya turned to Egypt as a counterbalance to both the Mahdists and the British, the latter looked with greater favour on the Mahdists. Historiographically it is important to note that most, if not all, the research done on this period has been based on the colonial archives. No one has written on this period from the archives of the Mahdists or Khatmiyya, so we are dependent on British evaluations of the motives of the principal actors involved.

There are two comments that can be made in regard to attitudes towards Islam in the colonial period. First, the British brought to Sudan policies fashioned in India. Ultimately the legal system in Sudan as regards Muslims was derived from the Indian Penal Code of 1837 and the later Indian Civil Procedure Code.[15] To Muslims in matters of personal status (marriage, divorce, inheritance and the like), the Sharia was applied, but, as under the Funj and Darfur Sultanates, in criminal matters secular or state law obtained. However, an important British legacy was the institutionalization of law: the creation of institutions for training *qadis* or Islamic judges, the formalization and codification of distinctions between state and private-status law and a recognition of the potentiality for a conflict of law.[16]

The second point is that the political movements among the northern Sudanese as they emerged in the 1930s and 1940s, be they the Umma party based on the Mahdists with its primary allegiance to the Mahdi family or the Unionists based on the Khatmiyya brotherhood owing loyalty to the Mirghani family, were thus based on supra-ethnic, avowedly Islamic organizations. However, in the context of a, by 'normal' African standards, particularly complex anti-colonial struggle (because conducted against and in concert with two colonial powers, Britain and Egypt), the Sudanese parties did not put forward overtly Islamic or 'Islamist' policies. Their strength derived from Islamic sentiments of solidarity, but these were used to articulate basically secular nationalist positions. This discontinuity between mobilization at the grass roots and the policies advocated by the leadership, who successfully co-opted the graduates of the Gordon Memorial College (later, the University of Khartoum), was to provide an opening for a third group, the Muslim Brothers.

The return of Islam?

One interpretation of the Islamization of northern Sudanese politics since the 1960s is based on two arguments: disenchantment with the failure of Western-orientated politicians and intellectuals to provide effective leadership, a failure leading to a stripping away of the Westernized 'false consciousness' represented by this élite.[17] The preoccupation of this élite with a row of 'isms', pan-Arabism, communism, socialism, the one-party state (the Sudan Socialist Union under al-Numayri) concealed the truly Islamic nature of northern Sudanese society. Moreover, with increasing urbanization and education, more and more northern Sudanese were being exposed to an urban form of Islam that derived many of its patterns of behaviour from Egypt. It was into this void that the Muslim Brothers and other groups moved, crystallizing around the charismatic leadership of Dr al-Turabi.[18]

Another interpretation, in a sense complementary to that proposed above, is to see the Islamist movement in Sudan as a derivative of its counterpart in Egypt. The Muslim Brothers of Egypt, established in 1928, did not begin to spread in Sudan, either through missionary or *da'wa* activity or returned Sudanese students, until the mid 1940s, at about the same time as the foundation of the Sudanese Communist Party (1946). An independent Sudanese movement, uniting several smaller groups, was established in 1954, but it was in its first years a propaganda rather than political movement. It only began to operate as an effective political movement when al-Turabi returned from study abroad in 1962.

The Islamist movement in Sudan from the 1960s until the present day has been essentially a political and ideological movement. As such it stands in some contrast to the 'Republican Brothers' (*al-ikhwan al-jumhuriyyin*) of the late Mahmud Muhammad Taha (executed for apostasy in 1985), who are much concerned with social and economic issues.[19] In the democratic interlude of 1964–1969, between the military regimes of Abbud (1958–1964) and al-Numayri (1969–1985), the Muslim Brothers were concerned with two issues, the struggle against the communists, and the great issue in northern Sudanese politics, an Islamic constitution.[20] This latter issue has run like a thread through modern northern Sudanese politics since the early 1960s. Why is a complex question. John Voll suggests an answer:

> As more modern Sudanese receive a modern style education, simple institution maintenance is not a sufficient expression of their Islamic identity. As a result it is possible to see a growing specifically Islamic content in the programs and platforms of groups in the Sudan. As this takes place, these statements take on a more explicitly fundamentalist tone.[21]

The manifest aim of the Sudanese Islamists is to create a new Sudanese Islamic identity; their means are complex and include educational initiatives, control over money from Arab oil states, banking, and the conversion and acculturation of the influx of southerners and westerners into the north because of war and famine.[22] A central problem is that, until July 1989 and the military coup of Umar al-Bashir, they were only one force within the complex of northern Sudanese politics. Now (1993), they are effectively the government in the north.

The truth of Voll's observation may be seen impressionistically in the changing role of ideology in the north/south conflict in Sudan. During the first civil war, 1955–1972 (the latter the year of the Addis Ababa Agreement, which brought to an end the first civil war and attempted, however inadequately, to satisfy the political aspirations of both sides), the conflict was scarcely articulated ideologically at all. At one level, it was a 'law and order' issue, in the best colonial tradition. Southern spokesmen talked vaguely of the legacy of the slave trade (rebutted by northerners who stressed European involvement in it), the dangers of Arab Islamic domination (denied by northern liberals, who argued for Arabic as a neutral national language). In sum, the southerners blamed the northerners, the latter the British. Much of the problem in the years following Ja'far al-Numayri's takeover in 1969, when there was a will in Khartoum to try to find a settlement, was to establish the terms of reference within which the two sides could negotiate.[23] Since its outbreak in 1983, the second civil war has been characterized by an altogether more sophisticated ideological debate on both sides, wherein on the northern side the Islamists have effectively taken over the agenda and Dr John Garang and SPLA/SPLM have provided the first consciously articulated secularist southern opposition.[24] To answer how this came about requires a deeper study of the modern urban social and economic history of northern Sudan; surveys of the political highlights are not enough, and the former has yet to be undertaken.

The Sharia issue in independent Sudan

The ideological turning-point, when the Sharia became something other than a pious aspiration, was the introduction of what have become known as the 'September Laws' by al-Numayri in 1983.[25] These laws, among other matters, introduced the mandatory punishments required for *hadd* offences, that is theft, highway robbery, fornication, unproved accusation of fornication and the drinking of wine (some authorities add apostasy and rebellion to the list). These are offences for which the punishment is prescribed either by the Koran or the Sunna (Prophetic tradition), so there can be no discretion as to their being inflicted or not. The 'September Laws' fundamentally changed the ideological landscape of Sudan; as Professor An-Na'im puts it, 'Overnight, the debate over the public role of Islam was transformed: the question now was not whether to implement Sharia, but whether to repeal it.'[26]

Since this version of the Sharia was introduced, no Sudanese government has faced up to the fact that, so long as these laws are on the statute books, no non-Muslim political movements will make peace until they are removed. The north/south conflict has become a religious conflict.

There is the obvious point that the 'September Laws' were not introduced as the result of the democratically expressed wishes of the majority of the Muslims of Northern Sudan, let alone a majority of the Sudanese. Moreover, great publicity was given under al-Numayri to the carrying out of the *hadd* punishments – the amputation of limbs and whipping for drinking alcohol – and not all the victims were Muslim. In other words, non-Muslim Sudanese have a very clear idea what the

Sharia as understood by the Islamists means. And to the Muslim liberal intellectuals, hitherto a very strong group in northern Sudan, the execution in 1985 for apostasy of Mahmud Muhammad Taha was a frightening warning of how far the Islamists were prepared to go.[27]

Although the departure of al-Numayri in 1985 led to the effective freezing of the 'September Laws', neither the transitional regime of Suwar al-Dhahab nor the elected government of Sadiq al-Mahdi were prepared to remove them from the statute books. A striking exception to this pusillanimity (from a Western perspective) was the mission in November 1988 by Sayyid Muhammad Uthman al-Mirghani, present head of the Khatmiyya brotherhood, to negotiate a settlement with John Garang. Sayyid al-Mirghani brought back a settlement that included the freezing of the September Laws and which was greeted with a spontaneous outburst of support by the people of Khartoum. However, the settlement was sabotaged by the then Prime Minister, Sadiq al-Mahdi. Moreover, the present military regime of Umar al-Bashr has now reintroduced the laws, making it clear that they will be operative in the north even if the southern provinces are allowed to opt out. But Sudan no longer comprises a Muslim north and a non-Muslim south (if it ever did); war and famine have driven millions of southerners northwards. If the Sharia is to apply to them, as recent pronouncements make clear, then they will on any normal interpretation of that law be second-class citizens in their own country if they are Christian, and have no legal status whatsoever if they are pagan. The NIF position appears now to be that an autonomous south would be free to apply its own laws, but citizens in the north, whatever their religion, would be subject to the Sharia. This is, indeed, the standard Sharia position: non-Muslim subjects of recognized religions are under Sharia jurisdiction except where the Sharia itself specifically exempts them from punishment for an offence for which a Muslim would be liable, for example, the drinking of wine.

Sharia and the non-Muslim Sudanese

It is striking when reading the writings put out by NIF leaders, particularly al-Turabi, how little the Sharia and its significance for both Muslims and non-Muslims are discussed in concrete terms. In his most extended recent account of the Islamist movement and its ideology in Sudan, *al-Haraka al-Islamiyya fi'l-Sudan* ('The Islamic movement in Sudan' (Cairo, 1991)), Dr al-Turabi devotes four out of 302 pages to the south and on the question of law simply refers the reader to the NIF 'Charter' discussed below. It is difficult not to conclude, perhaps at the risk of a false charge of insincerity, that the call for the introduction of the Sharia seems more a slogan than an invitation to a serious debate among Muslims about the relationship between religion and state, let alone the relationship between Muslim and non-Muslim in a state where some 25 to 30 per cent at least of the population are non Muslim.[28] An exception to this generalization is a book (in English) by Dr Abdelwahab El-Affendi – a leading spokesman for the NIF – entitled *Who Needs an Islamic State?* (London, 1991); El-Affendi recognizes the problem of the incompatibility of Western notions of a secular nation state with the Islamist's desire to create a Sharia-based state, but proposes no solution.

This reluctance, inability or unwillingness to think through the implications of their position is nowhere more apparent than in the NIF's 'National Charter'. Even on the premises of the Sharia itself, the Charter is contradictory.

The Sharia is a divine law, a law given by God. It must of its nature take precedence over all other forms of law. It is theoretically immutable; if the Sharia says that such-and-such is God's law, then no earthly agency can say otherwise. If one bases the state on the Sharia, then democracy must logically be curtailed; if the 'source' (*masdar* – which actually has a stronger connotation than 'source' in English) of the law is the Sharia, then how can a parliament vote on a law that is contrary to the Sharia? If the Sharia says that the punishment for highway robbery (*qati' al-tariq*) is crucifixion or execution by the sword (Koran, 5: 37 ff.), then how can the parliament decide on another form of punishment? Iran under Khumayni has accepted the logic of this argument by establishing a 'Board of Guardians' who determine whether laws passed by the *majlis* in Tehran are in conformity with the Sharia or not.

To continue with the NIF's 'Charter': it promises 'Freedom of choice of religious creed and practice', but also says, 'Islamic jurisprudence (*al-Sharia*) shall be the general source (*masdar*) of law'. How are these to be reconciled? Can a Muslim wake up one day in Khartoum and decide to become a Christian? Will he not be guilty of *irtidad* or apostasy – a crime the Sharia regards as punishable by death? The 'Charter' says:

> The rules relating to marriage, cohabitation, divorce, parenthood, childhood and inheritance shall be based on the religious teachings of the couple. To Muslims shall apply the Sharia. To scriptural religious denominations shall apply their respective church laws. To the followers of local cults shall apply their special customs. Any one of these or others can of course choose to be governed by Sharia.

This formulation raises many problems. 'Scriptural religious denominations' – *al-millal al-kitabiyya* – cover, as understood in the Sharia, the Jews, Christians and Sabians, but 'followers of local cults' – *dhawi al-millal al-mahalliyya* – have no status in it. In this instance, the

NIF is forced by the exercise of *ijtihad* or individual initiative – itself a questionable procedure within the Sharia – to add a new category to the traditionally recognized 'People of the Book'. On the more personal level, will a Christian or Jewish man, not to talk of a pagan, be able to marry a Muslim woman? Must the children of such a marriage, unrecognized by the Sharia, be brought up as Muslims? How does one in equity deal with the problem of the unequal value of a Christian's testimony in court to that of a Muslim? Here, one is at the level of the classic 'conflict of laws': whose law will prevail in a dispute between a Muslim and non-Muslim?

The NIF Charter does not conceive of a non-religious citizen.

The Islamist perception of a theocracy based on the Sharia is based *de facto* on the Sharia reality that the only fully mature person in the eyes of that law is a mature, *compos mentis* Muslim male. The rights of all others – Christian, Jew, woman or minor – are less. A secular alternative, based upon some ultimately Western-inspired conception of human rights, is by definition unacceptable to the Islamists.[29] These are only a few of the issues involved if the Sharia remains the law of the land. Other issues include the position of women (increasingly under threat by the present regime), the discriminatory effect of Islamic banking on non-Muslims, and the question of intellectual freedom (the University of Khartoum is in a precarious position).[30]

While it would be naïve to say that the Sharia is the only obstacle to peace in Sudan – the breakdown of 'law and order' is perhaps the most comprehensive menace – so long as the laws remain, they serve as a profound barrier to peace in Sudan and, because of their ideological significance to the Islamists, perhaps the most intractable. It may be that the Islamists of the north in their quest to fulfil the Mahdi's dream of a pure Islamic theocracy, albeit under very different terms, will also follow the Mahdi's (and Khalifa's) first followers in effectively abandoning the south. But, while the division of Sudan may transform the country's problems, it will make their solution no easier.

Notes

1. There is by now a vast literature on the Islamist (a better term than 'fundamentalist') resurgence. A useful volume is John L. Esposito, ed., *Voices of Resurgence Islam* (New York, 1983). This includes articles by Sadiq al-Mahdi and Hasan al-Turabi.
2. Many of the principal figures – Drs al-Turabi, Mansour Khalid, John Garang, Francis Deng and several others – have published much of high quality in both languages.
3. See Africa Watch, *Denying the honour of living: Sudan – a human rights disaster.* (London and New York, 1990). This presents the most detailed coverage to date of the various ethnic, religious and other conflicts in Sudan. It may be supplemented by a valuable fortnightly newsletter, *Sudan Update*, put out by the Committee for Peace and Reconstruction in Sudan.

4. If I may be permitted a personal comment; reading the account of the slave-raiding by the cattle-keeping nomads of southern Kordofan and Darfur in *Denying the honour of living*, I am reminded of an article I wrote. 'Slavery and the slave trade in Dar Fur', *Journal of African History* 14, 1 (1973), pp. 29–43. The latter concerns the eighteenth and nineteenth centuries, but the way slave-raiding parties are organized remains the same.

5. The Arabic has *takunu al-shari'a masdar al-tashri'i bi-wajh 'amm* – the Arabic is stronger than the official English translation given above; National Islamic Front, *Sudan Charter* (Khartoum, n.d.).

6. The following discussion is partly based on my 'Islamic hegemonies in the Sudan', in Louis Brenner, ed., *Muslim identity and social change in sub-Saharan African* (London, 1993), pp. 21–35.

7. The most accessible survey of Islam in English is still J. S. Trimingham, *Islam in the Sudan* (Oxford, 1949). Specialized studies have replaced it on almost all the topics it discusses, but no general synthesis of recent research is available. A forthcoming book will greatly deepen our understanding of the Muslim 'holy man' in Sudanese history, namely Neil McHugh, *Holymen of the Blue Nile*. See also P. M. Holt, *Studies in the history of the Near East* (1973).

8. On this topic in regard to Darfur, see my *State and society in Dar Fur* (London, 1980), pp. 109–14, and, in greater detail, R. S. O'Fahey and M. I. Abu Salim, *Land in Dar Fur* (Cambridge, 1983).

9. See Jay Spaulding, *The heroic age in Sinnar* (East Lansing, 1985), pp. 150–98, for this process within the Funj Sultanate.

10. On this period, see my *The enigmatic saint: Ahmad ibn Idris and the Idrisi tradition* (London, 1990), and Ali Salih Karrar, *The Sufi brotherhoods of the northern Sudan* (London, 1992).

11. See, further, R. S. O'Fahey and Bernd Radtke, 'Neo-Sufism reconsidered', *Der Islam* (forthcoming).

12. See Dorothea McEwan, *A Catholic Sudan: Dream, mission, reality* (Rome, 1987).

13. The classic study is P. M. Holt, *The Mahdist state in the Sudan, 1881–1898*, 2nd edn. (Oxford, 1970).

14. See, for example, N. Levtzion, ed., *Conversion to Islam* (New York, 1979).

15. G. Warburg, *The Sudan under Wingate* (London, 1971), pp. 124–36.

16. Carolyn Fleuhr-Lobban, *Islamic law and society in the Sudan* (London, 1986). An earlier, and to a non-lawyer at least, fascinating study is C. D'Olivier Farran, *Matrimonial laws of the Sudan, being a study of the divergent religious and civil laws in an African society* (London, 1963).

17. On the failure, see the forceful critique by one of the same élite's most articulate representatives, Mansour Khalid, *The government they deserve: The role of the elite in Sudan's political evolution* (London, 1990).

18. For this interpretation, see Abdelwahab El-Affendi, *Turabi's revolution: Islam and power in the Sudan* (London, 1991), and id. ' "Discovering the South" : Sudanese dilemmas for Islam in Africa', *African Affairs* (1990), pp. 371–89.

19. For example, in combating the crushing burden of dowry (*mahr*) on young couples, an issue that Sadiq al-Mahdi, for example, has sought to remedy. On the 'Republican Brothers', see J. Rogalski. *Die republikanischen Brüder im Sudan. Ein Beitrag zur Ideologiegeschichte des Islam in der Gegenwart*, Magister thesis, Freie Universität Berlin (1990), and Isabel Stümpel, *Die Ideen eines sudanesischen Reformdenkers vor dem Tribunal der islamischen Religionsgelehrten – Mahmud Muhammad Taha und die Weiterentwicklung der shari'a*, Magister thesis, Albert-Ludwigs-Universität zu Freiburg i.Br. (1990).

20. See, further, Abdullah A. An-Na'im, 'The elusive Islamic constitution: the Sudanese experience', *Orient* 3 (1985), pp. 329–40. On the Islamist movement in this period, see Susanne Wolf, *The Muslim Brotherhood in the Sudan*, Magister thesis, University of Hamburg (1990).

R. S. O'Fahey

21. 'The evolution of Islamic fundamentalism in twentieth-century Sudan', in G. Warburg and U. Kupferschmidt, eds, *Islam, nationalism and radicalism in Egypt and the Sudan* (New York, 1983), p. 131.

22. Other aspects include the adoption of Western missionary and aid organization techniques by Islamist organizations, for example, the African Islamic Centre established in 1972 and the Islamic African Relief Agency established in the early 1980s.

23. Much of the above is based on personal observation while a resident in Sudan, 1967–1971 and during several subsequent visits.

24. See *John Garang speaks* (London, 1992).

25. Much has been written on the background to the 'September Laws' and what may be termed the 'Sharia factor' in Sudanese politics since their promulgation. For a legal study, see Ibrahim M. Zein, *Religion, legality and the state: 1983 Sudanese penal code*, PhD thesis, Temple University (1989): for a detailed *islamwissenschaft* study of 1983 and after, see Olav Köndgen, *Das islamisierte Strafrecht des Sudan von seiner Einführung bis Juli 1992*, Magister thesis, Freie Universität Berlin (1992). Mansour Khalid has written a ferocious denunciation in *al-Fajr al-kadhib. Numayri wa-tasrif al-shari'a* (Dar al-Hilal, n.p. (Beirut), n.d).

26. Abdullah An-Na'im, 'Islam and national integration in the Sudan', in John O. Hunwick, ed., *Religion and national integration in Africa* (Evanston, 1992), p. 28.

27. See Abdullah A. An-Na'im, 'The Islamic law of apostasy and its modern applicability: a case from the Sudan', *Religion* 16 (1986).

28. Abdullahi An-Na'im makes this charge of lack of seriousness about these issues in his criticism of al-Turabi's earlier writings: see An-Na'im, *Toward an Islamic reformation* (Syracuse, 1990), pp. 39–42. It is perhaps worth quoting from one of Dr al-Turabi's English writings on the matter:

> There may be a certain feeling of alienation [on the part of non-Muslim citizens of a Muslim state] because the public law generally will be Islamic law. However, the public law of Islam is one related rationally to justice and the general good and even a non-Muslim may appreciate its wisdom and fairness. Christians in particular who now, at least, do not seem to have a public law, should not mind the application of Islamic law as long as it does not interfere with their religion. (*Voices of resurgent Islam*, p. 250).

29. Hence the unacceptability to many Islamists of the United Nations' Universal Declaration of Human Rights.

30. See further, An-Na'im, 'Islam and national integration in the Sudan', pp. 11–37. In this article, Professor An-Na'im gives a detailed discussion of the implication for non-Muslims of being subject to the Sharia. As of April 1993 some 100 staff members of the University of Khartoum have lost their jobs.

Four

Idi Amin
'the Nubi' & Islam
in Ugandan Politics
1971–1979

OMARI H. KOKOLE*

This chapter reconsiders the Nubi factor in Ugandan politics during the years between 1971 and 1979. The Nubi have featured in Uganda's history and politics for almost a century.[1] But here we focus on Idi Amin's Uganda, amongst other things because that period is still regarded by many people as an era of 'Nubi rule' in that country.

It has not been possible to acquire hard data about the immediate national origins of all Nubi who joined Idi Amin's political coalition in Uganda in the 1970s. Nor are demographic data about the Nubi presence in Eastern Africa as a whole at a later date very readily accessible. None the less, despite those research constraints, it is clear that the regional effects and side-effects of Idi Amin's years in power were considerable and deserve greater scholarly scrutiny than so far accorded to them.

It is arguable that had Idi Amin exclusively depended on his own tribe or ethnic group – the Kakwa – he would have been forced to be less favourable to Islam than he turned out to be. After all, the Kakwa are multi-religious (Christians as well as Muslims and others). But such a tribal base would have been dangerously narrow in plural and multi-ethnic Uganda. It was the addition of the Nubi constituency to the historically related and overlapping Kakwa/West Nile base which tilted

*I am grateful to Dr Edward Kannyo, Dr Al-Amin K. Mazrui, Professor Ali A. Mazrui and Professor Ibrahim Juma Wani for taking the trouble to read an earlier version of this chapter and for offering many very useful comments.

the balance more clearly in favour of Islam, the Nile Valley and the Arab world more broadly. On the whole, the Nubi overlapped with, and reinforced, the Kakwa and other Bari-speakers as ethnic groups. The Nubi factor also made Idi Amin's regime more ethnically mixed than otherwise it would have been. The two primary and defining characteristics of the Nubi – Islam and the Arabic language – cut across ethnic or 'tribal' boundaries.

Historically, the Nubi language evolved out of the military and related profession(s). Nubi was certainly the lingua franca among the forces that Khedive Muhammad Ali of Ottoman Egypt mobilized to conquer Sudan in the nineteenth century. Although his initial troops were from upper Egypt and northern Sudan, as their mission took them farther southwards the imperative of further recruitment took in men from a variety of diverse ethnic backgrounds. Mutual intelligibility under those circumstances was impossible without a lingua franca. The southern recruits enriched the ethnic composition of those forces, even as they also affected the form of Arabic spoken.

The three East African countries of Tanganyika, Uganda and Kenya were decolonized in the early 1960s. Tanganyika and Zanzibar united to form the United Republic of Tanzania in 1964. The first generation of leaders of the three newly independent states (Julius K. Nyerere in Tanzania, Jomo Kenyatta in Kenya and Apolo Milton Obote in Uganda) briefly toyed with the idea of regional integration. But Obote's Uganda soon developed cold feet over the prospects for regional integration in East Africa. In this respect, Obote's administration in the 1960s was not behaving differently towards regional East African integration from the way the Baganda under their last king had responded in the previous decades. Nevertheless, the creation of the East African Community (EAC) preserved functional links between the three contiguous states as regards airways, railways and research. For the first decade of its life as an independent country, Uganda's links to the Indian Ocean therefore remained strong.

It was under Idi Amin's rule in the 1970s that intergovernmentally Uganda began to shift away from its Indian Ocean partners towards the Nile Valley. At the subgovernmental level, the Nubi factor also kept Uganda and Kenya fairly close together politically. Some Kenyan Nubi did cross over to Uganda to work for the Amin regime. Nationals of other neighbouring countries came to Amin's Uganda because they claimed to be Nubi, or because they were Muslims by faith, or because they said they were both. Overlapping Nubi and Bari identities also facilitated a pro-Nile Valley orientation. A Nubi is defined primarily by language (Arabic) and faith (Islam). A Bari-speaker is a Nilote whose native tongue is part of a family of approximately nine languages.[2] These languages include Idi Amin's mother tongue, Kakwa. Bari-speakers nowadays reside in Zaïre, Sudan and of course Uganda. These two forces, the Nubi and the Bari, strengthened Uganda's relations not only with the southern Sudan and Mobutu's Zaïre but also with the Arab world farther afield.

As Uganda's links with the Indian Ocean partners atrophied somewhat (the EAC finally collapsed in 1977), relations with the Nile Valley were reinforced by Bari-ization and Arabization. The Nubi language is a creolized version of Arabic. This language is understood by many people with Nile Valley origins or connections. Amin's support of Arabic led to plans to establish a college of languages in Uganda, in which Arabic was to be a first among equals. Amin's Arabophilia also led him to authorize regular radio programmes in Arabic on Radio Uganda.

Under Amin, Uganda became staunchly pro-Arab in foreign policy. He abruptly expelled the Israelis in 1972 and established relatively consistent and cordial ties with both Saudi Arabia and Libya. Both Saudi King Feisal and President Muammar Qaddafi paid official visits to Uganda during the 1970s. These were the first visits ever to Uganda by leaders of those two Arab countries.

Idi Amin's identity as a Kakwa had already led him to sympathize with the southern Sudanese in their first civil war (1955–1972). Amin's links with the southern Sudanese, in turn, led him to befriend the Israelis, who were then major benefactor of the southern Sudanese. But Amin had other identities apart from Kakwa. As a Muslim Kakwa, Amin had cultural links with the Nubi. Cultural ties with the Nubi increasingly tilted Amin in a pro-Arab direction, without necessarily undermining his pro-Bari proclivity. Many of the Bari-speakers of the southern Sudan were part of the Anya Nya movement. The Anya Nya movement had political and military ties with the Jewish state; the Nubi had cultural ties (linguistic and religious) with the Arabs. Initially, the Bari factor had a greater influence than the Nubi element in the Amin coalition of forces.

In 1972, Africa's longest civil war (the first Sudanese civil war) finally came to an end. The Addis Ababa accords between the Khartoum regime and the Anya Nya spelt out the terms of reconciliation between the two sides. In the same year (1972) Idi Amin broke off Uganda's diplomatic relations with Israel and expelled all Israelis from Uganda. It is possible that Amin found it easy to expel his Israeli friends because Israelis were no longer useful to the Anya Nya movement, to which many of Amin's fellow Bari-speakers belonged. Once the Anya Nya ceased to need the Israelis, Idi Amin also had less use for them.

Whichever way one looks at the issues, it is clear that both the Nubi and the Bari factors intensified the new orientation of Amin's Uganda towards the Nile Valley. In the same vein, the termination of the very long first round of the Sudanese civil war enabled Amin to adopt a pro-Arab foreign policy without alienating his fellow Bari-speakers and the Anya Nya movement in general. Unlike his predecessor Obote, the southern Sudanese never needed to accuse Amin of 'betraying' them.[3]

Amin's years in power, therefore, were characterized by a weakening of Uganda's interstate relations with its Indian Ocean partners in the East African Community – Kenya and Tanzania – and a reorientation towards the Nile Valley and the Arab world. It was the cultural and ethnic links which Amin had with both the Bari and the Nubi which helped him towards a pro-Nile Valley perspective. The links with the Nubi, the Libyans and the Saudis also helped to Arabize the foreign policy of Amin's Uganda. The Nubi were part of both processes. The political geography of Uganda's international options was by these means temporarily transformed.[4]

Muslims in Uganda remain a small and disadvantaged minority.[5] Because Muslims in black Africa also tend to be the least culturally Westernized, they have often been left behind by others in their respective societies. It is therefore understandable that many Muslims in Uganda welcomed Idi Amin's advent to power and equated it with the political elevation of Islam in the country at a whole. Of course, events were to prove celebration here both premature and misplaced.

Under Idi Amin's reign (1971–1979), there were strong incentives for non-Muslim Ugandans to convert, sometimes for opportunistic reasons, to the Islamic faith. And many did precisely that.[6] But to have been merely a Muslim under Amin was not fully satisfactory. It did not propel one into the innermost chambers of authority or on to the commanding heights of political power. An additional qualification was needed. To religion one had to add language, a version of Arabic: Nubi.

A Nubi need not necessarily be someone whose mother tongue (or first language) is Nubi. The mere capacity to handle this creolized Arabic effectively, either as first, second, third or even fourth language, suffices for one to qualify as Nubi. This is an additional consideration supporting the proposition that Nubi are less of a 'tribe' in the usual sense and more of a 'club'.[7]

When he captured supreme power in January 1971 Idi Amin's political debt was more to non-Muslims (Christians, Jews and believers in traditional African religions) than to fellow Muslims. Among the factors that helped to propel Amin to power, Islamic solidarity was probably less important than either multi-religious support for him amongst the armed forces of Uganda or Israeli (Jewish) assistance. Two factors, one internal, the other external, shifted Amin's regime towards a pro-Islamic posture. The internal factor consisted of the Arabic-speaking Muslims, the Nubi, who cultivated Amin, and on whom Amin increasingly depended despite the fact that some notable Nubi had previously sided with the political leader Amin had just overthrown –

President Apolo Milton Obote. The external factor was Arab financial support.

A very wide variety of peoples, including the Kakwa, Lugbara, Avukaya, Logo, Moru, Azande, Alur, Makaraka and many others, were absorbed into this force. For example, two of the most important commanders of these forces have been identified as Lugbara and Makaraka in terms of tribal or ethnic ancestry. Comments John Agami, 'These soldiers were of various tribes in Sudan (now southern Sudan) under the command of Fadl el Mula (a 6 feet 4 inches tall Lugbara) and Selim Bey (a giant Makaraka).' We should hasten to point out that the Lugbara people, divided by colonial boundaries three ways between Uganda, Sudan and Zaïre, are ethnically distinct from the Makaraka, an exclusively southern Sudanese group. But, like a variety of other tribes or ethnic groups in that part of Africa, both the Lugbara and the Makaraka contributed members to the Nubi Muslim melting-pot.

What Agami does not tell us is that, even by the late nineteenth century, modern Uganda as we know it today did not exist. The whole of what is now northern Uganda was then foreign to 'Uganda'. What this means is that it is not entirely correct to say that the Nubi are of wholly Sudanese extraction because the area of recruitment was later divided three ways – part Sudanese, part Zaïrean and part Ugandan. This is one reason why, under Amin's rule, the Nubi and Islam were among the forces tilting Uganda towards the Nile Valley and the Arabs.·

Later on the British inherited this heterogeneous force, known for convenience as 'Sudanese soldiers' or 'Nubian mercenaries', and used them to serve their own imperial objectives and ambitions as opposed to Egypt's. But, by the time the British adopted them and made them the core of the King's African Rifles (KAR) in 1905, an inchoate identity of Muslims who spoke some variety of Arabic and had been bound together by history in the military profession had begun to emerge. Over time these soldiers and their descendants and relatives because known as 'Nubi'. A new Semitic breed was in the making.[7]

By the time Idi Amin joined the KAR in the 1940s, the Nubi had already existed in this manner for at least a generation. As a young Kakwa Muslim serving in the British colonial army, it was inevitable that Amin would be in touch with that Nubi circle, even as the army continued to absorb divergent groups. His own father had briefly served in the colonial army during the Second World War before returning to his career in the police force of colonial Uganda. Thus history and a lifelong military profession had partially 'Nubi-ized' Idi Amin. In addition to being Kakwa, he was also black and male, a Ugandan, a West Niler, an African, a father, a husband, a man, a *Keya* (a corruption of the abbreviation KAR) or soldier, a military officer, a Muslim, a political figure, a historical character, a sportsman and culturally, yes, a 'Nubi' of sorts, as well as a 'Mswahili' in a specialized military and Ugandan sense.

In the politics leading up to the coup of 1971 which ushered him into power, Islam played a contradictory role. Within the upper echelons of the military, the officers were not split very sharply between Idi Amin's Muslim supporters and Obote's non-Muslim allies. On the contrary, two top Nubi officers – Brigadier–General Hussein Suleiman and Colonel Juma Musa – were both staunch pro-Obote men, whom Obote even used to try to displace Amin. Indeed, while Obote was attending the Commonwealth summit conference in Singapore in January 1971, he wanted Amin either incarcerated or liquidated in his absence by a clique of Nubi men loyal to Obote. These high-ranking Nubi officials included Army Chief of Staff Brigadier-General Hussein Suleiman, Air Force Chief of Staff Colonel Juma Musa, Buganda Regional Police Commissioner Suleiman Dusman and Police Chief Constable Abdu Sebbi.[8]

Within the military at least, Idi Amin did not count heavily on the Nubi for support before the 1971 coup. In that phase of Uganda's history, it was Idi Amin's identity as a Kakwa which seemed to serve him well. Virtually all Kakwa troops – Muslim or non-Muslim, Catholic or Protestant, believer or atheist – rallied behind their ethnic compatriot in that supreme confrontation between Uganda's topmost politician, President Apolo Milton Obote, and his supporters on one side and on the other side Uganda's topmost soldier, General Idi Amin.

Indeed, the single most important Kakwa military officer after Amin in the Uganda armed force both before the 1971 coup and up until March 1974 was Roman Catholic – Brigadier-General Charles Arube (a captain in the First Battalion at Jinja before 1971). When Amin made his first, and almost reckless, trip abroad as head of state in mid-1971, he left the affairs of state in the hands of two fellow West Nilers, both of whom were Christian.[9] Acting as president was a Lugbara soldier, Colonel Obitre Gama. But real power lay with the man left in charge of the armed forces as a whole: a fellow Kakwa and Christian Brigadier Charles Arube.[10]

Also within the military there was a West Nile solidarity at that stage which Amin benefited from. The identity of West Niler also reaped dividends for Amin. The Lugbara, Madi, Alur, Lendu, Aringa, Kebu and other assorted groups of the West Nile (regardless of religious affiliation) rallied behind their Kakwa general, partly because the Kakwa as a people were fellow West Nilers. In any struggle for survival between a Kakwa and a Langi, West Nilers naturally decided, by and large, to side with the Kakwa.

The majority of non-Nilotic soldiers also sided with Amin. It was partly a marriage of convenience. The Bantu and non-Nilotic soldiers and officers sympathized with Amin, partly because they saw a little of themselves in Amin. Although definitely a Kakwa himself, Amin was not surrounded by fellow Kakwa military officers. As an ethnic group, the Kakwa were a minority, not just in the country as a whole but even in the very army that Amin himself headed. And, within the officer corps particularly, the Kakwa were especially under-represented.

In contrast, by 1970 Obote's people – the Langi and their Lwo cousins, the Acholi – were over-represented in the army, especially at the officer level.[11] This caused resentment among non-Lwo officers and troops. This resentment in turn contributed to the success of Idi Amin's coup. This basis fact remains woefully unacknowledged in the written history of modern Uganda.

But, while Islam was marginal in the plotting and counter-plotting within the Uganda armed forces that resulted in Obote's downfall on 25 January 1971, outside the army in the civilian sections of the population Amin seemed deliberately to cultivate a Muslim constituency. By the mid-1960s there were two divergent branches of Islam in Uganda. On the one hand there was a pro-Obote wing, dominated from behind the scene by his Muslim cousin Abubaker Adoko Nekyon (then also a minister in Obote's cabinet).[12] Called the National Association for the Advancement of Muslims (NAAM), it was created in 1964 and was widely recognized as the pro-government wing of the Muslim *ummah*. Its main mosque was located at Wandegeya near Makerere University (north Kampala).[13]

The contrary grouping was the Uganda Muslim Community (UMC) led by Mutesa II's uncle, Prince Badru Kakungulu Wasajja, with its main mosque at Kibuli on the opposite side of Uganda's capital city, Kampala. This other, older faction was widely recognized as the anti-government Muslim group, partly because it contained so many Baganda.[14] The Baganda were generally hostile to Obote because many of them believed that Obote had mistreated them, and had dealt with them as 'a conquered people'. As if this were not enough, Obote had also abolished their old and cherished monarchy. Partly because these Muslims were headed by the uncle of the last Kabaka, whom Obote had hounded into undignified exile before abolishing the monarchy, they were not his friends.

Ironically, the Obote forces who attacked the Kabaka's palace (Lubiri) in mid-1966 were themselves commanded by the then Colonel Idi Amin himself.[15] Because of this, one would have expected the Baganda Muslims to be as hostile to Idi Amin as they were to Milton Obote. After all, Idi Amin had done Obote's 'dirty work' against their king. Moreover, between 1964 and 1969 it was well known that Milton Obote and Idi Amin were very close political allies. Both men came from the north. Before 1970, too, Amin had distanced himself from Badru Kakungulu's Muslim group. Not to have done so would have been incongruous with his high-profile role as Obote's right-hand man and strongman. All pro-government Muslim officials were expected to be members of NAAM. Idi Amin conformed to this expectation until 1969.

By 1970 Uganda was abuzz with rumours that, for whatever reasons, there had developed a serious rift between President Obote and his chief of the armed forces and for some time staunch political ally, General Amin. Many believed that it was a matter of time before the final day of reckoning came. It was during that period that Idi Amin decided to publicly switch his allegiance from NAAM to Prince Kakungulu's group. To have publicly fraternized with anti-government Muslims was daring enough, but Amin decided to behave even more theatrically. He was not merely going to pray together with anti-Obote Muslims; he was also going to say publicly defiant things obviously aimed at Obote. So on one Friday afternoon in late 1970, in a speech to fellow Muslims following prayers at Kibuli mosque, Idi Amin asserted, 'I fear no one but God.' Whom was he addressing? Many realized that those remarks were aimed at non-other than President Apolo M. Obote himself.[16] The two men were estranged by then, and many knew publicly about their split.[17]

By saying this in 1970, was Amin guilty of politicizing religion in Uganda? Akena Adoko suggests that Amin behaved inappropriately when he made those remarks. That may or may not be a fair criticism. But it would be wrong to hold Amin responsible for initiating the process by which religion and politics have become so deeply intertwined in Uganda. Historically, more than elsewhere in East Africa, religion and politics in Uganda have interacted intensely before, during and after Idi Amin. As A.G.G. Gingyera-Pinycwa remarks:

> The fact is that religion and the modern political Uganda were like Siamese twins that saw the light of day at the same time. And, to continue with the metaphor, the two had not been really separated even when independence came some eighty years after.[18]

Or, as President Yoweri Museveni himself has observed:

> The politics of Uganda at Independence was unabashedly sectarian: DP [Democratic Party] mainly for Catholics, UPC [Uganda People's Congress] mainly for Protestants outside Buganda and KY [Kabaka Yekka] for Protestants in Buganda.[19]

Indeed, Obote and even his cousin Akena Adoko himself were both keen players in the game of mixing religion and Uganda's politics. Amin did not set any precedent in fusing religion and Ugandan politics: he merely continued it.

Upon seizing power in January 1971, it was important for Amin to widen his primary base. Because the Kakwa numbered less than 100,000 in a population of over 10 million, it was wise to turn to the

Nubi too. Furthermore, Nubi could absorb non-Nubi much faster than the indigenous Kakwa could absorb non-Kakwa. As Michael Twaddle has pointed out:

> Sociologically the Nubians form a fascinating category for scholars to study forming as they do . . . a secondary and expansible social category capable of assimilating Ugandans previously classified under other tribal names.[20]

Amin's fellow Kakwa and Kakwa-related peoples (Bari-speakers) were already pro-Amin in sympathy and political inclination. Now there were Nubi too. But in the long run the Nubi club was to prove potentially fragile and unpredictable.

An important internal source of wealth that helped to hold together the pro-Amin alliance consisted of the property of 'Asian' Ugandans, whom Amin abruptly expelled in late 1972.[21] It would be false to suggest that only the Kakwa, or the Nubi, or the Muslims, or for that matter only soldiers, benefited from the redistribution of the Indian 'loot' or largesse. However, it is true that many Muslims took advantage of this opportunity to redress some of their earlier economic grievances. In the same vein, the first pan-Islamic organization Uganda has ever had (created under Amin's impetus) – the Uganda Muslim Supreme Council (UMSC) – became, as a consequence, one of the largest collective landlords in the economic history of independent Uganda. Many of the buildings and houses previously owned by these economically privileged 'Indians' were allocated to the UMSC.

Fortunately for Amin, there were in addition external factors which tilted him in a pro-Islamic direction. Internally, Islam could enlarge his primary constituency of support. From the outside, Islam could bring much needed foreign aid from the Muslim world.

Generally, the 1970s were the heyday of the Organization of Petroleum Exporting Countries (OPEC), and OPEC was Arab-led. Under Amin, and despite the fact that Muslims were locally and demographically in a minority, Uganda benefited considerably from OPEC sources. Basically, this was because Idi Amin himself was a Muslim head of state. He was also staunchly pro-Palestinian as well as a dedicated and consistent friend of the Arabs, once he had taken the decision to break ties with the Israelis in 1972. Amin's relatively consistent – perhaps the most consistent aspect of his policies as President of Uganda – anti-Israeli/anti-Zionist orientation and strong pro-Palestinian/pro-Arab stand have continued to pay off, even since his violent overthrow in April 1979. Amin is now enjoying Saudi hospitality and generosity, partly in return for his dedicated pro-Arabism and his Islamic identity during his years in power.

During the time when he ruled Uganda (1971–1979), non-Muslim Ugandans converted to Islam, partly for opportunistic reasons. Some of these conversions occurred at public ceremonies at which Amin was

Omari H. Kokole

personally present. The total figures of those who actually converted are difficult to compute, as too are their current religious affiliations. But few seriously doubt that in the 1970s new converts to Islam in Uganda are to be numbered in their thousands. Some of those new Muslims also became 'Nubi' – partly because it was easy to do so and partly because it seemed politically advantageous to be identified as one at that time.

Notes

1. See Aidan Southall, 'General Amin and the coup: Great man or historical inevitability?', *Journal of Modern African Studies* 13, 1 (1975); Barri A. Wanji, 'The Nubi community: An Islamic and social structure in East Africa', Makerere University, Sociology Working Paper No. 115; and Holger Bernt Hansen, 'Pre-colonial immigrants and colonial servants: The Nubians in Uganda revisited', *African Affairs* 90 (1991), pp. 559-590.
2. These include Kuku, Mundari, Kakwa, Pojulu, Nyepu, Bari, Rigbo and Nyangwarra. See *Encyclopedia Britannica* (Chicago, London, etc., Encyclopedia Britannica Inc., 1986), Micropaedia Series, Vol. 1, p. 896. Groups that were split two ways between Uganda and Sudan include the Madi, Acholi and Langi. Communities split two ways between Uganda and Zaïre include the Alur, Jonam and Kebu. Groups split three ways between Uganda, Sudan and Zaïre include the Kakwa, Lugbara and Logo.
3. Because Obote was ethnically Langi and given that southern Sudan has its own Langi, many Anya Nya operatives expected Obote to sympathize with their cause. That he did not naturally disappointed most of them. Source: private discussions with several southern Sudanese. Also see Dunstan M. Wai, *The African–Arab conflict in the Sudan* (New York, Africana, 1981), pp. 130-133.
5. See, for example, Suleiman I. Kiggundu and Isa K. K. Lukwago, 'The status of the Muslim community in Uganda', *Journal of the Institute of Muslim Minority Affairs* 4, 1/2 (1982) pp. 120-131.
6. 'Conversion to Islam during Amin's rule was often a strategic decision. The Catholic priest in Yei [southern Sudan] took pleasure in pointing out certain prominent Ugandans, now Muslim, whose time of baptism as a Catholic [*sic*] he could remember' (B. Harrell-Bond, *Imposing Aid* (Oxford, 1986), p. 139).
7. Both Bernd Heine and David Dalby refer to the Nubi as 'new Semites'. See Heine, *The Nubi language of Kibera — an Arabic Creole*, p. 17, and Dalby, *Language map of Africa and the adjacent islands* (London, International African Institute, 1977), p. 24.
8. See, further, David Martin, *General Amin* (London, Faber and Faber, 1974).
9. 'Almost reckless' because the previous head of state (Obote) had been overthrown while abroad and here was Idi Amin venturing to leave the country to visit Israel and Britain after being in power for less than six months.
10. The late Charles Arube remains the kindest and most thoughtful of all military officers to be associated with the Amin regime. He was also highly respected as a human being by those who got to know him well, including this writer. See, for example, Princess Elizabeth of Toro, *African princess: The story of Princess Elizabeth of Toro* (London, Hamish Hamilton, 1983), pp. 135-136.
11. For example, of the 171 military officers the Uganda Army had by late 1966, 49 were either Acholi or Langi. Considering that Uganda comprises 44 ethnic groups, 49 out of 171 (28.65%) for just two (4.55%) related ethnic groups was definitely an over-representation. If one adds to the 49 officers other generic Lwo-speakers (Alur, Jonam

54

and Kumam, a total of 15 officers), the Lwo factor then becomes even more disproportionately pronounced. See Amii Omara-Otunnu, *Politics and the military in Uganda, 1890–1985* (New York, St Martin's Press, 1987), p. 80. In contrast, by 1966 there were only three Kakwa officers (out of 171, or 1.75%) in the Uganda Army; Idi Amin was, of course, one of those three officers (ibid., p. 80).

12. It remains to be confirmed whether Adoko Nekyon's Muslim (first) name was Abubaker or Akbar (or whether Akbar is a contraction of Abubaker in his case). I am grateful to Edward Kannyo for drawing my attention to this issue.

13. See A. G. G. Gingyera-Pinycwa, *Apolo Milton Obote and his times* (New York, London and Lagos, NOK Publishers, 1978), especially pp. 137–151.

14. See Abdu B. Kasozi, 'The Uganda Muslim Supreme Council: An experiment in Muslim administrative centralization and institutionalization', *Journal Institute of Muslim Minority Affairs* 6, 1 (March 1985), p. 39.

15. Mutesa II comments on Amin's role in the so-called 'Battle of the Palace': 'I did not see Colonel Amin, but I expect he was in command. Obote remained well away from the scene.' See 'King Freddie' the Kabaka of Buganda, *Desecration of my kingdom* (London, Constable, 1967), p. 192.

16. Milton Obote's cousin and chief of intelligence at the time, Naftali Akena Adoko, refers to that challenge in his book *From Obote to Obote* (New Delhi, Vikas Publishing House, 1983). Akena Adoko writes:

> In a language highly political
> And rather incongruous
> In a place like the Mosque.
> He stated amongst other things,
> 'I fear no one but God.'
> Then [*sic*] question asked was thus:
> 'To whom was he referring?' (p. 142)

Also see Henry Kyemba, *A state of blood: The inside story of Idi Amin* (New York, Ace Books, 1977). Kyemba comments: '[Amin] also stated publicly that he "feared no one but God" – a deliberate challenge to Obote' p. 32.

17. See Semakula Kiwanuka, *Amin and the tragedy of Uganda* (Munich and London, Weltforum Verlag, 1979), pp. 34–35.

18. A. G. G. Gingyera-Pinycwa, *Apolo Milton Obote and his times* (New York, London and Lagos, NOK Publishers, 1978), p. 23.

19. See the ten-point programme of the NRM, reprinted in Y. Museveni, ed., *Selected articles on the Uganda resistance war* (Kampala, NRM, 1986), p. 52.

20. Michael Twaddle, 'The ousting of Amin', *The Round Table* (London) 275 (July 1979), p. 221.

21. See, for example, Jan J. Jørgensen, *Uganda: a modern history* (London, Croom Helm, 1981), pp. 267–330; Michael Twaddle, ed., *Expulsion of a minority: Essays on Uganda Asians* (London Athlone Press, 1975) and Mahmood Mamdani, *From citizen to refugee: Uganda Asians come to Britain* (London, Frances Pinter, 1973).

Part Two

Christianity, Sectarianism
&
Politics in Uganda

Five

The Holy Spirit Movement
& the Forces of Nature
in the North of Uganda
1985–1987

HEIKE BEHREND

The increasing destruction of nature in the industrial societies has not only led to the growth of various environmental movements, but also to attempts to rethink the relationship between nature and society and to develop a concept of the political that includes society and nature. Thus, for example, in his book *Le Contrat naturel* (1990), Michel Serre calls for the development of a philosophical ecology which, in addition to the social contract that excludes war and violence from society, would also involve now entering a contract with nature, limiting real as well as symbolic violence against the latter. In the study of history, there has been interest only in heroes and wars, and not in the destruction of place. This, he says, now must change.

This new interest in ecology and nature has sharpened our view of environmental problems and the unfamiliar ways in which cultures of the so-called Third World deal with nature. In the following account, I want to use the example of the Holy Spirit Movement (HSM) in Uganda to introduce a concept of the political that includes nature and which can, in a certain sense, be regarded as avant-garde with regard to 'green consciousness'.

In 1986, in a situation of existential crisis, the HSM was formed in Acholi, in the north of Uganda. From a local perspective, a holy spirit, called the Lakwena,[2] was sent to Uganda by the Christian God. Under the leadership of the spirit, his medium, Alice Auma, a young woman of Gulu, built up the Holy Spirit Mobile Forces (HSMF) to overthrow the government, to cleanse the world of evil (see Behrend, 1992) and to build a new world in which man and nature were reconciled. Former

Holy Spirit soldiers told me that, to achieve these goals, not only men and women fought as Holy Spirit soldiers, but also 140,000 spirits and parts of animate and inanimate nature – bees, snakes, rivers, rocks and mountains. The war of the HSM was a cosmic uprising in which human forces, spiritual forces and the forces of nature actively took part together.

That bush fighters and guerrillas develop a special relationship to their natural surroundings – the bush or the wilderness – is well known. The Mau Mau forest fighters in Kenya, for example, were protected against the enemy by the forces of nature. Elephants and other dangerous animals did not attack them, while birds and monkeys warned them when British patrols were approaching (personal communication from Robert Buijtenhuijs). During the war of liberation in Zimbabwe, the freedom fighters were not allowed to kill wild animals in the bush (Lan, 1985, p. 159) because these animals did not attack them and even helped them to escape the enemy (pp. 162–163). The eagle, for example, gave the comrades warnings (p. 157). David J. Maxwell, who worked in the Northern Nyanga District of Zimbabwe, was also told that nature and the spirits were very faithful to the freedom fighters and tried to ease their task, and that animals provided signs and warnings to comrades (Maxwell, n.d., pp. 5–6).

While the significance of nature in the two movements mentioned above (and in many others) is rather a passive, protective one, the Holy Spirit soldiers won over the powers of nature as active allies in their struggle. To understand this perhaps unique aspect, in the following account I would like to present, first of all, the discourse engaged in by the HSM 'intellectuals' regarding their relationship to nature. Further I will try to show how this discourse about nature was put into practice in rituals invented in the course of the history of the movement. Then I want to determine which aspects of the Acholi 'cultural archive' (see James, 1988; and Foucault, 1972) were used, activated and transformed by the HSM and to show how Alice and her followers had recourse to a political and religious concept of pre-colonial times, which they reinvented and used to include the forces of nature in their fight against evil. And, finally, I will make a few tentative remarks about Christian influence on the ideology of the HSM in the area of its specific relationship to nature.

This study is only a preliminary essay, the result of a six-month stay in Kampala and Gulu from October 1989 to April 1990. Later, I hope to treat more thoroughly some of the themes here touched upon.[3]

The Holy Spirit Movement's 'myth of origin'

On 11 November 1958, Alice's father, Saverino Lukoya,[4] fell from the top of a roof, 'and sustained serious injury, and remained unconscious for some time. It was during this spell of unconsciousness that he felt his spirit leaving his body and going straight to the chief clerk of the Heavens'.[5] In heaven he was told that one of his children had been chosen to receive a great number of holy spirits.

On 2 January 1985, God sent the spirit Lakwena to Uganda and it happened on this day 'that Saverino realized that it was his daughter Alice who was the chosen child. She began to preach the words of salvation and repentance from sins to the people.' At this time, civil war was raging in Uganda, in which especially the Acholi, who provided many soldiers of the government army, were fighting the National Resistance Army (NRA) of Yoweri Museveni. It was a bloody, often brutal, civil war which cost many casualties, including many civilians.

On 24 May 1985, the spirit Lakwena sent Alice together with her father to Paraa in the Murchison Falls National Park. It is the story of the journey to Paraa which has become the founding myth of the HSM. I found two reports of this journey. One was written down by a former Holy Spirit member, who had belonged to the Front-line Co-ordination Team (FCT).[6] The other version is based on an interview with Alice's father, Saverino Lukoya, which Caroline Lamwaka[7] recorded in the barracks of Gulu on 4 and 5 September 1989, and which she kindly made available to me. I will present both versions here in a slightly shortened form.

FIRST VERSION

Under the command of the holy spirit, the Lakwena, Saverino and his daughter Alice set off for the wilderness on 24 May 1985. They arrived at Anaka on 26 May 1985, and the following day, 27 May 1985, they were at Wang Kwar. Under the command of the same spirit, on 28 May 1985 judgment was passed on all the animals at Paraa Park. The next day, 29 May 1985, judgment was passed on the water and the creatures in it. Under the command of the Lakwena, the waterfalls and the air around them remained still, obeying the command. The Lakwena then said 'Let all creatures in you multiply and fill you, because I have found you sinless.' They left the waterfalls, on 30 May 1985, and travelled back to Opit[8] to prepare for yet another journey to Mount Kilak. They started off for Mount Kilak on 3 June 1985, and arrived on 6 June 1985. The following day, 7 June 1985, at about 10 a.m., local time, Mount Kilak exploded three times to welcome Alice and Saverino. An appointment was made for 10 p.m., local time, to go back to the mountainside again. Later on in the night, Alice and Saverino went back to Mount Kilak, but arrived at midnight when it was very dark. A very bright light came from the mountain top, and led them up to a certain spot where there was a pool of water for curing people. The light was as bright as a star. That water for curing sickness was collected and they carried the same back to Opit, arriving there on 12 June 1985, ready to begin healing all sicknesses, including wounds, blindness, deafness, etc. The holy spirit then ordered Saverino to prepare a holy offering as was offered by Abraham. He secured a lamb for the holy offering.

Later on, they set off again for the wilderness, under the command of the holy spirit, to review the judgment the spirit had passed on 'water' and 'animals'. The wild animals complained about harassment by man, and that man continued to hunt them from their havens. Creatures which lived in the waters also complained about man not staying at peace with other creatures. This evil nature of man encouraged him to practise witchcraft. The Lakweha ordered that, forthwith, all practices of witchcraft must stop. All the holy spirits should embark on healing and converting man to God.

After leaving the Paraa Park on 20 June 1985, they travelled to Mount Kilak to review the judgment. The mountain complained that man was still sinful. The holy spirit, the Lakwena, was also given the power to cure all diseases.

When the day for the holy offering was approaching, they set off, on 3 July 1985. Saverino cried out to the Lord, 'What shall I do, since I am a poor man?' His prayer was answered when the Lord sent some people to assist him . . . After the holy offering the Lord said that in Uganda there is one tribe which is hated everywhere. It is the Acholi tribe. The Lord ordered that a lamb be found and offered for the atonement of their sins, and to stop bloodshed in Acholiland. The lamb was presented to the Lord by Saverino . . . It was after all these events that the holy spirit, the Lakwena, started operating through Alice, healing people and stationed at Opit.

SECOND VERSION (FROM SAVERINO LUKOYA)

On 15 May, 1985, the spirit told me to go to the servant [to Alice] in Opit. She was staying there for 40 days without food [fasting]. I raised my hand and put it on her head. We agreed to go to Paraa to ask the water about the sins on earth and the reasons for bloodshed. We began walking on 25 May 1985. On the 28th we reached the Falls. Alice put on the skin of a *kworo* [the skin of a civet cat, which the *ajwakas* – pagan spirit mediums – wear when working]. Lakwena[9] asked the animals: 'You animals, God sent me to ask you if bloodshed is with you? Are you the ones shedding blood?' The animals denied this, and the buffalo showed a wound in the thigh. Lakwena said: 'You really do not have sins. You should continue to multiply.'

Later we travelled to the elephants and told the elephants that the fault was theirs. The elephants denied this and went to a cave. We reached the gate of Paraa at 3 p.m. and found a gate-man there who was called Agha Khan. For 45 minutes he refused to open the gate. But the Lakwena took us through the gate by force, up to the chief warden, who received us kindly. Lakwena told him that she was sent to judge the living and the dead and that the gate-keeper did not know his job. We complained and asked that he be sacked. They sacked him. Lakwena asked the chief warden to take us to the water. He agreed and said that a boat was available. He gave us five people.

The next morning, at 7 a.m., Lakwena asked the waterfall: 'You water, I have come to ask you about the sins and the bloodshed in this world. I want to ask the leader of the water so that you cool down.' The water cooled down. We asked the animals for the reasons for the bloodshed. Crocodiles and hippos and all the other animals of the water were showing their wounds. A hippo showed one wound in the arm at 9 a.m. The crocodiles said they had no sins because they do not leave the water.

We reached the Falls. Lakwena told the Falls to calm down. He asked: 'Who are the sinners? Who are the leaders of bloodshed?' And the water answered: 'The people are sinners, the people with two legs, they kill their, brothers and throw them in the water.'

Lakwena asked what the water would do to the sinners. And the water said: 'I will fight against the sinners because they are the ones causing bloodshed.' The water said: 'You fight against sinful people because they throw their brothers into the water.'

And the water asked me to bring something to appease the spirits of the dead. I was asked to bring a red sheep, silver coins, 150 old coins, cowrie shells and some other things.

The water said: 'Come with these things, but first go to my brother, the rock.' The water promised to give holy water to nurse injuries and take away sins and for the people to multiply and to heal people's sickness.

We went to the rock on 9 June 1985. The rock told us to come at 10 p.m. It was very dark, and it had rained. Lakwena asked God: 'Save me and my people because we can't go to the place required.'

I went with 70 people at 10 a.m. When the rock saw me, he started shaking three times to welcome me, and people thought it could have been Koreans who shot at the rock. The place shook like during an earthquake and people were surprised. I knew God had come to reveal himself in the power of the rock. Later, at 10 p.m., I prayed together with Lakwena and we saw a star in front of us. It took us to some water near the rock surrounded by trees. Lakwena asked the rock: 'God has sent me to ask why there is theft in the world.' And the rock said: 'I have gone nowhere to steal anybody's child. But people come here and name other people whom they want me to kill. Some go and look for medicine. That is the sin done by men . . . I will give you water to nurse injuries and leprosy and other sicknesses. But for sins, I will fight.'

That was the promise of the rock and the water for judgment. Three times we went back to ask whether things were going well.

We went back to the water to ask if things had gone well. The water had made judgment on those who fornicated. Some people lost power [the Okellos]. The water said: 'Not everybody listens to the Word of God.' When they came the third time to make a sacrifice, the water was turning and the new world came into being. Christ wants people to be cleansed by the holy spirit.

On 2 July 1986, we went to the water and stayed 40 days. The spirit took Alice for two days. Then we returned to Opit on 15 August 1986. We made another sacrifice in the form of bananas, cassava, maize, chicken, birds, etc. to feed the spirits of creatures. On 17 August 1986, we saw soldiers of the UPDA[10] in Opit. They began to hit the railway. The railway driver was chased up to Lakwena's house. The UPDA soldiers shot at Alice, but the bullets bounced and produced smoke. Alice was protecting the railway driver. When the soldiers saw that Alice had power, they asked her to give them spiritual support.[11]

Under the command of the holy spirit, Alice healed and cleansed people in Opit. But, on 6 August 1986, the spirit changed his order and asked Alice to build up the HSMF and to fight evil. This evil revealed itself in various ways: first, as external enemy in the form of the NRA under Yoweri Museveni, who deposed Tito Okello in January 1986, taking control of state power; second, as internal enemy in the form of impure soldiers, witches and sorcerers. On orders from the spirit, Alice recruited into the HSMF primarily former soldiers who, after Museveni's victory, had fled to the north and who had tried to lead a peasant life again in their villages. In a complex cleansing ritual, these soldiers were cleansed of evil and initiated into the movement. The spirit Lakwena promised them mystical protection, which, however, was only effective if they conformed with the twenty 'Holy Spirit safety precautions', rules of moral conduct issued by the spirit.

The HSMF fought according to the 'Holy Spirit tactic': before every battle, Alice was possessed by one or more spirits, who through her, gave instructions regarding where and how to fight. Aside from the spirit Lakwena, who was High Commander of the HSMF, there were other spirits, such as Wrong Element, Franko, Ching Po and others, who were to take care of supplies, logistics or the intelligence service.

With her army, Alice moved from Acholi to Lira, Soroti, Mbale and Tororo, and from there to Busoga. In October 1987 at Jinja, about 50 km before Kampala, the HSMF were finally defeated by the NRA. Alice fled with some faithful followers to Kenya, where she remains in hiding to this day.

The myth in practice

As was mentioned above, in addition to the Holy Spirit soldiers and

140,000 spirits, parts of animate and inanimate nature – bees, snakes, rivers, rocks and mountains – also fought in the HSMF.

The task of the bees was 'to preserve the infrastructure of the country'. But sometimes they also participated directly in the struggle, flying to the front and driving the enemies to flight, as former Holy Spirit soldiers told me. The bees also gave honey for the production of a medicine, the 'Holy Spirit drug', a mixture of honey, water and oil, which had to be shaken for at least half an hour while praying before being applied to wounds. The Lakwena had given the recipe to Alice and the medicine was produced and applied according to his directions.

Snakes had the task of watching over the Holy Spirit soldiers. After the victory and the fall of the government, snakes would punish those who did not repent of their sins. If Holy Spirit soldiers encountered a snake, they said: 'You are my fellow soldier. Give me respect!' Some snakes were kept in the 'yard', the ritual centre of the defence. Others fought actively on the side of the Holy Spirit soldiers and flushed out NRA soldiers, forcing them to step out of hiding or cover, so that they could be killed by the Holy Spirit soldiers.

Among the twenty Holy Spirit safety precautions issued by the spirit Lakwena were prohibitions against killing bees or snakes because they had been won over as allies of the HSMF.

Water in general and rivers in particular were of great importance in the HSM. Thus Alice received the spirit Lakwena in the waters of the Nile at Murchison Falls, and, together with her father, she returned to this location at the command of the spirit in order to pass judgment on the forces of nature. Here she also received the holy water, which found broad application in the ritual practice of the HSM. The soldiers who joined the movement were initiated with water. They were sprinkled with water and thus purified of all evil. Before a battle, water was carried in front of the soldiers by the 'controllers', magical helpers who, by sprinkling the water, opened the way for the soldiers. In the yard, the 'technicians' – another set of ritual assistants – fought magically by sprinkling water on models of weapons made of wire, which were put in the fire of little charcoal stoves to cool down the danger of the enemy.

The soldiers of the HSM called themselves soldiers of the water, in contrast to the soldiers of the UPDA, who were soldiers of the land. While the soldiers of the land were impure and sinful, even if they fought for the same political goal, the soldiers of the water claimed to be purified, free of sin and holy.[12] They said: 'I am a soldier of the water. I am holy. Give me respect.' Each time that a river had to be crossed on the march to Kampala,[13] it was 'bought' by a technician.[14] They gave it cowrie shells and coins, with this offering moving it to support them. If a river had been bought, then water could be taken and the river crossed without difficulty. But, if a river refused to support the HSM, and they crossed it nevertheless, then it punished them, for example by letting the NRA come and win a battle. After fairly fruitless battles near Awere, the holy spirit appeared and said: 'Why have you crossed the Aswa river? The river was not bought!' And it ordered the punishment of Alice and the soldiers. Alice received six strokes of the lash, the soldiers only four each.

When the soldiers crossed a river, they showed it respect by not speaking. The rivers that had been bought and won over as allies allowed Holy Spirit soldiers to pass, but began to swell when NRA soldiers wanted to cross. Or they sent floods that consumed the NRA soldiers.

The holy spirit Lakwena also prophesied that, shortly before Jinja on the way to Kampala, they would not cross the Nile on a bridge, but that, like Jesus, they would walk on the water. Only the sinners would remain behind.

With the help of the holy spirit, Alice was also able to make rain. On her orders, the chief technicians shook pots filled with water in the yard and commanded the rain clouds to come or to disappear.

On the march to Kampala, when the Holy Spirit soldiers passed a rock or mountain, they had to purchase it as well. The technicians gave it cowrie shells and coins, and as a reciprocal present they were allowed to collect stones, which they brought to the yard. There, a lamb was sacrificed and its blood shaken over the stones. These began to glitter and gleam mysteriously. Soldiers and technicians prayed, and the stones were transformed into stone grenades, 'which could kill at least 25 enemy soldiers at one time, as if driven by electricity'. Before the battle, the stone grenades were distributed among the soldiers who went to the front. The soldiers prayed and 'the grenades began to shake in their hands; they flew and exploded at least three times'.

A former Holy Spirit soldier told me that the HSM was not able to fight in Kitgum because there were many rocks there that Alice had not been able to buy. If they had fought there, then the rocks would not have helped, but would have contributed to their defeat.

In Tororo, according to the same soldier, a Holy Spirit intelligence officer was sent out to make a survey of the locations of the rocks, so that they could be bought.

While a large number of holy spirits, bees, snakes, rivers and rocks were won over by the HSM as allies and took an active part in the fighting, other parts of nature were excluded. Thus, it was forbidden for Holy Spirit soldiers to remain in the neighbourhood of trees and termite hills, because magic charms for sorcery were made of the wood of the trees and because God had damned the trees and termite hills. They were also regarded as the dwelling of evil spirits, called *cen* in Acholi.

Thus it was not the entirety of nature that had been won for the

HSM's struggle. The part of nature that was associated with sorcery and the evil spirits of the dead who had died a bad death, the *cen*, was excluded from participation for being sinful.

Nature in Acholi[15]

In the HSM myth of origin, Alice and her father went into the wilderness, into the National Park at Paraa, in order to pass judgment on parts of animate and inanimate nature. The wilderness – in Acholi, *tim* – is the place not cultivated by humans, the untouched forest or bush, whose cultivation is at least forgotten. However, *tim* is also distant, foreign parts, space lying outside the Acholi culture, for example Kampala, where migrant workers go to earn money. The wild and the alien are associated with *tim*. Within the wider context of Acholi cosmological ideas, the homestead, the domestic domain and the wilderness are separate and conflicting worlds. In the wilderness live wild animals and various spirits, which are called *jok* or, in plural, *jogi*. These spirits dwell near rivers, rocks and mountains, but they can also take possession of humans, animals and things. Women, especially, were exposed to the *jogi* when they fetched water at the river or when they gathered firewood in the wilderness. They mediated between the domains. If they were possessed by a *jok* and became sick, then they could only be healed if a healer and diviner, an *ajakwa*, herself the medium of a *jok*, identified the spirit and drove it away or killed it, or else the sick person had to submit to a long and involved initiation and learn to domesticate the spirit and become an *ajakwa* herself.

The power of the different *jogi* was ambivalent. It could be used and manipulated for good and bad purposes. While in pre-colonial times the chief – in Acholi, *rwot* – and the priest of the chiefdom *jok* – in Acholi, *won ngom* – used the power of their *jogi* to advance the well-being and fertility of the land and the people, many of the *ajwaka*, mediums of the 'free' *jogi*, who had come from outside the Acholi culture, from Bunyoro, from Europe or from Sudan, used the power or their *jogi* for witchcraft and sorcery to harm people.

The *jogi* were held responsible for misfortune and catastrophes that hit Acholi, and at the same time they were a power against them. They could be appeased by sacrifices. But the *jogi* were not the only ones responsible for catastrophes in Acholi; a more or less immoral or unclean state of the society was primarily responsible. When the hearts of the people were not clean, when there was bitterness and hatred, witchcraft and sorcery, when people quarrelled and killed each other, then the *jogi* would become angry and sent natural or social catastrophes.

In Acholi, the order of nature and the moral order were thus not separate, but formed a continuum, which made it possible to causally connect natural events with moral feelings. A catastrophe could be seen as punishment for infringing upon the natural or social order, and the end of a plague could be seen as forgiveness. While for Europeans, since Descartes and the separation made by him between mind and matter, nature has become mere inanimate material that waits to be worked, ruled and exploited by humans, in Acholi it is a plurality of independent powers, with which it is possible to speak, negotiate and trade. These powers – the *jogi* and their mediums (mainly women) – mediate between nature and society and establish their unity.

In pre-colonial times, the wilderness belonged to the *rwot* – the chieftain and 'owner of the land'. In it, he instituted game preserves under the charge of a game warden, *won tim*, master of the wilderness, nominated by him. Hunting was strictly prohibited in these preserves. Only once a year did the *won tim* seek permission from the *rwot* for the people to join in a big hunt (Ocheng, 1955, p. 58).

An infringement of or a prohibited attack on the powers of the wilderness raised the danger of retaliation. The killing of a wild animal, as well as the killing of a person, had to be atoned for by a sacrifice to the spirit of the animal or person. If this was not done, then the injury or insult to the forces of the wilderness irrevocably led to a counter-attack. The powers of the wilderness became active to carry out retaliation.

During the civil war, the wilderness and the wild animals living in it were also subjected to damage. There were robbery, pillage and poaching. The prohibitions of the *rwot* or the *won tim* were disregarded, and purification and reconciliation rituals were not carried out.

In the 'myth of origin' of the way to Paraa in the National Park, Alice and her father listen to the complaints of injured and insulted nature. The animals show their wounds and the water complains about the contamination that occurred due to the many corpses thrown into it. Alice and her father pass judgment and recognize the innocence of wild animals, water and rocks, which themselves have become victims. But they demand retribution, order the fight. And it is this right to retaliation, to revenge, that Alice recognized and knew how to mobilize and activate for her movement.

In pre-colonial but also in colonial times, the *rwot*, together with the priest of the chiefdom *jok*, was responsible for the rain and for the fertility of land and people. Before sowing and after the harvest, rituals were carried out under his guidance, in which sacrifices were made to the chiefdom *jok*.

In times of catastrophic threat, the *rwot* and the elders had the task of ensuring that the moral state of the society improved and that the people had clean hearts again. To achieve this, they made various regulations forbidding quarrelling, killing, witchcraft and sorcery, and sexual union. If the people didn't obey the prohibitions, then the catastrophe intensified and demanded many victims. However, if the people obeyed the prohibitions, then the moral community reconstituted itself and the catastrophes came to an end (personal communication from R. M. Nono).

The secularization and bureaucratization of government during the colonial period and afterwards pushed the religious and moral duties of the *rwot* – particularly in regard to nature – more and more into the background. Ecological concern declined in general in Acholi and although today the sacrifices to the clan and chiefdom *jok* are still carried out once a year, so that rain and the well-being of the community are guaranteed, it is seldom the chief but rather the elders who carry out this ritual, on a lower, local level.

Alice had had recourse to the role of the *rwot* (pl. *rwodi*) in pre-colonial times and activated particularly those aspects that had retreated into the background since the colonial period, namely the ecological concerns. Like a *rwot*, she ensured the rain and made sacrifices to reconcile injured and insulted nature. Like a *rwot*, she passed judgment and set up regulations (the twenty Holy Spirit safety precautions), so that the people once again had clean hearts and the moral community was reconstituted. And, like a *rwot*, she made war against her enemies.

But, unlike the *rwodi*, she encountered an injured, insulted nature, which demanded revenge and whom she was thus able to win over as an active ally in the fight against evil. The reconciliation with nature was not only a distant goal of the movement; it had already occurred on the way to Paraa. The alliance between the HSM and nature proved its firmness and reality in the struggle and could be intensified through Christian ideas. Alice and her followers were able to connect certain motifs from the Acholi 'cultural archive' with certain aspects from Christian mythology. The motif of the 'divided river' (Baumann, 1936, pp. 260 ff.) which Alice took up, was generally known in Acholiland. Thus, in a myth about the Lwoo migration, there is a report about a quarrel between two brothers, who then parted company. One threw himself into the river, which divided in front of him so that he could pass safely, while the other remained behind on the riverbank (Crazzolara, 1937, p. 12). Like the rivers, the mountains also played an important role in the myths of the Lwoo migration. Mount Kilak, for example, is remembered as the place

> where a longer stop seems to have been made – perhaps as a visible sight at some distance from the place where the stop was made ... From such a place, messengers were sent in various directions to report on the country and the possibilities of settling there (ibid., p. 10).

It is also remembered 'that at Kilak a very heavy quarrel started which has had far-reaching consequences and has ever since been deeply impressed on the minds of the descendants of those implicated as being the event which has so largely decided their future' (ibid., p. 10). It was this Mount Kilak that Alice and her father visited several times, which greeted them with three explosions and which ordered them to fight. They won it over as an ally.

Rivers and mountains are also of particular importance in Christian mythology. In the ideology and practice of the HSM, their semantic field combined with the symbolism possessed by mountains and rivers in Acholi myths and increased to powerful metaphors.

Additionally, Alice and her followers succeeded in reinforcing the 'instant millennium' (Willis, 1970), which they inaugurated by cleansing their followers from witchcraft and sorcery, through Christian eschatological expectations. History has shown itself to be a history of catastrophes for the Acholi. The HSM took historical failure not only as a sign of judgment but also as a promise of redemption to be won. Alice announced that the Last Judgment was at hand. In the new world, which already existed, all creatures had equal fights. When the war was over, a general resurrection would take place. Not only humans, but the animals, too, would have their own yards. And, like St Paul, she promised that all creatures would be redeemed, even the stones.[16]

Notes

1. There have been several 'holy spirit movements' at various times. As far as I know, only the movement of Josef Kony in Acholi is still active today. While the HSM of Alice Auma called itself the Holy Spirit Mobile Forces, Josef Kony's movement changed its name to Salvation Army and later to Uganda People's Democratic Christian Army (UPDCA). All the holy spirit movements – including the one founded by Alice's father, Saverino Lukoya – were led by the holy spirit Lakwena. In the following I deal mainly with the HSM of Alice Auma.
2. Lakwena means 'messenger' and 'apostle' in Acholi.
3. I am deeply indebted to the Special Research Programme of the University of Bayreuth, which sponsored my research in Acholiland.
4. Saverino Lukoya built up his own HSM after his daughter Alice had fled to Kenya. When his followers left him and joined Josef Kony, in 1989, he turned himself in to the NRA and has been incarcerated in the barracks of Gulu. I was not permitted to interview him.
5. This and the following quotation are taken from the interview conducted by Caroline Lamwaka with Saverino Lukoya in Gulu in September 1989.
6. I was told the movement was led by the spirit Lakwena himself, who was also the chairman of the movement. He was represented by the Commander of the Forces (CF). Under the CF were four companies: A, B, C, and headquarters company. The civilian wing of the movement was the FCT, whose duties were to provide moral education for the people, to preach the message of the Lakwena to the people and to provide moral and political education for the troops.
7. I would like to express my thanks to Caroline Lamwaka, the late R. M. Nono and Mike Ocan for the their support and help.
8. In Opit, Alice built a shrine, performed a sacrifice and worked as a healer before the holy spirit commanded her to fight.

9. Here I use the name Lakwena, also used in the original text, when Alice is possessed by Lakwena, i.e. when it is the spirit that speaks and acts through her.

10. The UPDA (Ugandan People's Democratic Army) was formed in 1986 by former Uganda National Liberation Army (UNLA) soldiers to overthrow Museveni. Many soldiers of the UPDA joined the HSMF after Alice had gained several victories over the NRA.

11. This version is only one of many regarding the origin of Alice's leadership.

12. The Catholic missionaries used the 'Acholi word *maleng*, which means 'pure', to translate 'holy'. *Tipu maleng*, the holy spirit or holy ghost, also means 'the pure spirit'.

13. On the march to Kampala, Alice took the same route as the Lwoo-speaking people took when they migrated from Sudan into their present area of settlement a few centuries ago.

14. The 'purchase' of rivers and mountains or rocks may be traceable to Revelation 14: 3 and 1: 4.

15. In Acholi there is no exact equivalent to the Western concept of nature. In the following, I attempt to approach the Acholi by translating *tim* as 'wilderness'. 'Wilderness' and 'nature', however, are not contrasted, but rather a continuum: in colonial and post-colonial times, the Acholi concept began to approach our ideas of nature, moulded by science. Alice tried to reverse this process.

16. I am indebted to Mitch Cohen for translating this chapter from German to English. A further discussion and list of references appears in my monograph just published in German, *Alice und die Geister: Krieg im Norden Ugandas* (Munich, Germany: Trickster Verlag 1993).

References

Baumann, Hermann (1936) *Schöpfung und Urzeit des Menschen im Mythos afrikanischer Völker*, Berlin.

Behrend, Heike (1991) 'Is Alice Lakwena a witch? The Holy Spirit Movement and its fight against evil in the north of Uganda', in Hansen, Holger Bernt and Twaddle, Michael, eds, *Changing Uganda*.

Behrend, Heike (1992) 'Violence dans le nord de l'Ouganda: Le mouvement de Saint-Esprit', *Politique Africaine* 48.

Buijtenhuijs, Robert (1971) *Le Mouvement Mau-Mau*, The Hague and Paris.

Crazzolara, J. P. (1937) 'The Lwoo people', *Uganda Journal* 5, pp. 1–21.

Foucault, Michel (1972) *The archeology of knowledge*, London.

James, Wendy (1988) *The listening ebony: moral knowledge, religion, and power among the Uduk of Sudan*, Oxford.

Lan, David (1985) *Guns and rain: Guerrillas and spirit mediums in Zimbabwe*, London and Harare.

Maxwell, David J. (n.d.) 'Religion and the war in Northern Nyanga District Zimbabwe', unpublished manuscript, Oxford.

Ocheng, D. O. (1955) 'Land tenure in Acholi', *Uganda Journal* 19, pp. 57–61.

p'Bitek, Okot (1970) *African religions in Western scholarship*, Nairobi.

Serre, Michel (1990) *Le Contrat naturel*, Paris.

Willis, R. G. (1970) 'Instant millennium: The sociology of Africa witch-cleansing cults', in Mary Douglas, ed., *Witchcraft confessions and accusations*, London.

Six

The Church of Uganda
amidst Conflict

The Interplay between Church & Politics
in Uganda since 1962

KEVIN WARD

Both the Roman Catholic and the Anglican Churches in Uganda are great 'folk' churches; that is, they have become integrated at a very basic level into the social, cultural and political fabric of Uganda, both at the local and the national level. But this has operated in very different ways in the life of the two churches. The Catholic Church lost the battle for political power in the 1890s and concentrated on building up a 'spiritual kingdom', parallel to the state but not in direct competition with it, loyally co-operating with the colonial government in a more or less apolitical way. By the 1950s the Catholics had begun to have ambitions to reverse their subordinate position in an independent Uganda, and a good number of church leaders saw the Democratic Party as a suitable vehicle to achieve that end.[1] But, in the event, political power has constantly eluded the Catholics as a body even in independent Uganda, despite the fact that they are the largest religious body and probably a majority of the Ugandan population as a whole.[2] The sense that it has been denied its rightful position has helped to give the Catholic Church a certain degree of internal unity and cohesion, and a powerful critical voice *vis-à-vis* the state.

The Anglican Church (the Church of Uganda), in contrast, has had a rather more complex and ambiguous relationship to the state since independence. As a quasi-establishment during the colonial period, it has tended at times to cling on to that position in the very different situations of independent Uganda. Sometimes this has given the impression of an Erastian institution, following the line of whatever regime happens to be in power. In fact, the Church of Uganda has reflected –

or, rather, embodied – the tensions and conflicts operating within state and society. The unity and cohesion of both church and state have been fragile in the extreme. The relationship of the Anglican Church to the political parties has also been rather ambiguous. Granted the leaders of both the Uganda People's Congress (UPC) and Kabaka Yekka (KY) tended to be Protestant laymen.[3] But important sections of the Anglican Church have had their doubts about both parties as suitable vehicles for a 'Christian' view of society – suspecting the 'socialism' of UPC rhetoric, and the cultural chauvinism of KY. If the relationship of the Catholic hierarchy to DP seems more straightforward, that may, of course, be largely because DP has never been given the chance (apart from Kiwanuka's transitional government just before full independence) to exercise power.

The Anglican Church and the question of Buganda 1961–1973

THE PROBLEM

The issue which preoccupied politicians in the years leading up to and immediately after independence was the question of the status of Buganda. This was equally true for the Church of Uganda. The deportation of the Kabaka in 1953 had precipitated a crisis in the relationship between the Baganda and the Anglican Church. It was widely believed that the new bishop, Leslie Brown (who had only just arrived in the country), had been a party to Governor Cohen's decision to deport Kabaka Muteesa. Brown always denied that he knew anything about the matter beforehand, but a lingering suspicion always remained and his silence on the issue was compared unfavourably with the vocal condemnation of the former bishop, Stuart (by then in England). In any case, the traditional collaboration between Anglican Church and colonial state now served to alienate an awakened Kiganda nationalism from the church.[4]

Meanwhile, constitutional developments were taking place in the church too, with the aim of creating an independent province of the Anglican communion. If the Baganda were preoccupied with fears of losing their status and integrity as a nation in an independent Uganda, other ethnic groups were equally apprehensive about renewed domination by Buganda. In Anglican terms, this was expressed in fears that the Upper Nile diocese would be swamped by the more highly developed diocese of Uganda (and particularly by the Baganda), once they were united in a single province. The Archbishop of Canterbury even made what he called 'the bold suggestion' of having two provinces in the Church of Uganda, with an archbishop of Kampala and an archbishop of Mbale. Bishop Usher Wilson did not think this a good idea at all: 'It is unity more than anything else that we want, and to have two provinces would perpetuate a division which exists politically.'[5] Indeed, the north has always seen its best interests to lie in a single province, and has strenuously resisted all attempts, emanating from the south, to create more than one province.

The 1961 constitution created a province of the Church of Uganda, with five dioceses from the old diocese of Uganda and three from Upper Nile. The archbishop would be elected from the diocesan bishops and would retain his diocese. Namirembe cathedral, the 'mother church' of Ugandan Anglicanism, would be the cathedral both of Namirembe diocese and of the province. The ambiguities and tensions inherent in this settlement, in view of the delicate political situation with regard to the position of Buganda, were avoided at first by the election of Leslie Brown, first bishop of Namirembe, as archbishop. But they became all the more troublesome when in 1965 Erika Sabiiti, the bishop of Ruwenzori, was elected as archbishop.

ARCHBISHOP SABIITI[6]

Political considerations were not paramount in the election of the first African archbishop; nor would it have been considered right that they should have been. Sabiiti was elected for his spiritual qualities. Sabiiti belonged to the Balokole fellowship. Since the 1930s the Balokole had been waging a campaign for the renewal and moral regeneration of the church. By 1960 the Church of Uganda had more or less learned to accept and value their witness, not least as a counter-weight to the forces of nationalism within the church. Sabiiti (1903–1988) was a Muhima from a chiefly family in Ankole, educated at King's College, Budo, and Makerere College. He was one of the first clergy of the Church of Uganda to identify himself wholly with the revival. The fact that he was 'saved' (*omulokole*) and a 'brother' (*ow'oluganda*) was for him the most significant fact of his life and far outweighed all class, ethnic, political or even church loyalties. He was not interested in politics, nor did he have the politician's skills of compromise and flexibility. Compromise was alien to Balokole vocabulary. Balokole honesty – or bluntness – had at times led Sabiiti into situations of conflict: with his bishop, with the Bahima chiefs (including his own brother Chief Katungi) and with his congregation at Bweranyangi in west Ankole. His election as bishop of Ruwenzori in 1960 had been opposed by a group calling itself the Ruwenzori Christian Association. They criticized Sabiiti for being a member of the traditional ruling class and for being a *mulokole* who had had problems with Christians in Ankole. They wanted a more locally acceptable man. On the other hand, the Association was not exactly representative of opinion throughout the diocese: this 'Batoro clique', as it was dubbed, ignored Banyoro and Bakonzo opinion, and was regarded by some as little more than a group of the new educated 'UPC' élite.

Sabiiti's election as archbishop was not popular in Buganda. Kiganda cultural nationalism had always been resentful of the idea of a non-Muganda bishop occupying the throne of Namirembe cathedral. In 1947 there had been a protest against the consecration of Aberi Balya (of Toro) as the first Ugandan Anglican bishop. Why had a Muganda not been chosen? Were there not many well-educated Baganda clergy, much more educated than Balya? Was it not an insult to the Buganda church and nation to ordain a non-Muganda bishop in Namirembe?

> The Cathedral at Namirembe belongs to the Kabaka of Buganda and to the Baganda and is not for other nationalities . . . We ask that a Muganda be consecrated because we were given power to rule ourselves and the 1900 Agreement does not allow people of other tribes to sit on our councils.[7]

In 1965 the Baganda felt just as strongly that it would be fitting for a Muganda to become the first Ugandan archbishop. But the dearth of really suitable Baganda clergy was a problem. The reasons for this state of affairs are complex. They include the low status of the clerical office in Buganda compared with secular professions, the alienation of the Anglican Church from Kiganda nationalist sentiment since at least the 1940s and the expulsion of so many spiritually keen Balokole ordinands from the theological college in 1941.[8] Dunstan Nsubuga, the most likely candidate, had only become a diocesan bishop on the retirement of Archbishop Brown, and was hardly considered as eligible for immediate promotion. Many Baganda blamed Brown (somewhat unreasonably) for this situation.

Under the 1961 church constitution, Namirembe cathedral was to be, for ordinary purposes, the cathedral of the diocese of Namirembe. For national occasions the dean and chapter would make the cathedral available to the archbishop. A similar arrangement was hardly possible in terms of the Kampala residence of the archbishop. On this issue Baganda Christians interpreted the 1961 constitution in this way (and here they were supported by Brown): the diocese of Namirembe was the legal successor of the old diocese of Uganda, which had been divided in 1960. The province of Uganda had come into being a year later as a result of the agreement of all those dioceses previously included in the old dioceses of Uganda and Upper Nile. The position of archbishop was thus a new creation, and it was the duty of the new province to provide suitable accommodation at the capital for the archbishop. As long as the archbishop was also bishop of Namirembe, the problem of accommodation in Kampala did not arise. But Archbishop Sabiiti was bishop of Ruwenzori – his home was at Fort Portal, nearly 200 miles away from Kampala. On Brown's retirement, Bishop Nsubuga as the new bishop of Namirembe lost no time in moving into the old house of the bishop of Uganda, as he considered his right. He offered Archbishop Sabiiti the guest-house attached to the bishop's house – the 'boys' quarters' as it was dismissively called. A government commission of inquiry in 1973 put it this way:

> we have seen that the new Archbishop was thus subjected to ignominious humility, disrespect and complacent callousness in having to put up in the Retreat House which lacked even a bathroom . . . All this could have been avoided had the authorities concerned exhibited the slightest iota of common sense and Christian goodwill.[9]

Starting from these very different legal premisses, the commission came to some very different conclusions from those of Namirembe diocese and Bishop Brown. The commission held that land and property had been held, not in the name of individual dioceses, but in the name of the 'Native Anglican Church', a legal corporation whose successor was the province of the Church of Uganda. Whatever the legal strength of this opinion, undoubtedly this accorded with the sentiment of Anglicans outside Buganda, who were outraged by the treatment of the archbishop. Eventually, a new house was built for the archbishop, next to the bishop of Namirembe's and a little lower down the hill. A symbolic if somewhat hollow victory for Buganda in the light of historical events.

THE DESECRATION OF THE KINGDOM

Sabiiti was elected archbishop in January 1966. In February the *Lubiri* (the Kabaka's palace) was stormed by the central government of Obote. The Kabaka fled and went into exile. In 1967 Obote introduced a new state constitution, abolishing the old kingdoms and any trace of 'federalism' and stressing the unitary nature of Uganda.

Bishop Nsubuga recounts this story:[10] just before fleeing Kabaka Muteesa II visited the bishop secretly. The Kabaka said this: 'Ffe tugenda. Naye Obuganda mubukuume.' (We are going. You should look after Buganda.) The 'you' (plural) referred to religious leaders, specifically Bishop Nsubuga and the Catholic archbishop. Nsubuga took this to be a commission to guard the traditions and cultural heritage of Buganda – you might say the soul of Buganda. This story has a strong symbolic value. In late colonial times the Anglican Church had become increasingly alienated from Buganda's cultural and nationalist aspirations. Now the two began to come together again. In the absence of a Kabaka, the bishops (especially Dunstan Nsubuga and Cardinal Emmanuel Nsubuga) became the focus of loyalty for many Baganda. They served as guardians of Buganda in an increasingly hostile and dangerous world.

The events of 1966 and 1967 in national affairs made Baganda Anglicans all the more intransigent and determined to retain their cathedral and keep the 'province' in its place. It did not make the task of Archbishop Sabiiti at all easy. Baganda came to identify him as a 'UPC' and Obote man, despite his lack of interest in politics. Two seemingly trivial things branded Sabiiti as an Obote man for many Baganda: that the furnishings for the archbishop's house were provided by the government and that Sabiiti went to Lira to baptize Obote's children. This was a surprisingly emotive issue in Buganda because in the 1950s Bishop Brown had refused to allow the baptism of two of the Kabaka's children on the grounds that they were born out of wedlock, and he had suspended a clergyman who had secretly gone ahead with the ceremony. The fact is that Sabiiti was merely continuing the old colonial pattern by which the bishop of Uganda established a good working relationship with the governor in Entebbe. All the traditions of the church and the present expectations of Ugandans outside Buganda demanded this. But, on a personal level, Sabiiti hoped that his Balokole principle of openness and 'walking in the light' would enable him to be reconciled with his Baganda Christian brethren. As he wrote in a personal letter to Bishop Nsubuga:

> I think we are living in a very difficult time in the history of our Church and nation. I think we, the leaders of the Church, need God's grace to help us to catch a vision of our responsibility to bring about the unification of the Church. I am not now referring to being united with people of other denominations . . . but to a real unity in our own Church of Uganda, which is at present torn by tribal and political strifes . . . I am very sorry that Satan has been very active in creating misunderstandings . . . [but] at present, I feel there is nothing which is not in light between you and me. And I will keep being in the light.[11]

THE STRUGGLE FOR A NEW CHURCH CONSTITUTION

The political crises of 1966/1967 showed the impracticability of having an archbishop based in Fort Portal, far from the capital. Constitutional change was necessary. But the imposition of Obote's 1967 constitution, with its strong stress on the unitary state and on the powers of the central government, made the Baganda all the more tenacious of their institutions and traditions, not least in the church. The 'province' of the Church of Uganda was equated with central government; constitutional change in the church was likely to take it along the road of the 1967 constitution in the state.

In 1968 the Canon Law and Constitution Commission recommended to the executive of the Provincial Assembly that a new diocese of Kampala be created, as the archbishop's see. This could only happen by carving out a new diocese from Namirembe diocese. Namirembe synod accepted that the province could initiate changes in the provincial constitution, but denied that it could tamper with boundaries except with the consent of the diocese concerned. The synod made an alternative suggestion – that the archbishop continued to be bishop of his own diocese, but that he appoint a suffragen to do the main work there. The archbishop would reside in Kampala, but not have any diocesan responsibilities there. Negotiations with Yona Okoth, the provincial secretary, resulted in an agreement that there would be full consultations with Namirembe before definite proposals were formulated and submitted to the Provincial Assembly.

As far as Namirembe was concerned the publication in April 1969 of the Bikangaga Report shattered this accord. This was a survey of administration and finance in the Church of Uganda – but it touched on much more sensitive areas than 'administration' and 'finance' might suggest. John Bikangaga was a prominent Anglican churchman from Kigezi, a highly respected civil servant. As a representative of the Protestant educated élite from outside Buganda, deeply involved in the UPC politics of his home area, Bikangaga was unlikely to be very sympathetic to the Kiganda point of view. The Baganda were indeed alarmed at his proposals. They had already virtually rejected the idea of a diocese of Kampala, excised from Namirembe. They also rejected the proposal to strengthen the powers of the archbishop – this, they felt, was interference in diocesan affairs and gave him a 'quasi-papal' role, contrary to Anglican tradition. A suggestion that the house of bishops alone should be responsible for electing new bishops (rather than responding to names suggested by the diocese) was also rejected as undemocratic. Behind this suggestion was the idea that the episcopate should not be tied to a particular locality and ethnic group; bishops should not be 'tribal bishops' but should represent the whole church and be available for transfer to any part of Uganda. This was a very different concept from that of 'father of the people' as embodied in Kabaka Muteesa's parting commission to Bishop Nsubuga. To Buganda it smacked of the UPC policy of 'mobilization', the creation of a political cadre of civil servants and politicians responsive not to factional and regional divisions, but to national priorities as formulated by the central organs of party and government.

Perhaps the most sensitive issue of all was the proposal to set up Church Commissioners, responsible to the province and responsible for administering all land held by the Church of Uganda, any revenues accruing to help towards financing the administration of the province. Now, the great bulk of church land was in Buganda; much of it had been given as *mailo* land under the 1900 Agreement or by individual Baganda landowners. This proposal seemed a threat by the central organ of the church to alienate the *ttaka* (soil) of Buganda, which could encourage the central government to make even more drastic land reforms in the name of a nationalist or socialist policy.

Namirembe diocesan synod angrily rejected the report, claiming that its aim is the ambition to place all church matters under the jurisdiction of the Province. To do that violates the very nature of our belief in Christianity and our relationship and co-operation in the Church. To put all power in the jurisdiction of the Province is not the tradition of our Church in which we have our faith. Devolution of powers is the freedom of our Church but not centralisation of all power in the hands of one man. The main tie in our church is not the Province but the Diocese.[12]

Nevertheless a draft constitution drawn up in 1970 largely followed the recommendations of the Bikangaga Report. As Mr E. M. K. Mulira, a prominent lay member of Namirembe diocese, put it:

The constitution was proto-type with the thinking of the time. It was hierarchical in character – i.e. a 'mobilising' type of Constitution, which tried to accumulate all power to the centre; as such it was robbing the dioceses of some of their federal rights, thus departing from the tradition of the churches in the Anglican Communion.[13]

In other words, from a Kiganda point of view, it was an 'Obote' constitution, a UPC blueprint for the church.

The two Baganda dioceses of Namirembe and West Buganda (nicknamed the 'twins' (*Balongo*)) were determined to resist the new constitution. When they made little progress in delaying or amending its provisions at the Provincial Assembly held in Mukono in December 1970, the delegates of the 'twin' dioceses walked out. The assembly went ahead to vote for the new constitution. The Baganda dioceses talked openly of seceding from the province and establishing their own Buganda province (something which had first been mooted in 1965 when Sabiiti became archbishop). A synod of Namirembe diocese on 23 January 1971 voted for this course of action. Two days later Obote was toppled in Amin's coup. Undoubtedly political feelings in the church had reached fever pitch during these months, and there has been talk of intimidatory practices on both sides: the presence of spies of the General Service Unit (Obote's much feared intelligence network) at the Provincial Assembly in December, and threats by extremists against the moderates at the synod in January.

The Amin years 1971–1979

THE RESOLUTION OF THE SECESSION CONFLICT[14]

The overthrow of Obote was naturally greeted with jubilation in Buganda. Bishop Lutaaya of west Buganda diocese is reported to have hailed Amin as 'Our redeemer and the light of God'. But it was not only Baganda Anglicans that felt a great relief. Practically all sections of society had some reason to hope. If one commentator talked (in the hyperbole which many used at the time and were later bitterly to regret) of Amin emerging as a 'national symbol of unity, peace and social justice', many Baganda Anglicans saw events as providing the opportunity to pursue their own separatist aims with renewed vigour. Thus, the ending of the Obote regime did not immediately end the crisis within the Church of Uganda.[15]

Sabiiti was the target of bitter invective, accusing him of being behind Obote's 'master plan' to control and manipulate the churches, and that Sabiiti himself was a 'dictating politician' who, as archbishop, merely wanted to make the bishops his instruments. The most notorious incident was Sabiiti's exclusion from Namirembe cathedral on 31 January 1971, where he was due to preach at the thanksgiving service for the release of political detainees. The wardens refused to listen to Bishop Nsubuga's pleas that the archbishop be admitted – one later claimed that they wanted to avoid an assassination, alluding to the incident in 1949 when the Katikkiro (Prime Minister) of Buganda, Martin Luther Nsibirwa, had been assassinated on the steps of the cathedral. Both Nsibirwa and Sabiiti had become deeply unpopular because of their association with widely resented government policies. The House of Bishops condemned the incident as 'the most unfortunate and shameful of our era'. Sabiiti was also excluded from any official role in the ceremonies connected with the interment of the Kabaka's remains at Kasubi in April.

There were unrealistic hopes at this time for the restoration of the kingdom by the government and also that the government would support the creation of a separate Anglican province. Quite apart from the illusion that Amin, the 'simple soldier', could easily be manipulated, there was the fact that the first Amin government was in a sense a 'ministry of all the talents', including disillusioned UPC supporters and educated Protestants from all over Uganda. They had no intention of furthering the cause of Kiganda separatism. Amin put a great emphasis in these early months on healing the divisions within Ugandan society, including religious divisions, and set about bringing reconciliation within his own faction-ridden Muslim community. The resolution of the Anglican divisions was entrusted to Engineer Zikusooka, a Musoga Anglican layman who therefore belonged to Namirembe diocese without being subject to the pressures of Kiganda nationalism (as a Musoga).[16] A meeting was convened at Kabale in May and an accord was provisionally arrived at, based on the provisions of the 1970 draft constitution. But this was almost immediately disowned by Namirembe diocese and it was clear that the intransigents in Namirembe and west Buganda dioceses were holding out for much greater concessions. Amin, becoming impatient with this prevarication, began to put on the pressure. He summoned the Baganda leaders to meet him and was most annoyed to find that Bishop Nsubuga went ahead with a pre-arranged trip abroad and was not present: 'he is showing utter contempt for me personally and his attitude is . . . close to that of a rebel'.[17] Nsubuga, a moderate at heart, was subject to pressure to compromise from the government and to remain intransigent from many of the more outspoken Baganda leaders. Eventually, at a conference in the International Conference Centre in Kampala, held between 25 and 29 November, the government prevailed upon the Baganda leaders to accept a settlement. Amin was spoken of as the 'Constantine' of the affair – the disinterested ruler, concerned only for national and religious unity. It was a defeat for the Baganda separatists. The idea of Church Commissioners for the whole united province was approved; and a Land Commission, set up in 1972, was extremely critical of the position taken by Namirembe on land issues. Namirembe was also prevailed upon to agree to the creation of Kampala diocese, while insisting that its boundaries be as restricted as possible and that places like Nateete and Kasubi remain part of Namirembe. The resulting division of Kampala rather resembled the old colonial boundaries between the municipality of Kampala and the Kibuga of Mengo, which has been under the Kabaka's administration. Kampala as a diocese has always been hampered by its small size, which has made financial viability difficult to attain. But in churches within Kampala diocese where there has been a substantial Baganda element in the congregation, and where the boundaries with Namirembe are close, there has been a tendency for some Christians to hive off and establish a new church just over the border so that they can continue under Namirembe diocese – one example of this would be the new parish of Makerere West (in Namirembe) which was created as a result of defections from Makerere parish (in Kampala).[18]

THE CHURCH AND HUMAN RIGHTS UNDER AMIN

The compromise more or less imposed on the church in November 1971 was embodied in the 1972 constitution. After that the whole issue quickly faded into relative insignificance in the face of the increasing lawlessness and carnage of Amin's regime, which affected all classes, regions and ethnic and religious groups. A unity in oppression and misery was forged – between Buganda and the rest of Uganda, between Catholic and Protestant, and within the Church of Uganda itself. Unfortunately, it was a unity which was difficult to sustain once the Amin years were over. Dr Louise Pirouet, in her article 'Religion in Uganda under Amin', written shortly after Amin's overthrow, underlines the complexity of the religious situation under Amin.[19] It was not a straightforward persecution of Christians by Muslims. Muslims were also victims. Some Muslims profited from the regime at some times – for example, economically from the expropriation of Asian property in 1972 (though being an army man was perhaps a more important criterion than simply being Muslim). There was a perceived advantage in being Muslim if you were in business, and there was a small trickle of conversions from Christianity for economic reasons. The numbers were insignificant. Amin's most serious effort to improve the status of Islam was to make Friday a day of rest, in addition to Sunday. This was at the end of 1975, just before the murder of Archbishop Luwum, and it was part of a campaign of increasing pressure on the churches. But it hardly amounted to persecution. Its main effect was probably, again, in the economy – introducing, in effect, a four-day working week in many sectors of society, and thus striking another blow to the already shattered economy. Apart from the particular case of the attack on the Muslim community living near Kabwohe in Ankole in 1979, after the fall of Amin, there was little sense of outrage on the part of Christians against Muslims.[20] The Muslim community in Uganda has continued much as before – a small, rather underprivileged minority of about 7 per cent of the country, but one which, especially in Buganda, has deep roots in the society and which lives at peace with the Christian majority.

But it is true that the Christian churches were feared by Amin. The small independent and pentecostal groups were regarded with suspicion because of their foreign connections, real or imagined. Those which escaped banning in earlier years were proscribed in 1977. The Catholic and Anglican Churches were feared for the opposite reason – the fact that they were deeply indigenous, popular institutions which commanded the loyalty of a majority of Ugandans. By 1973 the Amin regime had squandered whatever legitimacy it might have claimed at the beginning (in terms of its claims to restore personal human rights, democracy and national unity). Such claims were quickly vitiated by an army leadership motivated by greed and envy, practising brutality and murder and unrestrained by law and morality. Could the churches have done more to resist this descent into barbarism? Dr Pirouet is right to point to certain weaknesses in the Church of Uganda which inhibited an effective response – its quasi-establishment tradition, its internal factionalism, its failure to confront the erosion of human rights early enough, during the Obote regime. One has also to acknowledge that the religious rivalries, especially the impact of Catholic–Protestant tensions on party politics, helped to create the very conditions which led to military rule. Yet, once the Amin regime was in power, it has to be said that many of the classic forms of protest against oppressive regimes were hardly viable options. Amin's regime was not exactly totalitarian – arbitrary, whimsical, anarchical might be better descriptions. To protest was not to risk some definable punishment which could be calculated in advance. Rather it was to risk unspecified ills involving looting of property, torture, imprisonment and death, not to mention reprisals on one's family. And this might be for some quite trivial offence as much as for a great stand on a matter of principle. Silence and ironic humour – an 'internal emigration' – might be the only weapons remaining to survive in Amin's Uganda. But for those who did escape into exile there was the possibility of more overt opposition.

It was the corporate strength of the churches which was seen as such a threat – their immovable presence when all other institutions (political parties, judiciary, press, etc.) had collapsed. Amin increasingly feared the churches as the embodiment of discontent against his arbitrary rule. It was said that during an attempted coup in 1974 of Charles Arube and other Christian officers from West Nile, the hymn 'Onward Christian Soldiers' was played for a time on the radio before the rising was crushed. From this time Amin expressed his dislike for such a martial hymn – though the hymn continued to be sung and with considerable gusto. Amin was also fearful that church collections might be used to help finance an invading force. This was an accusation made against the Protestant church in Ankole at the time of the 1972 invasion. The sale of badges and cloth for the 1977 centenary celebrations also gave rise to suspicion. Having proved his mastery over the church after the death of Luwum, Amin accepted the gift of a centenary shirt and rather liked being photographed wearing it. The fact that Bishop Nsubuga had got the right size must have been due to divine guidance, he felt.[21] Again in 1979, as the invading forces advanced from the south, the churches in Ankole were accused of collecting money to help the enemy.

AMIN AND ARCHBISHOP JANANI LUWUM

The Church of Uganda has been accused of 'having a tendency to elect men who were not necessarily popular to the believers, but simply because they were in the good books of the Government in power at the time'.[22] Whatever the general truth of this assessment, it does not apply to the election of Janani Luwum as archbishop of Uganda in 1974. In fact, here the church set itself firmly against the stream. Luwum was from Acholi, which had suffered so severely under Amin because the Acholi had been the backbone of Obote's army and they were the victims of an ongoing purge by the Nubian and West Nile elements of the army, who were now in power. Moreover, in political terms Luwum inevitably was seen as 'UPC'. Notoriously, Luwum's consecration as bishop of northern Uganda in 1969 in Gulu stadium had been manipulated by the UPC government for its own political purposes. But Luwum's election was not meant as a deliberate snub to Amin. The bishops were not thinking in political terms. Luwum was elected because he was felt to be, spiritually and intellectually, the most competent person. Luwum was the most prominent Mulokole in Acholi, an area where the Balokole movement was not strong but where it had developed the rather extreme tendencies of what was known as the Trumpeters (a name referring to the improvised megaphones or 'trumpets' with which this group broadcast its news to gatherings outside churches.) In fact, the Baganda brethren were at first rather suspicious of Luwum, fearing that he might be an adherent of this heterodox version of the Balokole. In his early months as archbishop, Luwum had to work hard to convince the Baganda brethren that he was not a 'Trumpeter'. He also had to overcome general Baganda suspicions of a northerner – moreover, from Obote's Lwo ethnic group. As more Baganda fell victims to Amin's terror, sharing a similar lot with Luwum's own kinsfolk, so these suspicions subsided.[23]

But, for the government, Luwum's ethnic origin could not be overlooked. Both as bishop in Gulu and as archbishop in Kampala, Luwum was called again and again to intervene on behalf of Langi and Acholi who had been taken away by the army. This required the constant lobbying of government ministers, army officers and police and intelligence officials to try to trace victims, to try to ensure that they did not simply 'disappear' and to try to secure their release before it was too late, or at least their proper legal detention. Undoubtedly, as archbishop, Luwum acted on behalf of victims from all parts of Uganda, but his role as protector of Langi and Acholi was central, just as, in times of crisis, Bishop Nsubuga had become protector of the Baganda. It was because he was an Acholi rather than because he was a Christian that Luwum was murdered in 1977. It seems certain that there was a plot to overthrow Amin and that Acholi were involved. As an Acholi 'elder', Luwum may have known something about what was going on, though, as a church leader, he is unlikely to have been directly involved. His strong Balokole commitment, undoubtedly the mainstay of his spiritual life, makes it extremely unlikely that he would directly involve himself in conspiracy. The archbishop's statement to those who came to his house in the early hours of 5 February 1977 in search of arms is that of a man of peace with nothing to hide:

> I did not come to Namirembe for the Acholi or the Langi but I was the Archbishop of Uganda, Rwanda, Burundi and Boga-Zaire and they (*sic*) were no arms in my house. Our house was God's house. We pray for the President. We pray for the security forces – whatever they do. We preach the Gospel and pray for others. That is our work, not keeping arms.[24]

The scandalous nature of the night raid on the archbishop's house and the attack on his person provoked the church, through its bishops, to issue its most eloquent defence of human rights:

> The Christians are asking if this is what is happening to our Bishops then where are we? The gun whose muzzle has been pressed against the Archbishop's stomach . . . is a gun which is being pointed at every Christian in the Church . . . The security of the ordinary Christian has been in jeopardy for quite a long time. It may be that what has happened to the Archbishop and the Bishop of Bukedi is a climax of what is consistently happening to our Christians. We have buried many who have died as a result

of being shot and there are many more whose bodies have not been found, yet their disappearance is connected with the activities of some members of the Security Forces.[25]

This letter from the House of Bishops to the President was dated 10 February 1977. Within a week Archbishop Luwum was dead, victim of the 'car accident' which also conveniently rid Amin of the two remaining Lwo members of his cabinet, Oryema (an Acholi) and Oboth Ofumbi (a Japadhola from eastern Uganda, Bukedi). As it happened both these men were Anglican Christians. Whether or not the government really believed that Luwum was involved in the plot may never be known, and is perhaps hardly relevant. Luwum died as a representative leader of the Acholi, who (with other Lwo groups) as a people were blamed for opposing Amin. But the impact of the bishops' letter and the 'Christian' opposition to Amin should not be discounted. Amin was no doubt extremely angry at this forthright exposé of the nature of his regime, and its production, with Luwum's signature at the head, may have sealed his fate. The murder of the archbishop was meant as a devastating response to the church's massive moral stature in society, a terrifying warning of the consequences simply of existing as a focus of discontent and opposition, however peaceful.

In emphasizing the ethnic element in Janani Luwum's death, I want in no way to detract from the idea that he died as a Christian martyr. Certainly he died as a witness to the truth for the sake of Christ and as a defender of the rights of the Ugandan people as a whole. The 16th of February is widely remembered as Janani Luwum Day – he is already in the Church of Uganda's calendar of saints, along with Bishop Hannington and the Uganda martyrs of 1886. But Luwum was and is the victim of the persistent force of ethnicity in Ugandan life. I vividly remember the lukewarmness with which the tenth anniversary of Luwum's death was commemorated in 1987. I spoke at St Francis' Chapel, Makerere University, to a congregation of two or three. Perhaps a failure of organization can be blamed for the failure of the occasion (the response was poor in the churches of Kampala generally). But I was left with the decided impression that politically the time was not ripe for a jubilant celebration of the memory of Archbishop Luwum. It was only a year since Obote's second UPC administration had been violently overthrown after a five-year civil war, in which Kampala and Buganda had suffered tremendously. People where in no mood to remember events in any way connected with what could be seen as a plan to restore Obote and the UPC to power.

In 1977 four other Anglican bishops had had to flee into exile to avoid the same fate as Archbishop Luwum. Three of them were, like Luwum, from the Lwo ethnic group – Benoni Ogwal, Janani's successor as bishop of northern Uganda, Melchizedek Otim of Lango and Yona

Okoth of Bukedi. Okoth had been arrested briefly at the beginning of the crisis, suspected of being implicated in the plot and bringing in arms over the border (Bukedi being strategically situated in eastern Uganda).[26] No arms were found at his home and he was released. The fourth bishop was not from the north and could not be implicated in the plot on an ethnic basis. He was Festo Kivengere, bishop of Kigezi.[27] He was a Muhima from the small Bahororo group of western Uganda. Only a few weeks before, at the consecration of Bishop Bamunoba as the first bishop of the new diocese of West Ankole, Kivengere had preached a powerful sermon warning government officials of their accountability before God for their deeds and calling attention to the robbery, violence and killing, which seemed to have official sanction. The consecration was held at Bushenyi, which made the sermon even more sensitive, since Bushenyi had been a centre of UPC support; it was to be the place chosen by Obote to stage his well-publicized return from exile in 1980. In Kampala, two weeks later, Kivengere was active in trying to find out what had happened to the archbishop when he was taken away by the soldiers on 16 February. Warned that soldiers were also looking for him, he slipped over the Rwanda border into exile a few days later. Beyond the specific plot which had precipitated the crisis, Amin was now taking the opportunity of ridding himself of a troublesome outspoken cleric and of smashing the organized power of the Anglican Church. The deportation of the only expatriate bishop, Brian Herd of Karamoja, meant that six out of the sixteen diocesan bishops had been eliminated in one way or another by Amin (one killed and five forced into exile) – nearly 40% of the episcopate.

The ten remaining diocesan bishops hastily met and chose Silvanus Wani as archbishop to succeed Luwum. The crisis certainly required speed if the church was to hold together as a body in the face of Amin's onslaught. But was the election of Wani a prima-facie case of the church electing a leader 'in the good books of the government in power at the time'? Wani was, in a loose sense, a kinsman of Amin, a Kakwa from Koboko county in West Nile district. But he was not an Amin appointee.[28] The bishops elected him because they hoped that he would be able to stand up to Amin, who claimed to respect him as an elder and who would therefore be willing to listen to him without immediately suspecting subversion. Wani was also familiar with army life, having served as an army chaplain during the Second World War, and he was popular within the ranks of Amin's army, among the West Nilers. In other respects, Wani's career in the church is remarkably like that of Luwum. Born in 1915, Wani was seven years older than Luwum, and became the first African bishop of northern Uganda in 1964, the post which Janani took over in 1969 when Wani became bishop of Madi and West Nile. Wani was the most prominent churchman in West Nile who had identified himself from the beginning with the Balokole movement. Like Luwum, Wani had suffered harassment from both church and state authorities because of his Balokole commitment during the early days. Both had avoided the excesses of the 'Trumpeters' and were concerned to see that the Balokole in northern Uganda should be fully integrated into the life of the church. Wani was a man of strong faith and personal courage. It can be argued that Wani played an important role in preserving the church from further senseless attacks by an increasingly embattled Amin, who now had cause to fear the power of the exiled bishops in helping to mobilize international opinion against his regime.

Liberation and Obote II 1979–1986

LIBERATION: THE REVIVAL OF POLITICAL FACTIONALISM
Kampala fell to the joint force of the Tanzanian army and the Uganda National Liberation Army (UNLA) on 11 April 1979 – Good Friday. The soldiers were greeted as *bakombozi* (liberators), and it was natural for those Christians who were able to get to church to worship on Easter Day to link the liberating power of the risen Christ with the momentous events which were happening in Uganda. But soon the very term *bakombozi* came to be used ironically, as the soldiers became notorious for 'liberating' people of their watches, radios, shoes and mattresses. Civilians at first had been encouraged to participate in this kind of liberation – freely taking sacks of sugar from government depots and looting office furniture with impunity. It was a dramatic enactment of the sense of liberation from oppression. But very quickly civilians became merely the victims, as the men with the guns demonstrated their superior liberating potentialities.

The period between the fall of Amin and the coming to power of Obote for his second term of office was a period of unprecedented violence, especially in Kampala, the centre of the political arena and the focus of struggle. One of the reasons for the level of violence was that the successive governments were so unstable and did not have effective control of the army. In fact, a national army hardly existed. Rather, bands of soldiers owed allegiance primarily to their own personal 'warlord' or wider political faction – or simply hired themselves out for the murder of political, economic or professional rivals. The loose coalition of exile groups which met in Moshi, Tanzania, in the last days of Amin, had chosen Professor Yusufu Lule (a Muganda Protestant) to head the new administration. But, in June 1979, after only two months in office, he was ousted. He was accused by his detractors of engineering a new order in which the particular interests of Buganda would be given priority. He was replaced by Godfrey Binaisa QC, the son of a Muganda Anglican clergyman. But his appointment was greeted with dismay by Baganda generally because he was held to be responsible for drafting the hated 1967 constitution, which had abolished the Kingdom of Buganda. Yet, within a year Binaisa's attempts to establish a 'non-party' system for Uganda as a whole, under the Uganda National Liberation Front (UNLF) 'umbrella', had so alienated the UPC elements in the government that he too was overthrown. He was replaced by a Military Commission headed by yet another Muganda Anglican, Paulo Muwanga. This administration was dominated by UPC, and was widely felt simply to be preparing the way for a UPC victory in the elections, which were set for December 1980. It was soon after Binaisa's dismissal that Obote staged his dramatic return from exile, landing at Bushenyi in west Ankole, an area where Protestants were dominant and support for UPC fervent. Throughout the Obote II period, 27 May was celebrated as 'Heroes' Day' and large-scale rallies were held at Bushenyi. As party politics revived under the Military Commission, one of the severe disadvantages under which laboured was that they could not hope to compete with UPC in terms of their armed strength.[29]

Both religion and ethnicity played vital roles in determining party allegiance and voting patterns in the December 1980 election, just as these had been controlling factors in the elections of the early 1960s. But the cocktail of religion, ethnicity and party was often mixed in very different ways. There was an expectation that religious affiliation could be crucial in some areas, and this led to the suspicion of gerrymandering in some areas in the delineation of constituency boundaries, especially in parts of Kigezi and Ankole, so that areas of high Catholic concentration (and therefore DP support) were split up and, it was hoped, neutralized by being included in constituencies with large Protestant (and therefore UPC) majorities. However, this equation could not apply in Buganda. There DP swept the board. There was no KY in 1980 and Mayanja Nkangi's Conservative Party (CP) was not considered to be a serious contender. Therefore Baganda, Catholic and Protestant, voted overwhelmingly for DP. Protestants realized that DP was the only party which had any chance of keeping the UPC out in Uganda as a whole. Lule's endorsement of DP was significant in persuading Protestants to vote DP. But it should be said that Protestant Baganda never felt any emotional attachment to DP as such; they have never felt totally at ease in a party with such close connections with Rubaga.

In the north and east, opposite considerations prevailed. DP had become inextricably linked in people's minds with the Baganda and therefore with fears of Kiganda hegemony. UPC could therefore reinforce its appeal and consolidate its base as the party for all non-

Baganda, but especially for Lwo (Acholi, Langi, Japadhola) and Ateso ethnic groups. Religious affiliation seemed to be an insignificant factor, though it was not entirely absent. Bugisu was strongly UPC, and there the Protestant preponderance was important. On the other hand, places like Acholi and Bukedi have big Catholic communities and the DP voice was repressed or submerged rather than non-existent – it has, for example, re-emerged in Bukedi since 1986. Brigadier Bazilio Okello, one of the 'Okellos' who overthrew Obote in 1985, was an Acholi Catholic, said to have links with DP. A similar configuration exists in West Nile, where Catholics outnumber Protestants. But in this area party politics never had a chance to resurrect. The 'liberating' forces of UNLA, consisting largely of Acholi and Langi soldiers, were intent on revenge against the 'Amin supporters' – the Lugbara and Kakwa. For example, on 15 October 1980, troops reached the Anglican theological college at Ringili, near Arua. They singled out Lugbara teachers and students, and sixteen were shot. The area was in no position to hold 'free' elections in December. The area remained disturbed by guerrilla incursions and UNLA counter-insurgency throughout the Obote II period.

The confrontation of UPC and DP on confessional lines was always at its starkest in western Uganda. However, the fairly simple lines of confrontation seen in Kigezi had always been complicated by Bahima–Bairu conflicts in Ankole, and by the 'Lost Counties' issue in Bunyoro (this latter was no longer a grievance by 1980). In 1980 a further complicating factor was the emergence of the Uganda Patriotic Movement (UPM), a party connected to Yoweri Museveni and his FRONASA soldiers. The UPM had a strong appeal to younger, more educated Protestants, tired of what they considered to be the dirty politics of the old guard of UPC, and of confessional rivalries generally. The Bahima cattle-keepers of Ankole (Museveni's people) were traditionally linked with DP. Though Protestant, they feared the power of the UPC Protestant agriculturalist Banyankore (the *bairu*). But some Bahima understandably switched their support to the new UPM party.

THE IMPACT OF PARTY POLITICS ON THE CHURCH OF UGANDA

'Do not bring Politics into the Church but take the Church into Politics.'[30] Archbishop Wani made this injunction at a national conference of pastors of the Church of Uganda held at Makerere in June 1980, at a time when political fervour was mounting as the first elections for seventeen years drew near. It was a plea for the tenets of Christian morality to inform the conduct of party politics, and a warning that clergy should avoid identifying themselves too closely with a particular party. It was a remark long remembered, though it was fairly conventional advice – indeed, regarded at the time by some as a pious platitude enunciated by a churchman who represented a previous regime of little relevance to the new circumstances. There was little temptation for Baganda clergy to involve themselves very closely in DP affairs – 'politics' for Baganda was much more a matter of national solidarity than of party politics as such. It was mainly in western Uganda that there were strong pressures from local congregations for the clergyman to commit himself clearly to the UPC. Indeed, many of the older generation of clergy felt that the alliance of Protestant church and UPC was perfectly natural, even part of the divine, ordering of society. As a Munyoro clergyman put it:

> As the Bible teaches that there is one God, one heavenly Kingdom, therefore there is one party – UPC, one President – Obote. In a church when a priest is giving a blessing, he raises his arm and shows the symbol that is similar to that of UPC. Hence this means that it is only UPC that can bring blessings to Uganda.[31]

He was referring to the Ugandan Anglican practice of raising the open palm while pronouncing the benediction, and equating this to the UPC symbol of the open hand (as opposed to DP's clenched fist).

In a parish in west Ankole, on the other hand, some prominent lay people refused to accept the appointment of a pastor whose sons were known to have joined the UPM. When asked why, one of them replied that 'they could not imagine how a man who was doubted to be UPC could administer sacraments to them'. He also felt sure that Jesus would vote UPC.[32]

To take the example of the church in west Ankole, 'not bringing politics into the church' was a difficult concept to interpret, let alone implement. The Church of Uganda and UPC seemed to be two aspects of a single reality, operating in a community in which all activity was integrated. In Amin's time, of course, UPC had ceased to function, but the church grew in strength and status as other social organizations atrophied. Many of the Protestant élite, educated people and politicians had been killed or fled into exile. Others kept a low profile, 'retiring' to their home areas, often becoming pillars of the local church. This was a genuine response to a personal and spiritual catastrophe. There was an element of 'hiding in the church' – using the church as a refuge in troubled times and as an alternative base for exercising power and influence. This had economic consequences for the church – wealth (often obtained by participation in the *magendo* (black market) economy) was used to help construct a new church building or a pastor's house, to provide robes for the choir or to help pay the diocesan quota. With the revival of party politics, these pillars of the church renewed their political ambitions. They were keenly aware that the church was a useful platform, as indeed were those returning from exile. One of the complicating factors in Ankole politics has been the extraordinary rancour of UPC factionalism. The old divisions of the 1960s between UPC *enkomba* (concentrated) and UPC *omufunguro* (dilute) were revived in 1980, if only as abusive labels to discredit rivals. The rise of UPM was in this area viewed as a UPC 'heresy'. Later on, as the Obote regime became bogged down in the problems of the civil war, Ankole UPC became bitterly divided between the 'syndicate' and the 'science' factions.

All of these disputes divided the church too. A study of the impact of party politics on a particular parish in west Ankole, near the borders with north Kigezi, illustrates forcibly the intensity of feeling in the church.[33] A sub-parish had been striving to get its own separate parish status. But during the 1970s the little church had come to be dominated by a clique of ex-politicians who did not want their control compromised by the presence of a resident parish priest in the area. They blocked progress towards parish status. After liberation, the Christians were able to break away from the grip of this clique. They formed a committee to co-ordinate efforts to build a new church, getting support from a wider group of élite 'sons of the soil', businessmen working in Kampala, professional people, etc. A considerable amount of money was raised. But after the 1980 elections the triumphant politicians, basically the UPC 'old guard', accused the organizers of the fund-raising efforts of having 'DP elements' in them. The chairman of UPC wanted the church building to stop and he prevailed upon the new parish pastor to call a church meeting. Local UPC Youth Wingers were active in bringing out many of the ordinary church members – simple peasants and women who felt a deep loyalty to the old UPC, which had given them 'salt' and other necessities in the 1960s. The meeting was well attended and very heated and a vote was eventually taken which produced a very narrow majority for a halt to church construction. In the next few months, a number of those who had been active in the fund-raising were shot in mysterious circumstances or were arrested. As a result, people lost morale, church giving generally declined and no further progress was made on constructing the new church. '*Nituziika ekanisa efiire*' (We are burying a dead church).

The effects of political conflict on the church in the cattle-keeping areas of east Ankole (Ibanda, Kazo, Nyabashozi) were even more drastic, extensive and debilitating.[34] The Bahima, who are almost entirely Protestant, had supported either UPM or DP in the 1980 elections. The combined support of Catholics and Bahima meant that DP MPs were elected in the area; but nationally UPC had won and this meant in practice that local UPC committees (largely consisting of Protestant Bairu/agriculturalists) controlled the area. Land disputes between cattle-keepers and agriculturalists were intensifying and the charge of being anti-government was often a pretext for the arrest of Bahima and the expropriation of their land. Such accusations were intensified as Museveni's guerrilla war grew more serious, since Museveni was a Muhima from the area. One participant (and victim) describes the situation thus: 'People started sorting out words to talk in their homes for fear of uttering anything against the government.' He goes on to say that even praying at night was dangerous – in case spies were listening outside. Bahima lay readers of the church were arrested, accused of using 'bad words' in the church. Churches led by Bairu lay readers, on the other hand, were deserted by Bahima members of the congregation, who feared that the lay readers might be government spies, a fear intensified when people were picked up as they returned from attending service. Things got worse when, in June 1982, the Ankole UPC (under the influence of the hard-line 'syndicate' faction) began to demand the expulsion of Banyarwanda immigrants. They were mostly cattle-keepers and had strong links with the Bahima – their expulsion was partly bound up with the land issue, partly because they were suspected of supporting Museveni. This particularly affected the life of the Anglican church in this area because a quite disproportionate number of lay readers were from the Rwandan community, and so the church lost many of its valued workers, not to mention some of its most generous supporters. Some churches in the Kazo area (and elsewhere) collapsed once the Banyarwanda had gone. During the crisis, some evicted people congregated at church centres, vainly hoping that this would be a sanctuary. But church leaders seem to have despaired that the government would do anything to restrain the local UPC fanatics (or perhaps in some cases sympathized with the reasons for the campaign). Bishop Kivengere of Kigezi was the most outspoken in condemnation of the affair and in giving physical help to those who were put in camps. Even those local church people who did sympathize feared that if they showed too much active concern they would be accused of harbouring subversive elements and aiding the guerrillas. The depth of distrust between the two Banyankore ethnic groups was seen later, in 1982, when an agriculturalist archdeacon replaced a Muhima and there was an unseemly dispute about the gifts of a low-status bull and a prized heifer to the two men. The incident, petty as it was, was 'a scapegoat of political differences', especially important in a society where the gift of a cow (*empano*) has such ritual and symbolic significance.

These kinds of bitter internecine disputes within the Anglican Church were not confined to Ankole. Surprisingly perhaps, there is a parallel situation in Buganda, in Mukono diocese, which covered the two counties of Kyaggwe and Bugerere.[35] For many years, Bugerere had attracted immigrants from eastern Uganda, especially Bagwere and Banyole, small Bantu groups. There were also communities of Badama (Lwo Japadhola), Lugbara (connected with Lugazi sugar plantations) and Banyarwanda. By and large these groups (with the exception of Banyarwanda) were supporters of UPC, especially if they were Anglican. In fact the immigrants were often enthusiastic Anglicans, and those from eastern Uganda were important as lay readers and clergy – the diocese would find it difficult to function without them. Wealthy non-Baganda were also crucial in giving financial support to enable the creation of Mukono as a separate diocese in 1984. Politically, the area, reflecting its big Baganda majority, voted strongly for DP in the 1980 election. But, in this situation, local UPC committees, strengthened by the fact that UPC was in power nationally, exercised an extensive and unrepresentative power. Immigrants were heavily represented in UPC committees, as Youth Wingers and as security (NASA) agents. In both society and church, the immigrants as a group were to be feared by Baganda. There is a story of a Muganda clergyman in the diocese who one Sunday took as his text the story of Naaman the leper from 2 Kings: 5. He is reported as saying: 'This government, right from the President to the lowest chief, have got leprosy. Please, seek your creator, so that you may be healed.' The lay reader of the church, an immigrant, was so annoyed at this political sermon that he reported the matter to the authorities. The priest, fearing arrest, fled from the parish and spent the rest of the Obote regime as a 'refugee' in Kampala. With the fall of Obote, those church workers who were thought to have collaborated too closely with the UPC had a rough time. The archdeacon of Bugerere, an easterner whose whole ministry had been in Buganda, was forced to leave the diocese. But a majority stayed, and the diocese continues to rely heavily on the services of immigrants from eastern Uganda.

THE CHURCH AS AN EXPRESSION OF THE LOCAL COMMUNITY

'What power they [i.e. the churches] have is now more locally based and they have in many cases grown in popular credibility as much as governments have declined in that commodity.'[36] Adrian Hastings's dictum is amply supported by the experience of Ugandans during the Amin and Obote years. Even the above discussion on the impact of politics on the life of the local church, disturbing as this is for Christian theology, is evidence of the importance of the church in the local community. One of the features of this period has been the way in which local participation in and control of local decision-making have been eroded as people have been manipulated or suppressed, even terrorized, by politicians, Youth Wingers, security agents and the army, either acting 'officially' or as a mob. The importance of the church as an institution firmly rooted in the community has been underlined. This has expressed itself in the intense desire of many communities to achieve their own parish status. People have been willing to contribute generously to the local church to that end – since a minimum standard of church building and pastor's house and proof of an ability to support a pastor are required by dioceses before parishes are created. On the other hand, this concentration on collecting what has come to seem like a 'church tax' has at times created resentment among local church people, a resentment often focused on the local catechist or lay reader, who is responsible for collecting the 'pledges'. The status of the ordained clergyman (and now woman) has grown in this period. Local churches are anxious to have educated, theologically literate pastors. They encourage their local young people to offer for training. Equally, the clerical profession has become attractive to young people for the educational opportunities it offers and the possibility of a stable and satisfying job, especially at a time when government employment in its widest sense is ceasing to pay an adequate wage and could be positively dangerous (the educated élite have often been the victims of harassment). The fierce competition for places, especially to do a theological degree at Bishop Tucker College, has led some to complain that nepotism has become deeply ingrained in the selection procedures.[37]

A similar process has been operating in the creation of new dioceses in the Church of Uganda – in 1969 there were nine, by 1986 there were twenty. There is an impulse towards an ethnically homogeneous diocese, though the complexities of ethnic geography preclude any final achievement of this 'ideal'. We have seen how the Kabaka, in a way, passed on his mantle to the bishops in 1966. In other areas, too, the bishops have inherited the role of father of the people as a whole from traditional rulers. The bishops can (and do) expect gifts of cows on their confirmation and parish visitations; and it is extraordinarily difficult to distinguish personal from official gifts, which should go to the diocese.[38] The bishop is the diocese. There is thus a strong preference for a local man, of that tribe and area, as bishop. There was in 1981 a reshuffle ('translation' in ecclesiastical language) of bishops, in which a number returned to their home area as bishop, and new bishops were appointed from the locality. These developments were criticized by President Obote as creating a 'tribal' church – he returned to ideas of 'mobilization', by which bishops would be moved around by a central secretariat of the church, ideas which had been unpopular in the 1960s and were quite unrealistic in the conditions of the 1980s.

In fact, the UPC government was quite willing to assist local demands for a separate diocese where it suited them. In Kasese district, for example, the Bakonzo had long-standing grievances against Toro domination, going back to early colonial times. Soon after independence, the Rwenzururu disturbances had erupted and had been suppressed by the Obote government. However, in 1980 the local UPC official, Amon Bazira, had cultivated Bakonzo support for UPC as a counter-weight to DP strength in Toro. In 1982 the symbolic leader of the fighters, the *Iremangoma*, and his warriors symbolically laid down their weapons (there had continued to be sporadic fighting in the mountains) in Kasese town, in a demonstration of reconciliation with the government. This 'marriage of convenience' undoubtedly assisted the Bakonzo in their campaign for a separate Anglican diocese (though it is not suggested that it was the only or the most decisive factor). The diocese of Ruwenzori South was created in 1984 and in August of that year Bishop Masereka was consecrated. President Obote attended the celebrations and used the occasion as a political platform (as all Ugandan leaders have tended to do – Obote is by no means unique in this).[39]

On the other hand, a similar campaign for a separate diocese at the other side of the country possibly failed to come to fruition because it lacked any political weight behind it. This was the attempt by the people of Buhugu in north Bugisu to get their own diocese. Long-standing rivalries with south Bugisu compounded with resentment at a 'southern', somewhat autocratic bishop, elected in 1980 to replace Bishop Wasikye, who had been killed in the last days of Amin, led to a declaration of secession. Bishop Wesonga, however, a strong UPC man and friend of Obote, strongly resisted this unconstitutional action. In the absence of political clout, the people of Buhugu also lacked diplomatic skills to further their cause with the church as a whole, and the affair dragged on year after year. The bishop was unable to visit the dissident part of his diocese for years and was deprived of its financial contribution. But the dissidents did not achieve their objective, despite the fact that the community as a whole seemed to be in favour of having their own diocese, until Bishop Wesonga himself died in 1992.[40]

A similar case has occured since 1986 in the Iganga part of Busoga diocese. Here there are the same ingredients of local particularism (which would certainly welcome a local diocese) and widespread opposition to the bishop.[41] But where the whole community is solidly behind the move towards a separate diocese, and where the issue is handled in a diplomatic way, then the trend towards the creation of ethnically homogeneous dioceses continues apace under the National Resistance Movement (NRM) government. In January 1990 the diocese of Muhabura came into being among the Bafumbira people (who are ethnically close to the Banyarwanda). The creation of a separate diocese was regarded as a great step forward for the whole area and the government was strongly admonished to take note of this precedent and to go ahead with the creation of a separate administrative district in Kisoro. At the celebrations to inaugurate the new diocese and consecrate the bishop, it was asked how a place like the Ssese islands (which is a single Anglican parish of Namirembe diocese, with one pastor at Kalangala) could have achieved district status when a whole diocese should still only be a sub-district.[42]

Kevin Ward

THE CHURCH AND THE NATION: CIVIL WAR

To return from the manifold expressions of the Anglican Church at the local level to the national arena, I want to go back to 1979. Archbishop Wani was in an unenviable position with the fall of Amin (as Sabiiti had been in 1971). Wani was identified by many as Amin's man, despite his important role in holding the church together in the difficult final two years of Amin's rule. To many church people he was a man of the past, an anachronism in the new era of liberation. Wani had problems with Paulo Muwanga, Chairman of the Military Commission, and with the new army (the UNLA), particularly with the Chief of Staff, David Oyite-Ojok. Wani's close connections, as a Kakwa and a former soldier, with the old army, the rank and file dominated by West Nilers, made it difficult to establish a working relationship with the UNLA. Moreover, he was reported as having loudly condemned the Tanzanian invasion at the end of 1978. The UNLA entered West Nile in 1980, 'liberating' the area with great brutality, as seen in the massacres at the theological college at Ringili. Then, in October 1981, came the first guerrilla invasion. In the subsequent counter-insurgency, Arua and Wani's home town of Koboko were devastated by the UNLA. Wani, as a Kakwa, found it difficult to protest publicly and he lacked the influence with those in power to make his voice heard effectively. The army took a dim view even of his mild complaints and, after the attack on Mbuya barracks in April 1982, Wani was called in for questioning and accused of knowing who were responsible. In that year, there were two attacks on Wani's person by armed men, who stole his car (once it found its way to the Malire barracks). Wani felt that the UNLA were involved, and Oyite-Ojok in particular. In 1983, he retired and went to live in Arua, despite the continued disturbed condition of the area, living a life of great simplicity, a familiar figure riding his bicycle round town.[43]

Wani's successor as archbishop was Yona Okoth, bishop of Bukedi in eastern Uganda (Tororo is the main town). Okoth, a Japadhola (Lwo), had been forced to flee the country in 1977 after the death of Luwum. In his earlier days, in the 1960s, he had been provincial secretary and had been involved in the negotiations, bitter at times, over Buganda's threatened schism from the province. His sympathies then and in the 1980s were decidedly with Obote and the UPC government: his background as a Protestant in eastern Uganda and his experiences of Buganda in the 1960s combined to confirm this position. Okoth became archbishop at yet another critical time in Uganda's history. The guerrilla activities in both West Nile and the 'Luwero Triangle' in Buganda had been going on for some two years with rising intensity and the growing frustration of government and army. The House of Bishops may well have taken into consideration the fact that, in the light of Wani's ineffectiveness to moderate the government's tough stance and the contempt in which he was held by the army, it might be better to appoint an archbishop who had the confidence of government and army and who therefore might be listened to. They thus passed over a man like Bishop Festo Kivengere, who was known (like all the other previous Ugandan archbishops) as a leader of the Balokole and also for his fearless outspokenness on questions of human rights. On the other hand, Kivengere's Hima origins and his supposed UPM sympathies (during the elections he had stressed to his flock that one should not simply support UPC because he or she was a Protestant) might alienate the government and cause yet more problems for the church.

By 1983, the guerrilla campaign of the National Resistance Army (NRA) under Yoweri Museveni was two years old. The counter-insurgency of the UNLA had created a wilderness throughout much of Bulemezi and Ssingo counties in Buganda. The population were forced into concentration camps – which consisted largely of the old and young women with little children. Those with the opportunity had fled to areas which were slightly more secure, mainly in and around Kampala. Many young men had little alternative but to join the guerrillas, if they wished to avoid being killed by the UNLA as potential guerrillas. The appalling situation through which Buganda was passing reinforced the bishops' role as guardians of the people. For the Anglicans, this involved the bishops of Namirembe and Mityana – Dunstan Nsubuga, with his assistant bishop, Misaeri Kauma, and Yokanna Mukasa. Bishop Kauma's house at Namirembe and many of the cathedral buildings became the haven for hundreds of internal refugees forced to leave their homes. The bishops also tried to organize relief for the camps and to visit them. Archdeacon Sserubidde of Luwero was particularly assiduous in this work, remaining at his post throughout the civil war. Many clergy were forced to leave their parishes as their parishioners fled and community life disintegrated.[44]

One of the most appalling tragedies in the war took place outside the Luwero Triangle itself, at a place called Namugongo, some 7 miles east of Kampala. This was in May 1984. Namugongo is a place of the deepest significance for all three religions in Uganda as the site where Muslims were killed for their faith in 1876 and Christians in 1886.[45] It is a place of pilgrimage for Catholic and Protestant. The NRA, having launched an attack on the Mpoma Earth Satellite Station near Mukono, encamped in the forest at Namugongo. This led to the deployment of UNLA troops. In the ensuing operation, the Principal of the Anglican Martyrs' Seminary, Revd Godfrey Bazira, was killed, and some hundred local people also met their deaths. Many of the students were beaten up and some of the women were raped, as were nuns at the Catholic shrine. The mosque was desecrated. The Namugongo massacre was a particularly blatant example of the indiscipline and brutality of the UNLA. The fact that an Anglican theological principal was killed on the site where almost 100 years previously the Uganda martyrs met their deaths made it a particularly potent symbol, to be compared with the importance of the death of Janani Luwum in decisively turning international opinion against Amin. But in Uganda itself the case did not seem to be clear-cut to many. Baganda felt that the rest of the Church of Uganda was decidedly lukewarm in its sympathy. Outstandingly, Bishop Kivengere came to share in Buganda's mourning. He preached at the Martyrs' Day service at Namugongo in early June, just over a week after the massacres – when the shallow graves of those who had been killed were still everywhere in evidence. But there was a reluctance by Anglicans outside Buganda to make too much of an incident which, however tragic, had been provoked by guerrilla activity. Yet again, the Church of Uganda found itself on both sides of the conflict, which had become more bitter than ever. This prevented, for example, the bishops as a body from agreeing on any really united stand *vis-à-vis* the government about the worsening situation.

Conclusion:
Museveni and the NRM critique of religion and politics

Yoweri Museveni and the NRM took power in January 1986. (Obote had been overthrown in July 1985 by an army coup and for six months Uganda was ruled by the Okellos, Tito and Bazilio, Acholi army officers. Tito, the Protestant, was officially Head of State, with Bazilio in charge of army operations.) The NRM had radical plans for a 'fundamental change' in Ugandan political life. Both political parties and religious institutions were accused of 'divisionism' – aggravating existing conflicts in society and creating new ones. They bore a large measure of responsibility for Uganda's ills since independence. The empirical evidence made it difficult for the churches simply to deny this charge. But there was some anxiety that the new government might prove hostile to all religion, especially that the 'Political School' might be used for anti-religious indoctrination and propaganda. The Political School at Kyankwanzi in North Ssingo (where the guerrillas had operated over a long period) was an important instrument by which the NRM could convey its basic ideology to Ugandans. Volunteers trained as cadres (political mobilizers). Prominent people in the élite, in education and the civil service, were drafted to attend courses. Soldiers from the former UNLA were sent for retraining. The aim was to create among citizens political awareness and also some basic military training to enable civilians to feel some confidence in the face of the brutality of undisciplined soldiers, under whose tyranny Ugandans had been powerless for too long. The aim was to replicate as far as possible the conditions which the NRM soldiers had faced 'in the bush', in particular the political education which they had received and which had created such an impressive discipline and ideological commitment. At first, a rather negative attitude to religion was conveyed by many of the teachers, deploying a vulgar Marxist terminology. Those in training were discouraged from organizing Sunday worship, because that would bring in the very problems of denominational separation which the course was designed to overcome. These things made the churches rather suspicious of the Political School. But a number of intellectually alert clergy have attended courses, and this has enabled the NRM to see that it is possible to articulate a defence of Christian faith compatible with its social and political priorities. Also, experience in government soon convinced Museveni (if he ever needed to learn the lesson) of the need to ensure the co-operation of religious bodies rather than engage in disputes.[46]

Museveni has since tried to avoid both unnecessarily antagonizing the churches and using a particular church as an instrument for establishing power, which would be his criticism of UPC. Museveni is an Anglican by upbringing. At Nganwa High School, Mbarara, in the 1960s, he was active in the Balokole movement. The training in leadership, intellectual debate and moral commitment which the revival gave him was important in his development as a politician. But he came to reject the unworldly pietism and apolitical stance of the Balokole. Religious commitment was transformed into a strong political commitment, critical of many aspects of religious belief and practice. As President he has avoided getting involved in philosophical debates about religion and has stressed the importance of good relations between all religious bodies and the state. In June 1986 he attended the Martyrs Day celebrations at Namugongo. It was, of course, an important political gesture in view of the massacres of only two years before by the UNLA soldiers. Museveni commended the original martyrs of 1886 for their courage in face of the tyranny of Kabaka Mwanga. He said that the martyrs had been willing to die because they believed in the resurrection of the dead, and that all, including Mwanga and later politicians, will have to give an account of their actions. It was in many ways a remarkable speech for an African politician – one has become more used to hearing 'render unto Caesar' loudly trumpeted. It bears comparison with Kivengere's sermon at the consecration of Bishop Bamunoba in 1977, just before the murder of Luwum. Indeed, Museveni has shown his admiration for Bishop Kivengere, a man whose deep Balokole commitment transcended the apolitical limitations of revival pietism. Museveni spoke very warmly of Kivengere at his funeral in June 1988, praising him as a great Ugandan nationalist, whose integrity and courage had led him to struggle fearlessly for the truth. Kivengere had never been a party man, whether in terms of political party, denomination or keeping to the rigid orthodoxies of the more conservative Balokole.[47]

The NRM rhetoric against 'divisionism' is all very well – but it is quite another thing actually to eradicate these evils from Ugandan life. After all, they had been part of the political platform of Obote and UPC in theory and they had become victims of those very forces, seemingly so intractable, which dominate Ugandan society. One important innovation of the NRM has been the creation of the Resistance Councils (RC). At the 'RC1' level, the community itself elects its leaders and organizes itself to undertake local defence and to solve disputes. The aim has been to overcome the feeling of demoralization and impotence which has so eroded community life in both rural and urban areas since the 1960s. But where the community is divided on religious and political lines this might result in the incorporation of division into the very structures of NRM. In the first series of RC elections, late in 1986, Protestant ex-UPC supporters tended to be in some disarray and to keep a low profile. This led Catholic and DP elements to emerge in a dominant position in some RCs. This seens to have happened in Bukedi. Here, the emergence of the so-called Force Obote Back Again (FOBA) activities perpetuated sectarian feeling, with Protestants a target for accusations of being 'FOBA', with consequent harassment and arrest, and Catholic members of RCs sometimes being the victims of political assassination. The Anglican bishop of Bukedi, Nicodemus Okille, has found himself in a politically sensitive position, caught between the need to help members of his congregation, who look to him to help them, and the suspicion of the NRM government. Even the archbishop, who previously had been bishop of Bukedi, was accused by defendants at a treason trial earlier in 1990 of having FOBA sympathies.[48]

Bukedi's strategic position on the Kenya border has, since Amin's time, made it a particularly sensitive area. But in Ankole, also, the NRM has not been able entirely to overcome the old religious antagonisms. In the 1986 RC elections, the Protestant community was in great disarray in the wake of the bitter internal UPC schisms of the Obote regime. People were not, of course, allowed to campaign for election on a party basis. Former UPC officials sometimes feared to stand even on a personal basis. This allowed Protestant Bahima and Catholics to get elected in larger numbers than would otherwise have been likely. Moreover, the government appointed a Catholic as the Special District Administrator (SDA) for Mbarara. Protestants felt that he showed an anti-Protestant bias in his enthusiasm for redressing the previously underprivileged position of Catholics in Ankole. But by the time of the 1989 RC elections the Protestants were determined to reassert themselves, and in this they had a large measure of success. They were able to a large extent to throw off the burden of their UPC past and to identify themselves strongly with the NRM and with its position that the revival of party politics would not be in the best interests of Uganda. In contrast the fact that DP was strongly urging the government to allow multi-party elections (presuming that in a fair system DP had a good chance of winning) enabled Protestants to present Catholic members on RCs as only lukewarm supporters of the NRM. Thus the religious factor cannot be discounted, even under the 'fundamental change' of the NRM.

The NRM has also found it more difficult than it envisaged at first to overcome the problems of ethnicity. A stark north–south divide quickly seemed to emerge, with northerners regarding government and army as entirely a Bantu affair. Admittedly the Langi and West Nilers were anxious to co-operate with the new government and suspicious of Acholi resistance. West Nile had suffered from the UNLA for too long; and the Langi had suffered at the hands of Acholi soldiers in the aftermath of the coup which had toppled Obote in July 1985. Acholi and Teso were the areas of the most entrenched resistance to the NRM. The NRA faced similar problems in the north to those which had confronted UNLA in Luwero, and was accused of resorting to the very tactics which had so discredited Obote. In February 1987, Bishop Benoni Ogwal, Anglican bishop of northern Uganda, interviewed in Nairobi for the BBC World Service, bitterly attacked the NRA for what was going on in the north, saying that it was worse than anything which Amin had perpetrated. Many Christians in Uganda felt that Ogwal had overstated his case, or at the very least had spoken tactlessly, in a way hardly designed to help the situation. His quickness to complain about what was going on in Gulu was contrasted with his silence about what had happened in Luwero, over many years. The bishop decided not to return to Uganda but to go into exile for a second time (he had had to flee in Amin's time). The assistant bishop also left Gulu, though he did remain in the Kampala area. Thus the Church of Uganda, which had barely had a chance to recover from the severe assault on its existence during the Amin regime, was again deprived of its chief pastors. The Catholic Church was also in a weak position, with its major national seminary at Alokolum forced to close, and dissatisfaction over the appointment of a Lugbara (Luluga) as bishop of Gulu rather than an Acholi. The church in Acholi had never been strong. At a critical time it now faced a general crisis of leadership, and a collapse of the institutional life of the church.

This religious void, combined with the collapse of law and order, helps to explain the rise of Alice Lakwena and her Holy Spirit Movement. For a year she left the resistance to the NRA in Acholi and the north generally, finally embarking on her suicidal attempt to cross the Nile and reach Kampala, which led to her flight into Kenya and her capture on 26 December 1987. Her determination, in the face of what seemed like overwhelming defeat for the Acholi people, to use 'traditional' spiritual weapons in the struggle invites comparison with the Yakan cult (which had operated on the Uganda–Sudan border during the early days of colonialism), Maji Maji and even the Xhosa prophetess Nonquase. Her movement seem to be a fusion of Acholi and Christian elements. Alice Auma claimed to be the voice of 'Lakwena' – the 'messenger' of the Holy Spirit. She imposed a moral discipline on her soldiers, prohibiting charms, drunkenness, theft, smoking or rape before battle, but encouraging prayer and ritual cleansing, and the singing of Christian hymns before battle. "Only sinners die in war,' but butter, oil and cotton wool in the ears would also help to divert bullets. After her capture other prophets rose, including her father, who claimed to be 'Lubanga Won' (God the Father), and others claiming to be possessed by such heroes as 'Archbishop Luwum' and 'Phoebe Cave Brown Cave' – the Church Missionary Society (CMS) missionary who had died some years before, after living for over half a century in Acholi. But the suspicion and resistance of many pastors to these prophets and their scepticism about the viability of their desperate struggle led to their being attacked and beaten up by the prophetic bands.[49]

By 1990 there were signs that Acholi was settling down to an exhausted peace. In contrast, although Teso had suffered as much as Acholi, and had been the focus of more intense fighting in 1989 and 1990, church life there had survived in a coherent form to a much greater extent. The importance of Bishop Geresom Ilukor, who has remained based at Soroti throughout the crisis, cannot be exaggerated in giving morale to the pastors and Christians. Here the church has been able to play a role which can be compared with that of the church in Buganda during the Luwero troubles. In Teso there are stories of a revival of religious commitment in some of the camps and in the villages.[50]

Soon after the liberation of 1986, the Provincial Assembly of the church of Uganda, meeting at Mukono in August 1986, discussed a motion that the church be divided into a number of provinces. This was a very popular idea in Buganda, naturally; it now also had its attractions for the Anglicans of western Uganda. But it had no supporters at all from the delegates from northern Uganda (the old Upper Nile diocese). They felt that the much stronger church in the south seemed merely to be ridding itself of a troublesome burden, and they stressed the unity of the church as they stressed the unity of the nation. The sufferings of the church and people in the north since 1986 would add strength to that plea.[51]

The NRM has undoubtedly brought many advantages to the greater part of Uganda in terms of peace and stability, local democracy and a more disciplined army. The idea of the accountability of government officials, civil servants and the armed forces is beginning to be applied in the life of the church also. Popular pressure is mounting for the church also to practise a self-critique of its standards of public morality and administrative practice. The clergy grew in popularity as traditional chiefs, government-appointed officials and politicians lost all credibility and ceased to be responsive to local wishes. But increasingly it has been felt that the church has also shared in corruption of national life, and that it is facing a severe moral crisis which will erode its credibility if the issues are not tackled urgently. Financial accountability, especially in the use of foreign funds, a clerical preponderance in church life, nepotism in the training of ordinands, episcopal autocracy – these are some of the issues still requiring attention from Anglican leaders in Uganda.[52]

Notes

1. Cf. F. Welbourn, *Religion and politics in Uganda 1952–62* (Nairobi, 1963). Michael Twaddle has warned against a too facile identification of the DP with the Catholic Church in his 'The Democratic Party of Uganda as a political institution' in E. Fashole-Luke and others, eds, *Christianity in independent Africa* (London, 1978).

2. David Barrett estimates religious adherents for 1980 as a percentage of the total population of Uganda as:

Catholic	49.6%
Anglican	26.2%
Islam	6.6%

These figures are probably extrapolations of the 1959 Uganda census figures, the last to ask about religious affiliation. D. Barrett, *World Christian encyclopaedia* (Nairobi, OUP, 1982).

3. From Kabaka Muteesa II to Yoweri Museveni, all heads of state in Uganda have had an Anglican background – except for Idi Amin.

4. Leslie Brown, *Three worlds, one word* (London, Rex Collings).

5. *Lambeth Palace archives: The Fisher papers*, Volume 210: Fisher to Brown, 30.1.1958; Usher-Wilson to Fisher, 6.11.1958.

6. Important biographical and historical material about Sabiiti is to be found in Philemon Tinka, *Uganda's first Anglican archbishop: A biographical study of Eric Sabiti*, dissertation for the BD degree of the Association of Theological Institutions of Eastern Africa (ATIEA) (1987).

7. *Church Missionary Society Archives* (University of Birmingham): G3 A7. Letter of protest at Bishop's consecration, 14.10.1947.

8. See K. Ward, 'Uganda: The Mukono crisis of 1941; *Journal of Religion in Africa* 19, 3 (1989).

9. *Report of the Commission of Inquiry into land possessed, owned, acquired or otherwise held by the Church of Uganda or any diocese thereof for ecclesiastical purposes* (Entebbe, Republic of Uganda, Government Printer, 1973).

10. J. K. Sebalugga, *The life and contributions of Dunstan Nsubuga (bishop of Namirembe 1964–85) to the Church of Uganda*, dissertation for the Diploma in Theology, Makerere University (1988), p. 38. Sebalugga interviewed Bishop Nsubuga shortly before his death on a number of occasions. This particular interview was on 20.4.1986.

11. Sabiiti to Nsubuga, 7.7.1966. Quoted by the 1973 *Report of the Commission of Enquiry* (see Note 9).

12. Minutes of Namirembe Diocesan Synod, 6 May 1970. Quoted by E. M. K. Mulira in an unpublished history of Namirembe diocese (written *c.* 1979).
13. E. M. K. Mulira in his unpublished history of Namirembe diocese. I am grateful to Mr Mulira for letting me read this important manuscript.
14. Tinka, *Uganda's first Anglican archbishop*, Sebalugga, *Life and contributions*, and Mulira, 'Namirembe diocese', are sources for this section. See, also, Akiiki Mujaju, 'The political crisis of institutions in Uganda, *African Affairs* (January 1976). ·
15. These quotations, some taken from the *Uganda Argus* (e.g. Lutaaya's is from 2.2.71), are found in E. B. Muhima, *The fellowship of suffering: A theological interpretation of Christian suffering under Idi Amin*, PhD thesis, Northwestern University, Illinois (1981), pp. 22–24.
16. Mr Zikusooka was ordained in the diocese of Busoga many years later.
17. Amin's speech at the International Conference Centre, Kampala, 25–29 November 1971, quoted in Sebalugga, *Life and contribution*, pp. 53–54.
18. *The church of the province of Uganda: Provincial constitution 1972*, Kampala, Uganda Bookshop.
19. Louise Pirouet, 'Religion in Uganda under Amin', *Journal of Religion in Africa*, 11, 1 (1980).
20. See Alex Kagume's account in his study of *The expulsion of the Muslim community at Itendero, 1979*, dissertation for the Diploma in Theology, Makerere University (1981).
21. Sebalugga, *Life and contributions*, p. 60. Based on an interview with the Revd. S. Mpalanyi, 27 January 1988.
22. *Weekly Topic* (newspaper), 8 April (1987).
23. Basic biographical information and a good acount of Luwum's death can be found in Margaret Ford, *Janani: the making of a martyr* (London, 1978). For Luwum's Balokole background, and an account of the Trumpeters, see Kenneth Gong, *The history of the revival movement in Kitgum*, dissertation for the Diploma in Theology, Makerere University (1985).
24. 'Report of a very serious incident at the archbishop's house in the early hours of Saturday, 5th February 1977', *AACC Newsletter* 3, 3, 23 February (1977) *Special edition: The churches mourn the loss of Archbishop Janani Luwum*, printed in Nairobi.
25. 'Letter from the House of Bishops to President Amin, 10 February 1977', *AACC Newsletter* 3, 3 (1977) (see Note 24).
26. 'Report of Bishop Yona Okoth's arrest', *AACC Newsletter* 3, 3 (1977) (see Note 24).
27. A biography of Bishop Kivengere is in preparation, written by Anne Coomes, to be published by Kingsway Press.· The account of Bishop Bamunoba's consecration is based on my own recollections.
28. For details of Archbishop Wani's life, see Samuel Kermu, *The life and times of Bishop Silvanus G. Wani*, dissertation for the BD degree of ATIEA (1987).
29. For a fuller discussion of these years, see Holger Bernt Hansen and Michael Twaddle, eds, *Uganda now: Between decay and development* (London, 1988).
30. Quoted in Kermu, *Life and times*, p. 85.
31. Philip Musindi, *The National Resistance guerrilla war 1981–85: The Christian response in Hoima district*, dissertation for the Diploma in Theology, Makerere University (1987), p. 13. Musindi interviewed the parish priest.
32. This is quoted in Stephen Bangumya, *The impact of the revival of party politics on the life of the church – west Ankole diocese*, dissertation for the Diploma in Theology, Makerere University (1982).
33. I have withheld the name of the parish and the individuals involved, since this is still a sensitive issue in the area.
34. This paragraph is based on the account by Samuel Mugisha, *The impact of political conflict on the church in Kazo sub-county, Ankole, Uganda, 1979–86*, dissertation for the Diploma in Theology, Makerere University (1987).
35. James Bbumba, *The role of non-Baganda immigrants in Mukono COU diocese: Co-operation*

and conflict in the church 1981–87, dissertation for the Diploma in Theology, Makerere University (1988). For the story of the sermon of the pastor of Namugabi and its consequences, see p. 67.

36. Adrian Hastings, *A history of African Christianity 1950–75* (London, 1979), p. 263.

37. Kevin Ward, *Called to serve: Bishop Tucker Theological College, Mukono: A history 1913–1989* (Kampala, 1989).

38. At his consecration as Bishop of Muhabura, the twenty-first diocese in the Church of Uganda, Bishop Ernest Shalita made a point of stressing that the gifts of cows and goats which he received on that day were gifts for the diocese, not for himself.

39. David Kambere, *The Bakonzo Rwenzururu War 1962–1982: Its effects on the growth of the Anglican Church, S. Rwenzori district, Kasese*, dissertation for the BD degree of ATIEA, Nairobi (1987).

40. Sam Masaaba-Nambobi, *The schism within the Anglican diocese of Mbale: An analysis of the background and development*, dissertation for the BD degree ATIEA (1985).

41. Sam Isabirye, *The schism within Busoga diocese 1983–88: An analysis of causes, developments and effects*, dissertation for the BD degree of ATIEA (1989).

42. Speech made at the festivities in Kisoro, 14 January 1990, which I attended.

43. This paragraph is based on Kermu, *Life and times*.

44. There have been a number of studies of the situation in Mityana in these years. In particular, see Yonasani Lubanga, *The role of the church in the preservation of human rights in Africa. A case study of Mityana diocese area, Uganda, from 1979–87*, dissertation for the BD degree of ATIEA (1989). There is also an earlier study of the refugee camps in Ssingo by Elias Luzinda Kizito, research paper for Diploma in Theology, Makerere University (1984).

45. Information from A. S. Kasibante, letter, 9 July 1990. See also Charles Sserwambala, *The 1984 military attack on Namugongo village*, dissertation for the Diploma in Theology, Makerere University (1987).

46. Information from A. S. Kasibante, who was one of the first Anglican priests to attend a course of political education in 1987. See also the study of NRM political philosophy at Kyankwanzi, undertaken by Aaron Mwesigye as his dissertation for the Diploma in Theology (1987).

47. I was present at Museveni's visit to Namugongo in June 1986, and also at the funeral service of Festo Kivengere in June 1988 in Kabale.

48. Newspapers such as the *Uganda Times* (a daily) carried reports of the trial in the early months of 1990.

49. Wilson Atine, *The effects of civil wars since 1977, on the Anglican diocese of northern Uganda*, dissertation for the Diploma in Theology, Makerere University (1988). I am also grateful to Apollo Lukermoi and Nelson Owille for information.

50. Information from Mike Okwi and Sam R. Opol, of Serere, Teso, May 1990.

51. I was present at the debates.

52. Note on the sources for this study: For fourteen years, I was a tutor at Bishop Tucker Theological College, Mukono, the main theological college of the Church of Uganda. Much of the material for the second half of this paper (1976–1990) is therefore based on personal observation and recollection. But the most important sources for this study have been the research papers undertaken by students of Bishop Tucker College in their final year. The research paper is a compulsory paper for the Makerere University Diploma in Theology, and over the years a considerable body of material has been collected, based on oral interviewing and field research in parishes, on many different aspects of the life of the church and of Ugandan society. The dissertations are deposited in Makerere University, in the Department of Religious Studies. Copies are also available in Bishop Tucker College library.

Seven

The Catholic Church
& the Root-Cause of Political Instability
in Uganda

JOHN MARY WALIGGO

The success of the current constitution-making process in Uganda will largely depend on a proper identification of the root-cause of the country's political instability and a relevant as well as lasting solution to it. Classical philosophy and modern social analysis both place vital importance on asking why until the ultimate answer is reached.

To the question of why Uganda has been politically unstable since 1966, many scholars both within and outside Uganda have given divergent answers. The conclusions of the ordinary citizens on the issue also differ widely according to the education, socio-politico-religious grouping, region and experience of each. There are interpretations of the root-cause which are based on political personalities especially of Obote and Amin, the nature and training of the Army, the external factors of destabilization, religio-political groupings, racial and developmental differences between north and south, and the political ignorance of the masses.

This study has a limited scope. It tries to identify the root-causes from the individual and collective letters of the Catholic bishops of Uganda, the spokesmen of their church, in order to evaluate their position in the light of the current constitutional debate in Uganda. For the clarity of the argument, some background to the post-independence politics is given.

Bishop Joseph Kiwanuka on the root-cause

Bishop Kiwanuka was committed to a programme of political awareness to prepare people for the just and peaceful attainment of political independence and to guide them in the democratic system of government which alone, in his view, could guarantee justice, peace, unity and development for the country's future.

It was in 1947 that Kiwanuka as nationalist, Muganda patriot, trained canon lawyer and Church leader, came to a clear position on his role in secular matters:

> After much reflection, I discovered that the leadership people want me to exercise in the country is not political as such but leadership of offering good and wise education which will help our nation and put it on the right path. In such responsibility I can be a leader without necessarily annoying the political rulers.[1]

In an effort to combat the imagined threat of communism and advance the process of democracy and popular political awareness in Uganda at the start of the Cold War, Kiwanuka sent several of his priests and lay leaders to study sociology, economics and political sciences in universities and institutes abroad. He encouraged his priests to study political and economic principles, through regular conferences and privately given assignments, so that they could assist the laity to understand political affairs. He became a friend to many of the leading personalities, including the four traditional monarchs in Uganda. In many of his letters to them, he indicated the principles on which the future independent Uganda should be founded. Many appreciated, but not a few viewed his genuine concern as uncalled-for interference of the church in politics.

Muteesa II became king of Buganda in the same year that Kiwanuka became the first African Catholic bishop, entrusted with leading the diocese of Masaka-Buddu. The two cultivated their friendship from the very beginning. They exchanged letters and visits. They shared important events of joy and sadness. While Muteesa was still studying at Cambridge in 1947, Kiwanuka sent him the following message:

> Your country is well, the representatives you left seem to be governing well, although complaints are not missing, but we have to weigh them in the light of who are complaining. There is one thing that has saddened even those I call 'wise heads'. It is the attempt to change the boundaries of countries especially Busujju. The wise heads think it would be better for that decision to await your return since there is no cause for hurry. It would give you a chance to hear what the majority of your people have to say on it.[2]

In his Christmas wishes of 1950 to Muteesa, Kiwanuka expressed the feelings of his priests and Catholics in the diocese:

We want to assure you that we love you, we pray for you and have full confidence in you that under your leadership we shall enjoy justice and peace in the country and in practice of our religion.

On our part we vow before you to be always honest towards you and ready to do whatever duty you may assign us for the benefit of our country.[3]

When Muteesa was deported in 1953, Kiwanuka ordered special prayers to be said daily in all churches for his happy return. True to his previous promise, Kiwanuka agreed to serve on the Hancock Commission which drew up the draft of the 1955 Agreement, on the basis of which the king later triumphantly returned to Buganda.

In the exchange of letters during the exile, Muteesa once had this to say to Kiwanuka:

I thank you very much for all you are doing on my behalf and for the prayers for me all this while. I am well, but as you know my heart is there in Buganda all the time and thus my prayers for you there.

Greet all those who are on our side, the side of God and truth.[4]

In response Kiwanuka wrote:

Your people are still alive and love you very much. They feel very unhappy to see that your return is so much delayed. I am leaving today for Mengo, the Lukiiko starts today to discuss the Report we gave it. It appears there are some extremists who try to pull the Lukiiko on their side. Some want to get *all* at once. We shall try our best to explain them. And I hope the Lukiiko will decide what is best.

What I fear is this: Once the Report is passed, who will implement it *impartially*?

Another point I ask myself is: what should we do to accelerate your return? These two things still worry me.[5]

The question of impartiality or justice in Buganda, which Kiwanuka had worried about, came to the fore in the democratic election of the new Katikkiro in 1955. To contest this top position in the Kabaka's government were three candidates. One was Matayo Mugwanya, a Catholic, a former Chief Justice of Buganda, a man of outstanding ability and the grandson of the heroic Stanislaus Mugwanya. The two other contenders were Paul Kavuma and Michael Kintu, both Protestants.

Pre-election estimates of the voting of the Lukiiko, which was the electoral body, predicted a victory for Mugwanya. This immediately set the Protestants to feverish work in an effort to find ways to defeat Mugwanya, and defeat him they did, though with a slim majority. Thereafter, the Kabaka refused to allow him to take up even a mere Lukiiko seat to which he had been elected.[6]

Here was at work what Professor Gingyera-Pinycwa calls 'bureaucratic politics'. Others refer to it as sectarian politics, politics of exclusion or a 'closed political system'.

When Muteesa visited Kiwanuka and the Buddu Catholics for the first time after his return from exile, the Mugwanya instance of 'bureaucratic politics' had marred the good relations that had existed earlier. True to his character and personality, Kiwanuka used the occasion to underline at least four main points: the great joy of Catholics on seeing the Kabaka back as their hero and warrior; the love and respect Catholics have for their king; the pain they feel at the politics of exclusion at Mmengo; and the need for the Kabaka to see full justice done to all his subjects without any institutionalized discrimination.

Our most beloved Ssabasajja Kabaka

I stand here in the holy place, the seat of Catholicism in Buganda and Uganda as a whole. I stand here to welcome you and congratulate you in the name of all Catholics.

Ssabasajja thank you, thank you so much for achieving victory! You are our victorious warrior! They snatched you from us secretly, we never bid you farewell. For two full years you were out of our sight. That is why today we are overjoyed! If our eyes were able to devour, they would have devoured you today! You are an excellent Commander-in-Chief. You led us well and you never turned backwards.

We, your subjects, who remained here, fought likewise. I do not know whether you will ever be able to find out what role Catholics played in that struggle, given the fact that they rarely get a chance to be among those who keep by your side. When you get time, however, to penetrate the cloud you will discover that among your subjects none love you more in truth, without self-seeking motives, as the Catholics. You will then know that in the struggle for your return none fought as fiercely as the Catholics. Some acted as a security for you, some became hated on your account. You will also discover that none played such an active part in keeping peace in the country as the Catholics. Catholic leaders preached peace everywhere and people obeyed. You know well that of your people who are over a million, almost half is Catholic. To keep such large number calm was not a minor job. If they decided to become rebels, the entire country would have been disturbed.[7]

This speech of Kiwanuka started a series of discussions and debates, which, unfortunately, instead of leading to the end of closed, discriminatory and sectarian politics, culminated in direct conflict between Muteesa end Kiwanuka in November 1961.

After the reception at Kitovu, the king asked Kiwanuka to explain to him the cause of the Catholics' complaints. Kiwanuka did so very frankly, with plenty of examples. The king asked him to come to Mmengo to discuss them further. Kiwanuka did so, going with a well-worked out document on the subject.[8] After the discussion between the two, the king asked Kiwanuka to discuss the entire matter with the Katikkiro and his ministers, which he did. Soon afterwards, the Katikkiro disclosed the discussion in the newspapers. Kiwanuka wrote to the king in protest and threatened to say far more about the whole matter in public.[9]

What happened was that Mmengo's bureaucratic politics had found it impossible to become open and non-sectarian. The analysis of Gingyera-Pinycwa is helpful here:

It will be noted that while the new nationalist politics . . . sought to embrace everybody, this bureaucratic politics continued to divide up people on the basis of their religious denominations, thus to defeat the purpose of integrative politics that the new nationalist political parties were advocating. It is not surprising, therefore, that the Catholics and the Protestants, the chief protagonists, came to align themselves in the end in a manner reflective of the pattern of bureaucratic politics with regards to nationalist politics as well. The need for a Catholic party came to be felt quite easily; and it was perhaps proof that its origin had a lot to do with the bureaucratic politics at Mmengo, when the party – the Democratic Party – did come, it was Matayo Mugwanya, who had been badly frustrated by that regime, who took up the leadership.[10]

Gingyera Pinycwa continues by noting that

This is the unhappy historical background to such utterances as we hear from time to time from some of our leaders:

(a) 'Religion is a divisive factor in our society'
(b) 'Religion and politics should be kept apart'
(c) 'Our present political parties are sectarian'

These and many other similar feelings have truth in them. But to assert and leave them at that is banal or trivial. Equally undesirable is to proceed from such assertions to wrong solutions such as the banning of political parties, or the manipulation of religion to make it serve the purpose of a given political group at the expense of others.

What has been required all along is a clear understanding of the question: Why have religion and politics been tied up in a manner which so many Ugandans know is unhealthy?[11]

It is to this question that Bishop Kiwanuka and later on other Catholic bishops have tried to offer an answer in the interests of stability and democracy in Uganda.

In his stand for frankness and principles, Bishop Kiwanuka never allowed the tensions thereof to undermine his personal friendship with the king and other leaders. When he was promoted to be archbishop of Rubaga in early 1961, he immediately wrote to the king and the Katikkiro:

Ssabasajja Kabaka,

It may be possible that you have already received the news concerning the retirement of Archbishop Cabana, and how the Pope has chosen me, your servant, to succeed him. More responsibility has been placed on me, but in that position I hope to do more for the Church and our country Buganda than ever before.

Ssabasajja, as I will now be near you I shall get more opportunities to fight on your side than I could living far away from you.[12]

The king replied:

I congratulate you on your promotion to the post of Archbishop, which carries much responsibility for religion and our country. I feel sure the Pope has given us great honour and we must take rightful pride in ourselves thanking God who willed your promotion. We shall never forget that the responsibility placed on you is great indeed, and therefore we shall never cease to pray for you that you may always be guided by God in all you do.

As you are coming near here, I hope we shall see each other more often.[13]

This mutual hope of meeting each other more often and working closely together for the advancement of the country was soon destroyed by the birth of the Kabaka Yekka (KY) Movement,[14] the strongest weapon and device for preserving bureaucratic and sectarian politics ever to arise at Mmengo.

Church and state: guiding principles and the root-cause

By temperament and in his concern for seeing justice done to all, Bishop Kiwanuka fully agreed with Elie Wiesel, who upon accepting the Nobel Peace Prize in 1986 had this to say:

I swore never to be silent whenever and wherever human beings endure suffering and humiliation. We must take sides. Neutrality helps the oppressor, never the victim. Silence encourages the tormentor, never the tormented. Sometimes we must interfere. When human lives are endangered, when human dignity is in jeopardy, national borders and sensitivities become irrelevant. Whenever men and women are persecuted because of their race, religion or political views, that place must – at that moment – become the centre of the Universe.[15]

In November 1961 Archbishop Kiwanuka issued his best-known pastoral letter addressed to 'Beloved Children in Christ'.[16] The message, as he outlined in his introduction, was occasioned by several indicative developments: the general elections of March 1961, which many people in Buganda boycotted, the violation of lives and property belonging to those who had voted for and joined the Democratic Party, accusations from the London Conference discussing Uganda's independence that Catholics were denying Buganda the right 'to receive what belonged to her', and personal insult to himself on two occasions. Having reminded Catholics never to lose courage when insulted or abused, and always to love their enemies, and of the need to do good to those who hate and persecute them, he underlined this principle:

> However, remember also that religion does not prevent one to defend oneself
> against one's assailants, nor does it forbid one to fight to protect oneself or
> one's property. But if ever you have to do that, never act through contempt
> or hatred, or through a spirit of revenge; just defend yourself, or simply pre-
> vent the action of evil-doers who wish to harass you.[17]

He clearly exposed what he considered to be the root-cause of all
trouble:

> What contributed most to bring trouble to the Catholics, is the fact that in
> the present political evolution there are Catholic citizens who have decided
> to contend for places of leadership in government and they have found the
> support of other Catholics. This has induced others to attack them. Now you
> may ask me: 'What fault have they done to justify such attacks? Is it a sin
> to contest a place of leadership in Government?' My answer is: No, it is not
> wrong. Nevertheless it cannot be denied that this is what hurts many, this
> is what brings them to speak harshly in buses, in bars, in the press or
> elsewhere. This it is which incites people to molest others, to slash their crops
> and to do similar acts of aggression.[18]

Kiwanuka took the occasion of the pastoral letter to enlighten those who
were ignorant of the changes taking place in the democratic process in
Uganda and to offer clear guiding principles for the relations between
church and state.

The bureaucratic or sectarian politics at Mmengo were being
attacked at their very foundation. They put up the strongest opposition
machinery in the form of KY in order to survive. Resistance to
changing an unjust and old-fashioned political system became the root-
causes: 'those who had up to now controlled the government fear
that their monopoly might soon decline and they might even be
withdrawn altogether.[19] Having explained the origin of democracy
and the manner in which democracy operates, Kiwanuka warned his
people not to belong to movements such as KY which neither were
officially registered nor possessed clear manifestos. He concluded on a
prophetic note:

> Those [members of] 'Kabaka'Yekka' and the others who flatter themselves
> that they are the defenders of the Throne and of the King, are the ones who
> will spoil our royalty by dragging the king in the back-wash of politics. In
> fact they are just seeking their end.[20]

The origin of the root-cause Kiwanuka was describing has been
traced by many school to the last two decades of the nineteenth century.
It is evident in the successive agreements of Lugard, Macdonald,
Gerald Portal and Johnston.[21] Before Uganda's political independence
there was need for a fundamental change in the attitudes behind such

agreements and in the general understanding of open and popular democracy on which the future depended. Such a change, however did not take place in the minds of those who controlled power in Buganda. In the minds of many such, the old-time political hierarchy had to remain – whereby Protestants came first, Catholics second, Muslims third and traditionalists last.

Shaping our national destiny

Six days before independence, the Catholic hierarchy issued a pastoral letter expressing its good wishes for the new nation.

> Wisdom, a senses of responsibility, justice with charity, unity in diversity, are the qualities that will be required of leader and people for a prosperous, happy and peaceful Independent Uganda.[22]

Those qualities, as the subsequent writings of the bishops will show, have been to a large extent missing in Ugandan society since independence.

The Bishops emphasized that the future destiny of Uganda would be judged by respect and promotion of fundamental human rights, the equality of all people, a special concern for the promotion of the equality of women, and the spirit of patriotism. They concluded on the point of freedom, so vital for the survival and progress of any nation:

> We want a good standard of living for our people. Freedom to go hungry or to be unhealthy or to live our lives in fear is no freedom. We want economic freedom, because, without it, political freedom cannot exist and is empty. We want freedom in our personal lives because freedom must find its true expression at the level of the individual citizen. We want that freedom for all the citizens that virtue brings, because sin can only bring slavery. We want above all freedom to serve God, because His truth alone can make us truly free.
>
> May Religion, Justice, Unity, Peace be the pillars of Independent Uganda.[23]

Reading these words thirty years later, after years of misrule and chaos, of wars and disunity, of glaring injustices and corruption, of murder and disrespect for human rights, of disintegration and under-development, one is certainly once again faced with the questions: What went wrong? What has been the root-cause of Uganda's suffering?

Several people have rather uncritically glorified the performance of the first Obote government in the first four years of the country's independence in order to emphasize the point that the root-cause of Uganda's subsequent instability should be sought, not in the past, but in the crisis of 1966. Archbishop Kiwanuka was of an entirely different view. He had strongly opposed the indirect election of Buganda's representatives to the National Assembly, the continued existence of KY, and its alliance with the Uganda People's Congress (UPC). He had warned that the issue of the 'Lost Counties' would cause trouble, especially as the campaign to move Baganda into those areas was highly resented by the inhabitants of the counties. To him, Uganda had attained independence before eradicating completely the root-cause of sectarian politics. Whatever was to happen in the future was to be seen as the logical consequences of that stubborn refusal to redress injustice in the political system. Writing to a friend a few months before his death, Kiwanuka had this to say:

> When you hear all this (trouble), plus the weight of other responsibilities, you feel like telling the Lord: My Lord you can see the years I have served. They are sufficient. You better give the burden to another person to carry.[24]

Kiwanuka died at Rubaga Hospital at 10.50 p.m. on 22 February, 1966, the very day Obote suspended the Independence Constitution of 1962. This action further speeded a tragic and vicious circle of politics upheavals in the entire country, whose effects are still being witnessed today.

Reshaping our nation after Idi Amin

With the removal of Idi Amin by the joint 'liberation armies' of Tanzanians and Ugandans, the country had another rare opportunity to examine the root-cause of its instability and to plan for a better, peaceful and democratic future. The Catholic Bishops of Uganda seized the opportunity to issue a pastoral letter calling all to concentrate on two main duties: cultivating a sense and culture of justice and nation building.

> This new order of things, however, cannot be brought about unless a sense of justice is restored in the mind of people. A sense of justice means respect for the rights and property of other people, respect for each one's personal dignity and the acquisition of wealth through just and honest means.[25]

Although there seemed to be a general good will among the ordinary citizens to restore justice and start a new era of non-sectarian politics, the 'exile mentality' of most of the leaders of the liberation struggle and the desire of the foreign army frustrated any positive action to liberate Uganda from its root-cause of suffering.

Soon after the return of Milton Obote from exile in 1980, the lifting of the ban on political parties and the declaration a general election, sectarian politics once again started up, supported by some members of the Military Commission and the army. Soldiers, supported by their leaders, started an exercise of genocide in the districts of Arua and Moyo from June 1980. People were murdered in places of worship at Maracha and elsewhere. Thousands ran into exile. The Catholic bishops wrote a pastoral letter condemning violence, which they called 'the curse that has poisoned the lives of people all over the country'.[26] They identified the army and its leaders as the perpetrators of this violence. When they came to the root-cause of the instability, this was no longer seen and analysed in terms of Catholics and Buganda but as it affected most Ugandans throughout the country:

> The coming elections are an extraordinary event for our Nation and of vital importance for overcoming the evils we have mentioned.
>
> Therefore we are greatly concerned about them and the desire that each citizen may be able to express his free choice in a peaceful atmosphere. Many people across the country have expressed concern and sorrow over the high-handed tactics used in the political and social fields. Rigged registration lists and dishonest practices of intimidation have been reported in many parts of the country. Even duly appointed delegates to party conventions have seen their religious and/or tribal origin used against them. There is a pervading feeling of dejection among the common people, that stems from the fact that those who hold power seem to care little for the voice of the common citizen. This in itself is against the rights and dignity of honest and God-fearing Ugandans.[27]

What happened at Mmengo before the country's independence was now being done on a national level by a group of politicians and military men to reinforce bureaucratic politics. Justice was not going to be allowed to triumph. Uganda, therefore, was about to continue along the old path of war and chaos. This is exactly what happened after the highly rigged elections of December 1980.

By 1982 several anti-government fighting groups had been formed. Obote's government and its army ruthlessly began to hunt the 'enemies', both real and imaginary. Those areas and people who had openly rejected the UPC leadership during the 1980 general elections became the main targets of the security forces and the worst victims of the regime.

In their message of concern, the Catholic bishops once again pointed to the source of the problem: 'Party-politics, tribal and religious differences, social inequalities have kept us divided.'[28] Instead of offering an effective secular solution to the problem, the bishops chose to call all Ugandans to an inner spiritual conversion:

> We ask other Christian denominations in the country to join us in admitting honestly before God that we have failed to put a significant imprint in our country, because Christians have not been true to their name.[29]

The year of penance throughout the country which Bishops proclaimed would have been better appreciated and more effective had it combined penance with organized protest against the unjust government and its total disregard for people's human rights.

By November 1982 many people had began to despair. The bishops issued a message of consolation in which they described the operations and effects of institutionalized injustice.

> The thirst for power is even worse than the search for wealth. To acquire and hold on to power people are known to make recourse to deceit, all sorts of falsity, suspicion, and the most inhuman forms of violence. Mutual fear becomes the rule, competition becomes callous and deceitful, violence is exercised with weapons of death, the entire system of justice is set aside to make way for a system of spies, torture and illegal executions . . . This state of fear and suspicion, of lying and of injustice has given rise to the tragic situation in which we live and suffer.[30]

They referred to the historical root of divisions which prevent united action against state injustices:

> We know fully well how the painful facts of our history, the wars, the murders, the acts of revenge, have seriously weakened our national consciousness. People tend to isolate themselves within the limits of their tribe, their religion, their political party, looking at others as strangers and possible enemies. The role of the Church in this situation is that of educating the population in the understanding of a national conscience that embraces all citizens within the nation. Without this conscience no nation will ever be born to life and will ever be able to face its problems.[31]

The repeated appeals by Cardinal Emmanuel Nsubuga for a Round Table Conference with 'rebels' having been rejected by government, the role of the Bishops was reduced to noting the atrocities done to people and the corruption and injustices within the government, and to encouraging people never to despair to 'resolve to work together for the salvation of our country'.[32]

Fundamental change and the National Resistance Movement (NRM)

The Catholic bishops hailed the successful revolution of the NRM, which they described as 'a most welcome breath of fresh air for us in Uganda and an example to the rest of the world'.

In the NRM, the bishops had hopes that the root-cause of Uganda's instability could be effectively redressed: 'We have also been favourably impressed by the attempt on the part of Government to overcome tribal divisions and prejudices.'[33] They endorsed the swearing-in pledge of Museveni for fundamental change in Uganda:

A fundamental change is urgent and necessary in our country. Indeed, we have been calling for such a change for many years especially through our various Pastoral Letters. Indeed it is an essential part of the Church's mission promote such a change for the good of our country.[34]

They outlined the areas which were in urgent need of fundamental change: the dignity of the human person, the commitment to the common good without discrimination, moral rehabilitation and reconciliation, the cooperation between church and state, genuine political education, education in democracy, integral development, the recruitment and training of the security forces, and a spirit of patriotism and national unity.

If fundamental change was to have lasting effects on Ugandan society, the bishops rightly believed, it had to be enshrined in a new national constitution. They welcomed the plan of the government for the new constitution and promised their full co-operation. Having shown how the 1967 constitution was imposed on the nation, and how political leaders were not committed to uphold and defend it, excepting where their own personal interests were concerned, the Bishops indicated the ill effects of the people's ignorance of the content, implication, rights and duties contained in their existing national constitution.

We attach great importance to the work of revision, not only for juridical reasons as regards the setting up of public structures, but because of the human and social implications of such a body of legislation. The Constitution can help to unify the Nation and create a new mentality capable of overcoming the various divisive factors. Moreover legislation determines a way of life and consequently shapes people's moral standards and behaviour, making it easier for them to establish an orderly development in the life of both individuals and society as whole.[35]

They called for a popular constitution to be discussed by the entire population and approved by the people's elected representatives. Three years later, when Government set up the Uganda Constitutional Commission, the bishops called on all Ugandans to take it as a moral duty to actively participate in the making of the new Constitution.

At last the bishops were able not only to analyse the root-cause of Uganda's instability but also to offer a lasting solution within the new national constitution.

The political tensions of 1961–1962, in which Archbishop Kiwanuka was much involved, occurred during and immediately after the discussions preceding the Independence Constitution of 1962. Elements of bureaucratic politics had been made part of that constitution. Its undemocratic abolition in 1966 sparked off the further crisis which led the country into chaos in subsequent years. The importance of a national constitution in the Uganda context can hardly be overemphasized. People of various types of opinion and background look at the new constitution as the possible lasting solution to Uganda's chronic problems. As the religious groups which felt oppressed took a strong stand for justice in the discussions of the 1962 constitution, the women in Uganda today are taking a similar stand to see their complete equality recognized and defended by the new constitution.

Not all, however, realize that the constitution alone can never redress all types of injustices in society. Some of these injustices are created by people's attitudes and private behaviour. These can hardly be legislated against, not even by the current anti-sectarian law in the country. Besides the constitution there is need for genuine political education, a culture of justice, peace and constitutionality, dedicated leadership, and enlightened citizens to translate constitutional ideals into daily practice. For religious bodies in Uganda a vigorous educative campaign for genuine ecumenism is also indispensable.

Bishop Kiwanuka and the Catholic bishops after him, by identifying the root-cause of Uganda's instability in terms of political injustice rather than mere religious rivalry or bigotry, have made a case which demands special attention from historians of Uganda. The radical change of emphasis in the bishops's analyses after the fall of Amin in 1979 also deserves careful observation. From then on it was no longer political injustice, directed towards Catholics only but towards all whom government and its agents identified as 'enemies'. The religious dimension in Ugandan politics was no longer the key issue. The issue had come to be illegitimacy of government, and its use of divisive means to perpetuate dictatorship in the country.

In the *Ten-Point Programme of NRM*, the third point is: 'Consolidation of national unity and elimination of all forms of sectarianism'.[36] Under this point, which is considered the fundamental cause of trouble, the NRM vows to 'rigorously fight tribalism and religious sectarianism'.[37] Ugandans are critically observing, not without some disappointments, how seriously the NRM leaders are committed as a group to the full realization of this part of the Programme. There is already a joke in some circles, which must be taken seriously, that from knowing the tribe of a ministry's driver, one may accurately guess the tribe of the minister!

What, however, is emerging from the current constitutional debate is the seriousness and eagerness which Ugandans have to see Uganda find lasting solutions to its problems of divisive politics based on tribe, region, religion and political parties. Although the debate is conducted in an atmosphere of freedom, both of speech and press, one would not be entirely wrong to suspect that some people do not consider it 'culturally' proper to discuss all issues openly. The more sensitive an issue is, the more likely it is that it will be treated superficially in public. What, however, is of uttermost importance is the fact that an opportunity has been accorded to all Ugandans to critically discover the root-cause of their country's instability and underdevelopment and suggest a lasting solution to it. Should the choice of the majority ignore the root-cause, then Uganda will fall victim, once again, to the previous vicious circle. For, as the Catholic bishops stated in 1982: 'a political system that does not respect justice . . . has clearly abdicated both its dignity and its right to exist'.[38]

Notes

1. Bishop Kiwanuka to priests, Kitovu, 31 July 1947.
2. Bishop Kiwanuka to Muteesa II, Kitovu, 6 November 1947.
3. Bishop Kiwanuka to Muteesa II, Kitovu, 12 December 1950.
4. Muteesa II to Bishop Kiwanuka, London, 7 September 1954.
5. Bishop Kiwanuka to Muteesa II, Kitovu, 17 December 1954.
6. A.G.G. Ginyera-Pinycwa, 'Religion and politics: Some related constitutional issues' unpublished paper, pp. 17–18.
7. Bishop Kiwanuka's speech, Kitovu, 16 April, 1956.
8. 'Ebirowoozo bye Immyumyaami ne Kabaka' (Ideas to share with the king), 26 April 1956.
9. Bishop Kiwanuka to Muteesa II, Kitovu, 11 June 1956.
10. Gingyera-Pinycwa, 'Religion and politics', p. 18.
11. Ibid., pp. 18–19.
12. Archbishop Kiwanuka to Muteesa II, Kitovu, 18 January 1961.
13. Muteesa II to Archbishop Kiwanuka, Mmengo, 27 January 1961.
14. Kabaka Yekka = King alone.
15. UNESCO.
16. Archbishop J. Kiwanuka, *Church and state: Guiding principles* (Kisubi, 1961).
17. Ibid., p. 4.
18. Ibid., pp. 4–5.
19. Ibid., p. 8.
20. Ibid., p. 28.
21. Lugard in 1892, Macdonald in 1893, Portal in 1893 and Johnston in 1900.
22. Catholic Bishops, *Shaping our national destiny* (Kisubi, 1962), p. 3.
23. Ibid., pp. 39–40.
24. Archbishop Kiwanuka to Fr. Tourigny, July 1965.
25. Catholic Bishops, *Reshaping our nation* (Kisubi, 1980), pp. 5–6.
26. Catholic Bishops, *I have heard the cry of my people* (Kisubi, 1980), p. 5.
27. Ibid., pp. 6–7.
28. Catholic Bishops, *Be converted and live* (Kisubi, 1981), p. 5.
29. Ibid., p. 6.
30. Catholic Bishops, *In God we trust* (Kisubi, 1982), p. 6.
31. Ibid., p. 16.
32. *Message of Catholic bishops to the government and people of Uganda* (Kisubi, 1985), p. 3.
33. Catholic Bishops, *With a new heart and a new spirit* (Kisubi, 1986), p. 9.
34. Ibid., p. 10.
35. Ibid., p. 33, and Catholic Bishops, *Towards making a new national constitution* (Kisubi, 1989).
36. NRM Secretariat, *Ten-point programme of NRM* (1986), pp. 8–10.
37. Ibid., p. 9.
38. Catholic Bishops, *In God we trust*, p. 14.

Eight

Catholics
& Political Identity
in Toro[1]

RONALD KASSIMIR

Recent attention to the reconstruction of civil society in Africa raises the issue of what role religious institutions may play in this process. Michael Bratton has recently emphasized that religious organizations may be particularly significant as non-governmental organizations. 'The largest and most rapidly growing voluntary associations [in Africa] are the churches – Christian, Islamic and separatist – whose ministries increasingly address secular as well as spiritual concerns, and which are federated from parish to national and international levels' (Bratton, 1989, p. 426). In Uganda, the early establishment of Christian missions (some predating colonialism), and their moral authority, independent resource base and international connections, have protected churches from the efforts of authoritarian and centralizing governments to emasculate autonomous organizations of civil society. Churches have survived the years of political and economic chaos while other voluntary institutions (trade unions, co-operatives, etc.) and elements of the state apparatus itself have atrophied as a result of them. The comparatively autonomous position of the churches in Uganda – and especially the Catholic Church – has enabled religious institutions to maintain a fair degree of their social power. This places them in a unique position among the array of voluntary associations that are slowly rebuilding under the more open policies of the present National Resistance Movement (NRM) government in the country.

What remains an open question is what types of civil organization can be achieved by the churches, given their internal dynamics. This study offers a microanalysis of the capacity of a religious institution in Uganda to effect social mobilization through the forging of a community that shares common interests and a common vision. It is based on fieldwork among Catholics in the former kingdom of Toro (now encompassed by the diocese of Fort Portal) in western Uganda.

By concentrating on the internal constraints and possibilities of the Catholic Church for social mobilization, it is not my intention to minimize attention to the social and political environment within which the church operates. Clearly, the vast upheavals experienced by Ugandans in the past twenty-five years have not left the churches untouched. Also, some aspects of religiously activated mobilization in Uganda in the past have come under severe criticism by the present NRM government. The NRM has decried the politics of 'sectarianism' as a major source of political instability and corruption in Uganda's post-independence turmoil. Religious affiliation, with its perceived expression in political parties (Catholics for the Democratic Party (DP), Protestants for the Uganda People's Congress (UPC)), is considered an important basis for 'sectarianism', the other basis being ethnic identity. The NRM's analysis echoes earlier efforts to interpret the nationalist phase of Uganda's colonial past and post-independence politics, when the partisan competition which emerged along religious lines in the 1950s was seen as a natural extension of the religious wars fought in Buganda in the late nineteenth century.[2]

Catholic Church, Catholic community

One important surface contradiction in regard to religion in Toro and elsewhere in Uganda concerns the significance attached to membership of a world religious institution while the degree of doctrinal and social commitment to it varies widely among members. Few Batoro today would identify themselves as 'traditionalists'. Yet many regularly violate church norms, especially those involving sexual behaviour and the practices of traditional modes of healing, spirit possession and exorcism, and protection from witchcraft. Attachment to a Christian denomination is not merely a reflection of being born into a Christian family or of a desire to be associated with modernity. Many Batoro deeply value the communal bonds conferred by membership. Many also accept elements of Christian belief and practice as an essential part of their spiritual and social lives. One informant, an ex-seminarian, reported: 'For some, being a Mutoro or a member of your clan is not enough. They need to belong to a religious community.' But, with perhaps the exception of followers of recently established Pentecostal churches, there has been little systematic incorporation of Christian dogma and theology as promoted by church officials into behaviour and beliefs among many Catholics and Anglicans. For many there is a limited commitment to Christian religious practice, often signified by the term 'Sunday-goer'.[3]

Why Catholic 'Sunday-goers' value their religious identity is part of a broader conception of the Catholic Church. This has been discussed by many observers. In their work on élite and mass conceptions of Latin American Catholicism, Levine and Mainwaring (1986) write that 'The importance of analyzing the interaction between institutional and popular dimensions is especially clear for the Catholic Church, since elites and rank and file value the institutional link and strive to remain within its bounds' (p. 5).

Observation of Ugandan Catholicism indicates that the struggles by church leaders to maintain social unity on the one hand and doctrinal unity on the other often work at cross-purposes. And, as I shall argue below, the inclusive nature of Catholic membership influences the form of potential mobilization the church can undertake. Further, the extent to which Catholics 'value the institutional link and strive to remain within its bounds' must be placed in historical context, as this commitment varies across individuals and across time. Maintaining the institutional link is obviously not the only social and religious goal of Catholics, and the growing minority attracted to the Pentecostal and 'separatist' churches is evidence that formal membership is not an immutable, lifetime commitment.[4]

Catholicism in Toro

Unlike in Buganda, where missionaries preceded the arrival of colonial agents by thirteen years, in Toro Christianity and colonialism arrived simultaneously. Specifically, they appeared initially in the person of one man – Kasagama, a crown prince of the Toro kingdom, who first fled from his homeland in the 1870s when Kabarega, the Omukama (king) of Bunyoro, decided to reconquer a former part of his kingdom which had seceded about forty years earlier from Bunyoro itself. Kasagama returned triumphantly to Toro in 1891 under the protective wing of Frederick Lugard. Lugard reinstalled Kasagama as Omukama of Toro. Kasagama had been living in exile in Buganda. There he had met Lugard and been exposed to the Anglican faith. Shortly after his installation as Omukama, he sent for Ganda catechists to begin preaching the gospel in Toro.[5]

The relationship between Toro and the British was formalized through a series of agreements, beginning in 1894, which specified the limitations to Kasagama's powers while establishing a classic indirect rule pattern. As the title of Nyakazingo's (1973) essay on Kasagama – 'A despotic and missionary king' – indicates, Christianity initially spread in Toro from the top down, beginning with members of the royal clan (the Babito) and strongly encouraged by the king himself. In the next two years, both Anglican and Catholic missionaries appeared in Toro to open mission stations and win converts. In a pattern similar in some respects to what had been established in Buganda,[6] chiefships in Toro were distributed on a basis that greatly favoured Anglican converts.[7] As most appointments historically had gone to those who had established ties with the king through kinship or patronage, most chiefs adopted the king's Anglican faith as a sign of loyalty. However, Catholicism began to spread through the peasant majority (Bairu) as Catholic missionaries concentrated on converting the rural masses after being closed out (although not completely) from access to the Toro political class.[8]

Beginning with the first Catholic missionary in Toro, the White Father Augustine Achte, and continuing throughout the colonial period, Catholic missionaries regularly complained to the king and colonial officers about discrimination in the appointment of chiefs. This was because the missionary enterprise seemed so contingent upon the presence of sympathetic chiefs.[9] Indeed, this was also an important motivation for the establishment of mission stations as self-contained, relatively autonomous social spaces, with the parish priest possessing chief-like powers, both within and beyond its territorial bounds.

Thus, we can see how the seeds for a Catholic sense of grievance against the kingdom and the colonial state were sown at the start. But it must be specified which Catholics bore grievances. Catholics who felt cheated by Protestant privilege in appointments were those who might otherwise have been eligible for chiefships but were denied them because of their Catholic faith. Throughout the colonial period, very few Batoro, Anglican or Catholic, held the qualifications which would have made them eligible for chiefships. Personalistic ties to the King and, in the later colonial period, secondary-level education, were the basic qualifications.

I stress this point because it is assumed by many observers of Uganda politics that there was a general grievance among Catholics because of Protestant predominance in chiefships. But Catholics whose potential careers in the civil service were harmed by the very real discrimination against them were quite few. They were members of the small Catholic élite which grew up in the interstices of Anglican hegemony. In the early colonial period, it was mostly marginalized members of the political clan who sought out the Catholic missionaries in order to give themselves an alternative base of support. In the later colonial period, it was mostly school-teachers, clerical workers or sons of those few Catholics who were chiefs or members of the political class. This group was frequently to form cadres of the DP in Toro and elsewhere in Uganda.[10]

In what way were the Catholic masses – i.e. those who could never aspire to chiefships in the first place – affected by Protestant privilege?

Patronage is the most convincing answer. Chiefs had much discretionary decision-making power at the local level; and, in the area of jobs, land distribution and dispute settlement, it is likely that chiefs favoured fellow members of their faith, especially those with whom they had regular interaction at church services or in church lay groups. In addition, chiefs in the colonial period monopolized coercion in the countryside, and had much discretion in the use of police power, tax collection and forced labour. Since most chiefs were Protestants, everyday Catholics may have suffered disproportionately from the unchecked power of chiefs. [11] To the degree that this is the case, the Catholic masses may indeed have had grievances along with the élite members of their church and an interest in giving Catholics equal opportunity for chiefships. Also, the masses were certainly socialized into this sense of grievance by the missionaries, the African clergy and lay leaders. It was recognized that elected representatives would bring in new sources of patronage potentially outside control of the chiefs. This is a much more plausible account of Catholic support for DP than the idea that Catholics and Anglicans were 'naturally' irreconcilable. Also few of Toro's social networks – in family, clan, village and workplace – failed to include members of other faiths. Patronage patterns surely were mediated by these non-religious personal ties, and several informants explain that chiefs, especially at lower levels of the administration, were as likely to show favouritism to fellow clansmen or those wealthy enough to offer 'gifts' as they were to co-religionists. [12]

The importance of this for the present day is that, among older Catholics, the grievances established during the colonial days persist, although the basis for grievance has largely changed. Younger Catholics were exposed somewhat to the older pattern under the Obote II regime (1980–1985), when many DP followers were persecuted. Since most Toro Catholics (and many other Batoro) supported DP in the 1980 elections, [13] they were affected by the abuses of UPC-appointed chiefs. But, according to most accounts, chiefs were not so much abusive in this period as ineffective in preventing UPC party cadres from taking advantage of their positions against DP supporters.

Finally, the relationship between religious denomination and political parties in Toro in the early 1960s is both complex and contradictory. For one thing, several leading politicians did not fall into line. John Babiiha, Toro's best-known national-level politician, was a staunch UPC member, who happened to be a Catholic. A successful DP candidate in the 1962 elections prior to independence was a Protestant. In the thirteen months between the 1961 and 1962 national elections for Toro's four parliamentary seats, the DP went from winning one seat to UPC's two and one to an independent, to winning all four seats in 1962, its overall percentage of the vote jumping from 29 per cent to 62 per cent. [14] Clearly, the Catholic population of Toro did not go through a similar increase in that period. Some Batoro politically active at that time say that the DP's success, while certainly resting on its Catholic base, had more to do with fears of the Buganda–UPC alliance formed after the 1961 elections. The status of the Toro kingdom *vis-à-vis* Buganda seemed to be a primary concern. More prescient than the Mengo clique of Buganda, which entered into an ill-fated alliance with UPC, some Batoro political élite and many voters of both religions saw the UPC as a greater threat to the kingdom's federal status than the DP.

Fort Portal diocese

The four main regions of southwestern Uganda (Toro, Bunyoro, Kigezi and Ankole) were constituted as the vicariate of Rwenzori under the administration of the White Fathers in 1934. In 1953, the Catholic hierarchy of Uganda was established and the vicariate was transformed into the diocese of Mbarara.[15] In 1958, the American Holy Cross Fathers in Fort Portal arrived to assist and eventually take over the ministry in this part of the diocese.[16] In 1961, Fort Portal diocese was formed, and included the Toro and Bunyoro kingdoms. Fr Vincent McCauley of the Holy Cross Mission was named its first Bishop. In 1965, Bunyoro broke off to form the diocese of Hoima. The first Mutoro bishop, Serapio Magambo, was consecrated during Pope Paul VI's visit to Uganda in 1969. In 1972, Magambo took over the leadership of the diocese from Bishop McCauley. In 1989, the parishes in the ethnic Bakonzo region south of Fort Portal broke off to form the diocese of Kasese.

What can be observed is the breaking down of a large diocese into units which almost exactly correspond with the administrative boundaries of the Ugandan state, which in theory, if not always in practice, overlap with particular ethnic communities. A general policy of the Africanizing Ugandan Catholic Church has been to place all priests in their ethnic zones, though not necessarily in their home parishes. This is, in part, a linguistic practicality. But the churches have generally remained more 'federal' in their structure than the state, where functionaries are typically placed in districts outside their home areas and frequently transferred. In fact, there is no single head of the Ugandan church in the sense of absolute authority – the Cardinal and the archdiocese remain *primus inter pares* with no power over bishops of the other dioceses. The Uganda Episcopal Conference, essentially a council of bishops, most closely approaches a central policy-making body, but individual bishops have almost full autonomy in the day-to-day operation of their dioceses.

Fort Portal diocese is now comprised of thirteen parishes spread over the districts of Kabarole and Bwamba.[17] Eight of these parishes have been created since 1960, four of them since 1977. In terms of personnel there are about sixty priests, the great majority Batoro, under the authority of the bishop of Fort Portal. Those not working in the parishes do a variety of administrative and pastoral tasks for the diocese, serve as chaplains for church-owned schools and lay groups or teach at the minor seminary at Virika, the diocesan headquarters just south of Fort Portal town.

In addition to local and missionary priests, a large number of religious brothers and sisters, mostly local and some expatriate, serve a variety of functions for the diocese. The Brothers of St Joseph the Worker, established by Bishop Magambo in the early 1970s, perform various tasks at the diocese, including manning the treasury and running some of the church's development projects. All the brothers are trained in technical skills, such as carpentry and car mechanics, and are occasionally sent out to the parishes to assist the priests. The order of the Banyatereza Sisters number several hundred and are in charge of Virika Hospital. Some work as nurses and others have recently started a women's development centre. Many live at convents in the parishes, helping the priest, teaching catechism and working with local women's clubs.

These groups – the bishop, clergy, religious sisters and brothers, and the catechists spread throughout the mostly rural sub-parishes of the diocese – constitute the core of the church's institutional structure. They are what Pizzorno calls 'the identifiers' – those members of an organization whose loyalty is not based solely on cost/benefit calculations regarding their membership, but whose very social identity is inextricably woven with the institution.

The marked status differences express various levels of inclusiveness within Toro's Catholic community. Indeed, one diocesan-level lay leader referred to a class struggle between clergy and laity. This has become a deep and complex issue, with much misunderstanding on both sides. The entrenched paternalism of the missionary period, combined with the resources which the White Fathers and American priests were capable of obtaining from abroad, set a pattern of expectations on the part of the laity for cash, clothes, school fees, medical assistance and other material items. It also meant that the parishes were not so dependent on locally raised revenue through tithes, gifts and contributions to maintain and expand church activities. As the clergy began to Africanize, these outside resources from the mission societies, while not drying up entirely, have been significantly reduced. Priests have less patronage to dispense, and even greater demands are made upon them by family and clan members. But, while the priests have fewer material resources for their parishes, some have access to cars and luxury items, such as music systems, which they inherit when taking over a parish, purchased through the generosity of benefactors encountered on their studies in Europe and America or acquired with their own entrepreneurial skills. While the lifestyle of a priest in a rural parish cannot compare to that of the élite in Kampala or even Fort Portal, it is still higher than that of most of the peasants, teachers and civil servants whom the parish serves. For the laity, the relative plenty of the priests makes their stated inability to assist parishioners on material matters suspect. For the priest, the low level of financial contribution to the parish (no priest interviewed estimated tithes coming from more than 25 per cent of church members) is sufficient explanation for the church's fiscal crisis. This 'class struggle' also has a moral dimension. The moral authority of some priests has been greatly reduced in the eyes of some lay people because of alleged alcohol abuse and violation of celibacy vows. These changes have contributed to a subtle shift among some Catholics, who have begun to perceive their religious affiliation as somewhat distinct from loyalty to the church and its institutional representatives.

As the old paternalistic pattern proves less workable, the church and its 'identifiers' are groping to establish new frameworks for clergy–laity relations. In this context, the notions of what defines the boundaries of Catholic identity are more fluid and contestable.

Who is a Toro Catholic?

The first step in understanding the organizational potential of a group is to examine its membership criteria. The answer to the question 'Who is a Catholic in Toro?' may not be as obvious as it seems at first glance. For one thing, there are institutional and popular criteria – i.e. the institutions and their functionaries, on the one hand, and the Catholic masses, on the other, may stress different qualities, beliefs and practices in identifying themselves or others as Catholic. Secondly, both for analytical purposes and in popular discourse, we can talk about degrees of 'Catholic-ness'. That someone is or is not Catholic may be less consequential for group mobilization than the extent to which Catholicism infuses his or her social life. It should be clear that the criteria for evaluating the intensity of an individual's religious affiliation are inevitably contestable, although the scope of disagreement and the social groups that express different criteria can vary over time.

The statistics of the diocese of Fort Portal show an ever-increasing number of Catholics within its territorial boundaries. This numerical expansion of the community expresses the Church's extensive power – nominal claims over people within a given territory.[18] The formal, or institutional, criterion for church membership is baptism. Anyone baptized within the Catholic Church is a Catholic. The importance of gathering statistics is evident in the yearly account that each parish priest must provide to diocesan offices – statistics on marriages, catechumens, number of village churches and lay association membership, as well as baptisms and total number of Catholics. The Catholic total is typically the sum of the last year's total plus the number of new baptisms (it is not clear if the deaths of church members or those who have joined other churches are subtracted from the total). These statistics are periodically forwarded to the Vatican.

This emphasis on statistics has several purposes. In part, it is an expression of the competitive nature of evangelization in Toro and elsewhere in Uganda – the numbers are an implicit measure of the strength of various denominations. This has always been important for the Catholic Church, as its claim that it has suffered discrimination has greatly turned on the under-representation of its members in administrative posts and scholarships, given its status as the largest single denomination in Uganda and in most districts (including Toro). An implicit message in the discourse of some Catholics active in the DP has been that the majority of Ugandans (by which they mean Catholics) have been disenfranchised because the DP has never been able to assume power. Also, to be able to show an expanding community assists the church in the pursuit of outside funding. The signal to donors is that the church's institutional reach is great, thus increasing the likelihood that donor-sponsored projects will benefit more people. Finally, the statistical emphasis brings status to church officials, who can show with confidence that they are doing the job well.

Yet the formal criterion of baptism in defining who is a Catholic is not wholly satisfactory to many members of the clergy and laity. As is plain to all church members, baptism is no guarantee of commitment to the faith and to the institution. Spiritually, many Catholics look to attendance at mass and receiving the sacraments. Socially, they may evaluate actual behaviour, including avoidance of church-proscribed activities and general moral conduct in social interaction. Institutionally, they might consider the regular payment of tithes as a sign of commitment and group membership.

Participation in the sacrament of Holy Communion is the most powerful act a Catholic can undertake to signify membership in the Catholic community.[19] Two important aspects must be considered regarding the Holy Communion: the 'giving' and the 'taking', and how it has changed over time. In terms of 'giving' communion, the priest, based on advice he may receive from his catechist or church council leaders, has the authority to deny communion.[20] The justification of denial is based on knowledge of violations of church doctrine committed by a church member. In Toro, the most common violations are men and women living together outside church-recognized marriage, sexual 'promiscuity', participation in traditional 'pagan' ritual and witchcraft (including ritual actions taken to defend oneself against witchcraft).[21]

Although less common, the sacraments can be withheld because of evidence of consistent non-commitment to church activities, such as payment of tithes and participation in lay groups and church-building projects. In other words, both adherence to doctrine and socially orientated signs of institutional loyalty determine one's status regarding the sacraments. The final element in the giving of Holy Communion is, of course, confession. The private confession of sins to a priest 'cleanses' one, making one fit to receive the sacrament.

The 'taking' of communion is performed by individual members of the congregation. It is expected that during catechism, when all Catholics are taught the basics of the faith, the requirements mentioned above for receiving communion are internalized. Many sins potentially committed, especially pre- (official) marital sex, participation in traditional ritual and witchcraft, are done in secret and are often unknown to the priest and catechists. Catholics, if they do not go to confession, are expected to deny themselves the sacraments through an act of conscience. To receive the sacraments 'uncleansed' is a mortal sin, which one theologian describes as cutting oneself off 'from the principle of right living (the ultimate good), and this is like death' (Bullough, 1963, p. 138). In this sense, 'taking' communion, given that the institution's intelligence network in inherently limited, is largely a matter of individual choice.

The giving and taking of the sacraments has changed in Toro over time. As for giving, the early missionaries were much stricter regarding violations of doctrine (especially living out of official wedlock) and the necessity of confession. Modern African clergy and catechists, as well as expatriate priests moulded in the days of Vatican II, tend to take a gentler approach. One informant said that an American priest described his approach as 'giving the Christians enough rope to hang themselves' – i.e. stressing the 'taking' of communion, and the role of personal integrity in making the decision, based on the Christian's knowledge of doctrine learned in catechism and an assessment of his or her own actions.

The early Catholic converts were so heavily indoctrinated by the catechism that personal conscience and/or the fear of discovery were often causes enough to act according to church rules. More recently, catechism is a much less intense and totalizing process, reduced to one year from the three years introduced by the White Fathers. Today, few young people go to confession. As a result of less intensive catechical training and a sceptical attitude toward the moral authority of priests, some young Catholics insist on taking the sacraments in full knowledge that their personal actions, especially concerning sexuality, violate church norms. The question then arises, why do they bother at all? The answer seems to be twofold. First is a concern for reputation. Some people do not want the priest and others to assume that they are living sinfully. (Of course, for those who are aware of a violation, seeing that person take communion is a source of amusement or outrage.) Second, in spite of disagreement with church doctrine on social behaviour or even more serious spiritual disagreement, many young Catholics want to feel part of the church community, for which receiving the sacraments is a defining gesture.

We have seen that the taking of the sacraments is a significant criterion for membership in the Catholic community. Communion, literally 'sharing', is a ritual act performed collectively (by most of those attending mass), which symbolizes membership in a community. The fact that some go to mass but do not receive the sacraments is not insignificant. Whether they go for spiritual or social reasons or a combination of the two, they represent an alternative conception of membership from 'sacramental' criteria. Many attending mass without receiving communion disagree with church norms regarding sexuality and yet still want to be part of the collectivity and believe that they do lead 'Christian' lives in their actions toward others. Additionally, since taking Holy Communion today may be a social act which does not necessarily comply with church rules, it is not always a measure of religiosity. When someone takes the sacraments, this need not mean that he or she is a good Catholic but that the individual wants to feel and to be seen as part of the community.

In recent years, another criterion for membership has been introduced by a small portion of the Catholic community, but one with some influence within the church. The Catholic Charismatic Renewal Movement has the potential to divide the Ugandan Catholic Church in a similar manner as the revival movement (called Balokole – 'the saved') almost did in the Anglican Church fifty years before. Drawing on the experience of Catholic charismatics in the United States and elsewhere, the Charismatic Renewal Movement seeks a deepening of the faith among church members through greater knowledge of the Bible, more enthusiastic and expressive forms of religious practice, sharing of religious experiences through small encounter groups, a levelling of authority distinctions between clergy and laity and an emphasis on receiving the holy spirit and charisms – spiritual gifts that all Christians contain within them – including the gift of healing.

Some Catholics, including many priests, accuse the movement of labelling anyone who does not participate as not being a 'true' Catholic. The fear that the charismatics may become another Balokole movement within the Catholic Church, eschewing traditional forms of Catholic ritual and practice and adopting practices which the church had previously opposed and belittled. After a recent recruitment drive held at a rural parish by charismatic members from Virika, two priests debated the validity of the movement. The younger of the priests angrily stated: 'Catholics shouldn't pray like Protestants.' This even further complicates the criteria for Catholic membership. For this priest, the form of religious expression is at least as important as the substance of religious faith in establishing Catholic identity. For some, though not all, charismatics, there is a sense in which one's degree of religiosity, expressed not simply in receiving the sacraments and being a 'Sunday-goer' but in an everyday commitment to the faith through participation in the movement, is the true criterion for full group membership.

The charismatic movement in Fort Portal diocese has the support of some priests, sisters and lay people. It has taken off mostly in the urban centre of Fort Portal, but is slowly spreading to some rural parishes. Its recent expansion is, in part, a response by some Catholic leaders to the exodus of educated Catholics to the new Pentecostal churches, whose less hierarchical structure, more enthusiastic forms of worship and emphasis on Bible reading and individual interpretation of texts have attracted those who had become alienated from their original faith.

To sum up thus far, we can see that levels of religiosity form different criteria for identifying a Catholic, a 'good' Catholic and a 'true' Catholic. Baptism provides the broadest criterion for group membership. Typically done as a child, baptism confers membership without reference to levels of religious or institutional commitment. Church attendance and receiving (or taking) the sacraments is a deeper measure of religiosity, although the emphasis is on outward practice. A Catholic is one who goes to Catholic places – i.e. church. Finally, the most intense criterion in terms of religiosity is an unambiguous unity of outward practice and internal belief, expressed not just on Sunday but every day, and is best exemplified by participation in the charismatic community. It should be noted here that commitment to the faith and commitment to the institution are not inherently coterminous. Those opposed to the charismatic renewal may not question the sincerity of charismatic beliefs but criticize what they perceive as potentially corrosive effects on the institution and divisive effects on the community. These disparate notions of membership and the church's willingness to tolerate the ambiguities of institutional loyalties have implications for its capacity to mobilize its members. By sacrificing the intensity of commitment for purposes of inclusiveness, the moral and social content of Catholic membership is diffuse.

Social action: the Catholic councils

While there are several forums in which the laity participate in social activities, in this section I shall focus on the role of the laity in social action via the Catholic council system.[22] The council system is organized in a similar structure to that of the Resistance Councils (RCs), instituted by the NRM.[23] Local lay leaders at the village church level are elected by church members and are put in charge of various committees (social development, pastoral work, women, finances). These village churches then send a representative to the sub-parish council, who work in conjunction with the catechist assigned to their area. The sub-parishes elect representatives to the parish council, who meet with the priest and head catechist. Finally, a diocesan council, which confers with the bishop and the vicar-general, is formed from the parishes.

In terms of authority, the clergy and catechists have the final decision-making powers on the council, although the implementation of certain projects often rests with the laity. The councils serve as a forum where lay leaders express their opinions on the running of church affairs and on social and political activities that affect Catholics. The amount of autonomy given to the laity is mostly dependent on the attitude of individual priests, who are often torn between the desire to reduce their workload and the possible loss of control of parish affairs. In addition, the perceived religiosity of lay members was often determinant in deciding who would be permitted to serve on the councils. One priest reported that only recently have Catholics who do not regularly receive the sacraments been allowed to serve on the social and financial sub-committees of the councils. (They are still prohibited from serving on the liturgical and pastoral committees.)

The social base of the councils tends to be those church members with relatively more education and higher incomes, although their participation in pastoral groups also recommends them. It is probably only at the parish level where noticeable social differentiation between council members and the rank and file are significant. The diocesan level is mostly the preserve of the Catholic élite, and its history is instructive for understanding the social and political orientation of lay leaders, as well as the church's view on the social and political practices of élite members of the community.

The Toro Catholic council was formed in 1960, the year before Fort Portal was declared a diocese independent of Mbarara. Because of this action, it was able establish itself as somewhat independent of the hierarchy, although its constitution specifies that members are subject to approval of the bishop. Yet its executive committee was composed only of lay people. Members of the Toro kingdom government, led by the Omuhikirwa (Prime Minister) Samson Rusoke, accused the council of fronting for the DP in Toro and of conspiring with the Baamba and Bakonzo rebellion. On 16 October 1962, just after independence, the vicar-general of Fort Portal diocese received a letter from the Speaker of the Toro Rukurato claiming that 'members of the Toro Catholic council are a subsidiary of the Democratic Party'. In his response the vicar-general asserted the autonomy of the council from party politics: 'That members of political parties are also members of the Catholic Council can easily be explained. As citizens, they have the right to belong to a political party; as Catholics they have the right to form an organisation to promote and safeguard Human Rights according to their conscience' (24–11–62, in Virika Archives).

At about the same time, the council sent a letter to Omukama Rukidi complaining that the Rukurato had been dismissing Catholics from responsible positions. Relations between the council and the Rukurato worsened until, in July 1964, the Omuhikirwa proclaimed that, during a meeting held in 1964, the council had planned for a 'Catholic Revolt in the Kingdom of Toro' in conjunction with the Bakonzo rebels. The council vigorously denied this, of course. Still, it seems clear that the council's political activities were causing discomfort for the diocese, while from the other side the council felt that the church was deserting them in their hour of need. This conflict erupted in August 1965, when the council sent a letter to Bishop McCauley complaining about discrimination against Catholics in the kingdom and the church's reluctance to stand by the council. The council members told the bishop that: 'aloofness is developing between clergy and laity and this is causing a drawback in the diocese. Most of the Christians seem to have lost interest in the clergy in whom formerly they had much confidence'. More ominously, the council continued: 'By and large religion itself will lose its grasp on the people. It took less than forty days for the Hebrews to adore the calf and for us paganism is still on the threshold and naturally we are inclined to it.' Regarding politics, they wrote: 'we neither want or intend to drag you nor force or persuade any of your clergy into such entanglements but for some issues politics and religion are practically inseparable.'

A series of sarcastic and aggressive exchanges followed between the bishop and the council. In the meantime, the diocesan leaders began to look for ways to control the council. As we saw in the chaplain report for the lay apostolate for 1963, Bishop McCauley had already indicated his preference for Catholics to join 'neutral welfare organisations rather than create new Catholic ones'. The chaplain reiterated this theme in a memo to the bishop in late 1965. He wrote that this issue revolves around:

> whether the TCC [Toro Catholic council] should be an instrument for the defence of Church institutions or a means of penetrating the secular spheres . . . But lay people as a whole see the first, and they can shout about it, but get afraid of acting on it . . . [A]t parish level, most Parish priests would like the CC [Catholic council] to act as a means of implementing Parish policies concerning material things (*endoborwa* [tithes], up-keep of churches, collections, schools, pilgrimage to martyrs shrines . . .). It then acts as a Parish council, but the autonomy of this type of Council is illusory, and educated people in Fort Portal do not accept it.

Accepted or not, this type of highly dependent Catholic council became the norm for the diocese. In 1966, the Toro Catholic council was officially disbanded. The chaplain's report for 1966 stated, 'though a group of laymen and women were calling themselves lay apostles, they were constantly undermining the Diocesan authority and causing friction in the diocese'. A new association, the Diocesan Council of Lay Apostolate, was established. Its constitution, written by a committee of three priests and three laymen, read in part: 'no Catholic Association can be tolerated or allowed in a Diocese if its aims and actions as well as its procedures disturb the peace of the Church'.

The Diocesan council grew dormant over time and has only recently begun to revive. The parish councils remained, but mostly as a rubber stamp for clerical directives unless individual priests saw it as desirable to involve the laity more fully. The situation is more complicated than the one we are normally presented with regarding the role of the Catholics in Ugandan politics. In the Toro case, we have an example of the church attempting to extricate the laity from political activity in the name of the Catholic community. Indeed, the struggle between the diocese and the council was about who had the right to speak for the Catholic community: the clerical or lay élite. While the DP clearly had the support of the council, the diocese felt that it was more important not to embroil itself in politics than to join hands with the laity in political support of the party for whom both had clear sympathy. The point is that, to the degree that Toro Catholics supported DP, it was not at the overt instigation of the church.

Catholicism and politics in Toro

As mentioned earlier, past observers of Ugandan politics and the present NRM regime have viewed religion as a primordial division among Ugandans, manifesting itself in party politics. To what extent have recent developments in Toro been evidence of this? The 1980 elections, believed by many Ugandans to have been rigged, put Milton Obote and the UPC back in power and proved a trying time for most Batoro. Toro was a stronghold for DP and Yoweri Museveni's Uganda Patriotic Movement (UPM), and subsequently was punished by the Obote II government. Roads remained in a state of disrepair, and few development projects were directed toward the district. Soldiers, UPC officials and the notorious Youth Wingers hounded DP supporters and suspected National Resistance Army (NRA) sympathizers. While this seemed more an attempt to suppress opposition than overt anti-Catholicism, the distinction blurred as many DP members were Catholics. Certainly in the minds of many Toro Catholics, the UPC government was perceived as singling out Catholics for persecution.

When Obote appeared one Sunday morning at Virika cathedral with a military entourage, the bishop insisted that armed men not be allowed on church grounds. Still, the heavily pro-DP vote in Toro implies that a fair number of non-Catholics voted DP, and several Batoro informants commented to me that some Catholics benefited from UPC patronage and protection during the Obote II regime. But, importantly, these same informants condemned Catholic members of UPC for their acts, not as traitors to the Catholic community. Michael Twaddle's observation is especially relevant here: [T]here is a world of difference between a religious denomination providing the sociological material for political parties to work on and . . . that denomination also determining the character and course of party conflict' (1978, p. 256).[24]

Those Catholics who were harassed by UPC or who could not receive justice from corrupt officials often turned to their priests for spiritual consolation, financial support and mediation with state authorities. Some priests could not watch the oppression without responding and took great risks in defence of members of the congregation and the community at large. One priest attempted to prevent UPC officials from grabbing land from a large squatter settlement and tried to organize a teachers' strike directed against a corrupt UPC-appointed headmaster. He later assisted the NRA, and was forced to flee into exile in 1984.

Several Toro priests performed extensive intelligence work for NRA when they began operations to liberate Toro, as well as recruiting fighters, collecting supplies and arranging for repair of vehicles and weapons. They also brokered the surrender of Kabarole district (the second territorial conquest in Uganda[25]) to the NRM in July 1985. The final agreement with the local Uganda National Liberation Army (UNLA) commander was negotiated on the grounds of the diocese. After the NRM takeover, one priest has continued to serve in the NRM secretariat and the Ministry of Rehabilitation.

Since the NRM victory in January 1986, two priests have thrown themselves directly into politics by standing for parliamentary seats in the 1989 elections. Both were victorious, but were asked to step down by Cardinal Nsubuga. The priest from Mwenge country complied and has since been appointed vice-chairman of the important Non-Governmental Organizations Committee. The second priest, from Kitagwenda, refused to resign from parliament, but was removed by a successful petition brought against him by his opponent, which charged him with bribery and 'sectarianism', specifically that he wore his cassock to the polls on election day. Many Toro Catholics saw the priest's embarrassing dismissal from office as a Protestant plot, but were quick to point out that this is unique to Kitagwenda, whose people are 'not exactly Batoro' and which always has been an area of religious conflict.[26]

Lay Catholics of all social groups (and fellow priests) seem to be divided on whether holding elected office is an appropriate role for a clergyman. But it is a far cry from the mid-1960s, when diocesan leaders were adamant that church personnel must not be drawn into the political arena. I would argue that these priests have involved themselves in electoral politics in part because lay associational life in the church has been impoverished, leaving a social leadership vacuum that these clergymen were willing to fill. In some instances, the patron-client relationships which were traditionally the norm between priests and lay members may have intensified in recent years. But, most important, priests were generally seen as 'with the people' during the recent hard times in Toro. Interestingly, the social and political legitimacy of priests may have risen at the same time as their moral authority has come increasingly under question.

As for Catholic lay people, many did join Museveni in the bush, although it would be difficult to identify any specifically Catholic motives in their actions. Since the institution of the RC system, many lay leaders hold positions on both church councils and the RCs. This has been explained to me as the result of harsh experiences suffered under the UPC regime, where many Catholics had been demobilized from politics. The more open political climate under the NRM has provided many with the opportunity to re-enter political life at the local level. That their standing in the church community assisted their election to the RCs is clear. Also, the political activity of lay leaders is emblematic of their desire to participate more fully in other institutions – i.e. the church. Many are precisely the people pushing for a greater role of the laity in church affairs.

Conclusions

In his recent treatise on the history of social power, Michael Mann distinguishes between the 'extensive' and 'intensive' power of social organizations. Extensive power is 'the ability to organize large numbers of people over far-flung territories in order to engage in minimally stable cooperation'. Intensive power is 'the ability to organize tightly and command a high level of mobilization or commitment from the participants, whether the area and numbers covered are great or small' (Mann, 1986, p. 7). In this study, I have attempted to show that the Catholic Church, historically an institution of 'extensive' power second to none, has not converted this power into the 'intensive' variety in Toro. Therefore, there has emerged no seamless 'primordial' or 'natural' Catholic community in Toro. Instead, there are various definitions of what might constitute such a community or Catholic communities, with different criteria for membership. This is due to (i) different conceptions of religiosity and of the importance of religiosity for group membership; and (ii) alternative sources of identity and interest, and the social networks that sustain them. These have inhibited the establishment of a more uniform Toro Catholic community across localities and social categories (region, tribe, class, gender, clan). In fact, the sense of a Catholic community may be lessening over time, particularly as the lay associations established and directed by the church speak less to the needs of new generations of Catholics.

At the same time, many lay members maintain a symbolic connection to the institution and wish to speak 'to' it and not join other sects. For most Batoro, it is difficult to imagine not being a 'something' (Catholic, Anglican, Pentecostal, Muslim). As long as it is common sense to have an institutional religious affiliation, those who share a common denomination will continue to find symbolic importance in the notion of a religious community. But the paternalistic mode which has defined the history of the Catholic Church in Toro, while being challenged in some quarters, still influences its mode of social action. The different, and often contradictory, versions of community membership and increasingly moribund lay groups still limit Catholic leadership largely to the clergy. The devolution of responsibility to the church councils may change this situation, although it is resisted by some priests and many lay people, who accept the paternalistic pattern as 'natural'.

Finally, the church's historical sense of grievance, combined with a laity whose organizational coherence has grown even looser in a chaotic political environment, has orientated Catholic social action in a defensive direction. This defensiveness, I would argue, has less to do with any inherent quality in Catholic political culture transplanted to Uganda[22] than with certain institutional and symbolic patterns established under colonial rule. A siege mentality, born out of the intense sense of grievance of missionaries and Catholic élites, led to the formation of hierarchically controlled institutions, which attempted (with limited success) to close off Catholics from other social networks.[28] The community and the church would protect each other in an environment perceived as hostile. As we have seen, in the early 1960s in Toro, Bishop McCauley was recommending that Catholics join neutral social organizations rather than establish their own associations. McCauley and the Holy Cross Fathers, of course, had only recently arrived in Toro and therefore did not share the historical memories of grievance of the White Fathers they replaced. But, more important than a change in mission societies, the conditions that prompted the development of tightly bound Catholic institutions had themselves already begun to change. It is this institutional legacy, with symbolic structures connected to it, that has shaped Catholic social action as defensive in new social action as diffuse and defensive in new social and political contexts.

One expression of this new context is that younger Catholics are less likely to claim religious prejudice as an obstacle to their life chances than their parents. In short, the purposes for which church leaders needed to construct an inward-looking, hierarchically controlled Catholic community, which led to advancing claims as Catholics, are dissipating. Their capacity to turn nominal Catholics into 'identifiers', who define their interests principally as Catholic ones, has always been limited and it is decreasing with time.

Notes

1. The eighteen months of fieldwork on which this chapter is based was assisted by grants from a United States Department of Education Fulbright–Hays Dissertation Fellowship and from the Joint Committee on African Studies of the Social Science Research Council and the American Council of Learned Societies, with funds provided by the Rockefeller Foundation and the William and Flora Hewlett Foundation, and the Wilder House Center for Politics, History and Culture at the University of Chicago.

2. See Welbourn (1965), Rothchild and Rogin (1966) and Apter (1961). However, see Twaddle (1978) for a critique of the granting to 'religious allegiance . . . a high status in scholarly explanation' (p. 259), especially regarding the relationship between Catholicism and the DP.

3. Among 'Sunday-goers', this commitment may greatly intensify in times of personal and/or social stress, as evidenced by the levels of church attendance during the Amin and Obote II periods. One church official of Fort Portal diocese remarked the 'people were going through bullets to get to church on Holy Thursday' during the 1979 war.

4. Personal observation. The growth of Pentecostal churches in Uganda is a relatively recent and, thus far, mostly urban phenomenon.

5. See the accounts in Ingham (1975), Steinhart (1973) and, on catechists, Pirouet (1968–1969, 1978).

6. Hansen (1984) is now the most complete account of this process in Buganda. See Chapter 8 for a comparison with Toro.

7. Interestingly, Kisembo's data show that in 1939, the *saza* (county) chiefships were almost evenly divided between Protestant and Catholic – four and three, respectively. Huge disparities exist at the sub-county (*gomborra*) and parish (*muruka*) levels (Kisembo, 1974, p. 30). Richards, reporting on Taylor's data from 1951, shows that the number of Catholic *saza* chiefs had been reduced to one, the percentage of *gomborra* chiefs remained at about 14 per cent, and the number of *muruka* chiefs had doubled to about 33 per cent of the total (Richards, 1959, p. 143) At the time of independence, there were five Protestants and two Catholics among the seven *saza* chiefs (memorandum in Virika Archives).

8. See the chapter on Toro in Pirouet (1978). For a similar case in Ankole, see Doornbos (1976).

9. Given the spread of Catholicism in Toro and other parts of Uganda, this supposition may have been erroneous. In fact, not being the religion of power seems to correlate with greater success in nominal conversion.

10. See Gingyera-Pincywa (1976) on the social origins of DP cadres in Acholi.

11. I have some oral evidence from older Catholics on this issue. I want to thank Nelson Kasfir for reminding me of the coercive dimension.

12. Referring to the 1962 independence elections, Michael Twaddle writes, 'Vote-catching was more a matter of producing attractive patrons and policies . . . than a mindless positioning of the faithful' (1978, p. 261).

13. DP candidates won four of the five parliamentary seats in Kabarole district, as reported in Bwengye (1985, pp. 231–232).
14. See Mugaju (1982).
15. See Byabazaire (1979).
16. See Connelly (1981).
17. Bwamba, with a mixed Baamba and Bakonzo population, has only one parish and is not likely to be made into a diocese.
18. On extensive and intensive power, see Mann (1986, p. 7).
19. While I focus on Holy Communion in this section, another sacrament – 'ring marriage' (marriage recognized by the church and performed by a priest) – also has implications as a sign of commitment to the church.
20. It should be noted that catechists, sisters, and deacons are permitted to distribute Holy Communion, with or without the presence of a priest, once the host has been consecrated by a clergyman. In fact, many Catholics in rural areas most often receive the sacraments from their catechist, who periodically brings the consecrated hosts from the parish to the sub-parish centres.
21. In 1989, the bishop announced that attendance at meetings of an independent religious movement would be punished by requiring six months of catechism before being allowed to receive the sacraments.
22. Other socially orientated groups include women's clubs, which focus on handicrafts, home management, health care and literacy. With the development of the Women's Development Centre run by the Banyatereza Sisters, these groups are likely to become federated to the Centre. In addition, several lay members are employed to assist in the running of church development projects.
23. One priest at the National Catholic Secretariat claimed that the RC system was consciously modelled on the church council structure.
24. Elsewhere, Twaddle (1983) notes that, during the 1980 elections, the DP was popularly perceived in Buganda as constituting an ethnic party (i.e. for the Baganda) more than a religious one.
25. Bundibugyo district, one of the other two districts which were then part of Fort Portal diocese, was the first.
26. There is some precedent for the political activity of priests in Fort Portal diocese prior to the Obote II regime. One priest served briefly as mayor of Fort Portal town in the later years of Amin's regime, learning of his appointment on the radio without prior consultation. Another priest, now the vicar-general of the diocese, was treasurer of Kabarole district until mid-1980 under the interim Uganda National Liberation Front (UNLF) government after Amin's downfall.
27. Welbourn (1965, p. 10) refers to a 'regressive, minority culture' among Ugandan Catholics.
28. I discuss both the institutional and the symbolic expressions of this process for Buganda in Kassimir (1991).

References

Adutu, Jerome (1989) The laity and small Christian communities', Position Paper No. 7, Fort Portal Diocesan Synod.

Apter, David E. (1961) *The political kingdom in Uganda: A study of bureaucratic nationalism*, Princeton, (second edition 1967).

Bagaya, Princess Elizabeth of Toro (1983) *African princess*, London.

Bratton, Michael (1989) 'Review article: Beyond the state: Civil society and associational life in Africa', *World Politics* 41, 3, (1963) pp. 407–430.

Bullough, Sebastian (1963) *Roman Catholicism*, Baltimore, MD.

Bwengye, Francis A. W. (1985) *The Agony of Uganda: From Idi Amin to Obote*, London.

Byabazaire, Deogratias (1979) *The Contribution of the Christian churches to the development of western Uganda 1894-1974*, Frankfurt on Main.

Catholic Bishops of Uganda (1984) *Celebrating our ancestors in the faith*, Kisubi.

Connelly, James T. (1981) *Holy Cross in East Africa 1958-1980*, Notre Dame, IN.

Doornbos, Martin R. (1976) Ethnicity, Christianity, and the development of social stratification in colonial Ankole, Uganda', *International Journal of African Historical Studies*, 9, 4, pp. 555-575.

Gingyera-Pincywa, A. G. G. (1976) *Issues in pre-independence politics in Uganda: A case study on the contribution to political debate in Uganda in the decade 1952-1962*, Kampala.

Hansen, Holger Bernt (1984) *Mission, church and state in a colonial setting: Uganda 1890-1925*, London.

Ingham, Kenneth (1975) *The kingdom of Toro in Uganda*, London.

Kassimir, Ronald (1991) 'Complex martyrs: Symbols of Catholic Church formation and political differentiation in Uganda'. *African Affairs*, 90, 360, pp. 357-382.

Kisembo, Thomas (1974) *The planting of Christianity in Tooro with special reference to the Roman Catholic Church 1895-1928*, BA Thesis, Makerere University History Department.

Levine, Daniel H. (1981) *Religion and politics in Latin America: The Catholic Church in Venezuela and Colombia*, Princeton.

Levine, Daniel H. and Mainwaring Scott, (1986) 'Religion and popular protest in Latin America', Kellogg Institute Working Paper, No. 83, Notre Dame, IN.

Magambo, Bishop S. B. (1988) *The life and mission of lay people in Uganda*, Kisubi.

Mann, Michael (1986) *The sources of social power*, Volume 1, Cambridge.

Mugaju, J. B. (1982) 'The Uganda general election results of 1961, 1962 and 1980: A comparative study', University of Nairobi Department of History Paper No. 7.

Mulira, James (1980) 'The implications of "collaboration" between African nationalists and the communist world – a case study of Uganda 1945-62', *Uganda Journal* 39, pp. 1-17.

Nyakazingo, Moses (1973) 'Kasagama: A despotic and missionary king', *Occasional Research Papers in African Traditional Religion and Philosophy*, 9.

Pirouet, M. Louise (1968-1969) 'A comparison of the response of three societies to Christianity (Toro, Teso, Kikuyu)', University of East Africa Social Science Council Conference: Religious Studies Papers, pp. 36-50.

Pirouet, M. Louise (1978) *Black evangelists*, London.

Pizzomo, Alessandro (1986) 'Some other kinds of otherness: A critique of "rational choice" theories', in Foxley Alejandro, McPherson Michael S. and O'Donnell, Guillermo eds., *Development, democracy and the art of trespassing: Essays in honor of Albert O. Hirschman*, Notre Dame, IN.

Poggi, Gianfranco (1971) *Catholic action in Italy*, Stanford, CA.

Richards, A. I. (with Taylor, B. K.) (1959) 'The Toro', in Richards, Audrey I., ed., *East African chiefs*, London.

Rothchild, Donald and Rogin Michael, (1966) 'Uganda' in Carter, Gwendolyn M., ed., *National Unity and regionalism in eight African states*, Ithaca.

Steinhart, Edward I. (1973) 'Royal clientage and the beginnings of colonial modernization in Toro, 1891-1900', *International Journal of African Historical Studies*, 6, 2, pp. 265-285.

Twaddle, Michael (1978) 'Was the Democratic Party of Uganda a purely confessional party?', in Edward Fashole-Luke *et al.*, eds, *Christianity in independent Africa*, Bloomington, IN.

Twaddle, Michael (1983) Ethnic politics and support for political parties in Uganda', in Lyon, Peter, and Manor, James eds, *Transfer and transformation: Political institutions in the new Commonwealth: Essays in honour of W. H. Morris-Jones*, Leicester.

Waliggo, John Mary (1976) *The Catholic Church in the Buddu province of Buganda, 1879-1925*, History Department PhD Dissertation, Cambridge University.

Welbourn, F. B. (1965) *Religion and politics in Uganda 1952-62*, Nairobi.

Part Three

*Christians & Muslims
in Kenyan Politics*

Nine

'Render unto Caesar the Things that are Caesar's'

The Politics of Church–State Conflict in Kenya 1978–1990

DAVID THROUP

This essay will trace the growing political role of the main Protestant denominations and the Roman Catholic Church in Kenya since President Daniel arap Moi came to power in 1978. It suggests that the downfall of long-serving Attorney-General Charles Njonjo, just before the 1983 general election, had a profound effect on religious freedom. Njonjo's downfall coincided with the ascension of a new, populist generation of politicians in the ruling Kenya African National Union (KANU). The party's national executive after 1985 increasingly claimed authority to delineate the limits of legitimate political discourse, disciplining back-bench members of parliament (MPs) and clergy who overstepped the permitted bounds of debate. By 1990, with the death of Bishop Muge of Eldoret, this had produced a major crisis in church–state relations.

Church–state relations during the colonial period

During the colonial era all the main Protestant denominations active in Kenya had been politically quiescent. They 'possessed a very limited theology of secular power'. Most clergy and lay workers of the Church Missionary Society and the Church of Scotland Mission had belonged to the conservative evangelical tradition, with its belief in the strict authenticity of the Bible and the primacy of individual salvation. Both the Anglican and the Presbyterian Churches had developed a close, semi-establishment relationship with the state long before independence. From the 1920s, prominent clergymen, such as the Revd Dr Arthur of the Church of Scotland Mission in the 1920s and Archdeacon (later Bishop, then Archbishop) Beecher of the Church Missionary Society in the 1940s, had been nominated to represent African interests on the Legislative and Executive Councils.[1] The churches had been co-opted into the policy-making processes of the state. The onset of the Mau Mau emergency in 1952, with the Mau Mau fighters' avowedly anti-Christian ideology and the prominent role played by Kikuyu Christians in resisting the revolt, ensured that the mission societies and their successor African-controlled churches were identified with the colonial order.[2] This was particularly true of the Church Missionary Society. In his *Social history and Christian mission*, Max Warren, for many years General Secretary of the Church Missionary Society, pointed out that:

> Readers of Sir Michael Blundell's autobiography – *So Rough a Wind* – will find opposite page 192 a photograph taken at the new Legislative Council in Nairobi, Kenya, in 1951. In the foreground is Michael Blundell standing at the Despatch Box. In the background sits the Speaker under the Royal Arms. On the Speaker's right is the Governor-General in full uniform. On the Speaker's left is the Bishop of Mombasa in Convocation robes. In those days the boundaries of Mombasa coincided with the political territory of Kenya. That photograph is good documentary evidence of the reality of the Anglican quasi-establishment.[3]

And, as Adrian Hastings observed in *A history of African Christianity, 1950–1975*, so was the fact that the Bishop of Mombasa's residence in Nairobi was located 'immediately outside the gates of Government House'.[4]

This identification with the colonial order and consequent lack of nationalist legitimacy meant that the main denominational churches, including the Roman Catholics, were hesitant to become embroiled with the post-independence state, once the nationalists were in power. In contrast, the staff of the ecumenical National Christian Council of Kenya (NCCK), recruited in the 1950s to assist the post-Mau Mau reconstruction, were theologically more liberal and committed to a 'gospel as much social as individual'. The new recruits worked mainly in Nairobi and other towns, and they commented in NCCK-sponsored newspapers on political, social and economic developments during the last years of colonial rule. In Lonsdale's words, 'the NCCK was free to be "alongside" the new African politics ... in a way in which the local churches would have found difficult even if their leaders had thought it desirable'.[5]

The Kenyatta era

Throughout the Kenyatta era, relations between the government and the churches in Kenya remained relatively cordial. The president's brother-in-law Obadiah Kariuki had been the first African appointed an Anglican bishop in Kenya, while his wife's brother, Monsignor George Muhoho, served as Roman Catholic chaplain to the University of Nairobi. By independence in 1963, moreover, the NCCK had developed a co-operative relationship with the nationalist movement. There were, however, limits to this understanding. The attitude of many nationalist leaders, such as Tom Mboya, towards the churches and even the NCCK remained ambivalent. Mboya, in his book of collected speeches, *Freedom and after*, for example, 'in the same breath complained that the churches were slow to take up African grievances under colonialism, congratulated them when they did, and warned the church after independence to "preoccupy itself entirely with religious matters"'.[6]

During the 1960s, the theology taught at Saint Paul's United Theological College at Limuru, the training ground for young Protestant clergy in Kenya, shifted, reflecting the changing needs of the newly independent nation. In the early 1950s, the college had emphasized the conservative evangelical belief in individual salvation and had given little weight to the churches' Old Testament prophetic tradition. By the 1970s, however, new clergymen were being trained to preach a gospel of political and social responsibility.[7] Despite their hesitancy to become embroiled in politics, in 1969 the churches had spoken out against the oathing campaign among the Kikuyu, which began following the assassination of the Luo Minister Tom Mboya. While the secular press remained silent, unwilling to antagonize the government, the September 1969 issue of the NCCK-sponsored Target newspaper, under its first African editor, the Luo Henry Okullu – of whom we shall hear much more – had produced a front-page editorial, headlined 'Killing our unity', juxtaposed with a photograph of the administration of the sacrament, under the caption 'Taking the oath'.[8] This protest had been endorsed by all the churches, who issued statements condemning oathing, which soon ceased when action was taken against forced administration. As Kevin Ward pointed out, 'the churches' response to the oathing crisis showed the peculiar strength of the conservative evangelical tradition in repudiating the secular power – as incompatible with God's prior claims on Christian allegiance'.[9]

The political activism of both the NCCK and its constituent churches, however, had important limits. No church leader, for example, spoke out the following month when the opposition Kenya People's Union (KPU) was banned and its leaders detained without trial. Aware of the increasing Erastian influence of the state, Lonsdale, Booth-Clibborn and Hake concluded their article by warning that:

> The indigenous Kenyan tradition of evangelical Revival, clear-sighted in crisis and prophetic in its defence of Christian autonomy when need arises, is, because of its very suspicion of hierarchy and organization, peculiarly ill-fitted to perceive, let alone guard against, such routine envelopment.[10]

They considered that it remained to be determined whether 'the developing Kenyan evangelical tradition will in fact adopt a stance of "critical solidarity" with the State'.[11] The Anglican provost of Nairobi, Henry Okullu, who as editor of Target had led the 1969 campaign against oathing, agreed. In 1972, he warned the churches of the danger of living in 'the time of Constantine . . . who put the Church in his pocket by offering government protection'.[12] It is hardly surprising that Okullu, two decades later, remains one of Kenya's most outspoken clergymen.

Attorney-General Charles Njonjo was a prominent lay member of the Anglican Church of the Province of Kenya (CPK). From the mid-1960s until the early 1980s, Njonjo protected the churches from their critics within the ruling KANU. Njonjo and other cabinet ministers had, of course, periodically clashed with unruly clerics. As we have already noted, Henry Okullu had criticized the government on several occasions, castigating the pervasive materialist ethos and growing social inequality of Kenya's 'man eat man' society. Vocal pressure groups such as the All Africa Council of Churches, which had its headquarters in Nairobi, and its outspoken secretary-general, Canon Burgess Carr from Sierra Leone, had earned Njonjo's condemnation for criticizing Kenya's lukewarm condemnation of racialism in South Africa. The government eventually banned Carr from re-entering the country when he attempted to organize a human rights' conference, which Njonjo feared would be highly critical of Kenya.[13] Less influential church bodies also aroused the Attorney-General's suspicion, most notably Kenya's small community of Jehovah's Witnesses, who refused to swear an oath of allegiance to the state.[14] These instances, however, were rare. Church–state relations were in the main amicable. One reason for this was that the CPK, the Presbyterian Church of East Africa (PCEA) and the Roman Catholics after independence had all become increasingly dominated by Kikuyu churchmen and their congregations in Central Province, whose lay members often held influential positions in the government.

The early Moi years

The situation did not dramatically change during the first years of Daniel arap Moi's presidency. Njonjo remained Attorney-General until 1980, when he resigned from the civil service and was elected MP for Kikuyu in Kiambu district. Shortly afterwards he was reappointed to the cabinet as Minister for Constitutional Affairs, and continued to exert considerable influence within the government.[15] Moi's other main Kikuyu supporter was Mwai Kibaki, who became the new vice-president. Kibaki had been educated at Mangu High School, the leading Roman Catholic school, and had been the most prominent Catholic in the cabinet since the assassination of Tom Mboya in 1969. But, after the abortive attempted *coup d'état* of 1 August 1982, the situation rapidly changed. Two years earlier, the alliance between Kibaki and Njonjo had collapsed as the former Attorney-General attempted to undermine the vice-president's position, stigmatizing him as an unreconstructed protector of Kikuyu hegemony.[16] After the foiled coup, President Moi decided in 1983 to abandon his erstwhile ally in order to bolster his own political position. The president disliked over-mighty subjects who had built up their own network of supporters in the National Assembly. Thus, by 1983, the major churches had lost their two most influential defenders.[17]

Following Njonjo's downfall, President Moi attempted to purge the party of unreliable elements associated with the disgraced former Attorney-General. Gradually, during 1984, as the Commission of Inquiry into Njonjo's activities progressed, his supporters were expelled from KANU and driven out of the National Assembly.[18] Meanwhile, President Moi continued to reduce the influence of Kikuyu within the civil service and the military, and to shift state resources and patronage from Kikuyu areas and businesses to other parts of the country, especially to his own Kalenjin area in the Rift Valley and to Western Province. The purge of the state apparatus culminated in the 1985 KANU elections, when a new clique, closely identified with the president, swept to power at KANU national headquarters. The party now became the most important institution in the state, disciplining recalcitrant back-bench MPs as it sought to enforce support for Moi's *Nyayo* ideology of 'love, peace and unity'. No longer did President Moi promise, as in 1978, to follow in the footsteps of President Kenyatta, but increasingly he required others to accept his rulings and to follow in his footsteps as expounded by KANU's new national executive. Soon the main churches and the NCCK clashed with the revivified KANU, as the ruling party sought to silence criticism of the regime. By 1985, four church leaders had already been identified as critics of the ruling party – CPK bishops Henry Okullu, Alexander Kipsang Muge and David Gitari, and the Revd Dr Timothy Njoya of Saint Andrew's

Church, Nairobi, the most prominent Presbyterian congregation in the capital.[19]

Bishop Alexander Muge of Eldoret

The Right Revd Alexander Muge had served for several years in the élite paramilitary General Service Unit (GSU). Born at Kimn'goror in Nandi district in 1948, Muge had become a priest in the mid-1970s, and had been posted to Saint Mary's, a Nairobi parish. Muge had been an outspoken critic of Kikuyu domination of the CPK and of the Kenya state. Despatched to take a theology degree at King's College, London University, shortly before Kenyatta's death in 1978, he had returned to Kenya in 1982 to find the process of dismantling Kikuyu hegemony well advanced. Once again, Muge soon emerged as a stalwart opponent of Kikuyu power in and out of the church. From his new pulpit as vice-provost of Nairobi cathedral – an appointment itself demonstrating the decline of Kikuyu power within the Anglican Church – Muge assailed 'tribalism'. By 1982, however, Kikuyu influence in the civil service and leading positions in the parastatal sector and state support for Kikuyu businesses had already been drastically reduced since the Kenyatta era, as President Moi attempted to promote his own Kalenjin and Abaluhya supporters. When it was decided to divide the diocese of Nakuru into two parts, Muge was a popular choice to become the new bishop of Eldoret, the first Kalenjin bishop. Most people saw his election as a further manifestation of growing Kalenjin influence, as even the Kikuyu-dominated CPK sought to come to terms with the Moi regime by promoting a prominent Kalenjin cleric to the House of Bishops.[20]

Muge arrived in Eldoret shortly before the 1983 general election. Daniel arap Moi, a Tugen from Baringo district, had never been the most popular Kalenjin politician, despite the fact that he had occupied the vice-presidency since January 1967. Both Jean Marie Seroney from Nandi and Taita Towett from Kericho had resented Moi's abandonment of the former opposition party, Kenya African Democratic Union (KADU), shortly after independence, in order to come to terms with the emerging Kikuyu political hegemony. In 1979, therefore, the new president was determined to assert control over his own Kalenjin political balliwick, bringing the whole Kalenjin coalition, rather than simply Baringo district, under firm control. Both the provincial administration and the GSU were deployed to secure the victory of Moi's associates, ousting virtually every sitting Kalenjin MP. The 1983 elections in Nandi were also rigged to ensure the return of the president's supporters. Once again, the field administration and the GSU were deployed to support approved candidates, including an old school friend of President Moi's, Stanley Metto in Mosop, Bishop Muge's home constituency.[21]

Shocked by the behaviour of the GSU and by the widespread intimidation of voters, the newly arrived Muge had protested to the provincial commissioner, challenging the validity of Metto's election. Relations between the bishop and District Commissioner Cyrus Gituai, newly elected MP Metto, who was appointed Assistant Minister of Education, and Metto's allies on the Nandi Country Council never recovered. Metto was soon asserting that the bishop was a close associate of Njonjo's, distributing old photographs of Muge welcoming the disgraced Attorney-General to Nairobi cathedral. The MP claimed that Njonjo was secretly financing CPK schemes in order to create discord in the area. Metto even claimed that the bishop was plotting to murder him. The country council withdrew its authorization for the church to build a dispensary at Kimn'goror, Muge's home village, and began to remove CPK adherents from school boards throughout the district and to withdraw funding from CPK-sponsored schools, dispensaries and water projects.[22]

Muge was so concerned that he sought assistance from Archbishop Kuria and his fellow bishops. Bishop David Gitari was dispatched by his colleagues to see the Nandi district commissioner, while the secretary-general of the NCCK and the head of the Kenya Christian Educational Association sought an interview with the Permanent Secretary in the Ministry of Education to explain the CPK's problems with the political leadership in Nandi. Meanwhile, the situation in the district continued to deteriorate as rumours of the bishop's involvement with Njonjo and in the plot to murder Metto spread. Finally, Archbishop Kuria was forced to seek an interview with Police Commissioner Bernard Njinu in an attempt to clear Muge's name by securing the publication of the police report into the case. Thus, despite his identification with Moi's dismantling of Kikuyu hegemony, Bishop Muge fell foul of local political rivalries.[23]

Moi was especially concerned by criticism from his own Kalenjin base, recognizing that his popularity in Nandi and Kericho, the most populous and developed Kalenjin districts, was precarious. Eldoret, the site of Muge's diocesan cathedral, was a particularly sensitive area. It was a rapidly expanding town, whose population had grown from less than 20,000 at independence in 1963 to over 100,000 twenty years later, on the border between the Kalenjin and Abaluhya. The president's two main ethnic bases of support were locked in conflict to control the town's politics and its commercial and industrial expansion, while in the surrounding rural areas landless Abaluhya and Kalenjin were squatting on the farms of notables. The social and economic problems of the region exemplified not only Kenya's social tensions but also the ethnic and class strains within President Moi's precarious political coalition.[24]

Phase one of the queuing controversy

Since August 1986, the main Protestant churches and the NCCK, and
to a lesser extent the Roman Catholic hierarchy, have been locked in
conflict with Kenya's political leaders. The confrontation began when
KANU's national executive proposed to the party's annual delegates'
conference on 19 August that elections to the National Assembly should
be reformed. Technically, since the banning of the opposition KPU in
1969, Kenya's multi-candidate elections had been a primary within the
ruling party. The victor in the KANU primary had then been returned
unopposed in the general election to the National Assembly. Now
KANU proposed that National Assembly elections should be divided
into two parts: a formal KANU primary, where, as in other KANU
elections, only party members should be allowed to participate, and
a second-round run-off between the three leading candidates, where all
adult Kenyans could participate in those constituencies where no one
had secured more than 70 per cent of the primary vote. The most
contentious element of the proposals was the decision to abolish the
secret ballot in the first round, the KANU primary, so that voters would
have to queue behind the candidate of their choice. Even during the
1985 KANU elections, civil servants, teachers and clergymen had
protested that they should not have publicly to reveal their political
preferences, and had received an assurance from KANU's secretary-
general that an alternative would be devised.[25]

In contrast to the 1985 debate, the 1986 KANU decision ignited a
furore. The confrontation was exacerbated because the KANU delegates' conference coincided with a five-yearly gathering of clergy sponsored by the NCCK. Thus, criticism of the KANU national governing
council's decision to abolish the secret ballot and to institute a formal
KANU primary, consolidating party control over the electoral process,
appeared to come not from individual clergymen but from the Protestant churches as institutions. The NCCK and the Law Society seemed
to be directly opposing the will of the ruling party. NCCK Secretary-
General John Kamau issued a statement, cautiously requesting KANU
'to find an alternative method in which church leaders can exercise their
democratic rights as members of this nation'.[26]

Exasperated by the recent clashes between MPs and the churches,
many politicians seized the opportunity to demonstrate the primacy
of the party over all other institutions in the country. Prominent
clergymen, many argued, seemed to consider themselves absolved from
the normal rules of Kenyan political life. Certainly, they had got away
with allegations which would have resulted in detention for private
citizens or even dissident politicians. Some even contended that the
NCCK had chosen this late moment to express its disagreement as
a deliberate affront to KANU, which had considered the proposals at

length. KANU Chairman Amayo, for example, alleged that some clerics wanted a confrontation in order to cause misunderstanding and chaos. Biwott, the president's former private secretary, urged those churches which did not approve of the NCCK's declaration to leave the organization. Minister of Education Peter Oloo Aringo claimed that the NCCK was being used by foreigners to create chaos and to discredit the government.[27]

Under this barrage of pressure, some of the less well-established churches decided that it would be wise to disassociate from the NCCK. Bishop Daniel Kirugo of the African Independent Pentecostal Church and the annual conference of the Full Gospel Church, along with the Association of Baptist Churches in Nyeri and the United Pentecostal Church, all expressed support for KANU and the new electoral system. Indeed, Tadeo Mwaura, the national chairman of the African Independent Pentecostal Church endorsed some of the wilder allegations and urged that the NCCK should be investigated, warning that it 'should not be allowed to ruin the country'.[28]

Most church leaders, however, refused to back down. The most outspoken were the Revd Timothy Njoya of Saint Andrew's Presbyterian Church in Nairobi and Bishop Muge of Eldoret, both theological conservatives. Their forthright stance was supported by more moderate clerics, including Archbishop Kuria and the Right Revd Ndingi Mwanza a'Nzeki, the chairman of the Roman Catholic Episcopal Conference, despite the fact that the Roman Catholics were not members of the NCCK.[29] The archbishop warned that politicians should not underestimate the depth of popular discontent and opposition to the abolition of secret-ballot elections. Bishop Okullu of Maseno South also cautioned the nation's political leaders, pointing out that 'the number of people who were secretly in support of the NCCK's stand is too staggering to appreciate'. Unlike Kuria, who was known to have been favoured by Njonjo, Okullu was immune from attack from those who attempted to stigmatize Muge and the archbishop as associates of the disgraced politician.[30]

John Kamau, the NCCK secretary-general, attempted to defuse the crisis, assuring the press that the churches had not intended to provoke a conflict with KANU. In contrast, Muge, addressing the CPK Youth Organization, warned that 'the church couldn't compromise theological issues with secular or temporal matters'. He urged the church to protest 'when God-given rights and liberties are violated'. The church in Africa, where there were so many one-party states, Muge argued, had a special duty to 'give voice to the voiceless'. It was 'the role of the church to stand up against the pressures of totalitarianism in the name of one party systems and against the detention of political opponents without trial'.[31]

Bishop Muge and the politics of Nandi district

Muge's comments exacerbated his own problems in Nandi and Uasin Gishu districts. In his address to the NCCK conference session on 'Church and society in search of justice', Muge had been highly critical of KANU. He had highlighted several recent corruption cases, quoting sections from the 1983–1984 Public Accounts report in order to demonstrate 'how millions of shillings are lost through open fraud and misappropriation'. Few politicians had forgotten his caustic remarks and many suspected that Muge had been the driving force behind the NCCK's opposition to the electoral changes.[32]

His opponents in Nandi were determined to discredit the bishop. The attack was led by his old rival from Mosop, Stanley Metto, who was joined by Henry Kosgey, the only cabinet minister from the district, and Samuel arap Ngeny, the deputy speaker of the National Assembly. Hitherto, Kosgey, whose relations with President Moi were deteriorating as the president found more pliable allies, had carefully avoided taking sides in the dispute, while arap Ngeny appeared to sympathize with the bishop, having himself clashed with Metto for abusing his position as Assistant Minister for Education in his vendetta against the CPK. Both politicians now came under renewed political pressure to distance themselves from Muge and to rally round the district's KANU leaders. Arap Ngeny's position was particularly difficult as not only was he known to be a rival of Metto's, but he was also a prominent lay members of the CPK in Nandi. A similar meeting took place in Uasin Gishu district under the leadership of Councillor Noah Teigut, the local KANU boss and chairman of Wareng County Council. Here too, several speakers denounced Muge, accusing him of opposing the government and calling upon the CPK to dismiss him as bishop. As in Nandi, the Uasin Gishu leaders decided that Muge should not be allowed to address church meetings, especially a major Christian rally that was to take place the following weekend at Eldoret municipal stadium.[33]

The underlying cause of the conflict in Nandi was the long-running rivalry between adherents of the CPK and the African Inland Church. Over three-quarters of the councillors and local leaders, who had attended the meetings to condemn Muge, were members of the African Inland Church, to which President Moi belongs. By attacking Muge and identifying the CPK as anti-government, the Bishop and his supporters claimed the African Inland Church was attempting to weaken Anglican influence. 'AIC [African Inland Church] and CPK pastors', Muge observed, 'should come together, pray together and then go out and tell their followers that they serve the same God and should not allow politicians to use the church for their own gains.'[34]

Muliro, Rubia and wa Nyoike and the defence of political debate

Only three prominent politicians dared to support the NCCK's opposition to queuing. Former cabinet ministers Masinde Muliro and Charles Rubia had long had a reputation for independence. Muliro had been dropped from the cabinet in 1975 for supporting the back-bench revolt approving the inquiry into the murder of Josiah Mwangi Kariuki, the radical Kikuyu politician, while Rubia, who had been the first African mayor of Nairobi from 1963 to 1969, had been dropped by Kenyatta as an assistant minister in 1974, for being too sympathetic to radical back-benchers, and by President Moi in 1983, because he had proved too vociferous a defender of Kikuyu power. The third defender of the churches, Kimani wa Nyoike, was a flamboyant Kikuyu trades union official, who was soon to be detained for contacts with the dissident *Mwakenya* movement. Elected to Parliament in 1979, wa Nyoike had remained a political maverick even after becoming Assistant Minister of Labour.[35]

Muliro was Kenya's leading old-style liberal and defender of human rights and free speech. First elected to the National Assembly in 1958, he had been under attack since his 1975 dismissal from the cabinet from Kalenjin politicians in Kitale, who were allies of Bishop Muge's opponents in Eldoret and Nandi. He urged politicians to show respect for church leaders and asserted that democracy was not merely the preserve of politicians. Indeed, the country needed to be protected from their 'intolerance and arrogance'. Muliro declared that 'criticism of the proposed polling method should not be taken in bad faith, since such criticism could enhance Kenya's reputation as a democratic one-party state that works'.[36] Rubia also defended the NCCK, denouncing cabinet ministers and KANU officials at a press conference for undermining freedom of speech. The former Kikuyu cabinet minister observed that 'democracy is not the monopoly of politicians'.[37]

President Moi intervened to end the controversy, declaring that clergymen, civil servants and members of the armed forces would be exempt from queuing and would be permitted to vote in primary elections by proxy. Moi revealed his anger by declaring that the behaviour of the NCCK in recent weeks had made him doubt its protestations of loyalty to the ruling party. The Revd John Gatu, the former moderator of the Presbyterian Church, attempted to repair relations, praising the president for averting 'a situation that was pregnant with restlessness'. His decision, the moderator asserted, revealed 'the hand of the Holy Spirit which had guided him to arrive at the solution'.[38]

An attempt to undermine the National Christian Council

Despite Archbishop Kuria's attempt to reaffirm the CPK's loyalty to the government, assuring President Moi that the CPK supported the one-party system and that it 'would not act contrary to the interests of the government nor associate with those who aim to undermine the government', church–state relations remained poor. The revitalized KANU did not know how to accommodate conservative evangelical churchmen. Provocative sermons by Njoya, Muge and Okullu did little to improve the situation as they continued to castigate corruption and political harassment of the churches. On 5 October 1986, for example, Njoya in a sermon heavily laden with comments on current political issues, called for a debate among all Kenyans, including 'fugitives, dissidents and malcontents'. Even worse, the Presbyterian minister had criticized growing social inequalities and corruption, and had prayed for Odinga and Njonjo – the two arch-dissidents of Kenyan politics – and described the confrontation between the NCCK and KANU as one between the righteous and the unrighteous, with 'the righteous wanting to maximise reason in economics, politics and community, and the unrighteous wanting to maximise their own power and wealth unreasonably and by unreasonable means'.[39] President Moi responded in kind, denouncing 'subversion in the church', when he welcomed a delegation from the African Gospel Church of Kericho district to his Kabarnet home six days later, while Assistant Minister for Foreign Affairs Ochola Mak'Anyengo condemned Njoya for promoting the interests of Charles Njonjo. Many politicians doubted Njoya's loyalty to the regime, despite his support of the one-party state, and identified the cleric with the *Mwakenya* dissidents. The churches had moved a long way from their politically quiescent stance in the first years after independence.[40]

The queuing controversy came to life again in November 1986, when Attorney-General Muli finally introduced the Constitution of Kenya (Amendment) Bill, 1986. Opposition to the Bill was led by B. M. Kariuki, chairman of the Law Society, rather than by the NCCK, although the churches did point out that changes to the constitution should only have been introduced after a protracted public debate.[41] The NCCK also issued a memorandum, signed by Bishop Lawi Imathiu of the Methodist Church and NCCK General-Secretary John Kamau. Imathiu was probably the senior cleric with the best relations with the political establishment. Under President Kenyatta he had served a term as a nominated MP and had preserved close contact with KANU leaders under the Moi regime. Unlike some CPK bishops, Imathiu had adopted a conciliatory line during the queuing controversy, attempting to mediate between the NCCK and KANU. The NCCK's memorandum warned that:

> The constitution of Kenya was formulated after almost four years of careful considerations about the necessary elements that would guarantee and safeguard democracy and the interests of all Kenyans. It is important to recall that the political scenario within which the constitution was formulated assumed a multi-party state. It therefore provides checks and balances which, if tampered with, would undermine the very basis of the stability they are meant to safeguard. If that was the case for a multi-party state, it is even more so for a one-party state.[42]

Despite Imathiu's caution, Mombasa KANU chairman Sharriff Nassir seized the opportunity to criticize the churches once again. Minister of Labour Peter Okondo also joined the fray. President Moi reiterated his warning that 'religion must not be dragged into politics and church leaders should confine themselves to the spiritual aspect of life, leaving politics to the politicians'. Church pulpits, he asserted, 'should not be turned into political platforms'.[43]

The situation of the main Protestant churches became even worse towards the end of 1986, when one of the NCCK's employees, Dr Walter Osewe, was charged with being a member of *Mwakenya*. Osewe confessed that he had been recruited to enlist prominent clergymen in the CPK, Presbyterian and Roman Catholic Churches. His allegations appeared to confirm charges by Gakaara Wanjau, the Kikuyu author and former Mau Mau detainee, who had claimed in April 1986 that *Mwakenya* was attempting to manipulate church leaders and encouraging them to oppose the Moi government. It seemed to confirm the worst attacks of politicians, and encouraged David Onyancha, the MP for West Mugirango, to call for a full security investigation into the affairs of the NCCK and its relations with *Mwakenya*.[44]

The 1988 general election and the subsequent KANU election brought queuing back to the forefront of political debate. Once more, Bishop Muge claimed that the general election in Nandi district, which unseated moderate Cabinet Minister Henry Kosgey, had been rigged. Catholic Bishop Ndingi Mwanza a'Nzeki pointed out that queues could be manipulated and intimidated even more easily than voters in a secret-ballot election. Minister for National Guidance and Political Affairs James Njiru, CPK Bishop David Gitari's old foe in Kirinyaga, however, informed the press immediately after the final round that queuing was no longer an issue.[45]

The humbling of Njoya and Muge

The two most outspoken clerical critics of the regime – the Revd Dr Timothy Njoya of Saint Andrew's, Nairobi, and Bishop Muge of Eldoret – both faced major problems throughout 1987–1989, and were forced to come to terms with the government. Njoya, as noted earlier, had been denounced by President Moi for his 5 October 1986 sermon, urging the government to open debate with its critics, including *Mwakenya* members and other exiles who had fled abroad.' The Presbyterian minister seemed determined to antagonize the government, regardless of the interests of the PCEA, which, like the CPK, was dominated by Kikuyu clerics and Central Province congregations.

After failing to secure a reprimand for Njoya from Saint Andrew's presbytery, Wanjau, the PCEA's new moderator, decided that the Nairobi cleric would have to be moved. In February 1987, therefore, the moderator proposed that Njoya be transferred to Kirima presbytery in his home district of Nyeri. Wanjau's decision was supported by former Moderator John Gatu, and Presbyterian Church Secretary-General the Revd Dr Plawson Kuria. All three men, like Njoya, were Kikuyu. They were concerned that Njoya's outspoken remarks would endanger the Presbyterian Church's previously cordial relationship with the government, identifying it in the public mind as a bastion of Kikuyu power.[46] Njoya fought their decision but was finally overruled and opted to leave the ministry rather than go to Nyeri. After a year of continuing conflict with the church authorities, however, he was compelled to seek reconciliation and agreed to move to Nyeri, stripped of his position as a pastor.[47] Even in Kirima, Njoya continued to attract the interest of both the press and the Special Branch, appearing with members of his congregation to browbeat the district commissioner when he was summoned to appear before the Nyeri District Security Committee in August 1989. Although chastened by his banishment, Njoya refused to be silenced.[48]

In contrast, Bishop Muge in 1988 did not run foul of the CPK leadership, but came into open conflict with President Moi. Muge's Eldoret diocese covered six mainly Kalenjin districts – Nandi, Uasin Gishu, Trans Nzoia, Elgeyo-Marakwet, West Pokot and Turkana. Hitherto, although the bishop had alienated many Nandi leaders and politicians in Eldoret town and the surrounding Uasin Gishu district, the church had continued to operate relatively untroubled in the four other areas. In 1984, the most senior of the three Pokot MPs, Francis Lotodo, had been arrested and charged with subversion for arming some local residents to resist the *Ngoroko* bandit incursions from Karamoja.[49] Lotodo, however, had been readmitted to KANU just before the 1988 general election and had been triumphantly returned to parliament, along with his political ally, Samuel Poghisio. Both men were closely identified with the CPK and the local bishop, Muge. Before his election, Poghisio had been the diocesan development co-ordinator in the district and had worked closely with Bishop Muge. The district administration and the third Pokot MP, Assistant Minister Christopher Lomada, resented Lotodo's return to political prominence and were determined to discredit him. Because of Poghisio's prominent role in local CPK affairs, the church and Bishop Muge became identified with the pro-Lotodo faction.[50]

Muge had organized a press conference in Nairobi in mid-June 1988, on his return from a two-day tour of Kacheliba division, a semi-arid region, dependent on livestock, which had been severely hit by the 1984 drought and by continued cattle rustling. The bishop claimed that people throughout the area were suffering from acute malnutrition as a result of widespread famine, castigated the district administration's callous inactivity and claimed that it had hindered rather than assisted the church's relief efforts.[51] The bishop's remarks created a national uproar. President Moi visited the district, addressing a large rally at Makutano on 20 June, which had been organized rapidly by the local administration. Following the rally, the leadership of the local KANU branch was purged, and Lotodo and Poghisio were expelled from the ruling party and the National Assembly. At the ensuing by-elections, allies of Assistant Minister Lomada, sympathetic to District Commissioner Lagat, were returned. As the purge continued, virtually everyone associated with Lotodo or with the CPK was driven from office, including the Revd D. M. Tumkou, the chairman of the Kapenguria Urban Council, and the chairman, treasurer and two other senior officers of the local KANU branch. During the next year, the district commissioner dismissed eleven chiefs and fifteen assistant chiefs associated with the CPK. Meanwhile, the district administration and the CPK fought for control over several church-sponsored schools.[52]

The bishop was in the news again in September 1989, following a sermon at All Saints' Cathedral, Nairobi, in which he called upon the government to release all detainees and asserted that free discussion and constructive criticism were essential to the well-being of democracy. The same month the bishop denounced the administration in Pokot once again. Muge claimed that the district commissioner, in alliance with Assistant Minister Lomada, was systematically attempting to destroy the influence of the CPK in the district, obstructing the church's development schemes, interfering in CPK-sponsored schools and purging adherents from positions of influence throughout the district. When Education Minister Peter Oloo Aringo and the West Pokot KANU branch intervened to support the district commissioner, the confrontation threatened to develop into a wider controversy. The affair raised the issue of the power over such schools under the 1968 Education Act of sponsoring agencies, like the CPK and other churches.

The CPK, the Presbyterian Church and the Roman Catholics insisted upon 'the maintenance of the religious tradition' and Christian morality in the institutions they sponsored. Churches had the right to nominate the head-teacher with the agreement of the ministry and the Teachers' Service Commission. Thus, the local squabble threatened to draw the other churches, including the Roman Catholics, into confrontation with the state.[53]

Determined not to be intimidated by the district commissioner, who had banned him from the district on 13 September, the next day Bishop Muge assembled a massive procession of cars and trucks to escort him into West Pokot. He took with him most of the staff from diocesan headquarters in Eldoret and several journalists to record his progress from Eldoret through Kitale and Makutano – the main town in West Pokot – on to Ortum, a small shopping centre on the border with Turkana district in the north. The bishop declared that he would return, accompanied by Christians from throughout the diocese, on Sunday, 24 September. He warned:

> Not even persecution will deter me from visiting West Pokot or any other part of my diocese . . . Just as Amos was commissioned by God to fight evil, we have to challenge anything that is ungodly. God has appointed us to be watchmen against evil in West Pokot and Kenya as a whole.[54]

Bishop Muge appeared driven to become a martyr. His conservative evangelical faith underpinned the cleric's determination to resist state interference in church affairs and to proclaim the church's prophetic tradition of resistance to mere secular power.

The KANU secretary-general's attack on religious freedom

In the meantime, Bishop David Gitari of Mount Kenya East had aroused the anger of KANU's newly elected secretary-general, Moses Mudavadi, when he had dared to criticize the calibre of the delegates chosen to attend the annual KANU delegates' conference on 25 September 1988 and the openness of the debates. Gitari claimed that the delegates were unrepresentative of local opinion and had merely 'rubber-stamped' decisions that had been taken by the ruling party's national executive. Mudavadi condemned such an outright attack on the party and threatened that steps might be taken to curtail freedom of worship if clergymen continued to make such subversive claims.[55]

Secretary-General Mudavadi, however, had gone too far, uniting clergymen from all the main churches behind the CPK. The clerics not only stressed the constitution's commitment to freedom of worship, but invoked the name of God to defend this 'God-given right', which was 'not a privilege granted by governments'. Archbishop Kuria was outspoken in defence of his colleague, condemning politicians who seemed to seize every opportunity to criticize the church and to make false accusations of foreign involvement. Bishop of Eldoret Alexander Muge observed that the secretary-general's proposals would inevitably mean that 'our country will be made an atheistic state'. Muge warned that if such legislation was introduced the government would be confronted by massive civil disobedience because the majority of Christians 'will continue to worship, whether Mudavadi likes it, or not'.[56] It was clear that the government and KANU could not win such a confrontation with the churches. They were too widely respected among all levels of Kenya society, commanding the loyalty of the majority of the population at all social levels. Vice-President Karanja attempted to extricate KANU from the crisis, assuring the National Assembly that the government had no intention of curtailing freedom of worship or of interfering in church affairs. Quoting Archbishop Kuria's statement, the vice-president declared that the government was fully satisfied by the primate's assurance that the CPK supported the government. For once, the CPK emerged victorious. As the *Weekly Review* observed, Mudavadi had made 'a major blunder'.[57]

The churches as the voice of dissidence and the decline of Kikuyu power

Only church leaders have the freedom to criticize the government without risking detention. The CPK, Presbyterian and Roman Catholic Churches have occupied the ground emptied by the silencing of serious political opposition since the attempted coup and Njonjo's downfall in 1982–1983. KANU's rise to pre-eminence has produced a more paranoid era in Kenyan politics. Church–state controversy was not unknown during Kenyatta's presidency but confrontations between the religious and secular leadership have become much more frequent under President Moi. Although few clergymen oppose the regime, many are concerned that civil liberties have been curtailed and freedom of expression restricted. KANU has become so powerful since 1985, overriding the independence of MPs and even cabinet ministers, while the press has become much more cautious, until only senior ecclesiastical figures dare defend civil rights and condemn intimidation and corruption.[58]

The CPK and the Presbyterian church are the most powerful and 'established' of Kenya's Protestant churches. Both have grown out of colonial mission societies – the Anglican Church Missionary Society for the CPK and the Church of Scotland Mission for the Presbyterians. But, although both churches have moved far from their colonial past – indeed, the Right Revd David Gitari even called at the 1988 Lambeth Conference of Bishops for a more liberal attitude towards polygamy – they have preserved close contacts, like Kenya's Roman Catholic community, with the wider Christian world and can less easily be intimidated than the Kenya-based independent churches.[59]

Both churches have been dominated since independence by their Kikuyu congregations in Central Province and Nairobi. This identification reflects the former missionary societies' religious and educational concentration upon Central Province and the responsiveness of the Kikuyu to these new opportunities. But, whereas the political and business leadership has been opened under President Moi to incorporate Kalenjin, Abaluhya and Luo members, among others, many people still identify the CPK and the Presbyterian Church with Kikuyu domination. In September 1990, for example, after twelve years of the Moi presidency and the dismantling of Kikuyu hegemony in the state, five of the twelve CPK bishops were Kikuyu. The moderator, former moderator, and secretary-general of the Presbyterian Church were also Kikuyu. Both denominations, moreover, were weak in the Kalenjin heartland of President Moi. Bishop Muge of Eldoret was the first Kalenjin bishop and had himself, of course, first attracted press attention when serving in Nairobi as a critic of Kikuyu control within the CPK as well as in state institutions. As the *Weekly Review* commented:

> A number of Parliamentarians [have] declared that both the CPK and the PCEA represented 'foreign interests'. But there was also the view that both churches represented tribal interests; both have their biggest influence and most fervent congregations in Central Province, and in the politics of the day, they are bound to be looked at with suspicion when they seem to take a dissenting view from government or party policy.[60]

In contrast, the African Inland Church, which contemplated withdrawing from the NCCK, was strongest in the Kalenjin areas of the Rift Valley.

The Roman Catholic Church is less identified with one particular ethnic group, having spread throughout the country with congregations in virtually every district. Although the Right Revd Ndingi Mwana a'Nzeki, the Roman Catholic bishop of Nakuru and former secretary of the Kenya Catholic Bishops' Conference, has been as willing to speak out on political matters as any of the CPK or Presbyterian church leaders, he has attracted much less criticism than Gitari, Muge, Okullu, Kuria or Njoya. The Catholic Church invariably presented a united front to the political establishment, issuing pastoral letters signed by the whole Kenya hierarchy or making statements through the chairman of the Kenya Episcopal Conference rather than through individual sermons. As a result, these comments were regarded as the official view of the whole Catholic Church. Politicians who would have condemned individual priests or bishops hesitated to attack the whole Catholic, hierarchy.[61]

The Presbyterian Church has been viewed with suspicion ever since the beginnings of the Njonjo affair in 1983, when a prayer meeting at Ruringu in Kiambu district was denounced for appearing to support the disgraced minister. The situation had deteriorated after Njoya's 1984 sermon at Saint Andrew's Church in Nairobi. Although he had criticized the former Attorney-General as a self-righteous individual, whose arrogant behaviour in power had led to his downfall, many politicians had perceived his remarks as an attack upon the processes leading to the ex-minister's disgrace and a manifestation of Kikuyu ethnic solidarity by the Presbyterian clergyman, and perhaps by his distinguished, Kikuyu-dominated congregation and the whole Presbyterian Church. As we have noted, PCEA leaders attempted to distance the church from Njoya, but they failed to dispel the suspicion that its Kikuyu members and clergy were not fully behind the policies of the Moi government, especially its dismantling of Kikuyu hegemony.[62]

Although Archbishop Kuria sought to moderate the remarks of his more outspoken colleagues, especially Bishop Okullu, a Luo, and Bishop Muge, a Kalenjin, whom many had expected to be close to President Moi and his associates, the primate had even less control over disputatious bishops than the PCEA elders had over Njoya. Muge, Okullu and Gitari could only be disciplined by their own diocesan synods. The archbishop himself, ever since the queuing controversy of October 1986, had attempted to rebuild relations with KANU, but his efforts had been undemined by criticism of the party by other bishops and church leaders.[63]

Bishop Okullu and the Revd Dr Timothy Njoya question the future of the one-party state

Okullu was in the news once more at the end of 1989, when he drew a sharp comparison between events during 1989 in Eastern Europe, culminating in the overthrow of Ceauşescu's dictatorship in Romania, and the prevalence of dictatorships and one-party rule throughout Africa. The bishop predicted that African dictators would experience a similar fate within the next five years. The Revd Dr Timothy Njoya was even more outspoken in a New Year's Eve sermon to his former congregation at Saint Andrew's Church, Nairobi. Njoya asserted that recent events in Eastern Europe demonstrated that one-party states failed to meet the demands of their people and were inherently undemocratic. Kwame Nkrumah and Nyerere had imported them into Africa where they had degenerated, like the communist parties of Eastern Europe and the Soviet Union, into unpopular, corrupt tyrannies.[64]

The sermon provided an opportunity for KANU leaders to defend one-party rule and to castigate multi-party democracy as likely to lead to ethnic conflict and fragmentation. The limitations on political discourse in Kenya were revealed by Elijah Mwangale, who demanded that Njoya should be detained, while Nandi KANU Chaiman Mark arap Too and Minister for Energy Biwott denounced the Presbyterian cleric for making 'tribal and prejudicial statements under the cover of theology'. Assistant Minister for Livestock Development Reuben Cheshire even demanded that Njoya should be defrocked. More intemperate figures within the KANU leadership speculated about a conspiracy involving dissident clergy and journalists and wondered why the *Daily Nation* had devoted more attention to Njoya's sermon than to Vice-President Saitoti's considered defence of one-party rule.[65]

Presbyterian Church Moderator George Wanjau attempted to adopt an air of quiet indifference to the uproar, although he did try to disassociate the church from Njoya, saying that the sermon had merely expressed the clergyman's own opinion rather than the official attitude of the PCEA, and former moderator John Gatu explained that 'it would be a grievous mistake to assume that whatever a church minister says is the view of the entire congregation or even the church in question'. But both refused to condemn Njoya. Indeed, Wanjau acknowledged that the clergy had a duty to 'continue speaking the truth and not to remain quiet while things went wrong'.[66]

Politicians, in contrast, could not resist widening the scope of their attacks to denounce other unruly clerics as well as Njoya. The CPK had been even more critical of KANU than the Presbyterian Church. Bishops David Gitari, Alexander Muge and Henry Okullu had been particularly persistent critics of the ruling party, castigating the failings of the political establishment. The NCCK also posed an easy target under its new chairman, Okullu. Aringo, for one, denounced Bishop Okullu and declared that the NCCK was riddled with 'anti-government agitators' and had been transformed into an opposition faction. The Minister of Education, who had also been elected KANU national chairman in 1988, urged churches loyal to the regime to consider their membership, only to attract the withering condemnation of the new NCCK Secretary-General Samuel Kobia, who dismissed his remarks as 'utter nonsense'.[67] The prospects of church–state reconciliation in 1990 appeared dim. Muge even suggested that the three main Protestant churches – the CPK, the Presbyterians and the Methodists – should form a union to strengthen their influence, enabling them to speak out against social evils. This proposal was immediately condemned by MPs. Assistant Minister for Culture and Social Services

Ochola Mak'Anyengo claimed that Muge had advocated the union 'for political reasons', intending to form an opposition against KANU.[68]

At the end of April 1990, the Right Revd Henry Okullu returned to his critique of one-party rule and called again for free debate on Kenya's political and economic future. This could only be achieved, he suggested, when the 1982 constitutional amendment establishing a *de jure* one-party state was repealed. The bishop also proposed that future presidents should be limited to two five-year terms.[69] KANU leaders professed to want a debate on such questions, Okullu protested, but the party's increasingly authoritarian stance intimidated people from expressing their real views. The bishop's observations encouraged two more powerful critics of KANU's increasingly totalitarian stance to declare their opinions – former cabinet ministers Kenneth Matiba and Charles Rubia.[70]

Confronted by the end of communist rule in Eastern Europe and demands in other parts of Africa for the ending of one-party rule, KANU leaders at the end of February 1990 had launched 'a debate' on multi-party systems. Until Okullu's sermon two months later and the intervention of Matiba and Rubia the following week, the so-called 'multi-party debate' had amounted to nothing more than a reiteration of the official KANU defence of one-party rule as a guarantee against 'tribalism' and national fragmentation. KANU Secretary-General Joseph Kamotho had, however, announced in mid-April that there would be a major conference to consider 'the Kenya we want', which would include church leaders, prominent lawyers and the leaders of other national institutions, such as the Central Organization of Trades Unions (COTU).[71] Okullu could, therefore, claim that he was merely responding to the KANU secretary-general's invitation and drawing attention to a central issue which needed to be debated. The bishop was supported by the Revd Dr Timothy Njoya, Bishop David Gitari, the provost of Embu cathedral Canon Gideon Ireri, ex-detainee and prominent constitutional lawyer Gibson Kamau Kuria and Gitobu Imanyara, the editor of the *Nairobi Law Monthly*.[72]

Two prominent clergymen, however, supported KANU. Bishop of Eldoret the Right Revd Alexander Muge and Bishop Lawi Imathiu of the Methodist Church, who had been a nominated MP from 1974 to 1979, defended one-party rule, arguing like the politicians that a multi-party system would merely divide Kenyans on ethnic lines. 'Tribalism' rather than ideology, they contended, would differentiate the new parties. The two bishops did, however, acknowledge that powerful constitutional checks and balances were required to limit the power of the president and KANU. At present MPs owed their allegiance more to the party than to their electors, and the 1986 constitutional reforms, forced through by KANU, had denied many Kenyans the right to choose freely their rulers through democratic elections.[73]

The churches and the multi-party movement, May to July 1990

Following the entry of Matiba and Rubia into the argument with their 3 May press conference, the confrontation escalated. A week later President Moi, speaking in Kirinyaga and then at Kamukunji in Nairobi on 10 and 11 May, denounced Okullu and Bishop Gitari, who had supported Okullu. The president asserted that the CPK was involved in a plot to undermine the government.[74] On 14 May, Archbishop Kuria issued a forceful rebuttal, dismissing the president's claim and insisting that the CPK had nothing to hide from any security probe. Throughout the multi-party controversy, the archbishop adopted an unusually combative stance, rejecting claims that the multi-party movement was no more than a bid to restore Kikuyu hegemony. Part of the explanation for this may lie in the fact that Kuria's daughter was married to former minister Rubia's son, and that the archbishop had been angered by the continuing attacks on the CPK as a Kikuyu-dominated organization. Neither of the church's two most outspoken leaders – Bishop Okullu of Maseno South and Bishop Muge of Eldoret – were Kikuyu, and they had, in fact, themselves been noted critics of Kikuyu power within the CPK.[75] By this time, however, KANU Secretary-General Kamotho, who had originally supported a 'Kenya we want' conference, had just announced that the party had decided that there was no need for such a discussion as the public rallies addressed by President Moi in every province had enabled Kenyans to express their opinions and to reject a multi-party system.[76]

The churches' response to the detention of Matiba and Rubia and the riots in Kikuyuland

The multi-party debate took a new turn on 4 July, with the detention of Matiba, Rubia and Raila Odinga, former vice-president Oginga Odinga's son. Three prominent lawyers were also briefly detained, while Gibson Kamau Kuria sought political asylum in the American Embassy and Paul Muite, the radical candidate for the chairmanship of the Kenya Law Society, disappeared underground for three weeks before he came to terms with the regime. Following widespread rioting, the government moved to silence its critics, arresting three former detainees, including George Anyona, the former radical Gusii MP, and a KANU official from Embu who associated with them. All were sentenced to long prison sentences for possessing subversive literature.[77]

Many KANU leaders believed that the CPK, especially Bishop

Okullu, and the Revd Dr Timothy Njoya of the PCEA were deeply implicated in the multi-party movement. Matiba and Rubia, they believed, had been plotting to subvert the government and had organized the widespread rioting which erupted in Nairobi and many parts of Kikuyuland following the detention of the two ex-ministers. Assistant Minister in the Office of the President John Keen, for example, claimed to have the names of Matiba's cabinet, including Bishop Henry Okullu. In contrast, church leaders, including Bishop Lawi Imathiu, suggested that the revolt had been caused by poverty and lack of participation in political affairs. The clergymen considered that the riots proved them justified in demanding a national convention to discuss Kenya's future. They saw the rioting as 'symptomatic of deeper problems of poverty and lack of participation in the affairs of the nation'.[78]

Bishop Okullu, as usual, was even more forthright, castigating the government for driving the country to the crisis by failing to listen to the people's wishes. 'The blame,' he asserted, 'must lie on the KANU government which in spite of calls to arrange for a national convention, a dialogue with all the people and a democratic form of government, has insisted on doing things its own way.' The bishop also condemned the state's 'cowardly action' in detaining the advocates of multi-party democracy. Okullu now doubted KANU's will to reform and to heed popular protests.[79]

On 14 July, several prominent Protestant leaders, including Archbishop Kuria of the CPK, Moderator George Wanjau of the PCEA and Bishop Lawi Imathiu of the Methodist Church, urged President Moi to release the political detainees and to go ahead with a national convention to consider Kenya's future. Archbishop Zacchaeus Okoth, the Roman Catholic archbishop of Kisumu and Okullu's local counterpart, concurred, pointing out that the political crisis demonstrated the need for dialogue between all interested groups. The government, however, rejected such calls, insisting that the KANU review committee, appointed just before Matiba and Rubia were detained, would provide an adequate forum for discussion.[80]

Early in August the CPK and the NCCK presented their evidence to the KANU review committee. Chaired by Vice-President Saitoti, a moderate technocrat, the committee's ten initial members had all been prominent cabinet ministers and powerful local KANU chairmen. Two of Kenya's most outspoken opponents of reform, Elijah Mwangale and Sharriff Nassir, had been nominated, and there had been widespread concern that the committee would not provide a forum for critics of the ruling party, who wished to condemn the changes in the constitution, the abolition of the secret ballot in 1986 and the ending of security of tenure for High Court judges, the Attorney-General and the Comptroller and Auditor General in 1988. In order to improve the committee's credibility, both in Kenya and with the country's American and West European aid donors, President Moi had been compelled to appoint another nine members. These included former vice-president Mwai Kibaki, widely regarded as a moderate; representatives of the trades union movement, amongst them COTU Secretary-General Mugalla, who had earlier criticized church leaders for continuing to call for a national convention; Mrs Wilkista Onsando, the leader of the women's movement the *Maendeleo ya Wanawake ya Kenya*, which under Moi had been incorporated into KANU; and two clergymen – former Presbyterian Moderator John Gatu and Bishop Kitonga of the Redeemed Gospel Church. Gatu had been a close associate of the Kiambu élite under Kenyatta and was widely respected in both clerical and political circles, while Kitonga had joined Archbishop Kuria, Moderator Wanjau and Bishop Imathiu in mid-July, urging President Moi to provide some means by which people could discuss 'the kind of Kenya we would be working for'.[81]

In their evidence to the committee, the CPK and the NCCK proposed that queuing should be abandoned and election-rigging reduced by establishing an electoral commission, which should include church leaders as well as civil servants. The CPK's lengthy memorandum reiterated the call for a national conference which could debate proposals to establish a multi-party political system. The CPK did not consider the KANU review committee sufficiently impartial to command the nation's confidence. The Revd Timothy Njoya was equally unimpressed by the committee's members. Njoya considered that the committee would only command credibility when strong party critics were included, such as Bishop David Gitari; former MP Martin Shikuku; radical lawyer Gitobu Imanyara; Professor Wangari Mathai, head of the Green Belt movement, the Kenyan ecological forum; or other advocates of multi-party politics. The Presbyterian minister was also critical of the committee's two clergymen. Neither John Gatu, who rarely attended the sessions, nor the Revd, Arthur Kitonga of the Redeemed Gospel Church had played a prominent role in the debate on political and social issues.[82]

Bishop Muge's attack on corrupt politicians

Another critic of the commission and of KANU was Bishop Alexander Muge, who appeared before the Saitoti committee when it arrived in Eldoret. Muge aroused politicians' anger by suggesting that a coterie of party leaders and cabinet ministers was isolating the president. Quoting the example of Kwame Nkrumah's gradual alienation from the people, which had resulted in his overthrow in a coup d'état in February 1966, Muge warned that President Moi might suffer a similar fate. The riots, Muge contended, offered 'a telling and hair-raising signal', but the government had used the police to repress advocates of political reform. The bishop urged the president to establish a commission to investigate the activities of senior civil servants and ministers, who were alienating people from the president by seizing land in the Uasin Gishu and Trans Nzoia and castigating their critics as disloyal.[83]

For most of the past year, Muge had been relatively quiet. His zeal for conflict appeared to have diminished since his row with President Moi over the famine situation in West Pokot in 1988, as a result of which the anti-CPK faction had systematically attempted to reduce the church's influence in the district. As a result of these troubles, which had attracted renewed public attention in September 1989, when the district commissioner had banned the bishop from entering the district, the CPK had lost out in a struggle with the African Inland Church to take over the property and congregations of the proscribed American-financed Associated Christian Churches of Kenya (ACCK), despite the fact that Muge had reached an agreement with ACCK leader Richard Hamilton to transfer the churches' resources to the diocese of Eldoret. Following these setbacks, Muge had attempted to restore relations with President Moi and the local political leadership, especially Mark arap Too, KANU chairman in Nandi. Since September 1989, Muge had attracted little press attention. He had even supported KANU's claim that multi-party democracy would lead to increasing 'tribalism' and ethnic animosity, earning the praises of Minister of Energy Nicholas Biwott, KANU chairman in Elgeyo-Marakwet district and one of the president's closest allies. The bishop had also attempted to establish improved relations with the new slate of Nandi MPs elected in 1988.[84]

This about-turn had embarrassed certain of his colleagues in the CPK. Bishop Gitari of Mount Kenya East, for example, had been questioned by the Special Branch when he failed to report a meeting with representatives of *Mwakenya*, when he returned from a World Council of Churches meeting in Toronto late in 1989. In contrast, Muge, who had also attended the meeting on behalf of the CPK, had provided the security forces with a detailed account of the conversation when he reached Nairobi. Muge's attack on the 'clique of cabinet ministers' isolating the president and his assertion that ministers and senior civil servants had seized land from squatters in Uasin Gishu however, brought the wrath of the political establishment down upon the cleric. President Moi was clearly irritated by Muge's accusations and took the opportunity of a delegation of Nyanza politicians to assert that he fully understood Kenyans' aspirations and to deny that he was isolated from ordinary people. President Moi seemed to have been particularly displeased with his comparison to Nkrumah.[85]

Faced by these criticisms, Bishop Muge attempted to divert attention on to his local critics, whom he claimed were misleading the president and distorting his remarks. These were the same individuals who were isolating President Moi. The bishop urged the president to appoint an independent commission of inquiry to investigate his charges. One cabinet minister, he declared, had been involved in an 81 million shillings irregular deal with the Kenya Planters' Co-operative Union and had removed squatters from land which he had bought with government money. The bishop's anger seemed to be directed against Energy Minister Nicholas Biwott, who claimed that the church leaders were merely closing ranks after realizing the futility of their protests against the political establishment. The minister was supported by several Nandi and Uasin Gishu politicians, including Minister for Co-operative Development John Cheruiyot. Ever since Cheruiyot had been elected MP for Aldai constituency in Nandi district in 1988, relations with Muge had been strained, although the bishop and the minister both supported Nandi KANU chairman Mark arap Too. The conflict between the CPK and the African Inland Church still pervaded the district and Cheruiyot, the son of African Inland Church leader Bishop Ezekiel Birech, was clearly identified with the anti-CPK faction.[86]

The decline of political debate in Kenya: Minister of Labour Okondo threatens Bishop Muge

President Moi's allies were probably more firmly established in Western Province than in any other part of Kenya. Ministers Elijah Mwangale from Bungoma, Moses Mudavadi (the president's late brother-in-law) and Burudi Nabwera from Kakamega and Peter Okondo from Busia had all risen to power under the new regime, sweeping former Abaluhya leader Masinde Muliro into oblivion. All were forthright defenders of the political status quo.[87] Although Mwangale was the most combative and influential of the Abaluhya ministers within the cabinet and in the National Assembly, Nabwera and Mudavadi had occupied more senior positions in the KANU hierarchy, serving respectively as party secretary-general from 1985 to 1988 and from 1988 to 1989. In contrast, Okondo, who had been a minister since 1984, had failed to establish himself securely within either the government or the party executive. Since his election to parliament in 1983, Okondo had earned a reputation as a belligerent politician, willing to use KANU's disciplinary procedures to expel local political opponents and to intimidate national rivals. Like several others whose position in the cabinet was not entirely secure, Okondo seized every opportunity to castigate church leaders, especially Muge and Okullu, who had antagonized the ruling party.

Both Okondo and his colleague, Joash wa Mang'oli, the MP for Webuye, did not hesitate to threaten their critics. Thus, in late July, Mang'oli informed Bishop Henry Okullu that he would have to face the wrath of local Youth League members if he visited Webuye; 'warned' the *Weekly Review*, the prestigious Nairobi political magazine, to stop misreporting his statements; and proposed that the government should detain fifty-eight lawyers who had signed a memorandum to the KANU review committee recommending the dissolution of parliament and the introduction of multi-party democracy.[88] Okondo was soon to get himself into serious trouble when he threatened Bishop Muge not to visit Busia on pain of death.

Following the revivification of KANU since 1985, the party gradually reduced the autonomy of formerly independent interest groups and professional organizations, such as the *Maendeleo ya Wanawake ya Kenya*, the national women's movement, which had been an independent pressure group. Even the Law Society under the chairmanship of Fred Ojiambo appeared to have muted its opposition to the recent constitutional changes.[89] Several independent churches had withdrawn from the NCCK because of its clashes with KANU. Only the major Protestant churches and, to a lesser extent, the Roman Catholic Church refused to accept the party's new ascendancy, resisting the growth of a more totalitarian political culture. The development of a party state encouraged politicians to adopt a more paranoid style since it was imperative to remain in favour with the ruling coterie around President Moi, whose populist prejudices frustrated political debate. District commissioners and local KANU bosses felt free to threaten their rivals and to manipulate elections, while the press remained silent. Kikuyu Cabinet Minister Arthur Magugu, during the riots following the detention of Matiba and Rubia, had urged his supporters to arm themselves with pangas against those who threatened the nation's stability, and earlier Nakuru district KANU chairman Wilson Leitich had ordered KANU Youth League members to chop the fingers off those who gave the two-finger sign in support of multi-party democracy.[90] Okondo's threat that Okullu and Muge would 'see fire and may not leave alive' if they dared to visit Busia, therefore, was not unusual, and reflected the decline in political discourse during the 1980s.[91]

Immediately after Okondo's incautious threat, Bishop Muge had issued a press statement on Monday, 13 August 1990 – the same day that Assistant Minister Pancras Otwani was warning bishops not to 'preach politics' in his constituency – declaring that Okondo's remarks heralded a plot to kill the church leader in order to silence his accusations against senior politicians and civil servants. The bishop asserted that he would visit Busia, where he was prepared to die 'at the hands of the minister's gang of KANU youth-wingers', and had warned that he might meet a similar fate to murdered Foreign Minister Robert

Ouko, who was rumoured to have been murdered by cabinet colleagues who feared his investigations into government corruption. Although the bishop accepted President Moi's assertion that the government had not been involved in Dr Ouko's murder, he observed that this did not absolve individual ministers and he denounced 'professional murderers' within the cabinet. The Eldoret bishop concluded by prophetically forewarning his ministerial critic: 'let Okondo know that my innocent blood will haunt him for ever and he will not be in peace, for God does not approve murder'.[92]

Bishop Muge's death and the CPK's denunciation of KANU

As in September 1989, when he defiantly visited West Pokot ignoring the warnings of the district commissioner, Muge had received a warm welcome when he visited Busia the next day. After conducting a massive open-air service outside Saint Stephen's Church in the town, attracting street traders and local workers, the bishop had left in a four-car convoy, taking an indirect route back to Eldoret, skirting Kisumu before joining the Webuye–Eldoret road. A few miles from the town, Muge's car caught up with a large truck, and as it slowly climbed up a steep hill encountered an out-of-control milk truck, which careered down the hill, crossed the road, hitting the back of the truck in front of Muge's car before crashing head-on into the driver's side of the bishop's vehicle, dragging it 100 feet and crushing the bishop behind the steering-wheel in the mangled wreck. Although his three passengers survived, Bishop Muge died at the roadside. Kenya was plunged into crisis as suspicion of murder fell upon Minister of Labour Okondo and Bishop Muge's other critics in the political élite.[93]

Over the next few days, as the bishop's body lay in Nairobi and memorial services were held at All Saint's Cathedral on Thursday, 16 August and Monday, 20 August, popular frustration overflowed as the people vented their rage against the political establishment. Ministers known to be opposed to the reform of KANU were jostled and turned away from the cathedral. Even Minister of Tourism and Wildlife George Muhoho, who had been a prominent Roman Catholic clergyman before leaving the priesthood in the mid-1970s to get married, was turned away, although he had taken no part in the attack on the churches. A crowd of 10,000 waited outside to hear church leader after church leader denounce the government and praise Bishop Muge's fearless assault on corruption. Archbishop Kuria and Bishops Okullu and Gitari were cheered as they condemned KANU and called for an immediate general election and the establishment of a government of national unity which, unlike KANU, could command popular support.[94]

Political leaders rushed to distance themselves from Okondo. Even before the bishop's death, Busia KANU chairman Moody Awori, who had ousted Okondo as branch chairman in the 1988 KANU elections, had apologized to President Moi for the minister's remarks. Delegates of the Methodist annual conference had also condemned Okondo's 'irresponsible statements', while the Right Revd David Gitari and the provost of Nairobi cathedral had criticized them as an example of the 'poor leadership' Kenyans enjoyed. When news was received that Muge had actually been killed on his way back from Busia, few politicians were willing to support Okondo.[95] Only Minister of Agriculture Elijah Mwangale, the hard-liner of Western Province politics, speaking at a rally in Narok, the territory of another hard-line KANU leader, Local Government Minister William Ntimama, had dared to suggest that the uproar following the bishop's death would soon pass and the party would be able to reassert its authority.[96] Even Bishop Muge's most powerful Kalenjin opponent, Energy Minister Nicholas Biwott, whom many suspected had been the target of the bishop's attack on land grabbers inside the cabinet and ministerial murderers, attempted to effect a reconciliation with the Muge family, although he met a hostile reception when he attempted to visit the bishop's home and had ignominiously to flee the angry crowd of mourners.[97] Minister of Labour Okondo's career was destroyed. The NCCK's Director for Justice and Peace, the Revd Jephthah Gathaka, best summed up the minister's problem, observing: 'Okondo may be innocent but how will he now cleanse himself from the wrath of Bishop Muge's curse?'[98]

Despite their differences the CPK united to condemn belligerent politicians and the growing totalitarianism in Kenya politics. Joined by leaders of the other churches, including the Roman Catholics, in their condemnation of Kenya's repressive political atmosphere, in the latter part of August and early September 1990 the CPK House of Bishops appeared more united and more outspoken in their condemnation of KANU than ever before. Several church leaders, indeed, believed that witchcraft had been used to effect Bishop Muge's death, while others reported that the GSU and Special Branch had been involved, and that the 'turn-boy' on the milk truck was a police officer who had carried a walkie-talkie radio transmitter to co-ordinate the crash. Church–state relations had never before reached such a low ebb.[99]

Church–state relations in the aftermath
of Bishop Muge's death

The situation deteriorated further during the following year. The united church front has disintegrated as the government has used denominational rivalries to divide and rule. A similar strategy has been used to fragment the CPK into ethnically based factions. A major attempt has been made to discredit Bishop Okullu, who was then the most likely candidate to succeed Archbishop Kuria as primate when he retires in 1994. Anonymous letters have appeared in the national press, condemning his high-handed control of the diocese of Maseno South, his nepotism and his 'tribalism'.[100] The press has freely speculated upon the ethnic dynamics of the election to the primacy, suggesting that the block of five Kikuyu bishops, supported by, bishops from Embu and Ukambani and the two Abaluhya bishops, who opposed the formation of the independent Katakwa diocese, will block Okullu's election, as in 1980.[101] Bishop Gitari, the leading Kikuyu candidate, has also been denounced for impropriety.[102] Even Bishop Muge's Eldoret diocese divided into hostile factions during the election of his successor.[103]

Nationally, the political scene remained quiet. First Rubia and then Matiba were released from detention. KANU also made some further concessions but showed little zeal to implement the recommendations of the Saitoti committee, apart from abolishing queuing and the 70 per cent primary rule. Energy Minister Biwott was implicated in Robert Ouko's death by several witnesses before the Commission of Inquiry into the former Foreign Minister's murder.[104] Otherwise, President Moi and his associates remain firmly in control. Only prominent clergymen were permitted to criticize the regime's construction of an increasingly authoritarian state, with its vapid *Nyayo* populist ideology. No one, however, could doubt that Kenya's churches had come of age and demonstrated far more than 'a stance of "critical-solidarity" with the state'. Muge, Okullu, Gitari, Njoya and a'Nzeki had formulated an indigenous theology of resistance to the demands of a hostile secular authority. Meanwhile, the state was still trying to enforce its vision of a more Erastian church.[105]

President Moi's government still faces major problems from the opposition of the main churches. During the last decade, respect for church leaders has grown as they resisted intimidation from KANU and politicians' popular support declined. The government realizes that it cannot afford to alienate the churches and the NCCK completely. Nonetheless, the populists around Moi, including the president himself, are unused to such robust criticism and do not see how to re-establish cordial relations, short of dismantling the Moi state and the post-1985 KANU apparatus of controls. To many of the president's henchmen, this was, and is, too high a price for renewed collaboration with the churches, just as fair elections and a free press seemed to be too high a price to pay for Western aid and long-term stability. They seemed for a while to choose the course of further repression. However, multi-party elections were finally held in December 1992, to a large extent the result of international donors' pressure. Principally because opposition parties were divided, KANU was re-elected. The churches, commanding mass respect, still remain a lone voice of criticism. Their conservative ideology has thus enabled them in recent years, not only to discourse with an authoritarian pseudo-party state, but to serve as one of the last redoubts for secular liberalism and democracy in Kenya in the new multi-party era.

Notes

1. C. G. Rosberg and J. Nottingham, *The myth of 'Mau Mau': Nationalism in Kenya* (London, 1966), pp. 110-112, 143 and 222-223; and E. S. Atieno Odhiambo, 'A portrait of the missionaries in Kenya before 1939', *Kenya Historical Review* 1 (1973), pp. 1-14. See also Anne King, 'J. W. Arthur and African Interests', and B. E. Kipkorir, 'Carey Francies at the Alliance High School, Kikuyu 1940-1962', in B. E. Kipkorir, ed., *Biographical essays on imperialism and collaboration in colonial Kenya* (Nairobi, 1980), pp. 87-111 and 112-159.

2. J. M. Lonsdale, 'Mau Maus of the mind: Making Mau Mau and remaking Kenya', *Journal of African History* 31 (1990), pp. 393-421, provides a fascinating account of the ideology of the Kikuyu forest gangs. For a contemporary colonialist view, see also L. S. B. Leakey, *Mau Mau and the Kikuyu* (London, 1953) and *Defeating Mau Mau* (London, 1954).

3. M. Warren, *Social history and Christian mission* (London 1967), pp. 33-34, quoted in A. Hastings, *A history of African Christianity, 1950-1975* (London, 1979), p. 20.

4. Hastings, *History of African Christianity*, p. 20.

5. J. M. Lonsdale, S. Booth-Clibborn and A. Hake, 'The emerging pattern of church and state co-operation in Kenya', in E. Fashole-Luke, R. Gray, A. Hastings and G. Tasie, eds, *Christianity in Africa* (Bloomington and London, 1978), pp. 269-270.

6. T. Mboya, *Freedom and after* (London, 1963), pp. 22-23, quoted in Lonsdale *et al.*, 'Emerging pattern', p. 270.

7. Lonsdale *et al.*, 'Emerging pattern', pp. 271-272.

8. Ibid., pp. 280-281.

9. Ibid., quoted p. 282.

10. Ibid., p. 284.

11. Ibid., p. 283.

12. Henry Okullu, *Church and politics in East Africa* (Nairobi, 1974, pp. 3-6 and 12-13; and the *Weekly Review* (Nairobi), 26 January (1990), pp. 4-5 and 8-9, and 2 February (1990), pp. 13-15. The *Weekly Review* is quoted frequently in the following footnotes as the most readily accessible source of news about Kenya outside the country. Similar information can be found in the *Daily Nation* and the *Standard*, the two main Kenya newspapers, of the same dates. The *Kenya Times*, operated jointly by KANU and Robert Maxwell, the British newspaper publisher, in contrast, usually provides an account reflecting the views of the ruling party, its owners, and has therefore been more hostile to the churches and the NCCK. Although the

David Throup

Weekly Review is also now owned in part by the ruling party and senior politicians, it provides a balanced account of political developments, especially with regard to the conflicts between the churches and the state, although it is not as critical of the Moi government as it was of Kenyatta's from 1975 to 1978.

13. *Weekly Review*, 3 October (1986), pp. 19–20.
14. Ibid., p. 19; and Lonsdale *et al.*, 'Emerging pattern', p. 273. See also S. Cross, 'Independent churches and independent states: Jehovah's Witnesses in East and Central Africa', in Fashole-Luke *et al.*, eds, *Christianity in Africa*, pp. 304–315, which provides a detailed account of the sect's persecution in Zambia.
15. *Weekly Review*, 25 April (1980), pp. 4–8; 6 June (1980), pp. 4–7; and 27 June (1980), pp. 5–6.
16. *Weekly Review*, 17th June (1983), pp. 3–7.
17. *Weekly Review*, 4 May (1983), pp. 4–9; 20 May (1983), pp. 4–13; 1 July (1993), pp. 3–7; 8 July (1983), pp.4–5; 12 August (1983), pp. 4–9 and 11–12; and 28 October (1983), pp. 3–6, for a few of many accounts of Njonjo's downfall.
18. *Weekly Review*, 16 March (1984), pp. 3–7; 23 March (1984), pp. 8–11; 30 March (1984), pp. 3–7; 6 April (1984), pp. 4–6; and 8 June (1984), pp 9–10.
19. Okullu, *Church and politics in East Africa, passim*; *Weekly Review*, 25 April (1980), p. 16 for Njonjo's intervention to block Okullu and to secure Kuria, the bishop of Nakuru's election; 24 June (1983), pp. 3–4; and 22 June (1984), p. 13. For details of the PCEA and the Ruringu meeting, see *Weekly Review*, 3 May (1985), pp 4–7, for the dispute between defeated PCEA secretary-general the Revd Bernard Muindi and John Gatu and Timothy Njoya. For more recent comments by Archbishop Kuria on church–state relations, see *Weekly Review*, 30 June (1989), pp. 8–9.
20. *Weekly Review*, 13 May (1983), pp. 13'. See also D. W. Throup, 'The construction and destruction of the Kenyatta state', in M. G. Schatzberg, ed., *The political economy of Kenya* (New York, 1987), pp. 57–67, for an account of President Moi's attempt to dismantle Kikuyu influence in the civil service, the military and the business world.
21. Throup, 'Construction and destruction', pp. 43–46; *Weekly Review*, 18 July (1986), pp. 3–5; and interviews with people from Nandi district.
22. *Weekly Review*, 18 July (1986), pp. 3–5.
23. Ibid., and *Weekly Review* 9 May (1986), pp. 9–10.
24. J. Seeley, *Praise, prestige and power: The organization of welfare in a developing Kenya town*, unpublished PhD thesis, Cambridge University (1985), pp. 73–75, 131–138 and 268–275. See also *Weekly Review*, 26 August (1983), pp. 7–12; and Throup, 'Construction and destruction' pp. 53–57.
25. *Weekly Review*, 29 August (1986), pp. 3–6; and 5 September (1986), pp. 1–2 and 4–6. For details of the 1985 discussions see the issues for 7 June (1985), pp. 3–5; and 28 June (1985), p. 1 for Ng'weno's editorial and pp. 7–9 for reports and comments.
26. *Weekly Review*, 29 August (1986), pp. 3.
27. Ibid., p. 4.
28. Ibid., pp. 4–5.
29. Ibid., pp. 5.
30. Ibid.; and *Weekly Review*, 5 September (1986), pp. 4–5.
31. *Weekly Review*, 29 August (1986) p. 5.
32. *Weekly Review*, 19 September (1986), p. 4.
33. Ibid., p. 5.
34. Ibid., p. 6.
35. *Weekly Review*, 5 September (1986), p. 4; and 12 September (1986), p. 4. See also the issues for 6 February (1987), pp. 3–5; 13 February (1987), pp. 3–5; 1 May (1987), pp. 12–13; 12 June (1987), pp. 8–10; 19 June (1987), pp. 4–8; and 28 October (1988), pp. 4–7, for the saga of wa Nyoike's downfall.
36. *Weekly Review*, 5 September (1986), p. 6. See also the issue for 1 May (1987), pp. 3–8.

37. *Weekly Review*, 5 September (1986), pp. 5–6. See also the issue for 12 December (1986), pp. 3–7.
38. *Weekly Review*, 12 September (1986), pp. 4–5.
39. *Weekly Review*, 10 October (1986), pp. 3–4.
40. *Weekly Review*, 17 October (1986), pp. 3–5.
41. *Weekly Review*, 21 November (1986), pp. 4–9; 28 November (1986) pp. 3–10; and 5 December (1986), pp. 3–7.
42. *Weekly Review*, 28 November (1986), pp. 6–7. For criticism of the NCCK, see *Weekly Review*, 5 December (1986), pp. 7–11. Imathiu had earlier spoken out on social and political questions: see *Weekly Review*, 19 September (1986), pp. 7–8 and 17 October (1986), pp. 3–5.
43. *Weekly Review*, 28 November (1986), p. 3; and 5 December (1986), pp. 7–11.
44. *Weekly Review*, 12 December (1986), pp. 7–12.
45. *Weekly Review*, 22 April (1988), pp. 4–8; 29 April (1988), pp. 4–15; and 6 May (1988), pp. 10–13.
46. *Weekly Review*, 6 March (1987), pp. 5–6.
47. *Weekly Review*, 27 March (1987), pp. 5–6; and 12 June (1987), pp. 7–8.
48. *Weekly Review* 18 August (1989), pp. 28; and 12 January (1990), p. 5.
49. For details of Muge's stormy career, see *Weekly Review*, 24 April (1987), pp. 3–13. For Lotodo's dismissal as Assistant Minister for Information and Broadcasting in 1984, see *Weekly Review*, 2 March (1984), p. 12; and 16 March (1984), p. 15.
50. *Weekly Review*, 10 June (1988), pp. 8–9.
51. *Weekly Review*, 17 June (1988), pp. 21–23.
52. *Weekly Review*, 24 June (1988), pp. 9–12; and 1 July (1988), pp. 4–7. For a list of West Pokot politicians expelled from KANU, see *Weekly Review*, 23 June (1989), p. 6.
53. *Weekly Review*, 15 September (1989) pp. 7–12; and 22 September (1989), pp. 8–9.
54. *Weekly Review*, 22 September (1989), pp. 8–9.
55. *Weekly Review*, 7 October (1988), pp. 1 and 3–5. See also the issue for 14 April (1989), pp. 4–10.
56. *Weekly Review*, 7 October (1988), p. 5.
57. Ibid.
58. For the growing power of KANU, see *Weekly Review*, 8 May (1987), pp. 4–12; 5 August (1988), pp. 3–13; 14 October (1988), pp. 3–13; 11 November (1988), pp. 4–8; and 23 December (1988), pp. 14–15. For a more detailed account of political changes in Kenya and the rise of something approaching a 'party state', see Charles Hornsby and David Throup, 'Moi and the party: Elections and political change in Kenya', *Journal of Commonwealth and Comparative Politics* (November, 1991).
59. For divisions within the Presbyterian Church, see *Weekly Review*, 3 May (1985), pp. 4–10; and 5 August (1988), pp. 13–14.
60. *Weekly Review*, 14 October (1988), p. 25. For a denial of 'tribalism' in the CPK from Bishop Okullu, see *Weekly Review*, 28 September (1990), pp. 15–16.
61. *Weekly Review*, 12 January (1990). An example of political intervention by the Roman Catholic hierarchy can be found in *Weekly Review*, 26 February (1988), pp. 30–31, when the Catholic bishops bought advertising space to publish a pre-election pastoral letter.
62. *Weekly Review*, 3 May (1985), pp. 7–8; 6 March (1987), pp. 5–6; and 27 March (1987), pp. 5–6.
63. *Weekly Review*, 12 January (1990), p. 8; 2 February (1990), p. 15; and 18 May (1990), p. 10.
64. *Weekly Review*, 5 January (1990), pp. 5–6; and 12 January (1990), pp. 3–9. For earlier comments on the political system by the NCCK, see the issues for 8 December (1989), pp. 10; 15 December (1989), pp. 6–8; and 22 December (1989), pp. 13–14. Bishop Okullu was the new chairman of the NCCK.
65. *Weekly Review*, 12 January (1990), pp. 3–5.

66. Ibid., p. 5.
67. Ibid.
68. Ibid. p. 6. See also *Weekly Review*, 6 April (1990), pp. 17-18.
69. *Weekly Review*, 4 May (1990), pp. 6-9.
70. *Weekly Review*, 11 May (1990), pp. 6-2; and 18 May (1990), pp. 5-8.
71. *Weekly Review*, 4 May (1990), pp. 8 and 17-18.
72. Ibid., p. 7.
73. Ibid.
74. *Weekly Review*, 18 May (1990), pp. 5-8.
75. Ibid., pp. 9-10; and *Weekly Review*, 29 June (1990), pp. 21.
76. *Weekly Review*, 18 May (1990), pp. 5-8.
77. *Weekly Review*, 6 July (1990), *passim*; 13 July (1990), pp. 3-12 and 16-23; and 20 July (1990), pp. 17-19.
78. Weekly Review, 20 July (1990), pp. 5 and 14-15; and 27 July (1990) p. 13.
79. *Weekly Review*, 20 July (1990), pp. 5 and 14.
80. Ibid., pp. 14-15.
81. *Weekly Review*, 27 July (1990), pp. 3-8. For Mwangale's comments, see *Weekly Review*, 20 July (1990), p. 15.
82. *Weekly Review*, 3 August (1990), pp. 13-14.
83. *Weekly Review*, 10 August (1990), pp. 10-12.
84. Ibid., p. 12.
85. Ibid., p. 11.
86. Ibid., pp. 11-12. For further details on Nandi politics and relations between Cheruiyot, arap Too and the CPK, see *Weekly Review*, 20 January (1990), pp. 7-12.
87. *Weekly Review*, 1 May (1987), pp. 8-10; and 24 August (1990), pp. 21-24. See also the issues of 9 October (1987), pp. 4-28 and 4 December (1987), pp. 3-10, for a detailed consideration of political factionalism in Kakamega and Busia districts.
88. *Weekly Review*, 10 August (1990), pp. 14-15.
89. *Weekly Review* 8 May (1987), pp. 11-12; 3 November (1989), pp. 4-13; and 10 November (1989), pp. 10-12. For conflict in the Law Society of·Kenya, see the issue for 10 August (1990), pp. 16-18.
90. See the editorial in *Weekly Review*, 13 July (1990), p. 1; and articles from the issues of 20 July (1990), p. 15; 10 August (1990), p. 15; and 17 August (1990), pp. 6-9.
91. *Weekly Review*, 17 August (1990), pp. 4 and 6-9.
92. Ibid., p. 4.
93. Ibid., pp. 4-6 and 9-13.
94. *Weekly Review*, 24 August (1990), pp. 4-11.
95. Ibid., pp. 18-20.
96. Ibid., pp. 12-13.
97. Ibid., pp. 14; and *Weekly Review*, 31 August (1990), pp. 3-6.
98. *Weekly Review*, 24 August (1990), p. 5.
99. Ibid., pp. 4-11.
100. *Weekly Review*, 31 August (1990), pp. 11-13; and 7 September (1990), pp. 4-9.
101. Ibid., expecially, 7 September (1990), pp. 7-9.
102. *Weekly Review*, 5 October (1990), pp. 3 and 5-10.
103. *Weekly Review*, 30 November (1990), pp. 1 and 28-29; and 7 December (1990), pp. 27-28.
104. *Daily Nation* (Nairobi), 25 July (1991), pp. 1-2; 31 July (1991) pp. 1-2; and 6 August (1991), pp. 1-2.
105. The most significant works are Henry Okullu, *Church and politics in East Africa* and *Church and state in nation building and human development* (Nairobi), 1984); and T.M. Njoya, *Human dignity and national identity* (Nairobi 1987).

Ten

Ideological Politics versus Biblical Hermeneutics

Kenya's Protestant Churches & the Nyayo State

G.P. BENSON

In December 1991, the Kenyan National Assembly repealed Section 2A of the constitution. The effect was to legalize the formation of opposition political parties to compete with the Kenya African National Union (KANU) for power.

The repeal was forced on President Moi by the United States and other donor nations, which refused further aid to Kenya until its political system was reformed. It was an international humiliation for Moi, and a weakening of his domestic power. It was also an ideological challenge, undermining the basis on which he had been attempting to reconstruct Kenyan society for a decade. From 9 June 1982, when section 2A was passed into law, to its repeal on 10 December 1991, Moi had striven to refashion Kenya as the *Nyayo* state.

Discontent with the *Nyayo* state was widespread, but largely suppressed. In April 1992, the Justice and Peace Commission of the Church of the Province of Kenya (CPK) issued a pastoral letter which reflected on the experience of one-party government:

> Fear was the order of the day and before very long that fear became a new culture in the national life – the *culture of fear*. Other institutions which were critical of the government were also intimidated and some succumbed to silence. In the final analysis it appeared as if only the Church and the Law Society had the courage to speak on behalf of the people.[1]

At a time when many opposition figures had gone into exile, the churches – especially the non-Catholic main-line churches – became the vehicles for resistance to Moi's regime. The churches' critique of the *Nyayo* state was, however, determined by their own agendas, not by the exiled radicals.

The conflict between the *Nyayo* state and the churches resembled a contest between a Roman gladiator and an opponent armed with a net during the late Roman empire. The opponents were unequally armed and had different strategies. A study of the methods and objectives of both contestants is essential, and that is what is attempted here.

The *Nyayo* state 1982–1991: a functioning ideology

THE FIRST STEPS IN *NYAYO*

Moi assumed the presidency of Kenya on Kenyatta's death in August 1978. He confounded many observers by rapidly securing his position against either coup or political opposition.

The churches shared the widespread hope and expectation that Moi's administration would be more principled than Kenyatta's.[2] In this they were not to be disappointed, although the principle in question would not be to their liking. Moi was a convinced and vocal Christian. At the time of the Chai oathing in 1969, he had played a valuable mediating role between the Kiambu establishment, which orchestrated the oath, and the churches and the Kalenjin elders, who were among its most outspoken critics. He, with Mwai Kibaki, had made an effort to free himself from corrupt links with business. On assuming power, he won widespread good will by releasing political detainees and by launching a campaign against corruption in the civil service.

Shortly after Moi became president, he stated that the principle of *Nyayo* (footsteps) was to be of great importance in his administration. At first, the principal meaning was that Moi's administration would follow in Kenyatta's footsteps, but later it became plain that Kenyans were supposed to follow Moi's.[3] From an early date, *Nyayo* philosophy figured frequently in public statements, and was subsequently defined as 'peace, love and unity'. By 1982, anxiety was growing[4] that Nyayoism might be another name for a presidential personality cult. Moi began to show himself intolerant of opposition; KANU was made the sole political party *de jure* and political detention reappeared.

It was not until 1986 that the president laid all his cards on the table, with the publication of *Kenya African nationalism*.[5]

AN OUTLINE OF *NYAYO* PHILOSOPHY

The following summary is based on a reading of Moi's *Kenya African nationalism*. Page references are to this book.

Sources

In his book Moi claims that Nyayoism is derived from three sources: African traditions of public affairs; Christian faith; and pragmatism about the means to be used to reach governmental goals.[6] The three keywords of Nyayoism – unity, love and peace – are sometimes treated as the respective contributions of each of these three sources, and are sometimes said to be inherent in each source. From these sources, Moi derives a vision of a society in which individuals' desire to better themselves is, by common consent, encouraged and yet bounded and directed by a desire of the whole community. The possibility of private entrepreneurship, the need for welfare services and equitable distribution, and government by consensus are all implied.

Leadership

The strategy for achieving such a society relies heavily on a doctrine of leadership. Leadership is to 'identify the needs and resources of the society; and to visualise and plan the ways and means to satisfy those needs with those and other resources. Leadership liberates and galvanises the people's ability into a dynamic force' (p. 78).

A section (pp. 76–78) entitled 'The people's will: a priceless asset' concerns the nature of leadership and concludes: 'Genuine leadership is the people's will: a priceless asset'. This assertion fits well with the statement that 'Leadership by traditional African consensus or by the majority elective will of the people is a holy and divine office' (p. 76). Leadership is not contingent or mutable; it is a sacral office. This evaluation is confirmed when defects in leadership are described as 'pollution' (p. 101).

Leadership is described as a 'resource' to be 'managed' and 'planned' (p. 76 and *passim*). For this reason Moi deplores the wastage of leaders in civil wars elsewhere in Africa; and to this he attributes his desire to discipline leaders who have gone astray, and also to forgive them when they repent.

The leaders comprise a 'corps' (p. 86) distinct from the mass of the people: indeed, steps must be taken to ensure that this corps does not lose touch with the people.[7] The corps cannot function effectively unless it has a focus; and that focus is in commitment to *Nyayo* philosophy. Nor can it function unless it is integrated: that is, all members of the corps support one another in holding forth and implementing a single vision for society. The key to integration and focus is loyalty: to Kenya, to the head of state and to the government.

All leaders share a responsibility to be servants of the people and morale-building models of integrity, as well as to show zeal and skill in their tasks. This applies to all leaders, such as councillors and civil servants; but members of the provincial, administration receive special mention:

G. P. Benson

That authority of the Government must be functionally resident in some single individual at any one stage in the national hierarchy of responsibilities. Thus at the top of the national governmental authority is the President. He is the symbol and functional embodiment of Government and authority, but that functional embodiment must physically exist at all stages throughout the nation. That embodiment is institutionalised in the Provincial Administration, the PC [Provincial Commissioner], DC [District Commissioner], DO [District Officer], the Chief and sub-chief, (p. 139)

Each individual is thus placed in authority with respect to those lower down the hierarchy and in submission with respect to those above. Each leader's power is meant to be used for the benefit of all, and having secured the consent of all; but it is essentially the unfettered sovereignty of Kenya which he wields.

Politics from above

The top-down direction of *Nyayo* polity is quite explicit. The people choose the leaders, but thereafter the leaders embody the will of the people. The strategy for leading is to get the people to respond positively to leaders' ideas, so that their resources are mobilized.[8] The people are described as responding to, accepting and co-acting with the initiatives of the leaders. This is not to say that the people are treated as merely passive or as spectators of the political process. On the contrary, Moi, the arch-populist, became indefatigable in touring the country and building and sustaining links·with the people,[9] and he encouraged other leaders to do the same.

Moi's book sees the leader's task as being to educate the masses politically. Advocating the creation of a rural élite, he argues that 'Such groups, with their more enlightened comprehension of political and development policies, will politicize the countryside effectively' (p. 73). However, 'politicized' does not mean seizing the political initiative: it means that the people have been taught what policies the government has laid down, and are ready to make their contribution by implementing them imaginatively and enthusiastically.

Devolution

Although Nyayoism is intensely hierarchical, it is not centralist. Three pieces of evidence point in this direction. Firstly, the District Focus Strategy for Development (DFS) had a significant effect on all the ministries concerned with development. Power genuinely shifted to District Development Committees, which became responsible for approving and co-ordinating small-scale development at local level. Secondly, the policy of encouraging, *'jua kali'* (hot sun) artisans represented a recognition of the informal sector of the economy. Although little practical assistance resulted, the change of rhetoric made it easier for the informal sector to operate unmolested by officialdom.

Thirdly, the revitalization of KANU after Moi's accession compelled politicians to take a new kind of interest in grass-roots concerns (even if their interest sometimes seemed to be manifested mainly in the rigging of ballots).[10]

Nyayo *and debate*

A very important practical consequence of Nyayoism is that it makes open discussion of public policy practically impossible, for, once the system has fastened on a policy, evaluation becomes tantamount to disloyalty.

Moi reserves fierce criticism for those who live by debate, namely the intellectuals. The chapter devoted to 'Challenges of the one-party system' contains a diatribe against 'dis-indigenised African elites and ideological upstarts who hanker after foreign thought patterns, ideals and ideologies' (p. 177). In this chapter, it is with the greatest difficulty that Moi turns to address the arguments raised by critics. For him, the very existence of the critics is the crucial challenge, for they have not accepted the premise of loyalty and are not following the *Nyayo*. Moi sets out his own understanding of the proper role of the academic: 'The most useful intellectual is a constructive and balanced realist' (p. 128). 'The staff in . . . universities must take the intellectual lead in providing a scholastic/academic atmosphere in which the students can orient themselves toward positive thinking, national consciousness, and a predeliction for good work and social improvement' (p. 130). Moi writes, 'Thus, well prepared, the students will evolve into intellectual *homeguards* against intellectual *terrorism*, political agitation and sub-version in the universities' (p. 131, emphasis in original).

Even at the local level, Nyayoism serves to stifle rather than to promote debate. Thus, although Moi's description of DFS frequently refers to responding to the wishes and the contribution of local people, his understanding of decision-making is not fundamentally altered. The leadership corps has been broadened to include a new tier of local leaders (p. 63), who are chosen, incorporated into the national leadership structure and make plans to which the people respond just as before.

THE NYAYOIST STATE

Moi: a doctrinaire politician

The keynote of Kenyatta's administration was pragmatism. Whether we consider the pattern of government in the 1970s to be the work of the Old Man himself, as Chepkwony suspects, or whether we think that in later years he was more an observer of than a participant in Kenyan politics, as Tamarkin and Bienen believe,[11] the government was guided by the desire to promote the interests of its patrons.

Nyayo ideology is not stunningly original: it can be summarized as the old call for nation-building in more elaborate dress. Nevertheless, it is important that Moi, unlike Kenyatta, is an ideologue. Although he lacks Kenyatta's formal academic training, he is by no means unintelligent.[12] Moi has developed and articulated his philosophy of Nyayoism and has reorientated Kenyan life on this basis. When his actions have hampered the growth of a mature political culture in Kenya, this is the result of the flaws of Nyayoism rather than purely the consequence of cynical manipulation of power.

It is fashionable among Kenyan intellectuals to despise Moi as uneducated, a scorn of which Moi is aware and which he bitterly resents. The effect of their own scorn is to make critics of the government underrate the power of his ideas and fail to engage with them. They criticize the more grotesque manifestations of Moi's personality cult, without describing how this is intimately connected with a whole system of thought.[13]

Nyayo *leadership*

Moi's book is quite explicit that his understanding of leadership is the heart of Nyayoism. The inadequacies of the doctrine have been demonstrated repeatedly. Even within the corps itself, debate on matters of principle is impossible. Such a high premium has been placed on loyalty and unanimity that the minimal presentation of alternative viewpoints necessary for a debate becomes a questionable, subversive activity.

The KANU delegates' conference meeting, at Kasarani in December 1990, which debated the Saitoti Report, was a classic example of the weakness of debate in Nyayoism. The report itself – the result of an investigation into grass-roots grievances on the functioning of the party – had recommended the scrapping of queue-voting, the 70 per cent rule[14] and disciplinary expulsions from KANU. It was widely believed that the president favoured the retention of all these measures. Consequently, although a few brave souls (*Weekly Review* identified only five among the 3600 delegates) publicly stated their support for the committee's proposals, the majority of speakers were ready to reject them.

However, when President Moi spoke at the close of the debate, he endorsed the reforms: whereupon the delegates performed an embarrassing public volte-face. *Weekly Review* castigated the weakness of delegates who were ready first to ignore public opinion in order to entrench their position and later to vote against their own inclinations in order not to be out step with the president.[15]

As well as modifying KANU's rules, the Saitoti Committee criticized the institutional outworking of Nyayoism. Hitherto, the fact that all leaders belonged to the same corps was taken to be a licence for them to interfere indiscriminately in one another's fields. However, 'The distinction between the executive, the judiciary, the legislature and KANU is blurred, and a serious scrutiny is called for so that the organs can be effective and independent.' The weakness of the Nyayoist view of leadership extends to the periodic assessment of leaders at election-time. The conflicting requirements of unswerving loyalty to the leader and assessing him or her objectively through the ballot cannot be resolved. In the case of the president and a few locally prominent politicians, the conflict becomes so acute that unopposed election becomes imperative.

The development of KANU: Nyayoism in action
The contrast between Moi's agenda and that of the Kenyatta era may be illustrated from the history of KANU.

P. Anyang' Nyong'o[16] suggests that, at independence, KANU comprised a coalition of regional nationalist interests. By 1966 a conservative faction had become dominant and, once this faction had secured a *de facto* one-party state, it allowed the party to atrophy.[17] The party retained sufficient life to legitimize the faction's activities, but was too weak to be a means for other factions to achieve their objectives within the bounds of law. KANU elections, the clearest means of revitalizing the party, were not held between 1968 and 1978, although the party constitution called for them to be held every two years. As Chepkwony says, 'the weak and emasculated KANU was used to consolidate the power of the regime as well as functioning as an arena used by Kenyatta to let others fight for the acquisition and control of subsidiary resources'.[18]

The revival of KANU after Moi came to power was striking. We have to question Chepkwony's assessment of this revival:

> party 'revitalization drives' were announced on several occasions in order to divert people's attention from national issues. For example, the drive in 1970 was to divert attention from the murder of Tom Mboya. In 1975, it was to counteract criticism against the Government's cover up of Kariuki's death.
>
> Finally, in 1978, it was aimed at providing the new President, Daniel arap Moi, with a power base.[19]

The 1978 party revitalization may have served to consolidate Moi's hold on power; but it must now be clear that it went well beyond this and it is misleading to compare it with the exercises in window-dressing which were typical of the Kenyatta regime.

From about 1985, fundamental changes were made to Kenyan political life by the enhanced role of the party. The creation of a mass party,[20] the holding of regular party elections,[21] the entrusting to rank-and-file KANU members of the choice of candidates for public office, the enforcement of party discipline[22] through disciplinary committees and by Youth Wingers, the delegation to branch level of the issue of life membership certificates, and the partial eclipse of the National Assembly by KANU councils[23] all gave the party a role it never had in the Kenyatta era.

This restructuring was in accordance with Nyayoist doctrine. Under Kenyatta, the people were excluded from formal political processes (although Bienen[24] suggested that through their contacts with the civil service they had an alternative form of political participation). Nyayoism, however, gives the masses a vital role in politics: that of legitimizing the leadership corps, and working for national development under the direction of that corps. The Saitoti Committee's report, defending the continuation of a one-party state, explained:

> Inappropriate comparison has been made between KANU and single political parties which once operated in eastern Europe and the Soviet Union. KANU, unlike the ideological vanguard parties of those countries, is a mass party, a mobilizing force and a democratic instrument of social change and economic development.[25]

The Saitoti Committee itself was a striking example of the difference between Kenyatta's KANU and the *Nyayo* KANU: both because the public bothered to tell KANU what it thought of its rules and because KANU bothered to listen. The committee, established to provide a safe release of political pressure against the one-party state, received and reported evidence highly critical of current KANU practices from numerous individuals; and substantive changes were recommended and made as a result.

Nyayoism in context

The preceding analysis is meant to supplement, rather than to replace, the analyses of Kenyan politics offered by Gertzel, Bienen, Throup, Crawford Young, Atieno-Odhiambo and others. In suggesting that there was an ideological dimension to Kenyan politics in this period, we do not suggest that factional, ethnic, class and selfish personal interests had lost their influence in public life. Senior politicians from the president downwards continued to profit from the system: it is possible to be doctrinaire without being saintly.

Likewise, regional 'bosses'[26] did not lose their power, but the context in which they operated altered radically. The new arrangements made them increasingly vulnerable to pressures from outside their districts. They were answerable to their superiors in the Nyayoist hierarchy of leaders.

Nyayoism and the churches

It is now easier to perceive the ideological basis for the Nyayoist demand for a one-party state. There cannot be two or more competing philosophies in the leadership corps, or the struggle between them will effectively bring development to a halt.[27] The introduction of multi-parties was utterly alien to Nyayoism.

This is also why Moi treats the church as 'part and parcel of the government'.[28] Church leaders are, in his view, just leaders; and all leaders must be part of the leadership corps and *Nyayo* followers. It explains why in *Kenya African nationalism* Moi, who frequently refers to the vital importance of Christian faith, never once mentions the institutional church. The church is not considered as an entity over against the state.

The Saitoti Committee went further than Moi's book in recognizing the functional distinction between religious organizations and the state. However, it still maintained the intimate connection between the two sets of leaders:

> The public drew the committee's attention to the war of words among and between politicians and religious leaders. They said that they expected leaders to work in harmony and not to wash their dirty linen in public, since their public quarrels would reflect negatively on those they lead.

The committee recognized the corollary of this interconnection, that church leaders cannot be excluded from political discussions:

> The relationship between the State and religious organizations can only be understood by recognizing their functional independence, that religious organizations need the State just as the State needs them . . .
> In this kind of relationship, a demarcation line as to what is political or spiritual, secular or sacred is hard to mark, just as a coin has two sides and yet is still a coin.

What is true for the church is true for any other organized group in the nation: they are not ultimately separate from the government, because they should be part of the one leadership structure of the nation. The affiliation of *Maendeleo ya Wanawake* (national women's organization) to KANU and suggestions that other groups, such as the Central Organization of Trades Unions (COTU) or the Law Society of Kenya should be similarly affiliated result from this belief.

Nyayoism claims to base itself on Christianity. The Saitoti Committee gave partial recognition to the churches as entities functionally distinct from the state. Nevertheless, *Nyayo* theory absorbs the church leaders into the national leadership, bound by the same requirements of loyalty, that apply to other leaders. Their licence to criticize the state is closely circumscribed.

G. P. Benson

The basis for church dialogue with the *Nyayo* state

PRELIMINARY NOTE: THE STATE'S DIALOGUE PARTNER

Although 'the church' has been in dialogue with the state throughout Kenya's history, different organizations have maintained the church's end of the debate from time to time.

In 1978, Lonsdale, Booth-Clibborn and Hake[29] pointed out that during the colonial era dialogue with the authorities was maintained by the CCK (later NCCK).[30] At that time, the mainstream Protestant churches, being part of the colonial establishment, were virtually silent on political matters.

However, during Kenyatta's rule, the NCCK's development activities made it part of the 'establishment'; it was reluctant to intervene in political debate. Meanwhile, the leaders of the mainstream Protestant churches found their voice in dialogue with the state – as became evident in the crises of 1969. Lonsdale and co-authors were concerned that in future the churches might 'fail to maintain an implied critique of the State, for want of a continuing commitment of their own to practical justice in society'.

Since 1978, the shape of church–state debate has altered. The Kenyan churches have withdrawn from NCCK its implicit sole licence to act on their behalf in human development issues: many churches now have their own development programmes. On a range of issues, such as queue-voting (1986) and constitutional amendments (1986, 1988), the churches have 'for a moment found themselves at the head of a political opposition'.[31] At the same time, NCCK has become more forthright in political affairs. By the time Section 2A was repealed, it was difficult to distinguish between the NCCK's stance and that of the churches. They stood together in dialogue with the *Nyayo* state.

THEOLOGIES OF POWER

Lonsdale and his colleagues' 1978 article began with the words: 'Apart from the Roman Catholic Church, the churches in Kenya – and they are many – have historically possessed a very limited theology of secular power'. This crucial observation requires attention: for, although it is true, it overlooks the more significant fact that the churches of Kenya possess a very well developed biblical hermeneutic.

Available theologies of power

The Christian world is not short of theologies of power. Kenyan church leaders are aware of them.

Two relevant examples are South African 'black theology' and Latin American liberation theology. Black theology is particularly well known; many Kenyan church leaders have visited South Africa and are on terms of friendship with acknowledged black church leaders there. Liberation theology is known in Kenya mainly through the writings it has produced, although some Roman Catholic clergy, especially expatriates, have attempted to apply the methods of con- scientization and 'base communities' in a Kenyan context.[32] Yet, although these theologies are studied with respect and occasionally quoted, neither is prominent in Kenya.

It is typical of such theologies to link themselves to a particular biblical motif, which is used as a source of categories for understanding contemporary politics. The exodus motif, with the categories of oppression and liberation, is an obvious example. However, a survey of Kenyan preachers' texts does not suggest a particular focus on the exodus or any other single motif.

Kenyan theologies of power

Some Kenyan church leaders have attempted to lay their own founda- tions for a theology of power. The two most influential essays have been those of the Revd Timothy Njoya[33] and Bishop Henry Okullu.[34] Njoya proposes a criterion of 'human dignity', by which he means individual human worth upheld in a framework of relationships, understood in senses derived from traditional African culture. By this criterion, we may assess the behaviour of an individual or the structure and conduct of a church or a government. Whatever enhances dignity (our own and that of others) is to be commended; whatever undermines it is to be condemned. All human institutions are the products of expediency, intended to further the goal of dignity. State, church and tribe have no assured place in the scheme of values, save that which expediency gives them.

Okullu's alternative criterion is 'justice', which is the chief charac- teristic of God's intervention in the world. This 'justice' is not limited to retribution for wrongs or to holding the ring of society. It entails actively promoting righteousness and human well-being. Part of God's plan is that there should be both church and state – sharing a common calling to promote justice, but institutionally independent of one another. Tribe and other lesser units of society should also be valued as the building-blocks of national unity.

Interesting as these essays are, they have had little effect on the agenda of the churches as a whole. Their main significance is to disclose the integrating principles behind the ministries of their authors.[35] More significant than either of these essays is the Kenyan tradition of evangelical biblical hermeneutics – a tradition in which both Njoya and Okullu stand, and whose most articulate representative is Bishop David Gitari.

Gitari's criticism[36] of both essays is instructive: he regards them as being exegetically weak. Gitari rejects any theory which finds a single explanatory principle for what the Scriptures say about the duties of the state: it would require a procrustean approach to exegesis which he cannot endorse. His comment is rooted in the biblical hermeneutic typical of mainstream Protestantism in Kenya.

BIBLICAL HERMENEUTICS IN CHURCH-STATE DIALOGUE

Hermeneutics is broadly defined as 'the science of interpretation'[37] or 'the attempt to understand something that someone else has said or written'.[38] In the field of biblical studies, 'hermeneutics defines the rules one uses when seeking out the meaning of the scriptures';[39] it raises 'questions about the nature of knowledge, the use of language, and the scientific and ontological presuppositions operative in the mind of the exegete'.[40]

The claim of Protestant critics of the Kenya government – especially from the CPK and Presbyterian Church of East Africa (PCEA) – is that they are not ill-intentioned or politically motivated, but that their reading of the Bible compels them to oppose some of the actions and attitudes of the state. Bishop David Gitari is among those who has made the hermeneutical roots of his thinking explicit.

Authority

The evangelical mainstream Kenyan churches assign to the Bible a unique authority and importance. The Scriptures are understood not merely as a product of long-dead human authors, but as a present communication from the living God. Gitari writes: 'It is because it is inspired by God that the Bible is able to instruct us in the truth about God'.[41] Part of the hermeneutical task is to enable the text to make its intended appeal to the reader, and to identify the reader's appropriate response:

> No man who is seeking for the truth can ignore the Bible. In the Bible there is saving wisdom which cannot be found in any other book . . . All theologies and all ethical teaching are to be tested against the teaching of the Bible.

This acknowledgement of the Bible's authority is not confined to religious contexts. Kenyan churchmen's pronouncements are steeped in biblical quotation and allusion. It is impossible to understand the churches' political thought without unravelling its relationship to the Scriptures:

> The study of the scriptures is not a selfish exercise; we do not study them merely for our own private benefit or just for the salvation of our souls . . .
> True love is love in action. It is a response to the needs of people and of society as a whole. Paul tells Timothy to study the scriptures so that he can be well-equipped for every good work.

Inspiration

Christians give authority to the Bible because they believe it to be inspired by God. An article by F.F. Bruce contrasts a view of inspiration in 'the Platonic sense of utterance in a state of ecstatic possession' with the understanding that it is 'a divinely-given quickening of the writers' awareness and understanding'.[42]

Gitari takes the latter view: 'Every book of the Bible is the very word of God. Though the Bible was written by human beings, yet those who wrote it were moved by the Spirit of God to write what they wrote'.[43] Preaching on 2 Timothy 3 and 4. Gitari discusses the origin and proper handling of this and other Scriptures. He repeatedly points his hearers to the historical context, the relationships and the psychology which led Paul to write as he did:

> Realising that his time to leave this world was near, Paul was anxious to hand over his leadership of the Church to Timothy . . . Paul wrote this letter to encourage Timothy to accept the responsibility of leading the Church despite his shortcomings.[44]

Gitari sees the Bible as the product of God's interaction with the ancient writers and their particular circumstances. It is as truly a human document as it is a divine one. The Bible is the word of God because God interacts with its humanity.

Text and reader

The churches of the Reformation claimed that the Scriptures were intelligible and authoritative and could be understood by the ordinary processes of attentive reading and scholarship.

According to Young and Ford, this approach to biblical studies 'assumed that scripture had one true meaning and that that true meaning was its original meaning. But this hope has not been realized'.[45] The hope failed as scholars reached diametrically opposite conclusions about the meaning of texts, and as European and North American exegesis yielded results irrelevant to the life of the church outside these regions.

Hermeneutics was compelled to recognize that the interpreter brings a pre-understanding to the text, which partly controls the reading of the text. A 'hermeneutical circle' is thus set up. In the words of G. N. Stanton.

> The interpreter must allow his own presuppositions and his own pre-understanding to be modified or even completely reshaped by the text itself . . . There must be a constant dialogue between the interpreter and the text. The hermeneutical circle is not only unavoidable but desirable.[46]

Cultural presuppositions explicitly affect Kenyan churchmen's understanding of the Bible. Gitari's presentation to the 1988 Lambeth

Conference, 'Evangelisation and culture: Primary evangelism in northern Kenya',[47] illustrates the point:

> We have inherited from the Western Church a concept of evangelism as winning individuals to Jesus Christ . . . But an individual making a major decision in his life alone is alien to African culture . . . We are convinced that in our primary evangelism among nomadic peoples, our approach must not be that of rescuing individuals from a sinking boat but rather winning communities to Jesus Christ . . . St Paul preached and baptized in the household of Cornelius, and in that of the Philippian jailer. The gospel can also be preached in the household of a nomadic people, respecting and preserving their traditional communitarian culture.

Eschatology: a central hermeneutical concern

The interpreter's pre-understanding of the Bible includes assumptions concerning what the Bible, or the New Testament, is about. For much of this century, biblical studies have been dominated by interest in eschatology (the study of the end of this present world).

Eschatology received an important new interpretation by scholars as diverse as A. Schweitzer, R. Otto, C. H. Dodd, R. Bultmann, W. Pannenberg and J. Moltmann. In their view, when Jesus spoke of the coming of the 'kingdom of God' he was not referring solely to a future event at the end of time. Rather, 'in Jesus' teaching it had begun to break in: "from its futurity it already extends its operation into the present" (Otto).[48] For Bultmann,

> here every present moment is an 'eschatological' moment, in the sense that the answers and questions of the past meet one in the present and evoke the reaction of responsible choice which goes to make that new thing, the future.[49]

The Bible's message, it was claimed, demanded an immediate response to God in the choices of the moment. This approach was welcomed by many, especially within the World Council of Churches, who believed that Christians had a duty to intervene in political affairs. Eschatological interest was reflected in research into biblical words for time, and so to a suggested lexical distinction between *chronos* ('chronological time') and *kairos* ('the eschatological moment').

By the mid-1960s academic enthusiasm for such analyses was diminishing. Nevertheless, word studies remained influential in African theology. In 1986, South African churches published the '*Kairos* document', which argued that the critical moment had come for Christians to oppose the injustice of the apartheid state. In 1991 the National Council of Churches of Kenya published 'A *kairos* for Kenya', which addressed the unease over the Kenya government's increasing hostility to calls for a multi-party state. The titles of these documents reveal the continuing influence of an eschatologically centred hermeneutic in contemporary African, and specifically Kenyan, theology.

In Africa, theological interest in eschatology is clearly linked to political crisis. True to this eschatological concern, much Kenyan Protestant theology is written in the shadow of impending judgment. The judgment foreseen is not supernatural apocalypse: it is national, social and economic catastrophe, which the sins of leaders (and churches) will draw down on their own heads. NCCK's book *A Christian view of politics in Kenya* interprets Isaiah 28-33:

> These chapters in Isaiah show that peace and national security are inseparable from genuine justice; and that it is the responsibility of the national leader to uphold justice at all times. Isaiah lived at a time when government ministers were abusing their position by making the courts an instrument of injustice; such things he warned would certainly lead to judgement and not peace.[50]

Gitari's paper for the African Theological Fraternity, 'The Church's witness in seeking just structures', warns churches against either giving uncritical support to governments or attempting to be neutral in the face of injustice. Such attitudes invite judgment on the church itself:

> The Church must at all times take the side of the poor and on their behalf (and even better together with them) struggle for justice. It is to be regretted that atheism is now being promoted in countries with a long history of Christianity. It appears as if 'the salt has lost its taste' and 'is no longer good for anything except to be thrown out and trodden underfoot by men'.[51]

Gitari's preaching as a whole, especially when he touches on political issues, returns repeatedly to the eschatological theme of judgment on those who reject justice. Of the four sermons in *Let the bishop speak*, two – 'Idols of our times' on Jeremiah 1: 7 and 'The truth is always triumphant' on Daniel 6 – are largely concerned with this theme. His reading of the Scriptures emphasizes that we have to do with a holy God, whose blazing anger against injustice and oppression arises from love of all that he has made. God's determination to restore all things in Christ will bring mercy to those who accept it but judgment to those who persist in disobedience.

THE CHURCHES' ENGAGEMENT WITH THE STATE

The churches' reading of the Scriptures motivated and shaped their engagement with the *Nyayo* state. They believe themselves obliged to measure any state's actions by the standards of the Scriptures and to compel the state to attend to the Scriptures by lively preaching.

At the same time, the churches' reading of the Scriptures, restricted their critique to the practical consequences of Nyayoist policies and restrained the churches from entering into dialogue with the theory of Nyayoism.

The preacher as prophet

'The preacher is captive to the Holy Spirit and he has to preach on any issue the Holy Spirit leads him to touch'.[52] Kenyan politicians commonly attack as disingenuous remarks such as this by Gitari. Churchmen, it is alleged, wish to claim a privileged position from which they may interfere in political debates without themselves coming under attack. The churches attract the cynicism of journalists, such as *Weekly Review's* Hilary Ng'weno:

> In his perennial battles with politicians, the Rev. Timothy Njoya has often invoked Almighty God as his ally in whatever he pronounces. That is perhaps as it should be, for, after all, the Rev. Njoya is a man of God, and in questions of truth he must be given the benefit of the doubt when he is in disagreement with laymen, even when, as on many issues such as economics, he makes pronouncements on subjects way beyond his depth.[53]

Nevertheless, church leaders claim that their preaching is more than the offering of personal opinion – even well-informed and intelligent personal opinion. The substance of the preaching has arisen from a dialogue between the preacher and the biblical text, on the subject of the contemporary world.

Gitari describes the preacher's responsibility as being 'the prophetic ministry of judgement'. He writes:

> Judgement means that the Church will constantly remind people of the standard of righteousness and justice which alone exalts a nation. The Church will also take a lead in giving moral and practical support to the State when it upholds that standard, and will responsibly criticize the State or those in authority when they depart from it. When society accepts as normal racism, tribalism, corruption or the exploitation of fellow men, Christians cannot be silent. They, like the prophets of old, must speak out and pronounce the will and judgement of God. The Christian community must be an ever-present reminder to the State that it exists only as the servant of God and man.[54]

For Gitari, the church must show that the Scriptures are relevant to contemporary society, declaring what God requires and providing a yardstick for the nation and its leaders to assess their own conduct. The church has a duty to promote justice in society as well as to draw individuals and communities to worship God:

> Prophecy differs from witness in that it does not address people in order to convert them. Rather, 'Prophecy aims at people as personifications of institutions and situations which perpetuate circumstances that are contrary to the will of God for this world. In her prophecy, the Church confronts the powers that be and challenges them to employ their power for greater justice,

peace and freedom. In this way, she humanizes society, as Jesus did in respect of Samaritans, tax-gatherers, women and lepers, in the society in which he lived.' If the Church does not challenge wrong structures, she is unfaithful to her prophetic calling; for where unjust structures are not explicitly challenged, then they are consciously or unconsciously sanctioned by the Church.[55]

Bringing the Scriptures to bear on the world

The goal of a Christian reading of the Scriptures is not to discover a set of propositions about God; it is to hear his living voice. C. P. Michael and M. C. Norrisey[56] describe a method of engaging with the text of the Bible whose pedigree goes back to St Augustine:

In Augustinian prayer, one uses *creative imagination* to transpose the words of Sacred Scripture to our situation today. One tries to imagine (intuit) what meaning the words of Scripture would have if Jesus Christ, or God the Father, or the Holy Spirit appeared and spoke them to us at this moment. In Augustinian prayer we try to think of the words of the Bible as though they were a personal letter from God addressed to each one of us.

The sermons with which Protestant clergy annoy the Kenyan government generally follow this model. For example, Gitari's 1987 sermon on Daniel 6[57] contains informative historical material about the Persian empire which is the setting for the text; but the exegetical context is contemporary Kenya. The following examples are chosen from among very many:

[King Darius] chose three ministers who were to receive reports from the 120 administrators. We might describe them as 'Ministers in the Office of the President, responsible for provincial administration' . . .

If Daniel was an administrator in Kenya today, he would sell KANU tickets to every citizen who qualifies and he would not register anybody as a voter who was not supposed to be registered . . .

The conspirators having failed to find faults in Daniel's work, they had to look for faults elsewhere. After much consideration, they decided to remove Daniel by changing the constitution . . ..

King Darius made the mistake of allowing the constitution to be changed before this matter which affected fundamental human rights was thoroughly discussed by all concerned.

Ancient Persia is depicted so as to bring out most strongly its resemblances to Kenya today, so that God's actions then become warnings of what God is about to do now. It is not too strong to say that in this sermon Darius is a Kenyan president, Daniel is a minister of state in the Kenyan government and his opponents are an alliance of politicians and KANU leaders who regard an honest man as an obstacle to their plans.

Such a reading of the text makes it speak with prophetic immediacy to the preacher's contemporaries. After the Daniel sermon, this was the point to which the discomfited authorities took greatest exception:

> The KANU national chairman, Mr David Okiki Amayo, yesterday accused Bishop David Gitari of the Church of the Province of Kenya of 'seeking to create chaos, confusion and incite wananchi against their popularly elected leaders . . .
>
> 'Bishop Gitari's biblical reference to the Book of Daniel chapter 6, about Darius and Daniel, has no parallel in Kenya. Such comparison can only be made with the aim of confusing the God-fearing and peace-loving Kenyans'.[58]
>
> Preaching in Nyeri recently, the Rt Reverend Dr David M. Gitari . . . misinterpreted parts of the Old Testament in a vain effort aimed at justifying his own radical disposition . . .
>
> The bishop glibly talked about King Darius of Persia, adducing a patently irrelevant argument which cannot justifiably be applied to present-day Kenya.[59]

These vigorous reactions show how well Gitari had succeeded in his aim of bringing his hearers to the point of engagement with the word of God.

A pragmatic, not a theoretical critique

Church leaders quickly recognized the move from the political pragmatism of the Kenyatta era to the ideologically driven system of *Nyayo*. NCCK's book *A Christian view of politics in Kenya* addressed the *Nyayo* view of leadership:

> The Apostle Paul wrote: Be imitators of me, as I am of Christ (1 Corinthians 11.1). Paul was not afraid to offer his own *nyayo* for others to follow, since he was himself following the *nyayo* of Christ. Any Christian leader who offers himself as an example in this way takes on himself the heavy burden of being a good imitator of Christ. (Foreword)

It also recognized structural defects with pastoral implications:

> As for Kenya, it will never be known whether people wanted the one-party system legalized, or not, since the matter was not openly debated in public, and even had that been so, the question could still have remained: would the people have openly discussed it – lest they be branded anti-*Nyayo*? Similarly, it is unclear whether the banning of tribal welfare associations had the popular support in the country. (p. 45)

The churches, from their reading of the Bible, were committed to seeking justice and fair dealing (both economic and forensic), and freedom of expression, association and worship. The churches were agreed that the state has been established by God and deserves support and that the church has the duty of confronting it when it goes astray.

These are highly political concerns; yet the churches' engagement with Nyayoism was 'from below', from its practical effects, rather than 'from above', at the level of political theory. They battled against its pastoral consequences: rigged ballots, intimidation of voters, suppression of freedom of speech. When they addressed issues of political structure, it was because of the evil pastoral effects of the structure, not because of its inadequate theoretical nature.

The churches found it easier to reach agreement on pastoral matters than on matters of political theory. In 1986, the National Pastors' Conference resolution deploring KANU's adoption of queue-voting was based almost wholly on the threat to the clergy themselves.[60] The lukewarm reception accorded to Okullu's and Njoya's political theologies indicate that the Kenyan church was unready to commit itself to a theology of power. Yet the lack of a theoretical critique of Nyayoism was not a weakness, the result of inadequate theological tools: rather it was a matter of principle. Gitari writes:

> Whatever action we might take for the liberation of man from oppressive regimes, it should never be assumed that succeeding governments will be free of evil. As Studdert Kennedy once observed:
>
> When a country changes its government, it only pushes one set of sinners out and puts another set of sinners in. The most passionate idealists are never completely free from egocentricity and partisan bias.[61]

Gitari believes that the church cannot support one system of government against another, as in effect it will if it engages in debate at the level of political theory. The church's duty is to engage in critical collaboration with any state which attempts to respect God's purposes. The church makes scriptural data available to the state, so that it can fulfil its God-given calling. It may not develop a root-and-branch critique of any political system which is not explicitly organized to do evil.

Nevertheless, repeated confrontation with an ideological state forced the churches to attend to the state's political theory. They developed an alternative view, based on a reading of the Scriptures, on such crucial tenets of *Nyayo* as the institutional distinction between church and state; the nature of loyalty; and the proper relationship between the leader and the people.

The churches' understanding of leadership is a case in point. The Reformation-based mainstream churches emphasize the 'priesthood of all believers', the essential solidarity between leaders and people; the influential East African Revival gives emphatic anti-hierarchic teaching. The churches' understanding is the very antithesis of the *Nyayo* doctrine of sacral leadership.

In practice, church leadership is frequently autocratic; yet at their best the churches permit open debate on policy and strategy, and make room for loyal disagreements. The churches set before Kenyans a radical alternative to Nyayoism just by being there.

The alternative positions on leadership and other matters, then, informed their day-to-day preaching. The preaching itself concentrated on the immediate practical problems faced by congregations, and barely mentioned the theoretical framework from which these problems arose.

Conclusion: pragmatic theology and ideological politics

The Kenyan churches' vigorous involvement in politics is the result of a sustained hermeneutical enterprise. Yet in its engagement with the *Nyayo* state it was essentially reactive, offering a practical critique of *Nyayo*. As the *Nyayo* state tottered, the church had no coherent alternative system to put in its place. Church interventions in politics form a complex and often exciting history of robust defence of those who are oppressed by the state's power; but, in a phrase suggested by John Lonsdale, 'a history of pinpricks replaces a theology of power'.

The churches, however, did not consider it to be their task to develop a theology of power. Their own principal agenda in Kenya is essentially evangelistic, pastoral and developmental. They had no wish to engage in mortal combat with *Nyayo* as a system. Nevertheless, from the point of view of *Nyayo* itself, the churches threw down a challenge just by existing as separate institutions, outside the framework of the *Nyayo* leadership corps.

˙Notes

1. CPK Justice and Peace Commission, *A pastoral letter to all CPK congregations* (Nairobi, Easter 1992), p. 16. The letter was signed by Archbishop Kuria and Bishops Okullu and Gitari in the name of the CPK episcopate.
2. For a description of the official policies and unofficial manipulation for sectional interest of the organs of state in Kenyatta's Kenya, see, for example, Agnes Chepkwony, *The role of non-governmental organizations in development* (Uppsala, 1987), pp. 101 ff.
3. Cf. George I. Godia's summary of this development:

   Literally speaking, 'Nyayo' is a Kiswahili word that means 'footsteps'. It has, however, acquired a much deeper meaning since President Moi first used it at a political rally to mean that he would follow the footsteps of his predecessor, the late Mzee Jomo Kenyatta. The word 'Nyayo' is not just a political slogan . . . It has become a projection of President Moi's philosophy of national life. (*Understanding* Nyayo (Nairobi, Transafrica, 1984), p. 11) .

4. NCCK's book *A Christian view of politics in Kenya: Love, peace and unity* (Nairobi, Uzima, 1983) was largely written in 1982 and had been commissioned before the coup attempt on 1 August that year.
5. (London, Macmillan, 1986). With hindsight most of what the book says can be discovered in Moi's earlier speeches; but the book makes clear the central connecting themes.
6. This is clear even from the acknowledgements (Moi, *Kenya African nationalism*, p. xvi). It is stated more formally on pp. 21–22 (where African tradition is summed up as

'African socialism' on the example of Sessional Paper no. 10), pp. 31–32, pp. 35–36, etc. Kenyatta's *Harambee* is sometimes treated as a crystallization of African tradition (pp. 18–20) and sometimes as an embryonic form of Nyayoism (p. 89).

7. 'Apart from a *Harambee* rally, I know of no other regular occasion at which leaders from all walks of life and all parts of Kenya come together, with the people and for the people' (Moi, *Kenya African nationalism*, p. 30).

8. 'Identification of leadership is, of necessity, a solemn duty of all citizens. Once identified, leadership is a resource for the identification of national goals and for the achievement of the same' (p. 79).

9. From early in his rule, Moi was criticized by the intelligentsia for 'devaluing' the presidency by over-exposure. Comparison was made with Kenyatta's much rarer but more significant appearances. Moi claimed that his frequent appearances were the logical outcome of Nyayoism (p. 91).

10. Henry Bienen says that the restrictions placed on mass political activity by the Kenyatta regime after independence divorced élites from their constituencies, and so gave them freedom to compete in irresponsible ways (*Kenya: The politics of participation and control* (Princeton, 1974), Chapter 3). The implication must be that the rooting of élites in their constituencies will encourage or compel more responsible forms of competition.

11. Cited in Chepkwony, *Role of non-governmental organizations*, pp. 168f.

12. A former deputy speaker of the National Assembly has told me that he considers Moi to be a shrewder political operator than Kenyatta was. Likewise David Throup has described Moi as

> a hard-headed political realist. Throughout his career, until perhaps Njonjo's carefully orchestrated fall from power in 1983, Moi's rivals have underestimated his skills as a political tactician. In fact . . . Moi has demonstrated consummate ability to survive the dirtiest of political infighting. He is a master of back room coalition building. (D. Throup, 'The construction and destruction of the Kenyatta state', in M. G. Schatzberg, ed., *The political economy of Kenya* (New York, Praeger, 1987), p. 46)

13. Cf. Ngugi wa Thiong'o, speaking on BBC World Service in 1988. Ngugi referred to an occasion on which Moi had told Kenyan leaders that he wanted them to repeat his own ideas 'like parrots'. He laughed and said 'How do you criticize a man who is a parody of himself'? The implication, that this represents simply a character trait of Moi, fails to understand that it is actually characteristic of his philosophy.

The speech to which Ngugi referred was made on 13 September 1984. According to the *Daily Nation*, Moi said

> I call on all ministers, assistant ministers and every other person to sing like parrots. During Mzee Kenyatta's period, I persistently sang the Kenyatta tune until people said: this fellow has nothing to say, except to sing for Kenyatta. I said: I do not have ideas of my own. Who was I to have my own ideas? I was in Kenyatta's shoes, and therefore, I had to sing whatever Kenyatta wanted. If I had sung another song, do you think Kenyatta would have left me alone? Therefore, you ought to sing the song I sing. If I put a full stop, you should put a full stop. This is how the country will move forward. The day you become a big person, you will have the liberty to sing your own song and everybody will sing it. (Cited by Koigi wa Wamwere in *Index on Censorship* 7 (1990) at p. 17. I am grateful to Mr Hugh Dinwiddy for this reference).

14. That is, the rule that a candidate who secured 70 per cent or more of the vote in the party nominations for national and local elections was declared to be the sole candidate for the seat in question, and so was automatically elected without need for a secret ballot. This effectively disenfranchised non-KANU members, who were never given a chance to express a preference.

15. *Weekly Review*, 14 December (1990), p. 9.
16. In 'State and society in Kenya: The disintegration of the nationalist coalitions and the rise of presidential authoritarianism, 1963–78', *African Affairs* 88, 351 (April 1989). After the legalization of opposition parties in December 1991, Anyang' Nyong'o became the executive director of the Forum for the Restoration of Democracy (Ford) party.
17. Nevertheless, at grass-roots level, far from the centres of power, KANU showed surprising vitality in some areas. Andrew Hake (*An urban metropolis* (New York, St Martin's Press, 1977), p. 151) draws attention to the success of the Mathare Valley Village II leadership in 'surviving the onslaughts of officialdom and in achieving its status of "improveability"', and attributes this 'in large measure to the links which were forged with the KANU party machine'.
18. Chepkwony, *Role of non-governmental organizations*, p. 168.
19. Ibid., p. 167.
20. In 1985 KANU held a recruitment drive, following which the party claimed 5 million members. The following year another drive led to a claim of 6 million members. Fresh recruitment drives have preceded subsequent national and party elections.
21. The revised KANU constitution of May 1987 provided for elections for party officials every five years, to coincide with the period of national elections. Grass-roots party elections were held in 1985 and 1988.
22. After the National Delegates' Conference in December 1990, expulsion from the party ceased to be available as a disciplinary measure: 'temporary suspension' took its place.
23. Cf. the remark of the chairman of KANU's disciplinary committee, the late David Okiki Amayo, in April 1987:

    > At the time of independence, there was a multi-party system, so the ruling party could not assume the supremacy of the land. Supremacy was therefore vested in parliament. However when the constitution was amended to make Kenya a one-party state in 1982, supremacy, in practice, moved to the party; the relevant sections of the constitution were, however, not examined and rectified along with the change to the one-party state. (*Weekly Review*, 8 May (1987), p. 6)

24. Henry Bienen, *Kenya*.
25. As reproduced in *Weekly Review*, 7 December (1990), p. 14.
26. Cf. Cherry Gertzel, *The politics of independent Kenya* (Nairobi, EAPH 1970), p. 62 and *passim*.
27. Nevertheless, Moi always left a door open to considering a multi-party system in future: 'I am convinced that, whatever the future holds for Kenya, history will confirm that at this point in time our one-party decision was right' (Moi, *Kenya African nationalism*, p. 183). Cf. *Weekly Review*, 30 March (1990):

    > On Friday last week the president declared that multi-party systems were unsuitable for Africa 'at the moment' . . . President Moi did not completely rule out the possibility of introducing multi-party systems in African countries in the future, but contended that this would only be possible when ethnic groups became welded into a cohesive national community.

    However, despite this open door, it is hard to see how the multi-party state is theoretically compatible with Nyayoism. Although Moi's book mentions the danger of ethnic fragmentation as an argument for the one-party system, the principal rationale is the unitary nature of the Nyayoist leadership corps. This main plank of *Nyayo* demands a single-party state with a single loyalty focus. The repeal of Section 2A of the constitution was highly destabilizing for Nyayoism.
28. Quoted in J. Lonsdale, S. Booth-Clibborn and A. Hake, 'The emerging pattern of church and state co-operation in Kenya', in E. Fashole-Luke *et al.*, eds, *Christianity in independent Africa* (London, Rex Collings, 1978), p. 284.

29. Ibid.
30. CCK: Christian Council of Kenya. NCCK: National Christian Council of Kenya, later National Council of Churches of Kenya.
31. Lonsdale *et al.*, 'Emerging patterns', p. 281. Cf. *Weekly Review*, 5 October (1990), p. 4:

> the CPK as an institution remains the most resilient focus of dissent, with the political opposition largely having been silenced . . . the CPK remains the one institution that retains the capacity continually to raise issues embarrassing to the government.

32. In June 1990, the Kenyan Catholic Episcopal Conference issued a pastoral letter, which said in part: 'we are afraid that the philosophy of National Security *publicly condemned by our brethren in Latin America* in unison with the Pope in 1979, may become installed in our country' (my emphasis; *Daily Nation*, 21 August (1990).

    Thika parish is an example of an individual Roman Catholic parish which has attempted to apply the base community model.
33. In *Human dignity and national identity* (Nairobi, Jemisik Cultural Books, 1987).
34. In *Church and politics in East Africa* (Nairobi, Uzima, 1974); and with greater clarity in *Church and state in nation building and development* (Nairobi, Uzima, 1984).
35. In the case of Njoya, it is doubtful whether even this is possible, for the 'dignity principle' carefully described in his book is almost wholly absent from his collection of sermons published in the same month.
36. Frequently made in conversation.
37. J. B. Torrance in A. C. Thiselton, *The two horizons* (Exeter, Paternoster, 1980), p. xi.
38. I. H. Marshall (ed.) in *New Testament interpretation* (Exeter, Paternoster, 1977), p. 11.
39. D. McKim, *A guide to contemporary hermeneutics* (Grand Rapids, Eerdmans, 1986), p. xiii.
40. Torrance in Thiselton, *Two horizons*.
41. This and the following quotations are from D. M. Gitari, 'All Scripture is inspired by God', in *Let the bishop speak* (Nairobi, Uzima, 1988).
42. 'The history of New Testament study', in Marshall, ed., *New Testament*, p. 26.
43. Gitari, *Let the bishop speak*, p. 49.
44. P. 44.
45. F. Young and D. Ford, *Meaning and truth in 2 Corinthians* (London, SPCK, 1978), p. 2.
46. G. N. Stanton, 'Presuppositions in New Testament criticism', in Marshall, ed., *New Testament*, p. 68.
47. Published in V. Samuel and A. Hauser, eds., *Proclaiming Christ in Christ's way* (Oxford, Regnum, 1989), pp. 110, 113.
48. Bruce, 'History of New Testament study', p. 47.
49. Ibid., p. 48.
50. Pp. 29f. Gitari was the principal author of this book and jointly signed its foreword.
51. In D. Gitari and G. P. Benson, eds, *The living God* (Nairobi, Uzima, 1986), p. 122.
52. D. M. Gitari, *Let the Bishop speak*, p. 51.
53. *Weekly Review*, 4 January (1991).
54. In Gitari and Benson, *Living God*, p. 135.
55. Ibid., p. 36.
56. *Prayer and temperament* (Charlottesville, Open Door, 1984), p. 58.
57. 'The truth is always triumphant', in Gitari. *Let the Bishop speak*, p. 32.
58. *Daily Nation*, 27 June (1987).
59. *Kenya Times*, Editorial, 29 June (1987).
60. Bishop David Gitari, who chaired the conference, told me that there was no point in seeking agreement on a more wide-ranging resolution; the delegates could not have accepted it.
61. Gitari and Benson, *Living God*, p. 136.

Eleven

Coping
with the Christians
The Muslim Predicament
in Kenya

DONAL B. CRUISE O'BRIEN[1]

There is a special urgency in the recent movement of Islamic renewal
in Kenya, in that the small Muslim minority in this country, while
it is now under the hegemony of a massive Christian majority, can
also look back to a pre-colonial period when the Muslims ruled the
Indian Ocean coast. The colonial period, which saw the evangelization
of the up-country peoples and the development of the interior, was
disastrous for the development of Islam in Kenya. By the time of
Kenyan independence (1963), the Muslims of Coast Province were
finding great difficulties in meeting the competition of Christian-
educated job candidates – in what had been the home region of
Islam. This comparative disadvantage gives purpose to the programme
of educational modernization on the part of Muslim reformists in
Kenya.

An effectively organized Muslim reaction to the predicament of
marginality, their inheritance from the period of colonial rule, did not
emerge until the mid-1970s. This reaction has not only emphasized the
need for local Muslims to come to terms with modern education, but
also argued for the expansion of the Muslim community by means of
an organized preaching (*dawa*), which borrows from the example of
mission Christianity. The movement of renewal is not, however, to be
confused with modernization in any Western sense: it has also involved
the strenuous rejection of innovation (*bid'a*), of post-Prophetic accre-
tions in Islam. And the emulation of the organizational instruments
of Christianity has gone with a campaign to weaken Christian belief.
One may doubt whether the organized and planned response of Muslim

200

associations in Kenya represents the most effective defence of the local Muslim community. Conversions to Islam appear to develop on an individual basis through trading contacts, or through intermarriage, where the organized *dawa* can revive communal hostilities. The revival of these antagonisms has recently been assisted by the creation of an Islamic Party of Kenya (IPK) (in 1992) in what seems a hazardous gesture in such a Muslim minority situation. Perhaps this impetuosity is to be explained as an instance of the dangers of believing in one's own demographic propaganda.

The number of Muslims in Kenya cannot be precisely known, given the wilful agnosticism of official statistics on the subject since 1962, but the best available estimates would suggest a Muslim population of somewhere between 6 and 8 per cent of Kenya's total population, or between 1,000,000 and 1,300,000 believers, in 1983. Higher figures are indeed proposed by Muslim sources, 25 per cent by the Islamic Foundation in Kenya, 35 per cent or 4.5 million Kenyan Muslims according to international Muslim organizations – but always without indication of the statistical sources. It is possible that census data from colonial times would tend to underestimate Muslim numbers, given the ascendancy of Christianity and the likely tendency to identify oneself with the dominant party, but local and ethnographic knowledge does not allow a very wide margin of statistical error. One may therefore with some confidence assert that the Muslim population of Kenya cannot exceed 10 per cent or fall below 5 per cent, and is in all probability somewhere between 6 per cent and 8 per cent.[2]

Kenya's Muslim community thus exists in the shadow of the dominant Christian population (45 per cent by one Catholic estimate, with 73 per cent as the estimate of the *World Christian encyclopedia*[3]). Kenyan Christians are, of course, divided – Roman Catholics, various Protestant denominations, independent churches – but from a Muslim perspective they constitute a formidable mass of unbelief. The dynamic sectors of the Kenyan Christian community would appear to be among the Roman Catholics and the African independent churches. The churches have in any case provided for the education of the national élite and, indeed, that of much of the mass: missionary sources concur that the basic reason for this educational emphasis has been as a response to insistent African popular demand[4] – education, therefore, as the most promising instrument of evangelization. The Christian-educated clerk from an up-country tribe could thus be the vanguard element in this evangelization under colonial rule, and the descendants of such early converts have come to constitute today's national political élite – in the state bureaucracy, in the commercial sector and in the ruling party. The country's power and wealth are thus broadly in Christian rather than in Muslim hands, as the economic development of Kenya has been concentrated in what were historically the white highlands of colonial settlement – it is the African Christians who have inherited the colonial earth.

Not only is the Kenyan Muslim community numerically small, it is geographically divided into two main peripheral areas – the semi-desert north of the Somalis and the Indian Ocean coast of the Swahili, to which one should add a small Muslim area near Lake Victoria. These peripheral areas do not, furthermore, significantly intercommunicate. Kenya's Muslims are more than a little suspect as national citizens: the Somalis as a subject of irredentism from Somalia (represented by one point in the five-point national star of Somalia), the Swahili as erstwhile supporters of the *Mwambao* movement at the time of Kenyan independence. A legacy of mistrust on the part of central government has followed from *Mwambao*, a movement with a confused aspiration to coastal autonomy, to some form of co-sovereignty with Zanzibar or even to separate independence.[5] And it follows from such considerations that the task of Muslim self-assertion in today's Kenya should be undertaken with prudence and discretion. Muslims complain that the Christian missions play on the stranger character of Muslims in Kenya, assimilating 'Muslim' with 'Arab' on the coast, reminding their pupils of the coastal Muslim role in the pre-colonial slave trade (as Muslim intellectuals also tend to offer reminders of the colonial role in the spread of Christianity).

The Muslims of the Indian Ocean coast, who are the principal concern here, have thus inherited a situation of marginality in present-day Kenya. A large part of the problem lies in the past failure of Islam to penetrate far inland from the coastal settlements, as trade routes to the interior were barred by the waterless environment of the *Nyika* and by a hostile nomadic population. In the relative absence of pre-colonial trade between Muslims and pagans, there was a corresponding absence of conversion to Islam in the up-country areas. The Swahili settlements of the coast lived by a combination of fishing and farming, with an overseas trade, notably to the Hadramaut, regulated by the annual monsoon winds, and to the islands and the other coastal settlements. In Neville Chittick's elegant summary, 'it was seawards that the cities of the coast faced, looking out over the great maritime region constituted by the Indian Ocean and its coasts'.[6] The maritime orientation was advantageous to Islam in so far as it allowed regular commerce with the holy places of the Arabian peninsula, sustaining the devotional life of the coast, but it was also a liability in so far as it tended to exclude regular commerce with those who were perceived as the barbarians of the interior, the *washenzi*, and thus to limit the diffusion of the faith.

The coastal cities liked to be left to manage their own affairs, a preference in which they were then to some extent indulged by British colonial rule. 'Benign neglect' would be an apt enough characterization of colonial policy for the coast after the transfer of the territorial headquarters from the coastal city of Mombasa to the new up-country town of Nairobi (1907). Economic development would then be concentrated among the white settlers of the highlands around Nairobi, and Christian spiritual development among black Africans of the same geographical area. And, although the coast was left to stagnate, it was also allowed a factitious autonomy under colonial rule, which appears to have been of some consolation to the erstwhile Muslim rulers, with a ten-mile strip from the coast (the cultivable area) under the nominal co-sovereignty of Zanzibar (those of the ten-mile strip being 'British protected persons' rather than colonial subjects).

Colonial protection may have been soothing for some, but it had the effect of further isolating Kenya's Muslims from the development of the interior. The contrast with the neighbouring territory of Tanganyika may be instructive here: in pre-colonial times there were already caravan routes to the interior, notably through Bagamoyo, which allowed Swahili Muslim penetration and substantial conversion to Islam among the people affected by this trade. And under colonial rule (German and then British) Swahili intermediaries were given an importance in Tanganyika which they never attained in Kenya after 1907, allowing them to play an important role in the continuing process of conversion to Islam. It must also be noted, in this context, that the Sufi brotherhoods in Tanganyika (principally Qadiriyya, but also Shadhiliyya) allowed the emergence of an African Islamic leadership among some of the up-country peoples. The saint of the Sufi brotherhood, with the loyalty of a mass of disciples, was a person of economic and political substance, a valued intermediary and power-broker under colonial rule. The organizational instrument of the Sufi brotherhood thus served the diffusion of Islam, bringing about conversions and protecting the newly converted. This was the case in Tanganyika,[8] and of course elsewhere in Africa (notably in Senegal), but in Kenya it has remained the case that the Sufi brotherhood is a marginal presence. There are, indeed, brotherhoods in the north, among the Somali, but among the Muslims of the coast organized Sufism appears to have made little impression. The absence of brotherhoods among the Swahili perhaps reflects (or perhaps determines) the absence of power at their disposal in Kenya. One informant volunteered the explanation that: 'We've no brotherhoods because we've no power'; the Senegalese case might suggest an inversion of causality here – the Swahili Muslims having no power because the Sufi brotherhoods are so little developed among them. (A schoolchild in Mombasa, upon learning the role of brotherhoods in Senegal, declared he was willing to die in *jihad* to make Kenya follow the Senegalese example.)[9]

Not only was the economic development of Kenya under colonial rule concentrated in the non-Muslim interior, allowing a very substantial development of conversion to Christianity: worse than that, from the local Muslim viewpoint, was the descent of the up-country peoples to the coast, in quest of employment as labourers or clerks. The port of Mombasa was the principal city thus affected: 'in the nineteen-twenties, devout Muslims saw familial order crumbling, drunkenness and disobedience rampant and aliens invading the city'.[10] The up-country migrants resisted conversion to Islam, unlike the up-country slaves of pre-colonial times, who had been readily assimilated, and the migrants even brought a Christianity which sought its own conversions (although these remained very few, even among the newly Muslim). But migration from the interior none the less had the dramatic effect of making the city of Mombasa, pre-colonial Muslim capital of the coast, a city with a non-Muslim majority.[11] As literacy in English and English-language qualifications became the necessary basis for career success either in the public service or in the more elaborate forms of commercial enterprise, so the Christian-educated got ahead and the Muslims fell behind. A balance of contempt appears to have developed here: Swahili Muslims tended to disdain manual labour in the port, and they seldom acquired the English-language credentials necessary for clerical employment (a problem to which we shall return), as requiring a 'Christian-dominated' schooling. Such Muslims have viewed the up-country competition as lying between barbarism and unbelief. The up-country migrants, on the other hand, have tended to view the coast people as lazy, ill-educated and illiterate.

The advent of Kenyan independence (1963) found the Muslims altogether confused and unprepared: lulled by the fiction of separate status under colonial government, and perhaps soothed by the reassuring words of local colonial officials, they were slow to accept the reality of up-country domination in independent Kenya. Muslim hopes in the period immediately before independence were for some form of special arrangement with the Sultanate of Zanzibar, perhaps even a separate independence. In the cautious formulation of one notable coastal ex-politician, the '*Mwambao* movement had many different strands, the most consistent demand [being] for some kind of political autonomy for a coastal state'.[12] But *Mwambao*, of course, came to nothing, and the reality of the post-independence political situation has been that of up-country domination, as government in Mombasa and elsewhere in the Coast Province has been monopolized by non-Muslim appointments to the principal administrative positions (District Officer, District Commissioner, Provincial Commissioner). It is to be remarked that the elected members of parliament (MPs) do provide some political representation for Kenyan Islam (seven MPs, out of a total of 170, in January 1987). Such political representation has had to work through the clientelistic paths of presidential patronage, where it has offered a valued resource in access to the diplomatic and financial support of the wider Muslim world. Muslims see themselves as numerically under-represented in the Kenyan parliament, although this is on the basis of their own optimistic estimates of the total number of fellow-believers in the country. It is again to be remarked that in some cases Muslims have done well enough in parliamentary elections, as in Mombasa, where tribal divisions among the up-country voters and candidates have allowed three Muslims to be elected for the town's three seats, with an electorate in overall majority non-Muslim.[13] But the elected representatives appear to be quite widely distrusted by their own electorate, suspected of working for their own benefit rather than that of the Muslim community. Such opinions may reflect the jealousies of factional politics: one MP in particular, Sharif Nassir (Mombasa Central), has apparently been instrumental in raising substantial subsidies for Kenyan Islam from Gulf sources, although Nassir's numerous enemies would suggest that the funds so raised have served his personal uses (absence of accountancy being a recurrent complaint in the financial affairs of Kenyan Islam).

Deficient in political leadership and poorly organized, the Muslims of the coast have thus found themselves exposed to what is seen as an up-country 'invasion', with negative effects sketched in a local pamphlet:

> The large number of Coast youth who have left school and are looking for jobs is alarmingly growing . . . aggravated by a large number of up-country youth, sent in to be given jobs in Mombasa . . . Those leaders who are ferrying youngsters from their respective areas into Mombasa, for the purpose of giving them semi-skilled, clerical or lower management jobs . . . take jobs meant for indigenous youth and for the ones who have been permanently living at the Coast for some generations.[14]

The Swahili are understandably proud of the way in which their coastal culture has assimilated other invaders in the past, thus 'conquering the Arab conquerors' of pre-colonial times, but their reaction to the challenge of Kenyan independence thus remains uncertain.

An effectively organized Muslim response to the predicament of up-country Christian dominance does not appear to have emerged until the mid-1970s with a younger and more assertive organizing committee taking control of the National Union of Kenya Muslims, (NUKEM) (Coast Province). NUKEM presented itself as the only effective voice for the Muslims of the coast, putting the Muslim position to government on such contentious issues as the law of succession or inter-faith marriage, but concentrating on the issue of education. Education is the vector of the principal issues confronting Kenya's Muslim population, and educational modernization became the first objective of the younger generation of Muslim leadership, in the Ansaar Muslim Youth (created 1976) and the Muslim Education and

Welfare Association (MEWA) (created 1986, and concentrating its attention on primary education).

The thrust of reformist activity was first in the field of education. Kenyan independence began badly in this area, from the standpoint of the Muslim modernizer, with the state takeover of the Mombasa Institute of Muslim Education, which was converted into a government polytechnic in 1964. This institution might have become an Islamic university, as had been the hope of its Muslim founders, but as Mombasa Polytechnic it has less than one-tenth Muslim students.[15] Some reformists would blame the organizational incapacity of the institute's founders, although there is also a discreet reproach to the Kenyan government for its rejection of an Arab League offer to take over the institute. These reformists saw the ensuing decade (1964–1975) as a period of lethargy and inertia among the coastal Muslim ('We had fallen behind', 'We were asleep'). The disarray of coastal Islam should also, of course, be seen in the light of the abortive campaign for coastal autonomy, the *Mwambao* movement.

The new generation of Muslim leaders, with greatly increased financial support from Saudi Arabia and other Gulf sources after 1973, came into prominence with the NUKEM takeover of 1975. It was then seeking the establishment of a modern Islamic education which could equip Muslims for job competition with the up-country 'invasion'. The traditional *madrasah* might still be popularly seen as an Islamic alternative to state education, a superior Koran school and a guarantor of Muslim values, but it has not been an instrument to career success. Muslim parents might none the less still prefer to send their children to *madrasah* and to eschew the state schools, as in a well-publicized incident in Lamu in 1987.[16] One reformist compromise has been to promote the *madrasah* as a weekend school, allowing pupils to be also enrolled in the state school, but it is agreed both that Muslim enrolment in the state schools tends to be lower and that the performance of Muslim pupils (as measured in examinations) is relatively poor.

It was the Muslim parents who were to be blamed in the first instance, both for low enrolment and for the pupils' poor exam performance, in the view of the organizers of the new associations (Ansaar, MEWA). Muslim parental resistance was presented as the principal obstacle to the education of the young in government primary and secondary schools. Parental indifference accounted for the weakness of parent–teacher associations (PTAs) in Muslim areas, and thus for the relatively poor quality of teaching staff: a strong PTA, capable of lobbying its cause with state officialdom, will win the better teachers. Parental indifference, negligence or ignorance was again blamed for the virtual inexistence of pre-primary schooling in Muslim areas: pre-primary education, ensuring basic literacy and manipulative skill, is becoming a necessity for admission to state primary schools (this last being a special concern of MEWA).[17]

In order to overcome such parental resistance to modern education, the reformists saw it as imperative that there should be (English-language qualified) teachers of Islamics in the state schools. The situation was that Christian religious education (CRE) was readily available in coast schools, but Islamic religious education (IRE) less so, in the absence of teachers with English-language credentials, English being the state language of instruction. An adverse effect of this imbalance was that Muslim pupils had often taken the CRE exam, and even apparently that there had been some conversions of Muslim pupils to Christianity in the rural areas of Coast Province.[18]

In allocating the blame for the deplorable situation of education on the coast, the new Muslim leadership pointed first to the parents and then to the local political leadership – Muslim MPs who had rendered scant service to their constituents and who were 'not under enough pressure from below'.[19] One thing the new Muslim organizers wished to make clear was that their problem was not primarily with the government. It would be wrong to accuse the Kenyan government of neglecting the Coast Province in its provision of schools, in the view of the MEWA organizers in 1987, as 'the schools we have are not full . . . our problem is with the parents.[20]

Such a denial of government neglect is certainly not accepted by other Muslim notables of Coast Province, where there is a strong feeling that government resources in all fields have been allocated by up-country politicians to their own up-country areas; thus roads, official buildings and telecommunications are concentrated around Nairobi, while the coast is neglected. This regionalist disfavour does extend, furthermore to education as to everything else; thus, for example, it is a coastal complaint that the allocation of university places in Nairobi reflects an up-country bias, simply explained by the fact that the relevant committee of evaluation is made up exclusively of up-country staff.[21] The standard up-country rebuttal of such charges of anti-Muslim discrimination in educational matters has been to argue that selection is based only on merit, as measured in examinations where Muslims have performed poorly for 'historical and cultural reasons'. It is unlikely that this could be the whole story even in this particular area, and in general terms one may say that coastal distrust of central government remains widespread.

It would also be wrong, however, to convey the idea of a single coastal Muslim community, of a group united whether by religion or by common political purpose. Communications between the Muslims of the towns and cities, on the one hand, and those of the villages of the Coast Province, on the other, have remained highly imperfect. The Islam of the urban centres has of course been dominated by that of an Arab and Swahili population ('the Swahili-speaking people', in Professor A. I. Salim's useful phrase), who are sensitive to the movement of religious opinion in the Middle East.[22] The Islam of the villages, on the other hand, that of the Islamizing Mijikenda (Digo, Giriama, etc.), has been a more recent development, still with limited awareness of the wider Islamic world.

Communication between the urban reformists and the Mijikenda, including a substantial element of discord, has focused in recent years on controversy over what is or is not a forbidden innovation (*bid'a*). Thus the notion that it is forbidden to deliver an oration at a funeral or to celebrate the Prophet's birthday has gained ground over the past fifteen years, as the first Digo students have returned from Saudi Arabia. 'Until ten years ago only Arabs went to Saudi, and they never told us about *bid'a*',[23] said a Digo secondary schoolteacher, who also remarked that the recent popularization of new notions of *bid'a* owes much to the action of the Ansaar Muslim Youth. Ideas of *bid'a* were thus apparently then current in primary schools, not in secondary, because the Ansaar-affiliated teachers (with fourth-form education and a teacher training qualification) were qualified only to be primary teachers. But this impediment will be removed as the secondary teaching qualifications are acquired by the urban reformists, in this diffusionist outlook.

The controversy surrounding the Prophet's birthday, the *maulid*, is at least half a century old on the Kenyan coast, but again the balance of opinion appears to have shifted against this festival over the past decade. The influence of returning students from al-Azhar or Medina is cited in explanation of this opinion shift, together with the influence of returning migrant labourers from Saudi Arabia or the Gulf. Is this celebration itself a forbidden innovation? The general question of what is or is not *bid'a* tends to raise a good deal of popular confusion, and to suggest the continuing differences between the Islam of the Mijikenda and that of the city sophisticates. As a schoolteacher asked, Why is it not forbidden to take an aeroplane to the *hajj*?

There remains a substantial element of country distrust of city ways, it would appear, in the reaction of the Mijikenda to the new current of Islamic reform. Emblematic of this distrust is the half-finished mosque in the Digo location of Matuga, which was to have been built on very substantial lines with the financial assistance of the urban reformist association, NUKEM. Work stopped on this construction and an adjacent *madrasah* was demolished, after the villagers refused to turn over the title deeds to the site to NUKEM. The village elder who recounted these events put the problem down to the crafty city types, *werevu*, or tricky fellows.[24] This sort of distrust does have a perceived racial element, the city folk being often identified as 'Arabs' by the Digo (in contrast to 'Africans'). But it would also plainly be an error to overstate the adversarial quality of this relationship: those of the town (whether 'Arabs' or 'Swahili-speaking people') do have an ascendancy among the Muslims of Coast Province. It is recognized that they know more of Islam, the wistful reproach being 'that they haven't troubled to tell us, the Mijikenda'. It should also be noted that the migration of up-country people to town complicates the lines of social division. The political consciousness of the Muslims of the coast is more developed in the towns, but even in the big city, Mombasa, it has appeared to be curiously restricted. Coastal Muslims thus could be excited by political development in the wider Muslim world or by romanticized historical accounts of the Golden Age when the Sultan ruled the coast, but they have seemed to find little to say of their present situation in Kenya. The examples of Libya and Iran, which show how Islam can wield power in the modern world, in the face of Europe and the United States, were thus much discussed. Iranian political literature was freely available in the streets of Mombasa (cartoons of Saddam Hussein and Ronald Reagan). Pictures of Ayatollah Khomeini were common, and Colonel Qaddafi was also admired.[25] But the reality of the Kenyan political situation was perhaps too depressing to be considered worth extensive discussion – better to look out to sea, as the coastal Muslims had so long done.

One way out of the impasse in which the Kenyan Muslims find themselves would appear to lie in the development of an organized drive for the conversion of unbelievers to Islam. The notion of such a campaign of competitive conversion, by Muslim preaching or *dawa*, is obviously relevant in a Muslim minority situation such as this, although it also may be fraught with political hazards. Muslims must thus be sensitive to the Kenyan official view that such proselytization may be divisive, contrary to President Moi's *Nyayo* philosophy of 'peace, love and unity'. Thus Muslims are warned in a semi-official pamphlet that they should not

> be claiming that they are fighting against non-Muslims and that their faith calls for discrimination against non-Muslims . . . If they continue doing so in the *Nyayo* area, they must be warned that they are doing so at their own peril and the disservice of their own faith, Islam.[26]

Competitive conversion is thus to be undertaken discreetly under present Kenyan conditions. The idea has been to the fore among local Muslims at least since the Saudi-sponsored World Assembly of Muslim Youth chose *dawa* as a major theme in its Kenyan meeting of 1982. The Ansaar Muslim Youth did advertise a discussion, among secondary school students in October 1986, on the 'obligation of *dawa*'. But Muslim informants in interviews in 1987 either denied the existence of *dawa* or down-played its significance; such disclaimers are expedient, although it does also appear to be the case that the expansion of the faith works most effectively when it is least consciously planned or organized (as, for example, among the Giriama of the coast region). It may even be that a campaign of organized *dawa*, conspicuously sponsored by Arab benefactors, harms the diffusion of Islam by identifying it with outsiders; Christian prompters will no doubt come forward with reminders of the Arab role in Kenyan history, the legacy of the trade in slaves. The modern Muslim reform associations are at some pains to emphasize that they do not depend upon outside patronage, that they raise their own funds first from members and domestic sympathizers. Some non-Muslim informants, however, suggested that outside funding (especially from individual benefactors in Saudi Arabia) is critically important to the survival of these associations, and that the scale of this funding has been the cause of much personal rivalry and factionalism, this possibly being detrimental to the associations' purposes in the longer run.

However this may be, it does seem clear that the purpose of such Muslim reformist associations is to be understood in terms of an interaction of religions, involving the adoption of many of the institutional devices of the Christian churches. Thus dispensaries and social centres as well as *madrasah* schools are built near the principal mosques, identifying Islam with social utility in the manner of a Christian missionary church.[27] And, of course, the very idea of Muslim missionary activity, structured and organized along modern bureaucratic lines, is itself understandable as an emulation of the procedures which have promoted the diffusion of Christianity in Kenya.

The national Muslim association, bureaucratic at least in principle, may also (and again in principle) increase the political vulnerability of the Kenyan Islamic community. Thus François Constantin asks whether one should discern an 'Anglican syndrome' in the working of the Supreme Council of Kenya Muslims (SUPKEM), an instrument to ensure the state's domination of the Muslim community? Constantin, however, concludes that the reality of Muslim associational life in Kenya is such as to preclude any monolithic control.[28] The Muslims of Coast Province certainly appear to pay scant attention to the proclamations of SUPKEM, issued in their name. Associations of coastal Muslims appear to have much of an informal character, with affiliations to a variety of foreign donors, personal rivalries and mutual non-communication. NUKEM could thus be said to be no more national than SUPKEM is supreme. And there are local Muslims who remain sceptical as to the effectiveness of such associations in bringing about the expansion of the Muslim community.[29]

The Muslim campaign of competitive conversion appears none the less to have become appreciably greater over recent years, in the opinion of several informants. Two Catholic priests interviewed in Nairobi, however, knew nothing of *dawa*: 'Muslims don't try to win new converts: they concentrate on undermining our beliefs'. It was in this context that the priests first mentioned the *Gospel of Barnabas*, as a document recently in clandestine circulation in Catholic schools. The *Gospel of Barnabas* does seem to have served as the semi-secret weapon of Kenyan Islam, a formidable instrument for the destabilization of the hegemonic Christians (the priestly informants even chuckled in rueful appreciation of its effectiveness).[30]

Christian scholarship sees the *Gospel of Barnabas* as a forgery, probably dating from the sixteenth century, the work either of a Christian convert to Islam[31] or (more plausibly) of a Muslim writing in the shadow of the Spanish Inquisition.[32] The second hypothesis, closely argued, sees the origin of *Barnabas* as lying in the urgent Muslim need of textual weapons in their struggle against the church militant. Thus the city of Granada became the centre of a veritable industry of forgery, detectable in this instance through numerous geographical lapses and historical anachronisms. Geographical errors include an account of 'sailing' to Nazareth (which is, of course, in the mountains) and 'going up' to Capernaum (which is on the Sea of Galilee), and historical anachronisms include the existence of the Arabic and Spanish languages in the first century AD. The *Gospel of Barnabas* has Christ repeatedly denying His own divinity and presenting Himself as a prophet come to announce the future coming of the Messiah, whose name is Mohammad. There are also some fanciful touches in the domain of the miraculous, as that the name of Mohammad was written on Adam's fingernail.

The circumstances in which this text was probably produced, those of a Spanish Muslim community oppressed at Christian hands, have their distant echoes in the present situation of Islam in Kenya – although, of course, there is no inquisition here in sight, the realities of Christian domination and of Muslim marginality are present. *Barnabas* does seem to be in circulation in the Kenyan Muslim community: I found three copies, looking well used, on the Islamics shelf of a leading Muslim secondary school in Mombasa in 1987. As with other English-language versions of the *Gospel of Barnabas*, these latter three copies were photocopies of the Clarendon Press English-language translation of 1907 (L. Ragg and L. Ragg). It was this Oxford edition of *Barnabas* which apparently brought the text to the attention of the Muslim world (the sixteenth-century texts, one in Spanish and the other in Italian, having been out of circulation). The Raggs prefaced their 1907 edition with a dismissive introduction, which is, of course, omitted from the many subsequent Muslim reproductions of the translated text (Waqf publishers, Beirut, etc.). *Barnabas* thus translated, and with a reputable English publisher's imprint, does appear to be an effective instrument of *dawa*, a means to undermine Christian belief ('You see, they admit it themselves'). I was aggressively questioned by a Muslim schoolteacher in Mombasa (in front of his class) on the subject of the divinity of Christ, questions probably inspired by this text. This particular encounter may be a small part of the recently increased Muslim aggression, of which Christian sources in Kenya complain and which they would date from about 1984.

The position of Islam in Kenya in overall terms is none the less to be understood as having the weakness of minority status and of political marginality in a Christian-dominated state. Swahili Muslims find it difficult to cope with the development of the Kenyan economy, being handicapped by their educational backwardness: not only is development concentrated in Christian areas of the country, but development in the Muslim Coast Province has been dominated by up-country activity (port of Mombasa, tourism). One might be tempted, in such a context, to speak of the demoralization of the Muslim community in Kenya, as evidenced, for example, by the recent generalization of the habit of chewing the intoxicant *miraa* shoot (a natural amphetamine). Many Muslim informants complained of the social effect of this drug, an effect which some related to the high rate of unemployment among the Muslims of the coast. Sharif Khatamy, at the Lamu *maulid* in November 1986, remarked that 'while *miraa* chewing was confined to a few eccentrics a decade ago, it has now assumed epidemic proportions in our society', and he saw this new habit as directly related to Muslim educational shortcomings: 'The present high rate of failure of Muslim children can be directly correlated with this sinister habit in which parents spend less time in supervising their children's school work'.[33] But it would perhaps be unwise to develop a general argument from the changing fashions of drug abuse.

Social contact with Christians may pose another sort of challenge to the Muslims of Kenya, projected into the future by Sheikh Hyder Kindy:

> With the mixing of peoples in Mombasa I don't know what's to become of our Muslims in fifty years from now. As they mix with Christians, even marry them, they don't change faiths: but they do lose interest in Islam. I've seen it happen with my own children.[34]

If this be the challenge of secularization, it would probably be deferred to a distant future.

Muslims in Kenya, while currently a beleaguered minority, are not without their hidden assets in the politics of inter-faith competition. The Christian majority is deeply divided by tribal and denominational rivalries and lacks any common purpose with regard to Islam (thus a Muslim minority can still win all three parliamentary seats in Mombasa). The disfavour suffered by Coast Province does not, furthermore, mean that the Muslims of that area are without recourse. Many of the Swahili-speaking people have found employment even in the upper reaches of government service in Nairobi. The Swahili language furthermore continues to spread as a vernacular language in the up-country areas, the language of African trade. Swahili announcers on national radio and television (wearing the characteristic Muslim cap or *kofia*) further help to promote the association of Islam and modernity in the audience. And, lastly, the Middle Eastern sponsorship of Kenyan Muslims is a dependable asset, even in times of world recession. Allah will reward the generous benefactor, whose donation may help to bring about the diffusion of Islam through Kenya to Central Africa. But to list such assets, some hypothetical, is not to deny the seriousness of the challenge confronting the Muslim community in Kenya.

Conclusion: an Islamic political party?

The formation of IPK, announced in Nairobi in February 1992, still awaited legal recognition at the time this chapter was written (September 1992). There were good reasons to doubt that the legal process will come to a speedy or (for the IPK) a successful conclusion. The Christian-educated political establishment of Kenya had, and has, its apprehensions concerning the violent politics of international 'Islamic fundamentalism', reinforced in this by the national press. There were, of course, the local memories of the Arab slave trade of the past century, revived of late by President Moi: the stronghold of the IPK is the old port city of Mombasa. And there was also to be considered the general reluctance of African leaders to allow legal space for religiously based political parties. In the transatlantic idiom of one of the new party's defenders at that time, Professor Mohamed Bakari, of Nairobi University, the IPK 'has a snowball's chance in hell to be registered'.[35]

The itinerary of this project remains of interest, even if the professor's gloom was ultimately to prove justified. After the announcement of IPK's launch, at the International Press Centre, 'the IPK disappeared from the newspaper columns but reappeared in the street', notably in the streets of Mombasa. The party's speakers took up positions in the market 'alongside Christian street preachers'.[36] with speeches attacking the local Kenya African National Union (KANU) chief (and national Assistant Minister of Information), Sharif Nassir. The police then broke up the crowd at the market (19 May 1992), using tear gas, firing into the air and 'arresting the crowd-pulling Muslim preachers'. Riot ensued, with the stoning of government vehicles, burning of cars, chants of 'Allahu Akbar', 'Down with KANU' and 'IPK'. On the following night, in retaliation, anti-riot police 'stormed' a mosque in search of IPK activists, an action described in an IPK press release as 'the greatest violation of human rights any civilised society has witnessed since the fall of communism'.[37]

The national background to this escalating violence in Mombasa was in Kenya's move toward multi-party politics in 1992. The local background was in the daily gathering of 'hundreds of eager youths' at the Mwembe Tayari market in Mombasa, for the 'fiery sermons' of an IPK activist, Khalid Balala (a graduate of Medina University, Saudi Arabia), against the government, the ruling party and Kenya's other political parties; against 'massive corruption in the country, and especially within the Municipal Council of Mombasa'.[38] President Moi, having warned the country's Muslims to 'shun Islamic fundamentalism or risk reviving bitter memories of the era of slavery of more than a century ago' (1 June 1992)[39] took sterner action in July 1992. 'Sheikh' Khalid Balala was then arrested (20 July) and charged with treason, 'an offence which carries a mandatory death penalty'.[40] Such a sentence, if carried, out, would no doubt open another round of mass violence, bringing further state repression.

The constituency of the new IPK appeared to lie especially among young Muslims of Coast Province, and there was evidence that many senior Muslims in the country followed another political line. On 20 July 1992 (the day of the arrest of Sheikh Balala in Mombasa) a delegation of Muslims called upon President Moi at State House, Nakuru, dissociating themselves from the IPK and pledging their support to the president and the ruling party, KANU. This delegation was led by SUPKEM and included important Muslim religious leaders as well as businessmen and civil servants. The IPK threatened in advance to 'punish' Muslims who joined this delegation, but failed to deter several hundreds from doing so. The delegation presented its memorandum of Muslim grievances to the president, who responded by warning of 'tough action against IPK's lawlessness'.[41] And, of course, President Moi was as good as his word, on the same day, in Mombasa. Some Kenyan Muslims in these forbidding circumstances promoted the idea of non-partisan political action in defence of the Muslim community's interests, combating 'discrimination against Muslims in all sectors of life, land tenure,' education, support for the poor, etc.'.[42] If the IPK was not registered, Professor Bakari suggested, Muslims should be patient and 'exercise their democratic rights by throwing out those politicians they consider as detrimental to their collective interests'.[43]

Professor Bakari's article ('What ails the Muslims?'), published in *Africa Events* (London) in July 1992, could be read as a long-distance declaration of a political candidacy. The Muslim ailment in Kenya was seen there by him as, in the first place, a problem of political representation. Muslim MPs, whose number he estimated at twenty-four, 'have enriched themselves at the expense of their people', and furthermore were an ignorant lot – 'not a single one has benefited from post-secondary education'. Kenya's Muslims thus faced a 'leadership vacuum'. Non-Muslim politicians, on the other hand, in Bakari's view, 'have the sophistication to understand the intricacies of government and how to manipulate power for the benefit of their ethnic groups'. While some of them are 'fabulously rich, they have at least allowed something to percolate down to their constituents in the form of schools, dispensaries, and other social amenities'. Representation within the ruling party was presented overall implicitly in the terms of J. F. Bayart:[44] 'KANU is a big dinner. Anyone with an appetite for land and other goodies is ... invited to join'. The IPK, in contrast, was 'led by sophisticated people ... who want to make a clean break from the previous politics of conformism and a culture of subservience'. Hassan al-Turabi of Sudan was then quoted, in triumphalist vein: 'Islam is a new force that is going to come anyway, because it is a wave of history. It represents modernity in Islamic societies. It will come through evolution if it's allowed to come peacefully and gradually'.[45] An offer not to be refused? Professor Ali Mazrui warned of the danger of a 'black *intifadah*' if the Kenyan government denied the Muslims the right to their own political party.[46]

Turabi-style triumphalism or warnings of a Muslim uprising may need adjustment to the realities of the Muslim predicament in Kenya. Imagined statistics, showing the Muslims to be one-quarter or more of the national population, may be good for Islamic morale and for inter-faith propaganda, but they provided a dangerous basis in a real political confrontation: Muslims probably accounted for less than a tenth of Kenya's total population.[47] The project of an Islamic party in these circumstances would seem to have been misguidedly self-isolating. The regional grievances of Coast Province are real enough, a long record of governmental neglect and up-country domination, what Professor Mazrui calls 'internal colonisation',[48] but it is easy for the governing party to play on communal and other political rivalries in the province when confronted with the IPK, and difficult to see how the IPK could form political alliances. Perhaps one should leave the last word with Professor Mohamed Bakari: 'the missionary impact on Kenya is so powerful that many Kenyans, grateful for Western enlightenment and education, will ... believe virtually anything a white man says about Islam'.[49] If things are as bad as that, better to concentrate on education than to look for shortcuts to political power. In fact, as is now known, IPK was denied the right to register for the December 1992 elections in Kenya, and the complaints about this continue among Kenyan Muslims.[50]

Donal B. Cruise O'Brien

Notes

1. Field research for this article was conducted principally in Mombasa – from the end of December 1986 to early February 1987 and from mid-July to late August 1991. Warm thanks are due to many Muslim informants, several of whom are acknowledged separately below, and especially to Mahmud Welton and Seif Muhammad Seif. Thanks also to David Sperling for generously dispensing his knowledge of coast society and introducing me to many very useful informants, to Christian Coulon and François Constantin, who were equally generous in their assistance in the preparation of this research, and to Shaikh Yahya for his practical assistance and learned advice.

   Thanks are due finally to the Nuffield Foundation for funding the research (Patricia Thomas was understanding of the particular problems of disabled research) and to the School of Oriental and African Studies for granting the necessary research leave. My wife Rita gave generously of her own time in coming to Mombasa on both occasions, an indispensable assistance unstintingly given.

2. The lower end of solid estimation (6 per cent) is offered in D. B. Barrett, ed., *World Christian encyclopedia* (London, Oxford University Press, 1982). Father J. Cuoq plumps for the figure of 7.7 per cent, without indicating the basis of this estimate, in *Les Musulmans en Afrique* (Paris, Maisonneuve et Larose, 1975).

   F. Constantin, working on the basis of the 1979 census and extrapolating from the 1962 census, gives a maximum figure of 8 per cent, in *Les Communautés Musulmanes d'Afrique orientale* (Pau, Crepao, 1983), pp. 62–64. Such an estimate would include all the Swahili, all the Somali, almost all the Digo and the Upper Pokomo, and one-half of the recently Islamizing Giriama, together with some small coastal tribes and a very small Muslim minority in the larger up-country tribes.

   M. A. Kettani estimates the Muslim population at 30 per cent of Kenya's total, but his demographic methods are altogether obscure. See M. A. Kettani, 'Muslim East Africa: an overview', *Journal of the Institute of Muslim Minority Affairs* 4, 1–2 (1982), pp. 104–119.

   Muslim estimates quoted in Constantin, *Communautés Musulmanes*, p. 64. The figure of 25 per cent was also offered in interview by Professor A. I. Salim in Nairobi, 12 January 1987.

3. Forty-five per cent is the estimate for Christians in Kenya offered by Cuoq, *Musulmans*; 73 per cent by Barrett, *World Christian encyclopedia*, pp. 432–437; 45 per cent '*tres plausible*' in the view of Constantin, *Communautés Musulmanes*, p. 64.

4. See for example, A. J. Temu, *British Protestant missions* (London, Longman, 1972). The missionaries 'believed that education was a vital weapon for evangelisation and they undertook the schooling of their converts because it was necessary for them to read the Bible and the catechism' (p. 140). African demand for education was strongest in the younger generation, as among the Kikuyu, where parents, elders and headmen often opposed the establishment of mission schools as socially disruptive (p. 146).

5. A. I. Salim, *The Swahili-speaking peoples of Kenya's coast, 1895–1965* (Nairobi, East African Publishing House, 1973): 'little rational and serious thought was given to the economic and political implications of autonomy' (p. 226). Also interviews, Sheikh Hyder Kindy, Mombasa, January 1987, and Sheikh Hyder Kindy, *Life and politics in Mombasa* (Nairobi, East African Publishing House, 1972), p. 185.

6. N. Chittick, *Kilwa: An Islamic trading city on the East African coast* (Nairobi, British Institute in Eastern Africa, 1974), Vol. I (*History and archaeology*), p. 245.

7. Although there were such contacts at certain times and places. See R. Pouwels, *Horn and crescent: Cultural change and traditional Islam on the East African coast* (Cambridge: Cambridge University Press, 1987). Also J. De Vere Allen, 'Swahili culture reconsidered: Some historical implications of the material culture of the northern Kenya

coast in the eighteenth and nineteenth centuries', *Azania* (1974); and D. Sperling, 'Islamisation in the coastal region of Kenya to the end of the nineteenth century', in B. A. Ogot, ed., *Kenya in the nineteenth century* (Nairobi, Bookwise Ltd and Anyange Press Ltd, 1985) (*Hadith* 8), p. 76, where it is argued that rural Islamization 'began in the second half of the nineteenth century'.

Finally, the judgement of R. L. Bunger: 'Throughout the history of Coast, the northern [Kenyan] Swahili seem to have shown little interest in spreading Islam into the hinterland. Indeed one can even hear Swahili in Mombasa expressing their indignation and contempt toward mainland Africans who adopt 'their' religion and Muslim dress. (*Islamisation among the Upper Pokomo*, 2nd edn (Syracuse, Syracuse University Press, 1979), p. 43.

8. A. Nimtz, *Islam and politics in East Africa* (St Paul, University of Minnesota Press, 1980).

9. A number of talks in 1987 on the subject of Senegalese Islam, in different schools in the Mombasa area, brought out some interesting academic reactions. My thanks to the staff and pupils of Allidina Visram High School, Kwale School and Coast Girls' High School.

  Verdict on brotherhoods in Kenya from Mahmud Welton, in conversation. One should at least mention the significance of the Alawiyya brotherhood, a grouping of the learned *ulama*, but the Alawiyya spurns mass membership and does not act as an agency of conversion to Islam.

10. M. Strobel, *Muslim women in Mombasa, 1890–1975* (New Haven and London, Yale University Press, 1979), pp. 35–36, 103.

11. Ibid., p. 36: 'By the 1960s non-Muslims were in the majority in a once over-whelmingly Muslim town.'

12. Kindy, *Life and Politics*, p. 185.

13. Several interviews with Sheikh Hyder Kindy, Mombasa, January 1987.

14. F. Dumila, *Mombasa KANU on the move* (Mombasa, NISHA Printers, n.d.) p. 19.

15. Between 1 and 2 per cent in the estimation of M. A. Abdallah (Sabir), Headmaster, H. H. Sheikh Khalifa bin Zayed al-Nahyar Secondary and Technical School, inter-view, Mombasa, 29 January 1987. See also article in the *Weekly Review*, 7 April (1978), 'Mombasa/coast: The politics of institutes' (unsigned).

16. See two newspaper articles; 'Bausi: Introducing Islamic education', *Kenya Times*, 30 January (1987), and 'Official hits out at report over Islam', *Sunday Nation*, 1 February (1987).

17. Interview with a group of MEWA officers, Dr Rashid Mzee and Messrs Said Omar, Awadh Jezan and Swaleh Taib, Mombasa, 29 January 1987.

  See also the report of the *Maulid* of 27 November 1986, in *Africa Events* 3, 172 (January–February 1987), where one of the *ulama*, Sharif Khatamy, is reported as having spoken (to a crowd of 12,000) in the following terms:

> He spoke about the importance of education for Muslims. He reminded the audience about the stress Prophet Muhammad put on education as an obligation not only to men but also to women . . . He noted that we must interpret the concept of education on a much broader scale to embrace both secular and religious education, because Islam does not recognise any dichotomy between the two. The present state of education of Islamic societies, he observed, stemmed from the fact that the role of education has been relegated to an inferior position.

Sharif Khatamy then spoke of the parental responsibility in this matter, women being castigated for their laxity as first teachers of their children, with the result of 'the present high rate of failure on the part of Muslim children', ('Lamu: The Prophet is born', *Africa Events* 3, 172 (1987), p. 32.

18. Interview, Abdusalam Benadir, editor, the *Message*, and spokesman for Ansaar Muslim Youth, Mombasa, 1 February 1987.

Donal B. Cruise O'Brien

19. Ibid.
20. Interview, Dr Rashid Mzee *et al.* (see Note 17), Mombasa, 29 January 1987.
21. See also letter of Sharif Nassir in *the Weekly Review*, 13 February (1978), 'Discrimination against Muslim children at the coast', and M. Bakari *et al.* in the *Weekly Review*, 27 February (1978), 'Discrimination against Muslims', including the statement that 'the history of Muslim education in Kenya has been one of continual struggle between the Christian administrator-cum-educationist and the Muslim parent'. Also, A. A. Mohamed, 'Discrimination of Muslim at the coast', *Weekly Review*, 20 March (1978). My thanks to François Constantin for referring me to this correspondence.
22. Salim, *Swahili-speaking Peoples*, with this pertinent assessment:

> The core of East African Islam has always been at the coast. Its nearest approximation to the Arabian form has been maintained over centuries by the upper strata of Arab settlers who preserved a regular contact with the Arabian peninsula and the centres of Islam. Seasonal commercial links ran parallel with maritime cultural links which not merely brought fresh immigrants and cultural elements from Arabia, but preserved a significant amount of consciousness of belonging to another world – a consciousness that goes an appreciable way towards explaining subsequent Arab policies and motivation', (p. 140).

On the attitudes of the Mijikenda, torn between the requirements of strict Islam and the conventions of custom, see David Parkin, 'Swahili Mijikenda: Facing both ways' in 'Kenya', in D. Parkin and F. Constantin, eds, 'Social stratification in Swahili society', special issue of *Africa* 2, (1989).
23. Interview, Abdullah Kugula, Kwale High School, 27 January 1987.
24. Interview, Juma Abdullah, Diani, 25 January 1987.
25. R. Peake, in a study of Muslim 'clerks' (secondary school education and in salaried clerical jobs), in the coastal town of Malindi, thus comments that:

> 'Islam, its moral and spiritual superiority become the focus 'for clerks' future hopes. A belief arises that in some mysterious way Islam can provide the basis of a resurgence in Swahili and thereby clerks' fortunes comparable to their romantic image of the time of the Sultan.' (R. Peake, 'Notes on tourism and Swahili youth in Malindi old town', *Africa* 59, 2, (1989).

26. Dumila, *Mombasa KANU*, p. 45.

It may be of interest here that Habib Saleh's famous mosque college in Lamu was praised (in a magazine sympathetic to the Muslim cause) for having 'acted as a bastion of resistance against Christian missionary incursions by producing trained manpower that transcended the local objective of merely staffing local *madrassahs*'. Habib Saleh's son, Sayyid Ahmed Badawi Jamalilayl, was tutor to a cadre of scholars, sent out to the remotest parts of East Africa to embark on *dawah* activities. He sent out for students among the larger African tribes around the Lamu archipelago, the Pokomo, the Orma, the Somali and the Boni peoples' ('Lamu: The Prophet is born,' *Africa Events* 3, 172 (January–February 1987), p. 29 ('Riyadha mosque', anon.)).
27. Temu, *British Protestant Missions*. Early Christian converts 'agreed to be baptised because they were attracted by the material comforts and wealth of the missions' (p. 15). The mission appeal was especially felt by 'misfits and exiles from their own tribal society'.
28. F. Constantin, 'Quelques questions à partir de l'exemple de la bureaucratisation de l'Islam au Kenya: portée et limites du syndrome Anglican', Bordeaux, April 1987 (unpublished).
29. My thanks to Fuad Nahdi, a Muslim student from Mombasa, who expressed his opinion in seminar papers on the subject of *dawah* in the School of Oriental and African Studies, 1986–1987: F. Nahdi, 'Islamic *Dawah*: Muslim missionary activities

in contemporary Africa', and '*Dawah* and politics: Muslim missionary activity in contemporary Africa' (both unpublished).

30. Interview, Frs A. Shorter and Y. Gaudreault, Catholic Higher Institute for Central Africa, Nairobi, 13 January 1987.
31. J. Slomp, 'The Gospel in dispute', *Islamochristiana* 4 (1978).
32. M. de Epalza, 'Le milieu Hispano-Moresque de l'evangile Islamisant de Barnabe (XVIe-XVIIe siècle)', *Islamochristiana* 8 (1982).

     For a modern Islamic commentary, apparently by an ex-priest, M. H. Durrani, 'In defence of the Gospel of Barnabas', *al-Islam* (Nairobi) 7, 3, p. 29 (from Muslim World League journal, *Makkah*). Here it is claimed that the Gospel of Barnabas is one of the Gospels suppressed by the Trinitarians at the time of Constantine, being then liberated from the Pope's 'prison' in the sixteenth century.

33. Cited in 'Lamu: the Prophet is born', *Africa Events* 3, 172 (January-February 1987), p. 32. On *miraa* (also called *marungi* or *qat*), the young shoot of a tree chewed with its skin, see Peake, 'Notes on tourism', *Africa* 59, 2 (1989), pp. 3ff., 23.
34. Sheikh Hyder Kindy, interview, Mombasa, 31 January 1987. This pessimistic Muslim assessment of the results of intermarriage is to be set against the Christian complaint that intermarriage works in favour of Islam in so far as Muslim women can't marry Christian men, while Muslim men must get their wives to become Muslim (interview, Frs A. Shorter and Y. Gaudreault, Nairobi, 13 January 1987).
35. M. Bakari, 'What ails the Muslims?' *Africa Events* (July 1992).
36. 'The fire this time', *Africa Events* (June 1992).
37. Ibid.
38. Ibid.
39. 'State House visit deepens split: An IPK activist faces death', *Muslim* (July 1992).
40. Ibid.
41. Ibid.
42. 'How Muslims can wield strong influence without own party', *Muslim* (July 1992).
43. Bakari, 'What ails the Muslims?'.
44. J. F. Bayart, *The politics of the belly: The state in Africa* (Longman, 1993), being the translation of Bayart's *L'Etat en Afrique: la politique du ventre* (Paris, Fayard, 1989).
45. Bakari, 'What ails the Muslims?'.
46. *Kenya Times*, 15 July 1992.
47. See Note 2 for demographic estimates.
48. 'Repression will not solve the "Muslim question" - Mazrui', *Muslim* (July 1992), p. 3.
49. Bakari 'What ails the Muslims?'.
50. See Ali A. Mazrui, 'The unfinished Islamic agenda: Reflections after elections [of December 1992]', *Sunday Nation*, 14 February (1993), centre pages 11-12; and 'Speaking out for Muslims, *Weekly Review*, 26 February (1993), pp. 8-10.

Part Four

Cross-Cultural Complications

Twelve

Christian–Muslim Inputs into Public Policy Formation in Kenya, Tanzania & Uganda

A. B. K. KASOZI

Relations between Christians and Muslims in East Africa have been adversarial and competitive from the period of initial contact to the present time. Muslim writers have not left as many documents as Christians about dealings with their adversaries, but from the few we have and from oral evidence it is clear that their dealings with the followers of Christ have in most cases not been smooth.[1] Christians have regarded Islam not only as a religious danger but also as a political obstacle to the type of societies they wanted to create in East Africa. Islam was regarded as a stumbling-block to the development of societies based on Christian values, laws and ways of life. On the other hand, the Muslim peoples saw Christians (especially Christian missionaries and colonial officials) as political and commercial intruders who wanted to take the territory, markets and minds of the peoples of East Africa from them. The result was suspicion and confrontation.

That adversarial relationships have prevailed between Muslims and Christians in East Africa for a long time is not surprising. First, both Islam and Christianity are evangelizing religions aimed at winning converts.[2] Secondly, each religion represented a distinctly different cultural and political system preached by people of different racial extraction, who were proud of its uniqueness. Thirdly, each often believed in the conquest of territory for the nation or nations to which its preachers belonged. The competition was therefore not only religious but also cultural, political and racial. After Christianity and Islam were adopted in East Africa, competition was transformed into class struggle. Adherents of these foreign religions seized power within East African societies and redistributed resources on the basis of class whose foundation was either Christianity (in Uganda, for example) or Islam (in Zanzibar and on the Kenya coast). Competition for resources assumed and was often masked by religious competition.

Islam was, and still is, regarded as a religious danger by Christians as a competitor for converts. Both Christianity and Islam attempted to convert Africans from their traditional religions. It was only later that each realized the possibility of securing converts from each other. Christian writers saw Islam as a danger for the following reasons. First Islamic doctrine was easy to grasp and therefore tempting to Africans.[3] They pointed out that in the initial stages of conversion all Islam asks is the pronouncement of the *Shahada*, i.e. that there is one God and Mohammed is His prophet, after which one is accepted as a Muslim. This simplicity, they felt, would work in favour of Islam. Secondly, they believed that Islam would snatch more converts because its social demands were not very different from those already common in African societies: an African converting to Islam did not have to undergo a substantial cultural transformation. As one writer pointed out, 'Islam has been grafted to African customs so efficiently that one wonders if a custom is Islamic or African'.[4] Thirdly, they noted that Islam's legalistic bent tends to provide advice for every social action. Unlike Christianity, which teaches certain principles to be applied to different circumstances, Islam regulates everything to the last detail, a feature thought to give Islam an edge in the struggle for converts. Fourthly, there was a fear that Islam was a community religion that provided social security for its adherents, while Christianity was individualistic. Wherever Muslims lived, they built a community that gave complete social support to its members. Muslims were said to:

> help one another in burials, in marriage feasts, in trade, in agriculture . . . If there is a Muslim *duka* [shop] a Muslim will never buy elsewhere, whereas a Catholic will often buy from a Muslim even if there was a *duka* owned by a Catholic.[5]

The Christians in Uganda were said to be individualistic because they had completely abandoned African customary social life and adopted the Christian way of life. Each one lived for himself without caring what happened to his fellow Christians. The danger to Christianity of such an attitude to social life was that it gave Islam the edge. Muslim communal attitudes to social life were thought to encourage the expansion of Islam because 'a Muslim cannot live his religious life alone. If there are no Muslims, he will try to win some'. This tendency explained how Islam has managed to spread without the assistance of organized missionary societies and full-time missionaries. Finally, there was a concern that Muslims were using money acquired from business to expand their religion. In Uganda and most of East Africa, Muslims were successful in trade.[6] It was feared that they used their money to entice Christian girls to marry them at tender ages, in most cases against the wishes of their parents. Muslims were also feared to be using their money to organize lavish feasts at Mauledis, weddings, wrestling matches and football matches, all to convert Christians.[7]

For the Muslims, Christianity was seen as a threat to their goal of building an Islamic community, sentiments expressed by a number of Muslim leaders interviewed.[8] Their desire was to have Muslim political leaders leaders legislate in their favour. It is not surprising that a number of Muslims in Uganda welcomed Idi Amin although they did not participate in his rise or fall or significantly influence the way he directed Uganda.

As independence approached in each colony or protectorate, there was apprehension in both the Christian and Muslim communities over who would control the formulation and direction of social policy after the colonial officials left. Christian leaders, especially the Catholics, were very clear about their desire to guide the direction of policy and the type of political community they wanted to build: it was to be based on Christian values. They regarded Islam as a political danger that had to be handled carefully and firmly. In a study conducted for the Catholic Church in Uganda, the Revd F. Schildknecht pointed out that Islam was a political danger at the internal and external levels. Internally, it was a danger because it could slow down the building of a Christian community; externally, it had the capacity to influence how Uganda dealt with foreign Muslim nations.[9] He advised that the best way to counter the political danger of Islam was to take two actions. First, Catholics who were able to participate in politics should be groomed to advance Christian interests in the political field, using the existing pro-Christian media, and be prepared to defend Christian principles in that arena. Secondly, Catholics and other Christians in Uganda should be encouraged to go into business, break the Muslim control of commerce and thereby dispel the myth that only Muslims could get rich. Doing so would eliminate the idea that to become rich in Uganda one had to convert to Islam. Although Muslims have not written much on this matter, oral evidence indicates that they were very much aware of the renewed struggle to control and influence social policy. In a long interview with Prince Badru Kakungulu, and later in talks with Sheikh Abdu Kamulegeya, I was informed that the alliance Muslims made with the Protestant-based Uganda People's Congress (UPC) and the Kabaka Yekka was not *ad hoc* but was a result of protracted negotiations between Muslim and Protestant leaders.[10] As a minority, Muslims would not have had on impact on the post-colonial politics of Uganda. But the division of Christians between Anglican Protestants and Roman Catholics permitted Muslims to enter the arena of policy formation in Uganda from the 1950s.

A. B. K. Kasozi

The role of religion in East African society

Before the coming of Christianity and Islam to East Africa, social cleavages existed in most African societies that were based on specific relations within a given social system.

Existing religious belief systems reflected the power structures of a given society. Religious beliefs served not only to maintain the status quo but to persuade deprived groups to accept their position within the established power structures. Religious beliefs legitimized the status of rulers and of the poor, and gave a supernatural explanation for relations within society as determined by those who held power.

It is therefore not surprising that when Christianity and Islam were introduced into East African societies they were adopted not only for spiritual but also for practical, and in most cases for political, purposes. Social groups that held power or positions of privilege saw foreign religions like Christianity and Islam as new instruments of social control to maintain or enhance their positions or power. Social groups that aspired to power or to upward social mobility saw in Christianity and Islam new routes for advancement.

For the mass of the people, there were a number of reasons why Christianity and Islam were adopted. For many ordinary people, Christianity or Islam was adopted because these religions were thought to be more true or to be nearer the truth than were the African traditional religions. It seems that these two foreign religions not only explained the mysteries of the universe better, but they coped with practical reality in a more successful way. The European missionary doctor brought better results than the traditional medicine man; the European engineer performed more miracles than did the mediums of the traditional gods; and in physical confrontations with the representatives of traditional religion the Christian European soldiers came out on top. Also, ordinary people joined Islam or Christianity to improve their social status, since the leaders of the new religions soon acquired allocative powers wherever they took control. By taking social control, they obtained access to material products that the traditional religious establishment could no longer offer.

It is important to understand this continuing role of religion in East African societies in order to comprehend the influence of Christian-Muslim relations on the formation and implementation of law and public policy since 1900. This role was not interrupted by the introduction of Christianity and Islam. On the contrary, Christianity and Islam took over this role and performed the political and social functions that traditional religions had performed previously. Christianity and Islam were internalized by African societies – up to a point – and used for local goals. Both native and foreign peoples used Christianity or

Islam in struggles to control East African society and resources, and to influence social policy.

Thus, although Christianity and Islam are foreign religions, born and bred in foreign cultural systems, once imported and adopted they were internalized and domesticated. But the relationship was not one-sided. The foreign preachers of Christianity and Islam also used these religions as instruments of social control.

In a number of places, such as Buganda, there was an undeniable relationship between advocates of Christianity and the colonial establishment which formulated laws and public policy. When laws were formulated, they inevitably became partisan because of the partisan nature of Christianity itself. Yet the advocates of Christianity tried very hard, through debates, letters, lobbying and use of the mass media, to obscure the partisan nature of their views. Indirectly, and at times directly, these religious ideologues sought to prove the necessity of their social system for the rest of the population. On the other hand, religious leaders out of power sought, and often succeeded, in modifying the nature of laws and policies implemented by colonial administrations.

The role of religious ideas in justifying the status quo and as a basis of law formation has not been fully recognized by the generality of scholars. Christianity in Uganda and Islam on the East African coast became the ideologies of the rising class of new societies, colonial in the interior and merchant on the coast. They reflected the economic, social, and political interests of their ruling élites through state politics and laws. In this manner, in many East African societies religious consciousness became indistinguishable from political consciousness. Religious commitment became the most concentrated expression of the interests and objectives of certain groups of people. It also became the starting-point for expressing the attitude of a certain group of people towards other groups of people, the colonial state system (which was Christian in essence) and the course of history in general.

Led by a core of people who were, or were perceived to be, thoroughly committed to their religions, Christianity and Islam became potent forces replacing primordial loyalties in many East African societies. Through the leadership of core believers, religious groupings were reinforced by class as they obtained access to resources through possession of political power. Meanwhile, those who did not join foreign religions were marginalized. While for the masses religion fulfilled religious and philosophical needs, for the leaders it was also a source of political and hence economic power.

Using religion as a unifying ideology, these 'core leaders' inflenced the direction of social policy and political culture in East Africa. They have articulated stands on such social issues as education, family laws, economic affairs, and foreign affairs, as well as the nature of their societies. But, because Christianity and Islam are so fundamentally opposed to each other in interpreting what is considered to be the ideal life, it is not surprising that relations between the two have been so adversarial. This competitive and adversarial relationship has in turn influenced the nature of laws and policies legislated for the wider community.

While the colonial officials (who were Christian) and later African leaders (who were also Christian) wanted to build societies based on Christian principles, they were faced with the presence of Muslim peoples in East Africa whose view of life was fundamentally different from their own. Laws based on purely Christian values could not be acceptable to Muslims. To protect themselves, and of course to advance their interests, Muslims also sought to influence the political system in order to have Islamic values enshrined in the laws and policies of their societies.

For that reason, especially in Uganda, religious ideology became closely linked to political organizations and institutions through which values and interests were promoted. Political parties became bearers of religious consciousness. And even before the era of political parties, legal consciousness in the colonial days was closely linked with religious consciousness and hence with political consciousness too.

Christian and Muslim legal consciousness was both different and the same. That is, both were nurtured in particular economic and social contexts, and both were intended to generate in their followers an awareness of God, to define obligations towards Him and towards their fellow human beings and to set standards of behaviour. Each held its own belief system to be the only true one. Each was antagonistic to the other's.

Laws and policies

Laws formulated in both the colonial and independent periods were affected by the interplay of religious forces. These forces shaped the value systems from which many of the laws and policies were made. After the establishment of colonial rule in East Africa, the aim of colonial officials, both British and German, was to create a society built on Christian values. They co-operated with missionaries to achieve this goal.[11] Family laws in Uganda and Kenya, British colonial education policy and the constitutional developments discussed below are good examples of laws passed to modify life in such societies.

However, the presence of Muslim peoples in East Africa wanting to create a Muslim state posed obstacles, and competition between the two religions systems resulted in the failure to build a purely Christian society. The colonial officials and the black African presidents who followed them after independence found that, in a pluralistic state, utmost care was needed when making or implementing laws and policies, because no law or policy could be effective if opposed by a substantial section of society. In Kenya, Tanganyika and, to some extent, Uganda, those in power were confronted with two antagonistic value systems, each seeking to influence social policy to build a political community based on its own dogmas.

This competition led colonial officials to adopt policies that would not unduly hurt either religious system. When assessing courses of action, colonial officials took one of the following three options:

1 In the first option, they tried to modify laws perceived to enhance one religion at the expense of the other. A good example in Uganda is the Marriage Ordinance of 1902 discussed below.
2 In the second option, separate laws could be made for each religious community, as happened in Kenya, Tanganyika and Uganda. Many of the Muslims on the coast of Kenya, Zanzibar and coastal Tanganyika were administered under Islamic law, while the rest of the country was administered under British common law, whose values had been shaped in Christianity. However, there was a 'repugnancy' clause that made common law paramount in any conflict with Islam or African traditional religions.
3 In the third option, some laws or policies were dropped entirely when religious opposition to them was particularly strong. A good example was the policy to promote Kiswahili as the lingua franca and medium of instruction in Uganda.

Education policy in Uganda 1900–1965

Christian–Muslim interaction modified both the colonial and the first Obote government's education policy. Although a number of colonial officials believed that the Christian missionaries were doing good work in education, there was a desire to build and financially support a free secular system of education, to which children of all religions could go. However, the government was forced to modify, and in practical terms to reverse, its desired policy because of the objections of Christian missionaries. They saw such a policy as benefiting Muslims and undermining their efforts to socialize children through Christian-based education. When British government officials took over the administration of Uganda, they found that Christian missions offered education as part of their evangelization process. Education was not only a means controlled by missionaries to produce the type of citizens they desired but also a powerful vehicle of élite recruitment. It was an agent that literally recruited the élite of colonial society from the masses. It was also a means of upward social mobility for those caught up in its embrace.

Following the 1900 agreement, missionary educators concentrated on teaching the sons of chiefs in a Christian atmosphere to build an economically powerful élite that was Christian. The Anglican Bishop Willis put this point very clearly when he wrote that the control of schools gave the church 'a marvellous opportunity of moulding a nation at its formative stage'.[12]

As a result of criticisms of giving education through missions only, the colonial state attempted to make some changes. In 1921 the Young Baganda Association criticized the funding of education through Christian missionaries because it did not cater for women, Muslims and non-believers. They recommended such structural adjustments as the creation of a central inspectorate and abolishing the linkage between admission to school and religious affiliation.[13]

In 1924 it seemed as if the educational policy of the Protectorate might change. An expert, Eric Hussey, was recruited from Sudan to open up a Department of Education in Uganda. Among his recommendations was that the government run six non-denominational elementary and intermediate schools to serve disadvantaged areas and groups. He felt that it was the government's duty to educate all citizens, whether Christians or not.[14] Athough he became the first head of Uganda's Education Department, he could not implement this policy. The Anglican Bishop, J. J. Willis, criticized him for favouring Muslims, saying that 'to establish schools for the Muslim community was to practise a form of religious discrimination in favour of the least progressive element in the population'.[15] The Catholic missionaries agreed with Willis and mounted a joint opposition. Hussey had no alternative but to modify government educational policy. Only one non-sectarian school was established, but even that soon closed for lack of enrolment and funds. The new policy recognized that Christian missions controlled the schools and that government was to fund them and, the main addition, inspect them. The essence of the old policy – to fund an educational system controlled by the missionaries – remained intact.

This policy was not shaken until the period 1963–1964, when the newly independent African government under Milton Obote decided to tighten the control and running of secondary schools. A number of steps were taken to reduce the influence of the missionaries: unified inspectorate for all schools; creation of a powerful officials, the Chief Education Officer, to administer all schools; creation of a centralized system of recruiting, hiring and firing of teachers, to be controlled by the government; and a directive that schools should serve the communities in which they were located instead of religious groups.[16]

If this policy had been implemented, the greatest beneficiaries would have been Muslims and the losers would have been the Roman Catholics because they had the biggest number of schools. Because

Table 12.1 Number of government grant-aided primary schools in 1964 and 1968, by founding body

	1964	1968
Government	99	119
Church of Uganda	969	1,102
Roman Catholic	1,146	1,170
Muslim	178	187
Other	30	67
Total	2,422	2,645

Sources: Kathleen Lockard, 1974 (see Note 21); Ministry of Education, *Statistical Tables*, 1964; Ministry of Education, *Education Statistics*, 1968, Table 1.

Muslims had no missionaries, they did not receive a Western education in an Islamic environment. A Western education was available to Muslims only from missionary-controlled schools, which passed on their Christian baggage too.

Yet Muslims lagged very far behind in education. By 1960 there were very few Muslims in schools. They had only a smattering of good primary schools and only one secondary school, at Kibuli. Table 12.1 illustrates the plight of the Muslims and the extent to which Roman Catholics had overtaken the Anglicans in number of schools controlled. Christian missions controlled over 80 per cent of primary schools, Muslims less than 5 per cent. Roman Catholic gains in education had been made at both primary and secondary levels. Out of forty-four secondary schools in 1962, sixteen (or 34 per cent) were run by Roman. Catholics, fourteen (or 32 per cent) directly by the government, ten (or 23 per cent) by Anglicans; three (or 7 per cent) by Asian (Indo-Pakistani) Muslim and one (or 2.5 per cent) by African Muslims.

Missions administered schools through structures developed internally. Each mission that received a government grant-in-aid employed a secretary-general for education, a number of education secretaries and school supervisors, who acted as inspectors. No doubt the structure involved duplication of effort, but the Christian missions were happy to have a system they could control.

Although there is no concrete evidence of a conspiracy between Muslims and Anglicans to cut down Catholic gains in education, it is clear that the former two groups worked together throughout the controversy regarding the implementation of the 1963–1964 education policies. Muslims, who had more to gain by the secularizing of education, tried to influence policies by exploiting the discord between the two Christian groups.

In the controversy following the announcement of the new policies, the Protestants and Muslims took the government view (government was led by Protestants) and the Catholics the opposing view. The Minister of Education, Luyimbazi Zake, visited a Protestant Theological Seminary at Mukono and a Muslim Teacher Training College at Kibuli to explain the new policy. He was applauded by both audiences.[17] Ntege-Lubwaama, who replaced Abu Mayanja as the Kabaka's Minister of Education, said that educating all people is the responsibility of the state.[18]

The Catholic Church in Uganda resisted the new policy with all its energies, acutely aware that Muslims would benefit and that the Protestant élite would take political credit, in addition to cutting down an able competitor.

In 1963, Luyimbazi Zake, Obote's Minister of Education, announced that the government would no longer fund the missions' sectarian educational supervisory staff. He asked local government staff to take over their jobs.[19] Early in 1964, the government decided to discontinue paying the three sectarian secretary-generals of education, twelve education secretaries and some fifty school supervisors. The central government projected that this would save £47,000 annually. The Buganda Minister of Education, Abu Mayanja, who was a Muslim, took it upon himself to implement the new policy in the kingdom. The Buganda government, which had already made it possible for boys and girls to attend the same schools, announced that any new sectarian school would not be funded by the Kabaka's government.[20]

Although Luyimbazi Zake had said that the now policies would not deprive the owners of their schools – since they owned the land on which the schools were built – the Catholic community resisted and made the implementation of the new policies difficult. In 1965 Catholic teachers in Masaka went on strike because they perceived they were being discriminated against in promotional and retraining opportunities. By the time Obote was removed from power in 1971, Roman Catholic missionaries remained in control of the education they gave in their schools.

Because of determined opposition from a religious community that feared it would be put at a disadvantage, the government policy failed to achieve all of its aims in a short period. By 1968 'almost 82% of Catholic students were studying in schools of Catholic origin [foundation] and 77% of Anglicans were studying in schools founded by their church'. However, 'over twice as many Muslim and Hindu students were in Anglican-founded schools as in Catholic school'.[21]

Family laws in Kenya and Uganda

One of the areas in which religions all over the world maintain an interest is family law. Since the family is the basic and smallest unit of social organization, all religions have an interest in influencing it. By 'family law' is meant 'the law that governs agreements to marry and betrothals, formalities that bring marriage into existence, maintenance, separation, custody, adoption, nullity, divorce, property acquired during the marriage by spouses, devolution of property and succession to property after a person dies'.[22]

In East Africa, Christians and Muslims have sought to influence the formation and implementation of family law in accordance with their own beliefs and to oppose measures contravening their view of life. Since 1900, Christians in East Africa have fought to establish the model of a Christian family, based on the relationship of one man and one woman united until 'death doth part' the two. But Islam, which is more liberal on this issue, has, according to Christian leaders, hindered the realization of the ideal. By permitting polygamy, Islam set what Christians thought was a bad example.

Colonial officials sought to build Christian societies in East Africa. In Uganda, for example, a government circular pointed out that it was 'desirous of encouraging the spread of Christian principles', although the administration would tolerate other religions.[23] The missionaries and most colonial officials believed, quite correctly, that building a Christian society could be accomplished only on the foundation of a Christian family. But colonial officials in Uganda, Kenya and Tanganyika failed not only to legislate Christian monogamous marriages but also to harmonize family law in each of the three territories. Instead of making a single family law based on Christian values thoughout East Africa, colonial officials drafted different laws and ordinances for each social group. Muslims, Hindus, unconverted Africans and Christians each had separate laws. In Uganda these were the Marriage Ordinance of 1902 for Christians, the Native Marriage Ordinance of 1903 for unconverted Africans, the Mohammedan Marriage and Divorce Ordinance of 1906 for Muslims and the Hindu Marriage Ordinance of 1961 for Hindus.[24] Similar diversity was found in Kenya and Tanganika.

After independence, African rulers found it difficult to harmonize family law. In Uganda, a commission under W. W. Kalema sought to do so and to improve the status of women and block legal loopholes in family law. Although the report was published on schedule, Uganda's rulers were not bold enough to overcome the conflicting demands of Christians for monogamous marriages and of Muslims for polygamy.[25] Amin, who seized power in 1971, disregarded the report and signed a decree permitting both polygamy and customary law.

In Kenya, the government drafted the Law of Succession Act (Cap. 160 1982) to unify all family laws into a single code applicable to everyone. Muslims said it violated their religious beliefs and that they would not obey it. A number of secular-minded educated Kenyans thought that such a law would be difficult to implement.[26] It is very probable that Muslims would make the implementation of this law difficult. Whether they can influence its repeal is another question.[27]

Constitutional development in Kenya and Uganda

The history of writing constitutions in East Africa illustrates the impact of Christian–Muslim relations on the formulation and implementation of policy. While the British colonial officers responsible for devising East Africa's constitutional laws were interested in creating a society based on their own Christian values at the urging of missionaries, who were often companions in faith, they were also aware that East African peoples had strong alternative value systems, such as Islam, as well as traditional African beliefs. Among those espousing alternative value systems were such friendly Muslim rulers as the Sultan of Zanzibar, who had contributed very much to the establishment of British power in the region. The orders in council that created the legal foundations of British power reflected the impact of these belief systems. Although Christian missionaries did not like toleration of Islam, they were appeased by the fact that common law, whose moral foundations are deeply influenced by Christianity, was made supreme over Islamic and African customary laws. Moreover, the missionaries were given the means to influence future generations by their monopoly of education. The African educated élite who eventually took power from the British inherited the same problem of competing value systems that were demanding 'security in law'. As virtually all of them were products of missionary schools, they were seen as 'Christians' by Muslims, who, especially in Kenya, heightened their demands for constitutional guarantees. Initially, accommodation was granted, but later, for the sake of 'modernity' and uniformity, Kenya's African rulers would not accept 'apartheid' in law. There was a growing tendency to make uniform laws applicable to all people by adopting Western values, which many Muslims felt were not in their best interests.

KENYA: ADMINISTRATION IN THE COLONIAL PERIOD UP TO 1963

Muslim–Christian relations influenced the nature of Kenya's supreme law, its constitution. The 1963 independence constitution, developed from various British orders in council, was also influenced by the Christian–Muslim relationship. After the imposition of common law, the British realized there was a great need to accommodate the many Muslims in Kenya by written guarantees safeguarding their way of life. In the neighbouring German territory, Tanganyika, there had been rebellions against the imposition of laws derived from Christian

(European) values. Accommodating minority interests after independence in the Kenyan supreme law has resulted in a higher degree of toleration and the development of a more peaceful method of conflict resolution than is the case in surrounding countries.[28]

The application of common law in Kenya stems from the East Africa Order in Council of 1897. It stipulated that, in addition to statutes made by the colonial administration, the common law of England, equity and statutes of general application would apply in what is now Kenya, subject to local conditions and the customs of the people.

In 1895 Britain had begun to administer the ten-mile Kenyan coastal strip, while leaving it a possession of the Sultan of Zanzibar. Islam had been practised by the people of the Kenya coast for many centuries and various Muslim city states had risen and fallen as power brokers in the coastal city states.[29] The British promised that the Islamic way of life would be protected by written guarantees. The coastal strip became the Kenya Protectorate and later was joined for administrative purposes to the Kenya colony, i.e. the interior.[30] The 1897 East Africa Order in Council allowed the application of Islamic law to all coastal peoples, including, surprisingly enough, non-Muslims. Liwali, Mudirs and Kadhi administered not only Islamic matters but secular ones.[31] The coastal strip was therefore administered as an Islamic state within a larger jurisdiction where common law was supreme.

Thus in Kenya, colonial administrators used the second option and made separate laws for each community, while leaving common law supreme in cases of conflict.

The 1963 independence constitution negotiations reflected the power of the various cultural groups in Kenya.[32] The Muslims on the coast and the Somalis, who were 90 per cent Muslim, in the northeast realized that, unless they bargained for special guarantees, they would not be able to live an Islamic way of life in Kenya. They realized to their horror that the African 'blacks', whom they used to refer to as 'Washenzi' (pagan, uncouth), had benefited from Western (Christian) education and were bound to lead the new nation. A political movement on the coast began to develop and articulate the need to maintain an Islamic way of life. It crystallized as the Mwambao United Front, which sent delegates to the constitutional conference in London.[33] The Front pointed out that the coastal peoples were a distinct social group that should either be given autonomy or be allowed to secede to, or 'rejoin', Zanzibar. British commissions to look into the problems of Muslim subjects in the Northern Frontier District (NFD) and on the coastal strip noted in their reports of December 1962 that religion was a factor. The NFD report stated that 'opinions were influenced by religion, ethnic affiliation and way of life', but 'division of opinion almost exactly corresponds to the division between Moslem and non-Moslem'.[34] The Somalis boycotted the constitutional talks and the general elections that led to Kenya's independence in 1962. Agitation in the NFD continued and culminated in a general emergency declared immediately after independence. In 1966 emergency powers were extended to the Masabit, Isiolo, Tana River and Lamu districts by a constitutional amendment. The people of the coastal strip were accommodated without violence after protracted negotiations. The British government had appointed Sir James Robertson, the former Governor-General of Nigeria, to

> report to the Sultan of Zanzibar and Her Majesty's Government jointly on the changes which are considered to be advisable in the 1895 Agreement relating to the Coastal strip of Kenya as a result of the course of constitutional development in East Africa.[35]

He found that the coastal strip was not economically viable, and that its status was complicated by Mombasa's role as a port for most of East Africa (including Uganda, Kenya and Rwanda) and by the fact that it had always been administered as an integral part of Kenya. He therefore advised that Mombasa port and the coastal strip be incorporated into Kenya, provided the Sultan of Zanzibar was paid due compensation and given the following guarantees in the new Kenya constitution:

1 a declaration of human rights including security of religious worship;
2 safeguards for the maintenance of the Sharia law for Muslims and the retention of the Kadhis' courts;
3 arrangements for the future appointment of Muslim administrative officers;
4 an Education Board.

In short, Muslim culture and Islamic law should be enshrined in the new constitution.

The Sultan of Zanzibar, the government of Kenya and the United Kingdom signed an agreement in 1963 endorsing these recommendations. Kenya promised the Sultan that

> the free exercise of any creed or religion will at all times be safeguarded and in particular His Highness's present subjects who are of Muslim Faith and their descendants will at all times be ensured complete freedom of worship and preservation of their own religious buildings and institutions. The jurisdiction of the Chief Kadhi and of all other Kadhis, will at all material times be preserved and will extend to the determination of questions of Muslim law relating to personal status, for example marriage, divorce and inheritance in proceedings in which all parties profess the Muslim faith.[36]

This constitution is an example of an African supreme law made and maintained after extensive consultations with various social and ethnic groups.

The failure to integrate the Somali NFD was due not only to a failure to accommodate different ethnic and cultural groups but to the presence immediately next door of the Republic of Somalia, whose people are, like those of NFD, Somali.

UGANDA: THE COLONIAL PERIOD AND AFTER

The constitutional development of Uganda provides an example of how combative Christian–Muslim relationships within the same country can influence the supreme laws of a state, and how statutes so framed can further rigidify social groups into adversarial relationships. Long wars between Muslim and Christian factions in the late nineteenth century in Buganda resulted in bitter alienation and combativeness. As a result, society was compartmentalized into mutually antagonistic social groups.

The Uganda Order in Council of 1902 formalized the famous 1900 agreement with Buganda (the 1900 Uganda Agreement). Similar agreements were made with the kingdoms of Toro (1901), Ankole (1902) and Bunyoro (1933). The administration of indigenous law was left to Africans, but British common law, which was supreme, remained within the jurisdiction of the colonial government. The order in council provided for English statutes of general application, common law and equity to apply in Uganda so far as circumstances allowed. The so-called indirect rule policy was allowed to operate wherever and whenever practicable.

In Buganda province particularly, this policy meant formalizing the rule of the Protestant Christian (Anglican) faction. They had defeated the Muslims in 1889–1890, the Catholics in 1892 and the Muslims again in 1893 in the struggle to control Buganda.[37] They were helped by the Imperial British East African Company, whose agent, Captain Lugard, decided to intervene in Buganda's civil wars.

The 1900 agreement established the victorious Christian chiefs in positions of political and economic power; based chieftainship on religious affiliation; gave Christian chiefs freehold land; and created a landed Christian aristocracy with enormous local political power.[38]

Apart from Prince Mbogo, Muslims were not given land. Christian missions were given land but Muslims had no missionaries. Christianity was established as the source of secular law, although Islam provided social values for many of Buganda's citizens. This policy was extended to other parts of the Uganda Protectorate. Because there was no provision for Islamic courts in Uganda, as in Kenya, native Muslims were tried either in common law courts or in district customary courts. In the colonial period, Muslims remained an alienated, despised and embittered section of Uganda's society.[39]

Since independence in 1962, Uganda has failed to build a viable political community. It has been rocked by violence and constitutions have been violently overthrown. The 1911 order in council which had replaced that of 1902 was repealed by the Judicature Act of 1962 but made no fundamental changes. Nor did the 1966 constitution make changes regarding way of life. The 1962 and 1967 constitutions contain similar provisions. Thus, in Uganda, not only have Muslims been unable to influence legislation to their advantage, but their victorious Christian adversaries have written laws disadvantageous to the cause of Islam.

It was from this combative religious environment that Idi Amin emerged. He wished to change the course of history by making Uganda an Islamic state. Thus, at the Lahore Conference of 1974, he transformed Uganda, whose population is less than 15 percent Muslim, into an Islamic state on the feudal principle that 'the religion of the ruler is the official religion of the state'.[40] He made Friday a public holiday. He used the official media to propagate Islam and transferred marriage laws from common law principles to African customary values. In short, he tried to reduce the influence of Christianity through law and public policy. Being born into a society that despised Muslims doubtless made him vindictive. His lack of education contributed to his inability to realize the limits of political power in changing social values in a single generation.

The administration of justice in Kenya, Uganda and Tanzania

Christian–Muslim relations influencing the making and implementation of supreme laws naturally had an impact on the administration of justice. After all, the judicial system interpreted and reflected constitutional instruments. By the administration of justice is meant the working of 'the court system through which justice is dispensed'. In Africa, British common law, based on Judaeo-Christian values, came face to face with Islamic law (which was rigid) and African traditional customary laws (which could change and adapt to new circumstances with time). As a result, court systems were devised to harmonize conflicts between these various value systems.

THE KENYA CASE

Areas having a substantial number of Muslims who co-operated with Christians developed mechanisms to accommodate the two value systems. In Kenya a system of parallel courts was allowed to develop, with Islamic courts subordinate to common law courts. But in Uganda, where the relationship between religions was more combative, a single court system was developed by the dominant group.

In Kenya, the East African Order in Council of 1897 provided for a tripartite system of courts: colonial, native and Islamic. Appeals from the Islamic Liwali and Mudir courts could lead to provincial and district Kadhi courts.[41] Because all Islamic courts were under the jurisdiction of the High Court (the depository of common law), common law was supreme over Islamic courts. In cases involving Islamic law, the Chief Kadhi sat in the High Court as an assessor.

Common law was made supreme over Islamic or customary law by means of the Repugnancy Clause, which stated that if local custom (including Islamic law) was repugnant to morality, good conscience and written law it was void. Polygamy, which is acceptable in Islamic and customary law was judged 'immoral' in *Rex* v. *Amkeyo* (1917) because common law was considered to be the standard of morality. In the case of *Gwao bin Kilimo* v. *Kisunda bin Ifutish* in Tanganyika, Judge Wilson states that:

> Morality and justice are abstract conceptions and every community probably has an absolute standard of its own by which to decide what is justice and what is morality. . . . To what standard, then, does the Order in Council refer . . . I have no doubt whatever that the only standard of justice and morality which a British court in Africa can apply is its own British standard.[42]

Common law took the position that polygamous marriage was immoral and only monogamy was acceptable.

For Muslims in Kenya, however, a problem arose in that they not only regarded their court system as separate from the main colonial courts but as equal to them. They therefore looked forward to its continuity, though many Muslims were unaware that British colonial officials were not of the same opinion.

It was under these circumstances of assumed equality and fear of 'Christian' laws that Muslims demanded the inclusion of the Islamic courts into the Kenya independence constitution of 1963 (section 179). When presenting the bill to parliament for the Kadhis' Courts Act, Charles Njonjo, the Attorney-General, reminded his colleagues that 'the constitution also requires that the whole of the coastal strip shall be within the jurisdiction of the Kadhi's Courts'.[43] What is most surprising is that the bill sought to extend the jurisdiction of the Kadhis' courts to other areas of Kenya, namely Nyanza Province, the Rift Valley, the Western Province and the North-East Province. The bill passed and established Kadhi courts as judicial institutions subordinate to the main common law High Court system. Two elderly Muslims interviewed in Eastleigh (Nairobi), believed the two systems were equal.

A. B. K. Kasozi

TANZANIA

In mainland Tanzania (Tanganyika), common law was applied on the basis of the 1920 Tanganyika Order in Council. It provided the constitutional scheme for this territory after it was taken over from the Germans at the close of the First World War. A number of edicts on Islamic and African traditional law were enacted and administered within the common law judicial system. Some of them were:

1 *Courts Ordinance, 1920.* This ordinance recognized Islamic and customary courts, presided over by Liwali, Kadhis and Akidas, as part of the main judicial system.
2 The *Native Courts Ordinance, No. 5, of 1929.* Under its terms all courts were made part of the executive machinery, in accordance with Cameron's indirect rule policy, except that Liwali's courts remained part of the main judicial system.
3 *Ordinance No. 15 of 1941.* Liwali courts were made part of the administration of justice.
4 *Local Courts Ordinance of 1951.* This reincorporated local courts into the judicial system.

Since independence, Islamic and customary law have continued to apply under the following statutes:

1 *Judicature and Application of Laws Ordinance.* This is the basis of applying law in independent Tanganyika. It also set up the country's courts of judicature. Under the act, customary law (including Islamic law) would apply in cases where the parties were natives, in as far as it was not repugnant to justice and morality or inconsistent with statutory law.
2 *Local Courts Ordinance–section 15.* This provided for the application of the law in similar terms.
3 *Magistrate's Court Act of 1963.* This replaced the Local Courts Ordinance. Section 9 of this Act specifically provides for the continued application of Islamic law in ordinary courts.
4 *Restatement of Islamic Law Act - 1969.* This Act provided for the minister in charge of legal affairs to make authoritative restatements of Islamic laws to be regarded as binding on various Islamic schools of law (or sects).
5 *Application of Islamic Law of Evidence.* This allowed Islamic Law of Evidence to apply in Khadhis' courts.[44] For example, an oath before a sheikh in a mosque was good evidence, if the evidence of the other side was not evenly balanced.

In Tanzania, as well as Kenya, Islamic law was allowed to operate alongside the established common law. In Kenya, 'separate' Islamic courts were allowed to operate, but, in Tanganyika, Islamic law was absorbed into the main court system. That is, Tanganyika developed a single court system, but this system was, unlike that of Uganda, tolerant of Islamic law.

In both Kenya and Tanzania, Islamic law, which is the junior law, has encountered conflicts:

1 First, if only one party is Muslim, Islamic law is *not* applicable.
2 Secondly, when a case is before a court other than an Islamic court there is no obligation to apply Islamic law, even if both parties are Muslims.
3 Thirdly, there was a problem of appeal to common law, i.e. non-Islamic, courts. In Kenya, the High Court is supreme over the Kadhi courts. Although Kadhis are permitted as assessors in the Kenya High Court when dealing with cases from lower Kadhi courts, the High Court has no obligation to apply Islamic law, even if both parties are Muslims.

It seems very likely that Islamic law will eventually give way to common law in East Africa, considering all the above circumstances, unless Muslims seek other means of influencing the practice of law. Education and changes in society are leading to the development of more secular societies. African secular society is more likely to apply common law than Islamic law.

UGANDA

In Uganda the earlier Christian–Muslim wars led the Christian victors to formulate laws and a system of justice reflecting their views of life, to the exclusion of their Muslim competitors.[45] Moreover, missionaries had more room for manoeuvre in the formulation of laws in Uganda than in Kenya or Tanzania. They had easier access to colonial law-makers. Many of them were in a position to influence policy. This was especially the case in the formative years of the Protectorate. The leader of the Anglican Protestants was Bishop Alfred Tucker (bishop 1890–1908 in Uganda). A legal expert on Uganda, H. F. Morris, has written of Bishop Tucker and his successors, that

> it must, of course, be remembered that in the early years of the [Uganda] Protectorate, the mission, and in particular the [Anglican] Church Missionary Society, played a vital part in framing and implementing of Protectorate policy, and the Anglican Bishop of Uganda was, in practice, in the position of honorary advisor to the commissioner (later Governor). To attempt to implement legislation against the wishes of the Bishop, particularly on such matters as marriage, would have been unthinkable.[46]

Indeed, Bishop Tucker was one of the key persons in the negotiations that led to the signing of the 1900 Agreement. He represented the

African Christian Baganda chiefs especially in transactions with the British colonial administration and in finding compromises on difficult issues. He helped formulate Uganda's educational policy, whereby the missions controlled the teaching of the young, and he was very much involved in the formulation of the Marriage Ordinances of 1902 and 1903 that were discussed earlier.

Muslims were unable to influence Ugandan policy until after independence, when they began to exploit the discord between Roman Catholics and Anglican Protestants. Their involvement in politics and organizations of state that formulated laws and public policy has been discussed.

One of the major results of the exclusion of Islamic influence from policy formulation in Uganda on the administration of justice was the development of a single court system revolving on the High Court, which applied common law wherever local custom allowed, provided that such a custom was not repugnant to Christian morality.

Public holidays

The presence of so many legal public holidays in Uganda is a reflection of the desire of the predominant religious social groups to have an influence on society. If you had visited Uganda in 1978, you would have a holiday on Friday and Sunday on top of a number of annual holidays, such as Christmas, Boxing Day, Good Friday, Easter, Idd-el-Fitr, Idd-el-Azhur and the birth of Mohammed, plus other holidays of a political nature, such as Independence Day, Coup d'Etat Day (25 January), etc. Since the fall of Amin, Friday and the birth of Mohammed have been knocked off the list, but the two Idds still remain. Kenya and Tanzania have, since independence, added the two Idds to the list of holidays to appease their Muslim populations.

Days set apart for resting in Uganda originated mainly from religious sentiments. The first official holiday was observed in Buganda on 5 October 1889. That was the day Baganda Christian exiles defeated the Muslims under Kabaka Nuhu Kalema. It was called 'Buganda Peace Day'. But the colonial government never gazetted it, although it was kept in Buganda up to independence. In the colonial period, most of the public holidays for the whole country were derived from Christian beliefs. In 1905, Bishop Tucker wrote to the Commissioner, Hayes Sadler, that Sunday should be observed as a public holiday. This followed an incident which had forced Baganda Christian converts to work on Sunday.[47] The Commissioner replied that, although he agreed with him in principle, no statute law could be enacted under current circumstances. However, in 1906, a number of days, including Sunday, were set apart as holidays for government employees.[48]

This action sparked off a Muslim reaction. Muslim soldiers wanted Friday to be added to the list of holidays given to government employees. The officer commanding troops of the Fourth King's African Rifles at Mbarara wanted to add Friday to the list of holidays, as he had many Muslim troops whose sentiments he wanted to honour.[49] The officer commanding troops at the headquarters wrote to the Commissioner about the same issue, but the Commissioner put the matter to rest by saying that 'the suggestion will receive due consideration'.[50] It was not until 1925, however, that a law formalized certain specific days as holidays. Besides confirming Sunday as a holiday, the ordinance spelled out New Year's Day, Good Friday, Easter Monday, Empire Day (24 May), Whit Monday, His Majesty's Birthday and Boxing Day.[51] For most of the colonial period, legal holidays remained identical to those listed in the Public Holidays Ordinance of 1925.

With the political campaigns leading to independence, Muslims were courted by the mainly Protestant-led UPC in the latter's desire to defeat the mainly Catholic-led Democratic Party. Protestantism had been developed as the established religion in the colonial period. Protestants occupied most administrative positions. But the Catholics concentrated on mass conversion and education. By 1950 they had overtaken the Protestants in numbers, in educational institutions and in the delivery of other social services to converts. If there were to be a vote conducted on the basis of universal suffrage, Catholics would win. The only way out for the Protestants was to court Muslims to vote for them. The Muslims were more at home with the Protestants, who allowed them in their schools and other educational institutions.[52] One of the key Muslim demands was to legalize Muslim days of prayer as public holidays. The UPC government decided to move with speed to draft the Public Holidays Act of 1965, which added Idd-el-Fitr as a gazetted holiday.[53]

When Amin took power, Muslim influence on the laws (or decrees) of the country also increased. Fanatical Muslim groups in the army, led by Sheikh Khamis Juma, had great influence on Amin. Among the civilian population, the Wandegeya Muslims gained much influence, at the expense of Kibuli Muslims, who entertained a rather different Islamic understanding of Uganda society. It is believed, though I do not have conclusive evidence, that these two Muslim groups influenced Amin to enact decrees favouring Muslims. Some of these lay in the sphere of public holidays. In 1976, Amin added Idd-el-Azhur to the annual public holidays. The following year, he added the birth of Mohammed, 12 Rabbi-al-awwal. In 1978 he issued decree no. 10, the Public Holidays Act (Amendment) Decree, 1978, which formalized his additions as well as making Friday a day of rest.[54] This latter addition was very unpopular among Christians. As soon as he fell from power

A. B. K. Kasozi

in March 1979, it was repealed. These and other actions by Amin deeply soured Christian–Muslim relations in Uganda in later years.

Notes

1. I conducted 130 oral interviews in Uganda in 1986–1987 and twenty in Kenya and fifteen in Uganda in August 1988.
2. Ali A. Mazrui, 'Islam, political leadership and economic radicalism in Africa', *Comparative Studies in Society and History* 9 (1967), pp. 274–279.
3. The Revd F. Schildknecht conducted a survey in Uganda for the Catholic Church in the period 1960–1961. On 11 August 1961, he presented his report at Gaba Seminary entitled 'Islam in Uganda'. I saw it at the White Fathers' Archives in Rome and quote it here at p. 21.
4. Schildknecht, 'Islam in Uganda', pp.2–6.
5. Schildknecht, 'Islam in Uganda', pp. 6.
6. This was the situation only in comparison to fellow Africans of the same social and educational level. The Indo-Pakistanis, whether Hindu, Muslim or Christian, dominated the most lucrative businesses.
7. J. Bamunoba, 'Islam in Ankole', *Dini na Mila* 2 (1967), pp. 5–17.
8. Interview with Haji Mbubi (70), Tororo, January 1987.
9. Schildknecht, 'Islam in Uganda', p. 2; L. P. Harries, *Islam in East Africa* (London, 1964).
10. In January and February 1987, I had five interviews with Prince Badru Kakungulu (84), the leader of Muslims in Uganda since 1921, and three with Sheikh Abdu Kamulegeya, who led, the National Association for the Advancement of Muslims (NAAM) in 1966–1971.
11. See H. B. Hansen, *Mission, church and state in a colonial setting: Uganda 1890–1925* (London, 1984), chapter 25; '*Moshi Records*, or "War with Germany: Islamic propaganda"', SMP 4784, Entebbe Government Archives, Uganda. In Article 6 of the Berlin Act, by which European nations agreed on how to partition Africa, it is stated that special protection was to be given to Christian missionaries, whose work was to be encouraged (Hansen, *Mission*, p. 26).
12. J. J. Willis, *Policy of the Uganda mission* (1912); privately printed by the Church Missionary Society.
13. Young Baganda Association to Chief Secretary, 12 March 1921; SMP 6538, Entebbe Government Archives, Sullivan to Chief Secretary 25 April 1921 and Young Baganda Association, same reference.
14. F. Carter, *Education in Uganda*, PhD Thesis, University of London (1967), p. 155.
15. Ibid., p. 161.
16. Circular no. 37 of 1963; Ministry of Education Act 1964, *Parliamentary Debates* (Entebbe, Government Printer, 1963/1964), vols 19–22, pp. 736–816, vol. 27, pp. 1917–1920; *Munno* editorials 3 June 1963, 1 June 1963, 8 June 1963, 29 September 1963, etc.
17. *New Day* 128 (July 1964); *Uganda Argus*, 21 December (1964).
18. *Uganda Argus*, 27 October (1964).
19. *New Day*, 5 April (1963).
20. *New Day*, 30 November (1962).
21. K. G. Lockard, *Religion and political development in Uganda, 1962–1972*, PhD Thesis, University of Wisconsin (1974), p. 346.
22. Gibson Kamau Kuria, 'Christianity and family law in Kenya', *East African Law Journal* 12, 1 (1967), pp. 33–82.
23. Circular No. 16 of 7 November 1917, SYMP 4844, Entebbe Government Archives.

24. H. F. Morris and J. S. Read, *Uganda: The development of its laws and constitution* (London, 1966); *Laws of Uganda*, Cap. 109, 111, 110, 112; A. Tucker to Sadler, 8 December 1902, A24, Entebbe Government Archives; H. F. Morris, 'Marriage laws in Uganda', *Uganda Journal* 24, 2 (1960), pp. 197–206; J. N. D. Anderson, *Islamic law in Africa* (London, Cass, 1920); copy of the draft law in SMP 6013, Entebbe Government Archives; H. F. Morris, 'Marriage law in Uganda: sixty years of attempted reform', in J. N. D. Anderson, ed., *Family law in Asia and Africa* (New York, 1968), pp. 34–48; *Nile Gazette* (July 1964); *New Day*, 23 December (1965).

25. Interview August 1988 with Sheikh Abdu Kamulegeya, then Vice-President of NAAM (see Note 10 above); *Report of the Commission on Marriages, Divorce and the Status of Women* (Entebbe Uganda Government Printer, 1965), p. 44; interview with Sheikh Ahmad Nsambu in 1970 at Natete, Uganda; *New Day* (December 1965); *Munno*, 23 August (1966); *Uganda Argus*, 22 August (1966); *Parliamentary Debates*, vol. 70, 1967, pp. 2203–2204; Edward Bakaitwako Muhima, *The fellowship of suffering: A theological interpretation of Christian suffering under Idi Amin*, Phd Thesis, Northwestern University, Evanston, Illinois (June 1981), pp. 35–42, 49–55.

26. Gibson Kamau Kuria, 'The Law of Succession Act', mimeo, paper given at the Regional Conference on Social Change and Legal Reform in East, Central and Southern Africa at Harare, Zimbabwe, on 13–16 January (1987), p. 2. More detail on this law appears in F. M. Kassam, 'Notes and comments on the report of the Commission on the Law of Succession: A comment', *East African Law Journal* 12 (1969), pp. 221–245; *National Assembly Debates*, Kenya, 19 November 1970, p. 2099; J. N. D. Anderson, 'Comments with reference to the Muslim community', *East African Law Journal*, Nairobi 5 (1969), pp. 5–20. For the delegation, see *Standard*, 15 September (1981), p. 1.

27. Mohammed Bakkar, Department of Linguistics, Nairobi, in *Nairobi Times*, 16 August (1981), p. 4.

28. D. Rothchild, *Racial bargaining in Kenya: A study of minorities and decolonisation* (London, 1973). He analyses negotiations of various ethnic and cultural minorities for safeguards in an independent Kenya.

29. Margaret Strobel, 'Mombasa society', in B. A. Ogot, ed., *History and social change in East Africia* (Nairobi, 1976), pp. 207–232; A. I. Salim, *The Swahili-speaking peoples of the Kenya coast, 1895–1965* (Nairobi, 1973); F. J. Berg, *Mombasa under the Busaidi Sultanate: The city and its hinterland*, PhD Thesis, University of Wisconsin (1971).

30. Y. P. Ghai and J. P. W. B. McAuslan, *Public law and political change in Kenya: A study of legal framework of government from colonial times to the present* (London 1970), p. 15.

31. Native Courts Regulation, 1897, EAPG, Orders and Regulations, Vol. 1, p. 65, made under the Orders in Council.

32. Ghai and McAuslan, *Public Law*.

33. *Report of the Kenya Constitutional Conference* (London, HMSO, 1962) pp. 8–9; O. S. Basadiq and Shaikh A. Nasir represented the Mwambao United Front.

34. *Report of the Northern Frontier District Commission*, Cmnd 1900; A. A. Castagno, 'The Somali–Kenya controversy', *Journal of Modern African Studies* 2; J. Drysdale, *The Somali dispute* (London, 1964).

35. *Report of the Commission on the Coastal Strip* (London, HMSO, 1961), Cmnd. 1585.

36. Gibson Kamau Kuria, 'Kenya's Law of Succession today', paper given at the Regional Conference on Social Change and Legal Reform in East, Central and Southern Africa at Harare, 13–16 January (1987), p. 7; Kenya Constitution: Section 179, 22 (k), etc.; Kadhi Courts Act, Cap. 11; *Laws of Kenya* (Kenya Government Printer, 1968), p. 2.

37. Michael Wright, *Buganda in the Heroic Age* (Nairobi, OUP, 1971); D. A. Low, *Buganda in Modern History* (London, 1971).

38. D. A. Low, *Religion and society in Buganda 1875–1900* (Makerere, 1957).

39. F. B. Welbourn, *Religion and politics in Uganda 1952–62* (Nairobi, 1965).

A. B. K. Kasozi

40. Ali A. Mazrui, 'Religious strangers in Uganda: From Emin Pasha to Amin Dada', *African Affairs* 302 (1977), pp. 21–38.
41. Native Courts Regulations 1897, EAPG, Order and Regulations, Vol. 1, p. 65, for more elaboration.
42. Quoted by J. B. Ojwang, 'Polygamy as a legal and social institution in Kenya', *East African Law Journal* 10, 1 (1974), pp. 63–91.
43. *National Assembly Debates*, Kenya, 23 May 1967, p. 67.
44. Judicial Advisory Report 1, p. 34.
45. F. B. Welbourn, *Religion and politics in Uganda* (Nairobi, 1965).
46. Morris, 'Marriage law in Uganda', pp. 34–48.
47. Tucker to Sadler, 29 September and 1 October 1905, A22/1, Entebbe Government Archives.
48. Circular 13, SMP 999, 1906, Entebbe Government Archives.
49. Officer Commanding Troops, Mbarara to DC, 13 September 1906, SMP 999, Entebbe Government Archives.
50. Acting Deputy Commissioner to Officer Commanding Troops, 31 October 1906, SMP 999, no. 4, Entebbe Government Archives.
51. Public Holidays Ordinance, 1925.
52. See, for example, the Annual Report of the Department of Education, Uganda, 1935, pp. 30–31.
53. Public Holidays Act, 29 July, 1965, *Laws of Uganda*.
54. Decree signed on 8 July 1978, Public Holidays Act, *Decree no. 10* (Government Printers, Entebbe, 1978).

Thirteen

The Churches &
Human Rights in Kenya & Uganda
since Independence

M. LOUISE PIROUET

When people talk about human rights, they are generally referring to civil and political rights, and it is these which this chapter will discuss. However, the UN Universal Declaration of Human Rights and the African Charter of Human and People's Rights both also deal with social, economic and cultural rights. Socialist writers, such as Osita C. Eze, Professor of Law at Imo State University, Nigeria (*Human Rights in Africa, Some Selected Problems*, 1984), and Professor Issa G. Shivji of Dar es Salaam (*The Concept of Human Rights in Africa*, 1989), argue for the primacy of social, economic and cultural rights, and believe that human rights are not universal but relative to a society's development towards socialism. The failure of socialist societies in Eastern Europe to progress towards the achievement of either of these two sets of human rights strengthens the counter-argument, that civil and political rights are basic and that, when these are denied, social, economic and cultural rights will be eroded.

In this study we shall also concentrate on official action by the churches, either alone or in co-operation with one another or with other religious bodies. Individual church leaders have often taken a lead in defending human rights: action by the churches as institutions is much rarer. Prior to independence, the missions generally showed an equal, if not greater, reluctance to come into conflict with government, and it was not easy for the churches to reverse this habit of acquiescence. They were extremely reluctant to endanger their relationship with government, and were rendered extra cautious when their control of the schools disappeared soon after independence when these were nationalized.

Most of the institutions devoted to monitoring and defending human rights are secular institutions, e.g. Amnesty International, the Minority Rights Group, Index on Censorship, Cultural Survival, International Alert and Africa Watch, the last two of these having come into being only in the latter half of the 1980s. Only the Roman Catholic Church, through its Justice and Peace Commission, has an effective instrument for educating its members in human rights, and helping them to find ways of establishing justice in public life. It represents official church teaching, and, although membership of it is voluntary, Catholics cannot argue against its existence. However, many church people are still suspicious of the human rights movement, and believe that because it is humanist in inspiration it must in some way be anti-religious, or that defending human rights involves interfering in politics, and that this is wrong for Christians. The Protestant churches are often divided on this issue.

Then, too, liberation theology has not caught on in Africa. Only in the Republic of South Africa has there been any systematic theological thinking on this issue. Arcbishop Desmond Tutu has commented:

> I fear that African theology has failed to produce a sufficiently sharp cutting edge . . . it has by and large failed to speak meaningfully in the face of a plethora of contemporary problems which assail the modern African. It has seemed to advocate disengagement from the hectic business of life, because very little has been offered that is pertinent, say, about the theology of power in the face of the epidemic of coups and military rule, about development, about poverty and disease and other equally urgent present day issues.[1]

Liberation theology, though inadequate in some respects, could provide a powerful corrective to much of the spirituality and theological thinking of the Kenyan and Ugandan churches, which are, in contrast, too concerned with individual salvation, personal devotion and sexual morality. The Anglican churches in these two countries are offshoots of the evangelical wing of the Church of England, which, for most of this century, has emphasized personal salvation at the expense of social concern, though this is beginning to change. The leadership of the Roman Catholic Church has sometimes seemed authoritarian and conservative, though some of the Catholic missions represent more liberal Catholic thinking, and the Pastoral Institute, formerly at Ggaba, Uganda, and now at Eldoret in Kenya, has done much to introduce liturgical innovation and the new thinking of Vatican II into East Africa. Right-wing fundamentalism from the USA is on the increase. It is not altogether surprising, then, that the churches as institutions have been slow to rock the political boat by acting in defence of human rights in the face of governments nervous of any kind of dissenting voice. Nevertheless, there have been important interventions by the churches, as well as by individual church leaders, and there have also been occasions when the churches should have acted and failed to do so.

With hindsight it is easy to detect the warning signals in Uganda. They began to appear almost immediately after independence. In 1964 the armies of the three East African states mutinied. Unlike his fellow presidents in Kenya and Tanzania, President Obote of Uganda gave in to all the army's demands and thus ensured that they, not he, would in future hold ultimate power in Uganda.[2] During the years that followed there were constant abuses of power by the security forces, culminating in the horrors of the Amin regime, and continuing under Obote II. During Obote I the churches at no time made any public statement about the misuse of power. The only public protest at the detention without trial of Rajat Neogy and Abu Mayanja, apparently for writing an article critical of the government in *Transition*, came from Professor Ali Mazrui, who wrote an open letter to Obote. As George Kanyeihamba points out, the use of detention without charge or trial was nothing new: 'Detention and Deportation Ordinances were promulgated almost simultaneously with the Declaration of the Protectorate.'[3] Everyone was used to the idea. By the time Amin seized power, civil liberties had already been seriously eroded. A crisis was widely expected, and few people were surprised by the 1971 coup, though it quickly emerged that it had little to do with rectifying previous misgovernment. Coups never do have. The extent to which human rights were abused and freedoms restricted during Obote I has often been underestimated because of what was to follow. It is frightening to look back on those years and note how quickly and quietly repression was able to take hold and become accepted.

The position of the churches in Kenya was somewhat different. First, there were far more of them. In Uganda Roman Catholics and the (Anglican) Church of Uganda had a near monopoly of the religious scene (it has become a little more varied since). A Joint Christian Council was established in 1964, but it was not very active in the social field. Kenya's National Christian Council (NCCK) was able to speak for all the major Protestant denominations in that much more varied ecclesiastical scene (although it did not speak for the Roman Catholics, who are proportionately much less strong in Kenya than in Uganda). As Lonsdale, Booth-Clibborn and Hake explain, the NCCK at the end of the colonial period and during the first few years of independence was far stronger and more autonomous than most of its African counterparts and recruited its own staff of more liberal and socially aware Christians than were usually to be found in the Kenyan Protestant churches.[4] The writers of this article comment on the NCCK's concern about living standards in the slums of Nairobi, and the NCCK's stand with the shanty-dwellers over against the City Council, which regarded the shanty towns as nests of thieves and vice (p. 279), as they still do. The writers go on to note the campaign against the 1969 resurgence of oathing among the Kikuyu, who vowed 'to keep the government of Kenya within the House of Mumbi ... However unintentionally, and perhaps reluctantly, the churches for a moment found themselves at the head of a political opposition.'[5] The church newspaper which ran this campaign, *Target*, was independent from but closely connected with the NCCK.

The Ugandan churches found themselves dragged, perhaps even more reluctantly because of the greater danger, into opposition to President Amin. At the time of the expulsion of the Asians, the churches appear to have made no public protest. However, the archbishops of both churches, together with the Chief Kadhi, did make known to Amin their concern at the manner of the expulsions, and this co-operation between the religious leaders set a pattern which was to be important for the future. It is reported that they said: 'Yes, we agree with the policy of Africanising the country's economy. We agree that the Asians with British passports should gradually leave the country. But we cannot agree with the manner of deportation, breaking up families, robbery and violence.'[6] Presumably it was on the basis of this that Uganda Radio claimed in a broadcast that Archbishop (later Cardinal) Emmanuel Nsubuga had approved the expulsions. The archbishop issued a strongly worded denial, but he found himself forced on to the defensive, as was to happen for one reason or another many times during the next few years.[7] If there are dangers in making public statements, there are also disadvantages in not publicizing them.

By 1976 the situation in Uganda had deteriorated still further. The Christian and Muslim clergy found themselves increasingly forced into opposition by having to care for widows and orphans bereaved by the slaughter, and by having to conduct the funerals of many of the victims of the regime. Some of these funerals became political protests, as thousands of mourners of all faiths came to them. Then, in early August 1976, Archbishop Janani Luwum of the Church of Uganda and Cardinal Nsubuga went together to Makerere University because of their concern at reports that violence had been used by the army against students and staff. They were assured by the vice-chancellor that all was over, but in fact the worst violence occurred during the night following their visit. Margaret Ford, Luwum's secretary, wrote in her short life of Luwum, 'neither the Catholic Church nor the Anglican Church in Uganda had any tradition of social or political criticism, but now they were forced to take up political positions'.[8]

Later that August, Christian and Muslim leaders, prompted by religious violence in Ankole, met together in conference at a church-owned centre just outside Kampala to discuss how the violence and insecurity engulfing the country might be met. The minutes of their deliberations noted that: 'People were arrested by members of the State Research Bureau and the Public Safety Unit and not taken to court where proper justice could be administered. Many of these people disappeared.' The minutes were also highly critical of the military police and described the deplorable levels of crime and violence in the country.[9] A meeting with the president was requested, and refused. Amin was furious to learn that this conference of religious leaders had taken place without his knowledge and permission, and terrified because Muslims as well as Christians had been involved. Were they all against him? He demanded to see the minutes. These had been signed by Luwum as chairman of the conference and no doubt sealed his fate. Within a few months, after a final courageous stand, Luwum was murdered, together with two government ministers, on 17 February 1977, tragically after a breakdown in communication between Catholics and Anglicans had left him isolated.

. With hindsight it is plain to see that the interventions by the religious leaders had come too late. Action had been needed when things first began to slip during Obote I, or during the first two or three months of Amin before matters had gone beyond the point of no return. It is doubtful whether approaches that are not publicized can achieve much. The only weapon the religious leaders used was words (in spite of Luwum being falsely accused by Amin of being involved in an armed plot), though we shall later find the Roman Catholic Church in Kenya turning to educating clergy and laity in human rights. The Ugandan religious leaders' minuted decision to 'fight evil and violence' in their country was misunderstood: bishops and clergy were accused of preaching sermons which incited violence when they preached sermons about the fight against evil.

If we turn to Kenya, we find much the same lack of willingness to speak out strongly in defence of civil and political rights in the last few years of Kenyatta's presidency. The Kenyan churches were by that time fairly comprehensively Kenyanized and perhaps less able to risk publicly opposing the government with a moral critique of the country's social and political situation, though individual church leaders, notably Bishop Henry Okullu, continued to do so on occasion. In comparison with most of her neighbours, Kenya was far freer, far better administered, far more stable and with much less need for outspokenness. Yet there were serious and glaring flaws, and Kenyans still had the freedom to be more outspoken, but the chance was missed. The murder of the politician J. M. Kariuki was never fully explained, though the government was possibly implicated. Church leaders who had previously been willing to take a stand over detention without charge or trial somehow allowed themselves to be persuaded that it was acceptable in the case of the professor and novelist Ngugi wa Thiong'o. Far from defending and helping refugees, the Joint Refugee Services of Kenya (JRSK), which were sponsored by the NCCK, cheated and exploited them. The chairman of JRSK, who was also the general secretary of the NCCK, tried, in 1978, to suppress a report which revealed gross mismanagement (the report was leaked and a copy is in the writer's possession). In 1980, JRSK was finally broken up and two of its senior officials were jailed on fraud charges.[10] Church leaders, with some honourable exceptions, were persuaded to do nothing for the Ugandan refugees, and the NCCK tried to prevent an agency set up to assist them from operating. The Most Revd Festo Olang', Archbishop of the Anglican Church of the Province of Kenya (CPK), refused to be cowed, and permitted money for Ugandan refugees to be channelled through CPK accounts. Corruption and smuggling were rife, but the churches for the most part remained silent. President Moi's accession brought about a temporary improvement. He won widespread acclaim by releasing all political detainees, and for a while the atmosphere in Kenya was freer and more relaxed.

In Uganda, by contrast, the overthrow of Amin did not bring relief. Political uncertainty and an undisciplined army quickly led to fears that the situation was slipping out of control. Once again, Uganda's religious leaders made a joint submission to the government about the state of the country. The memorandum, prepared by the cardinal, the Church of Uganda archbishop, the bishop of the Orthodox Church, who was now included for the first time, and the Chief Kadhi, was the first in a series of remarkably bold and outspoken documents sent by the religious leaders. The inclusion of the Chief Kadhi was important at a time when many people were tempted to take vengeance on Muslims for what they had suffered under the Muslim president, Amin. This first document was not made public.

It was sent in July 1979, after Yusufu Lule had been deposed from the presidency and detained. The religious leaders remonstrated with his successor, Godfrey Binaisa, about the manner of Lule's deposition and detention, about the intrusion of the army into government and politics, and about the breakdown of law and order, with soldiers responsible for much of the violence. The behaviour of the army troubled the religious leaders most:

> Members of the liberation army have diverted from the objectives of the Front and are acting in no better way than the soldiers in the previous regime. They are killing people and robbing people's property almost every night throughout the country. To everybody's dismay the situation is getting worse than before.[11]

They stated that the nomination of ten soldiers to the Consultative Council (the body then effectively running the country) 'is not exactly a measure calculated to restore democracy and stability to our country'. They demanded the demobilization of many hurriedly recruited soldiers and a restructuring of the army along the lines of a people's militia. Their demand that the army be confined to barracks seems to have been temporarily heeded,[12] but it was not long before the soldiers were at large again, and lawlessness and murder continued.

But when the Church of Uganda came to issue a pastoral letter, which it did at about the same time, it became clear that there was dissension among the bishops. Some were not prepared to speak out clearly. The pastoral letter was in a different vein from the statement of the religious leaders. It offered spiritual comfort to the suffering and bereaved, it exhorted the people to forgive and it spoke of the need to fight against evil. It admitted that many people had been murdered since the liberation, but it attributed this to 'forces which are difficult to identify'. The religious leaders acting together had had no such difficulty in identifying those responsible: not only the army, but quite certainly the army bore a large share of responsibility.

Less than a year later, the religious leaders again wrote to the government, but again they do not seem to have made their approach public. The occasion was the announcement that elections would take place in December 1980. This time their memorandum was firmly based on the UN Universal Declaration of Human Rights: President Binaisa had been a member of the International Commission of Jurists, 'a non-political, non-governmental organization of lawyers based in Geneva, devoted to the promotion of the rule of law and the legal protection of human rights in all parts of the world'.[13] The religious leaders claimed: 'We are facing a complete rejection of articles 3 (right to live), 5 (right to be spared torture), 12 and 17 (right to private property)'. They go on to refer to Article 21 ('everyone has the right to participate in the government of his country either by himself, or through others he has freely elected'). 'We are not satisfied', they said, 'that this article has been properly implemented in the way members of the National Consultative Council were selected, nor in the manner in which the leaders of "Mayumba 10" units were appointed.' The religious leaders concluded:

> If we have insisted here on the text of the Universal Declaration of Human Rights it is precisely because it is in full accordance with the teachings we, as religious leaders, are trying to instil in our faithful as a basis to our nation's moral rehabilitation, while at the same time it is an almost universally accepted charter among the member states of the United Nations, including Uganda.[14]

But the army and the Consultative Council, not Binaisa, were in control, and this fell on deaf ears. And such appeals to governments have even less chance of achieving anything if they are not made fully public, though there are also risks in that policy.

Less than a year after the disputed elections, which placed Obote in power for the second time, the religious leaders wrote the third in this series of memoranda, and this time it was published and was widely reported.[15] The sentence, 'The Uganda you lead is bleeding to death' caught everyone's attention. The document is a shocking indictment of the army's behaviour:

> Once they are sent in an area, they start shooting innocent people without discrimination. Property is looted, women and girls are raped, and many civilians desert their homes to save their lives . . . As soon as they [the army] appear on site [the civilians] run away . . . Official army vehicles have been seen carrying loads of civilian belongings and property . . . What they are not able to take is crushed to pieces and houses damaged . . . The road blocks have become places of torture, especially when mounted by army men . . . When you see the army men . . . search the women it is very unhealthy and harmful. At gunpoint they sometimes force the women to take off their clothes, they demand money even from children and old people.[16]

This seems to have been the last joint memorandum sent. Joint action between the Catholic and Anglican churches became increasingly difficult as old political allegiances reasserted themselves. The Church of Uganda had traditionally been associated with the Uganda People's Congress (UPC), Obote's ruling party, and the Catholics with the opposition Democratic Party (DP). The regime seems deliberately to have courted the Church of Uganda in order to drive a wedge between the churches and win Church of Uganda support. Bishop Festo Kivengere wrote in November 1983:

> We have a government in Uganda which is almost entirely made up of members of our church. That should make things very easy for us, you may think. But I am sure you know that that makes things very difficult for us. The government does not stand in our way at all . . . in fact we are constantly appealed to by members of the government to take the lead in 'spiritual rehabilitation' . . . this sounds tremendous but underneath it is very difficult because words do not mean actions . . . When the government is putting us in this position of favour, speaking the truth becomes doubly difficult.[17]

That same month great pressure was put on the Church of Uganda bishops to elect a UPC supporter as their new archbishop, and this they did. Thus the regime virtually ensured that the Church of Uganda's voice would be silenced.

Even after an appalling incident at Namugongo Martyrs' Shrine, in which over eighty people died, no joint public statement was made by the religious leaders, nor did the Church of Uganda, which suffered particularly seriously in this outrage, seize the opportunity to demand that the army be brought under proper control. That the army had admitted responsibility and 'apologized' seems irrelevant. So far as is known, no one was ever brought to justice for this massacre. It was left to the diocesan bishop, Misaeri Kauma, and his predecessor, the elderly Bishop Dunstan Nsubuga, to go to the theological college which the army had ransacked, and rescue the body of its principal, whom the army had murdered. In June a visitor from overseas wrote,

> The bishops in the Anglican Church of Uganda are divided in their response [to the barbarities of the regime and in particular to the massacre at Namugongo], and the Archbishop refuses to blame the army, preferring to try to exert influence privately on the government – whose members, including Obote, are predominantly Anglican. Many of the priests in Buganda feel bitter at this silence: one spoke to us of how the church should be the voice of the oppressed and terrified people, and her silence renders them speechless. On the other hand we heard priests in other parts of the country praising the church's refusal to become enmeshed in political controversy, its purpose being only the salvation of souls.[18]

This writer compared the Church of Uganda's silence with the determined stand made by the Catholics. In a news bulletin in July, they had spoken out forcefully against the 'barbaric acts' and 'indiscriminate killings' at Namugongo, so speaking for both churches, since the Church of Uganda had, in this instance, suffered much more severely. When Yoweri Museveni's National Resistance Movement (NRM) took power in 1986, the Church of Uganda found itself severely compromised. To a lesser extent the Catholic Church also found itself temporarily wrong-footed, since it was accused of supporting the DP rather than the NRM.

Recent events in Kenya are instructive in any consideration of the churches and the defence of human rights. In early 1988, a pastoral letter from the Catholic bishops was a call for the church to work for justice and peace, and a Kenya branch of the Justice and Peace Commission was established. This heralded a move into a different mode of action, since it involved, not just the issuing of statements by the church authorities, but educating people at grass-roots level in working for the defence of human rights – civil and political, and also social, economic and cultural – in a systematic fashion. The pastoral letter carefully justified the church's involvement in working for justice and peace by reference to the gospels and to papal encyclicals. The bishops noted 'a situation of growing injustice' in Kenya, both in the economic sphere and in the sphere of civil and political rights. The pastoral letter referred to the 'violation of human rights in detention without trial [and] the widespread corruption and abuse of power and privilege in structures that are meant to be of service to the people', and the objectives of the Justice and Peace Commission were set out in detail. Only the main points can be picked out here:

(a) To develop programmes for the education of people towards a stronger sense of justice.

(b) To guide and coordinate pastoral action in fostering justice and peace.

(c) To work for the eradication of injustice wherever it is seen to exist, for instance: the question of land distribution, unfair practices in agriculture, education, health, media, tourism, housing and habitat and etc. . . .

(d) To give advice, encouragement and support to all those involved in the promotion of justice and in opposition to injustice.

The pastoral letter concluded by speaking of the need for co-operation with 'other institutions and people working for human rights'. The Christian monthly *Beyond*, whose February 1988 issue published this, was itself suppressed later in the year for alleged subversion and its editor jailed, after he had produced a number which included a forthright article on human rights violations in Kenya and referred in detail to an Amnesty International Report on the torture of detainees, and a sermon by Bishop David Gitari, which *Beyond* headlined 'Another political murder'.

The establishment of the Justice and Peace Commission in Kenya meant that the Catholic Church was well placed to issue an official statement in June 1990, when a crisis was clearly looming over the government's refusal to consider any moves towards greater democracy, and Moi's outbursts against any hint of dissent were bordering on the paranoid and irrational. The Catholic hierarchy issued a balanced document, carefully referenced to official church pronouncements. It specifically criticized the superiority of the party over the authority of the Parliament', and constitutional changes which undermined the independence of the judiciary. The bishops stated:

We are afraid that the 'philosophy of the National Security' publicly condemned by our brethren, the Bishops of Latin America in union with the Pope in 1979, may become installed in our country leading to political murders, unlawful house searches, arbitrary detentions, confessions under torture and death squads' actions that escape the control of the public forces of order.

The bishops reiterated their concern about the queuing system for voting in elections 'whereby the secret ballot of the citizens was drastically diminished'. They suggested that a national conference should be called 'to analyze the main problems of our country, their root causes, and their possible solution', and they set out a list of conditions necessary before such a meeting could take place, including the need for 'some form of guarantee acceptable to all that no one will be victimised later as a result of opinions expressed or ideas proposed during the conference', a caveat which was an eloquent commentary on the insecurity in which many Kenyans were living.[19] This letter was read to the press on 21 June by Archbishops John Njenga and Zacchaeus Okoth, and was later read in all Catholic churches.[20]

But, because of the establishment of the Justice and Peace

Commission in Kenya, the matter did not rest there. The pastoral letter was accompanied by a 'Guide for group reflection' prepared by the Commission, some of which is worth quoting. The groups of readers were asked to

1. SEE

a) Read in your group the Pastoral Letter and list all the problems the Bishops are concerned about (e.g. superiority of the party, cost of living, forced Harambees, etc.).

b) Which additional problems are you experiencing in your family, parish area? Add them to your list. . . .

3. ACT

a) What is the course of action proposed by the Bishops?

b) What can we do in our own community (parish) to work towards a solution of one or other of these problems? Which of them are we able to start tackling NOW? WHO is doing WHAT, WHEN, HOW?

CONCLUSION

1. Discuss the argument FOR and AGAINST the Church's involvement in 'realms beyond the spiritual and religious'.

2. What can we do to spread the Pastoral Letter in our Small Christian Communities and parishes?

On 27 August 1990, the *Independent* carried a report by Tod Shields on the mounting discontent in Kenya, and the protests following the death in a 'road accident' of the Anglican Bishop Muge, after threats had been made against him by a cabinet minister, Peter Okondo. The reporter went on to note how the commission set up to gather views on reforming the ruling party had been obliged to widen its mandate to include the gathering of opinion on public life in general.

> The result was an outpouring of criticism. People from all walks of life – farmers, students, lawyers, businessmen, clergymen, and even one man who identified himself simply as a golfer – appeared before the Committee. Some observers believe the panel's work, by revealing the extent of discontent, has helped create a climate of opinion unlikely to be satisfied with timid reforms.

Some of those who appeared before this commission perhaps gave more thoughtful evidence than they might otherwise have done had they not been urged to study the Catholic bishops' pastoral letter, and church representatives were among those who made written submissions to the commission. Some of these were reprinted in the September issue, of the previously banned *Nairobi Law Monthly* for September 1990. The whole of this issue is taken up with submissions to the Saitoti Commission, and five of them were from the churches: from the Roman Catholic bishops, the NCCK, the Catholic diocese of Murang'a, the Catholic Justice and Peace Commission and the Christians of the (Anglican) diocese of Eldoret. One further submission was from an individual Christian, the Revd Dr Timothy Njoya. They make impressive reading.

Between 1990 and 1992, Roman Catholic bishops in a number of African countries (e.g. Sudan, Zaïre, Malawi, Cameroon) have made statements on human rights, sometimes at great risk to themselves. In Zaïre a key role in the attempts to move towards democracy through a constitutional conference has been played by Archbishop Monsengwo Pasinya, who has acted as its chairman and who has taken important initiatives in persuading President Mobutu to accept change. There is no way of telling how much the Roman Catholic Justice and Peace Commission has been involved in this championing of human rights by the Catholic hierarchies, or how much effect the work of the Commission has had on non-Catholic Christian groups. One can only guess that it has been considerable. The model provided by the Justice and Peace Commission is one which deserves to be widely copied by other churches. It is among the few institutions in Africa which have the capacity to help modify undemocratic and repressive governments.

We shall conclude with some words from Dr Njoya's submission to the Saitoti Commission:

> Having a single party or multi-parties are social preferences, political choices, that can be made peacefully without introducing state violence in the name of national security to silence one side of the debate. *We don't want to debate with guns, knives and rungus, but with reason, sanity and vision* ... Our task is to provide the moral alternative of non-violent reformation through communication and dialogue. (*Nairobi Law Monthly* 25 (September 1990), p. 36. Emphasis in original)

Notes

1. Reprinted from the *Journal of Religious Thought* 2 (1975), in J. Parratt, ed., *A reader in African Christian theology* (1987), p. 54.
2. A. Omara-Otunnu, *Politics and the military in Uganda 1890–1985* (1987), Chapters 4 and 5.
3. G. Kanyeihamba, *Constitutional law and government in Uganda* (1975), p. 430.
4. J. Lonsdale *et al.* 'The emerging pattern of church and state cooperation in Kenya', in E. Fashole-Luke and others, eds, *Christianity in independent Africa* (London, 1978).
5. Ibid., pp. 280–281.
6. Fr. Robert Gay, in *Petit Echo* (1978–1979), p. 477. This seems to be paraphrase written from memory.
7. M. L. Pirouet, 'Religion in Uganda under Amin', *Journal of Religion in Africa* 11 (1980), p. i.
8. M. Ford, *Janani: The making of a martyr* (1978), pp. 71–72.
9. Ibid., pp. 74–75.
10. *Nairobi Times*, 20 March (1980); *Daily Nation*, Nairobi, Official Notice, 1 August (1980).
11. p. 3, paragraph 4.
12. *Guardian*, 12 July (1979).

13. International Commission of Jurists, *Uganda and Human Rights* (1977), p. vii.
14. 'Memorandum by the religious leaders of Uganda to His Excellency President G. L. Binaisa on the current situation in Uganda', 18 April (1980).*
15. e.g. *Guardian*, 30 September; *Sunday Times*, 4 October; *Kenya Weekly Review*, 9 October (1981).
16. 'In search for peace and development for our nation Uganda', 24 September (1981).
17. Letter dated 9 November 1983.
18. Letter dated August 1984.
19. 'A pastoral letter of the Catholic bishops of Kenya on the present situation in our country', 20 June (1990).
20. *APS News and Features Bulletin*, Nairobi, 25 June (1990).

Fourteen

Church & State
in Eastern Africa:
Some Unresolved Questions

MARTIN DOORNBOS

'Guess what we talk about most of the time,' my friend asked as he ushered us into the house. Not waiting for an answer, he continued: 'trying to find out what we are doing here'. I had not seen him for a few years, a Roman Catholic missionary in an out-of-the-way Ugandan parish. But now there was a difference. The last time I visited, there had been a sense of purpose about the mission, inspired by a feeling that the station could provide needed tasks in social care, rudimentary education and other relief work. Today, though these welfare activities were continued, the air of purposefulness had waned: the two priests at the mission felt that their contacts with the people had often been more apparent than real and they had realized how foreign an element the church was in its present environment.

During most of the weekend we indeed talked about little else but what it was they were doing there. If they faced problems with that, it was not so much because the area was difficult practically. The parish they served was situated in a no man's land between regular government control and a rebellious movement, a situation demanding considerable tact and understanding in dealing with all sides. If anything, that fact should have helped a search for meaningful involvements, and to some extent it had done so. But, precisely because the area offered a seemingly ample but saliently unfulfilled scope for church engagement, the two priests not only derived a sense of inadequacy from their failure to be more relevant but were in a position to perceive the broader dilemmas of the missionary situation more sharply than many of their colleagues elsewhere.

The predicament they perceived was cultural, institutional, religious and also personal, mixed in a complex fashion as the larger transitional problems of the Roman Catholic Church were added to the specific difficulties of this particular situation. The cultural aspect was the frustration that communication and genuine involvement had not been forthcoming, notwithstanding enthusiastic effort and tolerant, if not positive, responses initially. The priests had found it difficult to relate to the population, in church affairs as well as in other matters; in their opinion, people often said one thing itself but did another. This was itself not an unusual judgement, except that the recent establishment of the parish – in the early 1950s – had perhaps left fresher expectations among its servants. Disappointments on this score were ultimately reflective of two different worlds meeting, a reality as easily overlooked as overestimated. Equally easy to overlook (but not to overestimate) was that the exotic element in this confrontation was formed by the Roman Catholic Church rather than by the African social setting.

Institutional dilemmas exacerbated the cultural deadlock. Even if the cultural gap could be successfully bridged, then what? Then small numbers of people who had been in touch with the mission, particularly school-age children who had been taught and fed for periods of about half a year, would return home to find no follow-up whatsoever to their training. There would be insufficient clergy to satisfy any curiosity aroused by the church's teaching and any embryonic religious interest would thus be left to itself – with potential psychological frustration for the initiated. 'It's not just that we don't seem to solve anything, but we may actually be adding to the problems,' one of the priests observed. One alternative, largely followed at this particular mission, was to abandon most proselytizing ambitions – at any rate of the conventional soul-winning kind – and do relief work at whatever rate possible. But this, too, raised questions. Not only did church policy demand a certain *acte de présence*, and hence the creation of some visible religious identity, but sooner or later one would still have to ask oneself why one had chosen certain tasks and by what criteria these had to be evaluated. Concentration on welfare work was not only unlikely to result in any actual impact, but its net effect might be that one merely took over government responsibilities and perhaps inadvertently caused stillbirths to local initiatives towards ameliorating conditions. Did the immediate needs of the situation outweigh these considerations?

In addition, there were questions about the nature of religious involvement. Vatican II had had a greater influence on some priests than others; for some, it was merely a belated and incomplete codification of what they had long felt to be the proper course of action. More profoundly even than in Europe, the reorientation involved raised questions about the kind of message that should be conveyed to the non- or newly initiated, about the role of the priesthood and about religion itself. 'Look at those nuns,' one or the priests said, 'they're Pavlovian. At the sound of the bell they come out for prayers, next they are back to reading, and so forth. To what purpose? Why are we doing that to these people?'

Critique and reconsideration

The questions raised in one parish are echoed in many others. Introspective and retrospective, the concerns are shared ones – often with a prefoundly personal dimension. More intensely than at any earlier moment, including independence, missionaries in Africa today are reconsidering assumptions and achievements which are no longer self-evident; it is another soul-searching, but of a different kind. There is a sense of urgency, as processes of Africanization and changes within the Roman Catholic Church at large combine to induce a critical stocktaking. 'We've talked them into it, now we have to talk them out of it', some expatriate priests remark. Dismayed at the inadequacy of a church structure allowed to grow into a hierarchical, status-conscious and liturgy-orientated edifice, they fear that it has encouraged seminarists and African clergy to affect a style of living which is not just exotic but increasingly antiquated and socially irrelevant. A 'penguin in the savannah', as the Roman Catholic Church in Africa has at times been called, with its white-robed officers, its somewhat mysterious aura and strange rites, it is perhaps not an unsympathetic creature, but at least a little out of place.

While many of the church's problems are recognized, dissected and theorized upon, their solution is complicated as a result of policies and principles. Some of these difficulties are readily understood when considering the clerical manpower situation. It is difficult to deny the anachronism that, many years after independence, often two-thirds of all priests in many African countries are still Europeans or Americans. The necessity of replacing expatriate clergy is generally acknowledged. None the less, disinclination to withdraw is not the issue. Most missionaries now in Africa are of an older generation whose retirement within a few years will be virtually automatic. (Already, quite a few parish churches have essentially become retirement homes for those who have come to identify fully with their adopted country; of the three priests in one Ugandan parish I visited some years ago, for instance, one had arrived in 1912 and the two others in the 1920s.) At the bottom of the age pyramid, only very few, perhaps 1 or 2 per cent, of the expatriates are recent seminarists, the interest in priesthood and missionary work having shrunk to an unprecedented low. Finally, at the intermediate age levels many priests presently opt out, because of either disillusionment or lack of confidence or in recognition of changed circumstances, often turning to marriage and other worldly pursuits.

Consequently, notwithstanding the continued European predominance, there is hardly a question of a resistant rearguard unwilling to make room. If the expatriate presence alone were the problem, it would solve itself. The point is rather that the structure cannot maintain its present form with their departure. For one thing, seminary training is too long, the intake and interest too little and the rate of student dropout too large to produce anywhere near the required number of African priests to replace the expatriate element in any foreseeable future. Besides, with the phasing out of foreign priests, a good deal of financial assistance is likely to dry up: already, some African churches are preparing themselves for 'self-reliance', engaging in reassessments of what local groups can contribute toward clerical maintenance. One thing this implies is that, in future, African priests will have to content themselves with more modest amenities than were enjoyed by their predecessors.

In one form or another, continuity is desired in many quarters. With the imminent expatriates' withdrawal and the lack of replacements, however, continuity can only be secured if some major reorientation is made. Discussions in this regard focus on the need to diversify the priesthood, through the lifting of celibacy, delegating priestly functions to catechists and lay members of the church, introducing worker priests, and reorientating and reducing the content of seminary training – all different propositions to help fill a gap and to ensure a continued and viable church leadership. Immediately linked to this, the need for increased relevance of the church to present-day problems of development in Africa is raised. A sense of crisis in church circles thus stimulates a critical rethinking of what the church should do and be.

However, virtually all suggested innovations encounter formidable obstacles at opposite extremes of the church structure. At one end, many proposed reforms strand on key church rulings. Married clergy and increased responsibilities of catechists, two of the most strategic ways of alleviating the manpower problem, conflict with basic policies and have no chance of early and officially sanctioned adoption. Reform or recruitment and training sufficiently drastic to meet the demands of the situation similarly clash with universals. Papal representatives with African churches leave no doubt that some of these topics are off limits, and usually their warnings are heeded. None the less, although a source of considerable delay in the search for effective adaptations, these barriers are not altogether insurmountable. Some meaningful experiments with a redistribution of tasks are being conducted in various areas. If these prove successful, the universal church may well at some point find it necessary to accept changes effected from within. Sooner or later, the ties with Rome themselves are bound to be subjected to reconsideration and this too might facilitate the granting of concessions.

At the other end, obstacles to change are potentially more tenacious. Any institution, church or otherwise, which is ingrained in society is pervaded with a certain image that covers all those who become involved in it. Profound reorientations may occur at the centre, or wherever innovation originates from, while the general image may not change or may change only after some delay. This pattern applies particularly to the Catholic Church in Africa.

The generation gap

Although caught up in the same situation, different categories of priests react to it in different ways. Somewhat arbitrarily, contrasting orientations may be distinguished between various age-groups of European priests (arbitrarily, because other factors, such as membership of different orders and personal backgrounds, play a role in erasing or reinforcing the age factor's importance). The older generation's perception of its social environment was usually given shape during an earlier decade, and often its members continue to act accordingly. Emotionally, some are probably closer to the pioneering days than to the present. They do not necessarily form a stumbling-block to change, in the sense of actively militating against it, but commonly constitute a dead weight in discussions of basic reforms – augmenting the 'revolutionary' self-image held by their younger colleagues.

Rethinking of the church situation appears to occur particularly among the 30–40 age-group. If age figures here as a variable, this is not in the last place due to the fact that this category is involved in a profoundly personal sense: its members are confronted with the church's predicaments at an age at which their chosen career must either be found meaningful or not. Often with enough experience and influence to carry weight, but without the burdens of officialdom that might hold them back, the debate, the experimentation and the demands are largely carried by individuals within this bracket. But their difficulty is not only to find new ways in the midst of dilemmas. It is also the growing recognition of being strangers in a situation which is not their own that increasingly raises the question as to what right they have to push for change, no matter in what direction.

This dilemma is of more than purely academic interest. Turning to perceptions and attitudes among African clergy, two broad categories may again be roughly distinguished, also partly based on age though less markedly so than on the European side. One of these is the group that has reached seniority, holding office as parish priests or bishops or other positions of authority. Most of them have persevered through a rigorous educational system at a time when it offered a manifestly different culture, infusing a Latin socialization in spirit if not in fact. To be sure, there are quite a few exceptional people among them whose personalities would carry weight in any culture or situation.

None the less, the fact that members of this group moved up in the system just as the Catholic Church reached full bloom, in the 1950s and 1960s, has not failed to leave its imprint. Not surprisingly, it tends to be the church of that period they represent, and which they will defend in the face of any challenges. This attitude entails a considerable deference towards Rome and a barely concealed appreciation of the symbolic and ceremonial sides of church life. Also involved is a taste for the prestige traditionally due to the church and its priests, often still seen as an intrinsic quality of religious leadership resting on command and status relationships.

It is particularly among their juniors, still in or just out of seminary, that different orientations are found. Some of these, who have studied in Rome or elsewhere, are noted for holding more critical views on the role of the church in African life than can be found in almost any other quarter. Partly, perhaps, their 'Young Turk' sentiments are a familiar concomitant of studentship, wearing off as they pass through subsequent states in life. None the less, it must be noted that they are being confronted with the need to scrutinize the church's role at a radically different stage from that of a decade or more ago, a stage in which the social relevance of the church, hence also its involvement and structure, are raised as prime issues. It is to be expected that these concerns will figure more significantly once these younger African priests take their turn at leadership.

Today, the double generation gap results in a stalemate. If, on the European side, the older missionaries are phasing out while the younger ones are trying to carry the ball, the older African clergy are increasingly gaining control while their juniors are still without effective voice. Mutual relationships and perceptions are marked accordingly. At the far ends, resignation and impatience are characteristic; the tension occurs in the middle. Expatriate activists fear that African clergy will assume exactly the type of role they are trying to discard. 'The Archbishop?' a militant in one East African country exclaimed. 'He is useless. He is concerned with trivialities, like raising money for an altar, altogether oblivious to the key issues we are facing.' Bitterly, they cite examples of African priests who sit reading on their porches, not to be disturbed by people who come to ask for held on rural development projects. They claim that some of the African clergy oppose reforms, particularly in the nature of the priesthood, because it would devalue the status positions they have reached after prolonged sacrifice. Also, they feel that not a few African bishops are blind to the collapse that is imminent unless timely adjustments are made. In part, these criticisms may be explained by the fact that many expatriates keep closely in touch with new currents within Roman Catholicism at large, which their counterparts are often not in a position to do. Only the younger African priests are supportive of these views, frequently in even more outspoken fashion.

The older African clergy's view of the expatriates is equally inimical. They are wary of people who keep pressing for reform and are apt to consider this as interference with the authority accorded to them. They feel they have a better insight into what is proper and called for in African society than Europeans and Americans can ever hope to develop, and see the repeated insistence on change as a new form of paternalism through which expatriate missionaries burden the African church with their own frustrations. 'Our people here are united in Christ and the task of the priest is to bring them light and lead them in worship. He is their spokesman before God' is often their time-honoured but elusive position. Through their bishops and cardinals, African priests tend to maintain a strong orientation to Rome, and they often seek support in papal directives to counter back-door strategies of expatriate experimental change. 'The Church is not owned by the Europeans, or didn't they mean that in the first place?'

Not surprisingly, then, calls are frequently made for the rapid decolonization of the church – but with different meanings. To the African cadre, decolonization means the early withdrawal of European staff, so that the African churches may assume their rightful place among the churches of the world. To the expatriates, it means undoing a structure which they wish had not developed, and trying to adjust it instead to African conditions. Debates on these issues, at conferences and study seminars, bring out these positions. On such occasions, a cardinal is likely to be brought in to support the African side, while the expatriates may try to use a modernist Roman prelate as a weapon. Joint declarations are commonly adopted about the role the church should play in nation-building, and a European contribution may well be (and has been on occasion) the insertion of a clause of congratulation that 'we are bringing Negritude into the universal Church'. But, beyond the declaratory stage, definition of that role awaits the breaching of an impasse. With the number of its adherents estimated at between fifty and one hundred and fifty million, an important record in education, health and additional fields and, not least, considerable resources in manpower, expertise on local conditions and preparedness to contribute, the Roman Catholic Church in Africa is one of the largest and relatively better-equipped bodies to take part in development efforts; often, in fact, it is second only to government in terms of capacity. Theoretically, at least, it should be possible to reach a formula whereby these resources can be more fully mobilized for development, an objective which few could argue would clash with religious imperatives. One prerequisite, however, is the need for long-term planning – not primarily focused on maintaining the number of converts or even gaining new ones, but rather of a type which is concerned with phasing out from certain fields and reorientation in others. If this were given timely consideration, a major breakdown might be averted. However, any such strategy would require a large degree of resolution in the decision-making process, a characteristic which, for all its hierarchical features, the Catholic Church involved in Africa does not appear to enjoy.

Church, state and society

The future position of the African church cannot be considered in isolation from the evolution of the state system in Africa. The relationship between church and state is one which needs to be 'sorted out' over and over again, anywhere. Whereas the post-colonial African state, just as, indeed, the church itself, is still in the process of developing its profile, it stands to reason that its relationship to the church(es) sooner or later will come up for more explicit scrutiny. At such a juncture their respective record and social role and significance will no doubt prove to be of considerable consequence.

It is useful to view the present dilemmas in and around the Roman Catholic church in the perspective of this reassessment and position identification. In a sense, they may well represent a foreboding of them. The careful, and at times overly cautious, way in which the African clergy has often defined its position *vis-à-vis* controversial socio-political issues, in fact, may not be unrelated to a rather basic sense of insecurity as to both its own role and position and the expected evolution and posture of the state system.

As regards the church's own role and position, what is of inescapable importance is the awareness that its leadership refers to an inherited complex structure which in essence is still being viewed as foreign. There is a relatively acute awareness that it will not be able to continue to have the support structure from Europe which it used to enjoy, while at the same time it is still insufficiently rooted to be genuinely sustained on the basis of African support, and in African style.

Beyond this, there is a lingering expectation that the understanding and working relations with the colonial state which had been gradually established will sooner or later be subjected to a critical reappraisal. Moreover, it is felt that, while the relationship to the post-colonial state will need to be worked out afresh, perhaps even from scratch, for the time being there is only a kind of status quo and a relative tolerance of church activities by those in political power. The latter themselves are often still relatively 'new' and insecure as to their own position and might not be able to avoid an element of suspicion of anything that might signify an autonomous basis and political stronghold among the population.

Not surprisingly, therefore, the attitude of various political leaders *vis-à-vis* the role of the church is rather manifestly ambivalent; one acknowledges the church's commitment and input as a significant potential contribution towards national development, but is none the less alert to what it might be able to mobilize – or 'withdraw' from the state – in terms of political loyalty. In turn, this may well strengthen, and be strengthened by, feelings ranging from mild jealousy to straight xenophobia in the extreme case. This 'strange duck' syndrome can be particularly pronounced in situations where efforts are made to emphasize 'authentic' cultural identities, such as in Zaïre. If one has opted for a narrowly nationalistic path as a way to create a new political identity, then few things will seem more plausible than to regard the church as essentially a residual colonial legacy, a recurrent intruder or an unwanted interferer. None of these allegations needs to be voiced aloud in order to be of some consequence. Latent feelings and insecurities reciprocally may contribute to an a priori attitude, particularly on the part of the church, which would seek to avoid conflict and try to give as little provocation as possible. This may lead to – at times, too large – a measure of circumspection, if not silence, especially as regards political issues but also in connection with human rights and wider social problems. More generally, it may imply a concentration on spiritual instead of worldly matters. Quite literally, as well as symbolically, this may amount to a withdrawal within a protective bastion, and to the nurturing of a kind of 'shell' complex.

It is not too difficult to point to a number of factors that have induced this defensive attitude. The closed, rather introvert atmosphere of many Catholic centres is one of them. That characteristic itself has something self-perpetuating about it. The lack of a tradition of militancy *vis-à-vis* social injustice is definitely another one. On questions of arbitrary state action, violation of human rights, poverty, violence and inequality, the church has been silent too long or too often. As a tradition of protest in this regard was evidently not established during the colonial period, or only very incidentally, it has now become much more difficult to create it. At the same time, it must be recognized that the church's own, inevitably durable, contacts and ideological ties with Europe, no matter how much these may also constitute a direct source of support and security, unmistakably act as a disincentive to any readiness and alertness to engage in the African political and national-cultural arena.

Finally, the shell complex may perpetuate itself in yet another way. It may imply insufficient familiarity with what is at issue within the wider context in social and political terms. In turn, this may lead to a lack of alertness in reacting to specific situations (and possibly to losing the right moment for action), and perhaps to a tendency to abandon oneself to a frustrated rejectionism *tout court*. Conversely, it might mean that, if one does not embark upon any social or political action, it may be conducted in a rather clumsy fashion, create adverse effects and, finally, only add to the feelings of frustration which lay at its basis to begin with.

Yet it is also, or precisely, the church's inclination to keep aloof from Africa's social problematics which will continue to raise questions and criticism. In Africa, too, particularly during times of social crises, a fundamental social commitment, which is to contribute to the regaining of moral self-confidence and social stability, is expected of virtually any religious current and religious institution.

In that regard, the current societal dislocation and crisis situation in many parts of Africa may definitely be identified as acute. In the absence of a close engagement with the problems concerned, the ecclesiastical institutional infrastructure runs the danger of losing its inspiration and, in the end, its credibility. New religious movements at the grass-roots level will increasingly be taking on a role in this regard, thus underscoring how much the adaptation in the post-colonial era of a Western into an African church may be doomed to fail.

The contours of the options open to the Catholic church in Africa are increasingly being delineated. If the transformation to an African institution is to have any chance of success, then it will be of crucial importance to find openings and establish linkages with religious renewal movements emerging at the grass-roots level.

Actually, the protective community which the Catholic Church forms in many situations might well serve as a point of departure, if not as a launching-pad, for new social action. To be sure, such reorientations may very well entail friction with Rome, as well as conflict with the state: friction with Rome, because in Africa, perhaps even more than elsewhere, the question as to what is or what should be universally binding, and what not, undoubtedly will be tested and fought over to the utmost limit. Sooner or later, a confrontation with the state is to be expected in any event, and it will by no means be 'cushioned' by an independent posture and social activism on the part of the church. On the contrary. But it is a cardinal question to what extent that should be a reason for a continued authority-abiding circumspection, particularly in cases concerning regimes which themselves may hardly claim legitimacy. This question at once implies the choice with which the church and its different components will find itself confronted: a choice between the continuation of a cautious status quo policy on the one hand, with all the uncertain certainties it involves, but also with a chance in the end of losing touch with firm ground altogether, and the adoption of a more militant orientation and closer identification with the African social world and it problematics, though in doing so risking a collision with the state, as well as friction with Rome as to what is still permissible in terms of universal norms.

How these choices will be made and with what results are as yet far from certain. What is clear, however, is who will make them: the younger generation of African priests and laymen.

Index

Index

Index

Index